COMMUNICATION DISORDERS FOLLOWING TRAUMATIC BRAIN INJURY

Communication disorders following traumatic brain injury

edited by

Skye McDonald
University of New South Wales, Australia

Leanne Togher
University of Sydney, Australia

Chris Code
University of Sydney, Australia and University of Exeter, UK

Psychology Press
a member of the Taylor & Francis group

Psychology Press Ltd, Publishers
27 Church Road
Hove
East Sussex
BN3 2FA
UK

British Library Cataloguing-in-Publication Data
A catalogue record for this book is available from the British Library

ISBN: 0-86377-724-4
ISSN: 0967-9944

Typeset by Action Publishing Technology, Gloucester, UK
Printed and bound in the UK by Biddles Ltd, Guildford and King's Lynn

Contents

Series preface

From being an area primarily on the periphery of mainstream behavioural and cognitive science, neuropsychology has developed in recent years into an area of central concern for a range of disciplines. We are witnessing not only a revolution in the way in which brain–behaviour–cognition relationships are viewed, but a widening of interest concerning developments in neuropsychology on the part of a range of workers in a variety of fields. Major advances in brain-imaging techniques and the cognitive modelling of the impairments following brain damage promise a wider understanding of the nature of the presentation of cognition and behavour in the damage and undamaged brain.

Neuropsychology is now centrally important for those working with brain-damaged people, but the very rate of expansion in the area makes it difficult to keep up with findings from current research. The aim of the *Brain Damage, Behaviour and Cognition* series is to publish a wide range of books that present comprehensive and up-to-date overviews of current developments in specific areas of interest.

These books will be of particular interest to those working with the brian-damaged. It is the editors' intention that undergraduates, postgraduates, clinicians and researches in psychology, speech pathology and medicine will find this series a useful source of information on important current developments. The authors and editors of the books in this series are experts in their respective fields, working at the forefront of contemporary research. They have produced texts that are accessible and scholarly. We thank them for their contribution and their hard work in fulfilling the aims of the series.

CC and GH
Sydney, Australia and Birmingham, UK
Series Editors

Brain Damage, Behavioural and Cognition Developments in Clinical Neuropsychology Titles in Series

Series Editors
Chris Code, University of Sydney, Australia, and University of Exeter, UK
Dave Müller, University College Suffolk, UK

Cognitive Retraining Using Mirocomputers
Veronica A. Bradley, John L. Welch, and Clive E. Skilbeck
The Characteristics of Aphasia
Chris Code (Ed.)
Classic Cases in Neuropsychology
Chris Code, Claus-W. Wallesch, Yves Joanette, and André Roch Lecours (Eds)
The Neuropsychology of Schizophrenia
Anthony S. David and John C. Cutting (Eds)
Neuropsychology and the Dementias
Siobhan Hart and James M. Semple
Clinical Neoropsychology of Alcoholism
Robert G. Knight and Barry E. Longmore
Neuropsychology of the Amnesic Syndrome
Alan J. Parkin and Nicholas R.C. Leng
Clinical and Neuropsychological Aspects of Closed Head Injury
John T.E. Richardson
Unilateral Neglect: Clinical and Experimental Studies
Ian H. Robertson and John C. Marshall (Eds)
Cognitive Rehabilitation in Perspective
Rodger Wood and Ian Fussey (Eds)

Series Editors
Chris Code, University of Sydney, Australia, and University of Exeter, UK
Glyn Humphreys, University of Birmingham, UK

Transcortical Aphasias
Marcelo L. Berthier
Communication Disorders Following Traumatic Brain Injury
Skye McDonald, Leanne Togher, and Chris Code (Eds)
Spatial Neglect: A Clinical Handbook for Diagnosis and Treatment
Ian H. Robertson and Peter W. Halligan
Apraxia: The Neuropsychology of Action
Leslie J. Gonzalez Rothi and Kenneth Heilman
Developmental Cognitive Neuropsychology
Christine Temple

Preface

Traumatic brain injury can result from injury to the head. Common causes are road traffic accidents, sporting injuries, missile wounds, and industrial accidents. Although there are many excellent books available on traumatic brain injury, there are very few concerned with the communication problems that accompany it. There are also many excellent volumes devoted to neurolinguistics and the neuropsychology of language for the reader to choose from, but there are few volumes available on the unique communication problems that can come with traumatic brain injury.

Recent years have seen an evolution from viewing the communication problems of traumatic brain-injured people as some form of aphasia to realising that their problems can be very different. There has emerged a realisation that these difficulties in communication are closely tied to the cognitive, behavioural, and social problems observed following traumatic brain injury. This is changing the way people with traumatic brain injury are assessed and is generating new approaches to rehabilitation.

For this book our aim was to bring together a comprehensive and contemporary collection of chapters that would present the best work being done in the area. We felt it was important to include good coverage of the exciting work that is examining social and functional linguistic behaviour. To this end we have included chapters on discourse, pragmatics, exchange structure, and social skills. These areas are inevitably inter-dependent, but we have attempted to keep repetition to a minimum.

Traumatic brain injury can also impair articulation and voice production, resulting in dysarthria, and we have therefore included a chapter that presents a comprehensive account of contemporary research and treatment. Children with traumatic brain injury have special difficulties and in recognition of this we have included a chapter focusing on contemporary research and rehabilitation with the paediatric population.

A few points on organisation. The book begins with a short chapter that briefly reviews communication problems in traumatic brain injury. This chapter also guides the reader to relevant chapters in the book. If you are coming new to the area we recommend you read this chapter first. In Chapter 2 we have attempted a comprehensive overview of the causes and consequences of traumatic brain injury. Again, if traumatic brain injury is a new area for you, or you want an up-to-date review, this chapter is recommended. We have resisted the temptation so far, but in the rest of this volume all authors use "TBI" instead of "traumatic brain injury" before they get too far into their chapters.

We think this book should be of interest to psychologists, speech pathologists and therapists, and linguists. Clinicians and researchers working with people with TBI, and their students, should find it a comprehensive source of contemporary approaches to characterising the communication problems of people with TBI and for planning rehabilitation.

Finally, we are grateful to our contributors for the work that has brought-this book to publication. It has been a privilege working with them. We will have to find new excuses to take long lunches together. It is our hope that improvements in our understanding of the communication problems will lead to improved outcomes for people with traumatic brain injury.

Skye McDonald
Leanne Togher
Chris Code

List of contributors

Richard Body, Community Brain Injury Rehabilitation Team, St. George's Community Health Centre, Winter Street, Sheffield, S3 7ND, UK.

Sandra Bond Chapman, Brain Research and Treatment Center, University of Texas at Dallas/Callier Center, 1966 Inwood Road, Dallas, Texas 75235, USA.

Chris Code, Brain Damage and Communication Research, School of Communication Sciences and Disorders, University of Sydney, Box 170, Lidcombe, NSW 2141, Australia, and School of Psychology, Washington Singer Labs, University of Exeter, Perry Road, Exeter, EX4 4QG, UK.

Carl A. Coelho, Department of Communication Sciences, U-85, University of Connecticut, Storrs, CT 06269-1085, USA.

Jacinta Douglas, School of Human Communication Sciences, Faculty of Health Sciences, Latrobe University, Bundoora, Victoria, 3083, Australia.

Linda Hand, School of Communication Sciences and Disorders, Faculty of Health Sciences, University of Sydney, PO Box, Lidcombe 2141, Australia.

Stacy L. Lawyer, Brain Research and Treatment Center, University of Texas at Dallas/Callier Center, 1966 Inwood Road, Dallas, Texas 75235, USA.

Harvey S. Levin, Department of Physical Medicine and Rehabilitation, Baylor College of Medicine in Houston, 1333 Moursund Avenue, AS2205, Houston, Texas, USA.

Nigel V. Marsh, Department of Psychology, University of Waikato, Private Bag 3105, Hamilton, New Zealand.

Skye McDonald, School of Psychology, University of New South Wales, Sydney 2052, Australia.

Bruce E. Murdoch, Motor Speech Research Unit, Department of Speech Pathology and Audiology, University of Queensland, St. Lucia, Brisbane, Queensland, Australia.

Mark Parker, Head Injury Rehabilitation Centre, Sheffield, S6 3EB, UK.

Michael Perkins, Department of Human Communication Sciences, University of Sheffield, 18/20 Claremont Crescent, Sheffield, S10 2TA, UK.

Pamela Snow, School of Human Communication Sciences, Faculty of Health Sciences, Latrobe University, Bundoora, Victoria, 3083, Australia.

Deborah G. Theodoros, Motor Speech Research Unit, Department of Speech

Pathology and Audiology, University of Queensland, St. Lucia, Brisbane, Queensland, Australia.

Leanne Togher, Brain Damage and Communications Research, School of Communication Sciences and Disorders, Faculty of Health Sciences, University of Sydney, Box 170, Lidcombe, NSW 2141, Australia.

CHAPTER ONE

Communication problems following traumatic brain injury

Leanne Togher
Brain Damage and Communication Research, School of Communication Sciences and Disorders, University of Sydney, Australia, and Liverpool Brain Injury Rehabilitation Unit, Australia

Skye McDonald
School of Psychology, University of New South Wales, Australia

Chris Code
Brain Damage and Communication Research, School of Communication Sciences and Disorders, University of Sydney, Australia, and Department of Psychology, Exeter University, UK

Traumatic brain injury is the most common form of brain injury in the modern Western world predominantly affecting young adults, many of whom suffer devastating disabilities without any truncation of life span. These disabilities span both physical and psychological domains of function. Communication impairment may be a consequence of disabilities within and across these domains and represents a unique area of investigation for clinicians and researchers alike. The past three decades have seen a major evolution in the way in which such disorders have been described, and this chapter will provide an overview and introduction to the various approaches used.

DEFINITIONS

The term "traumatic brain injury" refers to brain injury caused by trauma rather than disease, vascular accidents, alcohol, etc. Traumatic brain injury is a consequence of a head injury of sufficient severity to cause damage to the brain beneath and can be either penetrating or blunt. Penetrating or open head injuries are an uncommon cause of traumatic brain injury, with the exception of war-wounds. These occur when a missile, such as a bullet, pierces the skull and traverses the brain tissue. High-velocity missile wounds cause catastrophic focal and diffuse damage and are usually fatal, whereas low-velocity missiles or missile fragments produce focal lesions restricted to the area of direct damage (Grafman & Salazar, 1987). Loss of consciousness is relatively uncommon following such injuries (Salazar, Grafman, Vance, Weingarter, Dillon, & Ludlow, 1986) and the functional sequelae often closely resemble those of other kinds of focal neurological lesions frequently leading to discrete and specific kinds of cognitive impairment (Grafman & Salazar, 1987). Research into aphasia following penetrating head injuries has been important in the development of theoretical approaches to aphasia and aphasia classification. For instance, Goldstein (1942) developed hospital treatment for brain-injured soldiers in Frankfurt during the First World War where he assessed and treated over 2000 patients. This work influenced his theoretical approach, although he also had extensive experience with vascular lesions. Russell and Espir (1961) studied the records of 1166 brain-injured patients examined in Oxford during the Second World War. The researchers estimated that about 60% of left hemisphere damaged patients had aphasia of some degree. Perhaps the most well-known neuropsychologist whose approach to aphasia is influenced by his experience with penetrating head injury is Luria. His famous book, *Traumatic Aphasia* (1970) was first published in Russia in 1947 and details the theoretical approach that he developed during his work with Russian soldiers during the Second World War.

Blunt head injuries are, however, by far the most common type of head injury during peacetime (Grafman & Salazar, 1987) and are the major focus of this book. Blunt head injuries are often caused by the rapid acceleration and deceleration of the head such as occurs during motor vehicle accidents. This kind of injury produces multi-focal pathology in the brain, is associated with altered consciousness in the acute stages and generally causes widespread deficits quite unlike penetrating head injuries. Henceforth, the term "TBI" in this book will refer to traumatic brain injury caused by blunt head injuries. It should also be noted that the term "head injury" is sometimes used interchangeably in the ensuing chapters, because both this and the more specific term "closed head injury" have had wide usage in the TBI literature.

It is now well recognised that communication problems following TBI are distinctly different to those subsequent to a more focal lesion such as occurs in a cerebrovascular accident (or a penetrating head injury) and these require different approaches to assessment and remediation. This has come from the recognition that, due to the multi-focal nature of TBI, there is a complex interplay of cognitive, linguistic, physical, behavioural, and organic psychosocial factors that may contribute to the communication difficulties experienced. In turn, communication problems can have a significant effect on psychosocial outcomes. The ability to communicate successfully is crucial to being able to maintain relationships and to establishing vocational and leisure activities. It is therefore logical that by establishing ways of measuring and improving communication in these individuals, there may be a significant benefit in their everyday lives.

APPROACHES TO ASSESSING COMMUNICATION DISORDERS AFTER TRAUMATIC BRAIN INJURY

The complexity of communication following TBI has resulted in a range of approaches from varied theoretical backgrounds, including neuropsychology, psychosocial outcomes, pragmatics, sociolinguistics, social skills, discourse analysis, and neurophysiology. This chapter will provide a brief overview of these different and often confusing perspectives and will refer the reader to the relevant chapters within this book.

Language assessment from the perspective of aphasia

In the 1970s there were attempts to describe the ways in which TBI patients presented differently to patients with other types of neurological communication impairments. Communication problems following TBI were described as being unique (Groher, 1977; Halpern, Darley, & Brown, 1973). Communication was described as being confused (Groher, 1977), confabulatory (Hagan, 1982), tangential (Hagan, 1982; Levin, Grossman, Rose, & Teasdale, 1979; Thomsen, 1975), full of empty phrases (Heilman, Safran, & Geschwind, 1971), and failing to display logicosequential relationship between thoughts (Hagan, 1982). While recovery of language function was demonstrated at below the sentence level, it was frequently observed that TBI subjects did not manage at conversational levels (Groher, 1977; Halpern, Darley, & Brown, 1973; Levin, Benton, & Grossman, 1982).

In the absence of appropriate measurement tools, researchers were only able to provide a superficial description of the way their subjects communicated. Use of aphasia test batteries failed to delineate the problems that were observed in day-to-day communication leading to the creation of new definitions such as "subclinical aphasia" (Sarno, 1980) and subsequent debates as to what constitutes aphasic impairment (Holland, 1982). In aphasia the patient has problems that can be described in terms of representational linguistic levels of phonology, morphology, syntax, and lexical semantics (Code, 1991). A TBI may well result in aphasic disturbances. Early descriptions of language impairment following TBI suggested that aphasia occurred in 2% of 750 cases and 14% of 50 cases respectively (Heilman, Safran, & Geschwind, 1971; Levin, Grossman, & Kelly, 1976). But in addition, while Sarno and colleagues (1980, 1986) indicated that 32% of their TBI subjects evidenced frank aphasia, they also argued that many subjects suffered a form of subclinical aphasia, defined as "evidence of linguistic processing deficits on testing in the absence of clinical manifestations of clinical impairment" (Sarno, 1980, p.687). The linguistic deficits in the subclinical aphasia group included difficulties with visual naming, word fluency, and impaired performance on the Token Test, when compared with a matched dysarthric group. These results have been replicated in later studies with evidence of specific word-finding difficulties on naming and word fluency tasks being the most common finding when people with TBI are evaluated on tests of traditional language functioning (Adamovich & Henderson, 1984; Levin, Grossman, Sarwar, & Meyers, 1981; Lohman, Ziggas, & Pierce, 1989).

Difficulty with naming appears to be one of the most reported persisting communication problems following TBI. Thomsen's (1975) study of 50 patients with severe TBI found persistent oral expression impairment in half of the subjects when they were examined on average 33 months post-injury. Groher (1977) assessed a group of 14 severe TBI patients at monthly periods following resolution of coma. Patients demonstrated intact confrontation naming (on the Porch Index of Communicative Ability; Porch, 1967) four months after regaining consciousness, although their communication was described as lacking in conversational content. Levin, Grossman, and Kelly (1976) found in their sample of 50 severe TBI patients of varying severity that 40% evidenced impaired naming on the Multilingual Aphasia Examination (Benton, 1967). In a follow-up study of 21 subjects who had been acutely aphasic, Levin, Grossman, Sarwar, and Meyers (1981) found that 12 showed persistent naming impairments.

Naming impairments have been investigated more recently in children with TBI (Jordan, Ozanne, & Murdoch, 1990; Jordan, Cannon, & Murdoch, 1992) and with adults (Kerr, 1995) using an information-processing approach to assessment in the tradition of Coltheart (1987) and Shallice (1987). Kerr (1995) found that one of her six subjects had preserved semantic knowledge, whereas the other five subjects evidenced some central semantic impairment as a major contributing factor in their naming problem, but with concomitant visual and phonological breakdown. The information-processing approach to word finding impairments has been applied in treatment (Hillis, 1991) to successfully remediate both semantic and phonological impairments in one TBI patient. The sophistication of this approach, widely used in aphasia therapy in describing the nature of naming impairments, holds some promise for word-level analysis with TBI patients. The advantage of a psycholinguistic perspective is the control it allows over the context in which language production occurs.

Frank aphasic and specific naming deficits in TBI have been conventionally assessed using standard aphasia batteries such as the Western Aphasia Battery (Kertesz, 1982), the Boston Diagnostic Aphasia Examination (Goodglass & Kaplan, 1972), and the Multilingual Aphasia Examination (Benton & Hamsher, 1983), supplemented by specific tests of naming such as the Boston Naming Test (Kaplan, Goodglass, Weintraub, & Segal, 1983) and comprehension, like, for example, the Revised Token Test (McNeil & Prescott, 1978). The development of the psycholinguistic approach to language assessment has culminated in the production of assessment instruments based upon these principles such as the Psycholinguistic Assessment of Language Processing in Aphasia (Kay, Lesser, & Coltheart, 1992). However, while these instruments may be sensitive to basic linguistic deficits following TBI, the spectrum of communication deficits experienced in TBI are inadequately captured by such instruments. Nor do they take socially mediated aspects of language functioning into account.

Recognising the influence of other cognitive disorders

Sarno's term "subclinical aphasia" precipitated a debate regarding the terminology researchers and clinicians should be using when describing language impairment following TBI. Holland (1982) argued that language disorders following TBI are not aphasia but are secondary to cognitive and memory impairments. She objected to Sarno's term "subclinical aphasia" as inappropriate labelling. Braun and Baribeau (1987) further criticised Sarno for not reporting non-verbal psychological functions that they felt precluded the differentiation between generalised intellectual dysfunction and aphasia. This foreshadowed the interest that was to follow in the relationship between cognitive impairments and communication.

By the middle to late 1980s increasing awareness of the interplay between cognition and language led to the introduction of the term "cognitive-language disorder" (Hagan, 1984; Kennedy & DeRuyter, 1991). Researchers began to investigate the relationship between the cognitive disturbances that frequently follow TBI and psycholinguistic aspects of language. Hagan (1984) described the relationship between the commonly occurring cognitive impairments following TBI and their effects on language processing. For example, the impairments of attention, memory, sequencing, categorisation, and associative abilities are seen to result in an impaired capacity to organise and structure incoming information, emotional reactions, and the flow of thought. Such impairments, Hagan argued, cause a disorganisation of language processes. Cognitive disorganisation is reflected through language use that is characterised by irrelevant utterances that may not make sense, difficulty inhibiting inappropriate utterances, word-finding difficulties, and problems ordering words and propositions. Prigatano, Roueche, & Fordyce (1985) described non-aphasic language disturbances following TBI, including the problems of talkativeness, tangentiality, and fragmented thought processes. Some attempt was made to compare 8 TBI subjects who were described by relatives as "Talkative" on the Katz-R Adjustment Scale with 40 TBI subjects who were described as "Non-talkative" on their respective neuropsychological status (e.g. on the WAIS, WAIS-R Vocabulary, Block Design and Digit symbol scores) but no differences were found between the two groups. In addition, these authors described a single TBI subject who was subjectively noted to be tangential in a written text and who was found to evidence difficulty with short-term memory and with shifting cognitive set (as measured on the Trail Making Test). The only "language" problems noted were difficulties naming pictures, repeating sentences, and rapidly retrieving names on a word fluency task, although these deficits were not reported to be "obvious" in casual conversation. Prigatano et al. (1985) therefore argued that this tangential output was the result of the association of core neuropsychological impairments with tangential thinking and communication.

More recently the term "cognitive-communication disorder" has been used (Hartley, 1995). The focus on cognition arose from an examination of the underlying pathophysiology of TBI (described in detail in Chapter 2), which commonly results in multi-focal cerebral damage with a preponderance of injury to the frontal lobes. Cognition can be broadly described as "mental activities or operations involved in taking in, interpreting, encoding, storing, retrieving, and making use of knowledge or information and generating a response" (Ylvisaker & Szekeres, 1994, p.548). Examples of cognitive processes attributed to the frontal lobes include ability to focus attention to stimuli, remembering and learning, organising information, reasoning, and problem solving. In addition to specific cognitive processes, the frontal lobes appear to mediate executive control of thought and behaviour (Chapter 2). Such executive functions include goal setting, behaviour planning and sequencing, goal-oriented behaviour, and initiation and evaluation of behaviour (Lezak, 1993). It became increasingly obvious to researchers that it was impossible to assess language functioning without taking neuropsychological functioning into account.

Tacit recognition that TBI communication disturbances are likely to reflect other cognitive deficits influenced everyday clinical assessment procedures. Clinicians often rely upon the more difficult of conventional language tasks that appear to have an additional cognitive load in order to gain an indication of the presence of communication disturbances experienced by their TBI clientele. For example, verbal fluency, so often noted to be impaired in TBI, and attributed to subclinical aphasia by Sarno (1980), is a task independently recognised as having additional cognitive demands. The Controlled Oral Word Association Test, which forms part of the Multilingual Aphasia Examination (Benton & Hamsher, 1983) and the Neurosensory Centre Comprehensive Examination for Aphasia (Spreen & Benton, 1969) requires generativity of words in rapid succession according to specific rules. This task demands speed, productivity, and flexibility, in addition to linguistic competence, and is impaired in many forms of brain damage including frontal lobe dysfunction (Benton, 1968). Failure to perform on this task, in the absence of clear linguistic deficits on other parts of standard aphasia batteries, can therefore be taken to indicate the presence of cognitive deficits that are *impacting* upon language performance. Other verbal tasks with an emphasis on abstraction skills, such as the decoding of metaphor in the Right Hemisphere Language Battery (Bryan, 1989), proverbs in the Wechsler Adult Intelligence Scale–Revised (Wechsler, 1981), and other figurative language in the Test of Language Competence (expanded edition) (Wiig & Secord, 1989) can also give an indication of impaired language *performance* that can frequently be observed independent of linguistic deficits per se. Finally, more complex and difficult sentence structures such as those used in the Wiig–Semel Test of Linguistic Concepts (Wiig & Semel, 1976) or the Test for Reception of Grammar (Bishop, 1983) may elicit difficulties for TBI patients who perform relatively normally on the simpler tests of comprehension.

Although impaired performance on cognitively demanding language tasks may alert the clinician to the presence of communication disturbances, such assessment procedures fall a long way short of providing accurate, comprehensive, or ecologically relevant measures of impaired communication skills in TBI. How does the inability to think of words beginning with "f" translate into communication competence in the workplace, the home, and the general community? Obviously, in the case of Prigatano et al. (1985), such deficits did not appear to translate at all.

New approaches to language assessment and treatment with a focus on communication

By the end of the 1980s, researchers were focusing their attention less on isolated language functions and more on the impact of linguistic impairments on discourse functioning (e.g. Penn & Cleary, 1988), with discourse being defined by Ulatowska and Bond-Chapman (1989) as a unit of language that conveys a message. There are different types of discourse tasks that have also been referred to as different discourse "genres". A genre is a particular text type, which has its own structure and sequence. Some examples of discourse genres include narrative (or recounting a story), procedural (a set of instructions for doing something), expository (giving an opinion or discussing a topic in detail), and conversation. This change in focus represented a significant shift in the way communication problems following TBI were viewed. Developments in discourse analysis were related to a proliferation of interest across a number of disciplines including sociology (e.g. Hymes, 1986; Labov, 1970), psychology (e.g. Mandler & Johnson, 1977), artificial intelligence (e.g. Schank & Abelson, 1977), and linguistics (e.g. Grimes, 1975, van Dijk, 1977). Particular techniques in discourse analyses have been derived from both the psycholinguistic and sociolinguistic perspectives. The psycholinguistic analyses include measures of syntax

(Chapman, Culhane, Levin, Harward, Mendelsohn, Ewing-Cobbs, Fletcher, & Bruce, 1992; Glosser & Deser, 1990; Liles, Coelho, Duffy, & Zalagens, 1989), productivity (Hartley & Jensen, 1991; Mentis & Prutting, 1987), and content (Hartley & Jensen, 1991). On the other hand, sociolinguistic techniques include cohesion analysis (Coelho, Liles, & Duffy, 1991; Hartley & Jensen, 1991; McDonald, 1993; Mentis & Prutting, 1987), analysis of coherence (Chapman et al., 1992; Ehrlich & Barry, 1989; McDonald, 1993), analysis of topic (Mentis & Prutting, 1991), and compensatory strategies (Penn & Cleary, 1988). The practical application of these new methodologies to brain-injured populations has proven to be fruitful as a means of exemplifying communication disorders not apparent in traditional testing.

Discourse analysis was initially used to describe the communication of people with aphasia following stroke (Bottenberg, Lemme, & Hedberg, 1985; Ulatowska, North, & Macaluso-Haynes, 1981a, 1981b) which led to descriptions of treatment using discourse level tasks (Armstrong, 1993; Ulatowska & Bond-Chapman, 1989). Examining discourse as an index of communication following TBI occurred for the following reasons: (a) to address the need for scientific verification of clinical impressions of the discrepancy between TBI subjects' performance on traditional language tests and their impaired communicative functioning in social contexts; (b) to examine the relationship between language and cognition in connected speech tasks; and (c) to address the need for assessments to form the basis for treatment of communication in real life contexts taking into consideration the impact of communication impairment on disability and handicap. The application of discourse analysis in TBI is discussed by Carl Coelho in Chapter 3. This chapter provides an overview of microlinguistic discourse analysis (i.e. examining discourse at the word or sentence levels—e.g. phonological, lexical, and syntactic processes) and macrolinguistic discourse analyses (i.e. examining discourse across sentences and/or at the level of the entire text—e.g. cohesion and story structure) as well as other measures of productivity and content of TBI discourse.

Pragmatics. Embodied within the broader field of discourse analysis is the study of the pragmatic nature of interactions. Pragmatics is concerned with the way language is used and the context of its use rather than the forms language takes (Levinson, 1983). As communication problems following TBI have been described as a difficulty with language use rather than form (Holland, 1982) it is not surprising that the tenets of pragmatics have been applied to this population.

The application of pragmatics and its relationship to cognitive processing in TBI is described in Chapter 4 (Body, Perkins, & McDonald). This chapter provides an overview of some of the key concepts that have emerged from pragmatics, including the notions of semantic vs. pragmatic meaning, speech act theory, conversational implicature, relevance theory, and the relationship of cognitive impairments following TBI with pragmatic communication functioning. A further brief discussion of the relationship of pragmatic theory to the development of rating scales can also be found in Chapter 5 (Togher, Hand, & Code).

The importance of context. Since the early discourse studies (e.g. Mentis & Prutting, 1987; Milton, Prutting, & Binder, 1984) there has been increased attention to different types of discourse genres and an array of approaches has emerged to measure them. Most of these approaches have been borrowed from the disciplines of behavioural psychology, pragmatics, and sociolinguistics. With the development of these approaches there has been an increasing recognition of the complexity of language functioning as it occurs within social contexts. One approach emerging from sociolinguistics was Systemic Functional Linguistics (Halliday, 1985). This is a theory of language use that is based within a sociocultural framework. The language produced in an interaction is viewed as being interdependent with the contextual features of that situation. One of these contextual features is the relationship that exists between the participants (also called the "tenor"). For example, it is proposed that factors such as familiarity and social status will directly influence the language that is produced. To evaluate the way language is influenced by the context in which it occurs, the use of analyses from Systemic Functional Linguistics is described in Chapter 5 (Togher, Hand, & Code). Communication problems following TBI have been described as interactional in nature (Hartley, 1995), and this chapter focuses on the way interactions unfold according to who is involved. The two-way nature of interactions is also reflected in this analysis, with data being reported on the language produced from both TBI and control subjects and their communication partners.

Few studies have described the ways in which contributions of the communication partner may impact on the communication of the person with TBI (Bond & Godfrey, 1997; Coelho et al., 1991; Mentis & Prutting, 1991). The common observation from these studies is that the communication partner (i.e. the research assistant or speech pathologist) was required to take responsibility for maintaining the conversation as evidenced by increased frequency of question asking, prompting, and requesting clarification and interpretation. Similarly, communication partners have been reported to talk for a significantly shorter time with TBI subjects when compared with controls, possibly because they were less likely to find a topic of common interest with TBI subjects. They may also have been given few opportunities to speak or not encouraged to keep talking by TBI subjects. This has been suggested to lead to interactions that are judged to be less rewarding, interesting, and appropriate when compared with control interactions (Bond & Godfrey, 1997). When the tenor relationships between communication partners and TBI subjects are appraised in these studies, such results may have been expected. The way information is exchanged is dependent on the relationship between participants as well as the activity that is occurring, and on the structure that is expected to unfold. Taking the tenor relationship into account is a critical feature of the research presented in Chapter 5.

Some approaches to assessment and treatment of social communication have also been driven by a focus on language occurring in a social context (Hartley, 1995). The focus on functional communication (i.e. communication in natural environments) has led to assessment procedures that can be used to describe a TBI sufferer's communication outside the clinical environment. This recognition of the importance of examining discourse in social contexts has also led to increasing involvement of family, healthcare workers, and most importantly the person with TBI in the rehabilitation process.

One of the key aims of the rehabilitation process is to enable the person who has sustained a head injury to return as closely as possible to their previous level of functioning. After assessing cognitive and communication impairments, it is necessary to interpret the results with reference to disability and handicap. Measuring disability—i.e. the extent to which an individual is able to perform roles or tasks in the social environment (Crisp & Medulla, 1991)—has received increasing attention (Newton & Johnson, 1985; Prigatano et al., 1985). The extent of the contribution of cognitive and communication impairments to the long-term disability experienced by these patients remains unclear.

Psychosocial assessment. The assessment of the effect of psychosocial impairments on the individual with a TBI has focused on global rating scales, which are more reflective of handicap (Bond, 1976; Burton & Volpe, 1993; Tate, Broe, & Lulham, 1989). One of these scales is the Glasgow Assessment Scale, or GAS (Livingston & Livingston, 1985; Livingston & McCabe, 1990), where the patient is rated on clinical evidence and informant reports. For example, areas rated on the GAS include personality changes, subjective complaints, occupational functioning, cognitive functioning, physical examination, and activities of daily living. Cognitive functioning is measured according to tasks such as immediate recall and two-minute recall. Communication is measured only according to the presence or absence of dysarthria (i.e. motor weakness or incoordination of the articulators resulting in impaired speech and/or voice, see Chapter 8) or aphasia (language impairment) on the "physical" scale. This is a misnomer because aphasia is not a "physical" impairment. While scales such as the

GAS provide a measure of outcome evaluation in a broad sense, they do not shed light on the contributing factors to the known poor outcomes following TBI.

The study of psychosocial outcome following TBI has rarely incorporated specific communication or language measures. Levin, Grossman, Rose, and Teasdale (1979) assessed 27 TBI subjects using the Glasgow Outcome Scale (GOS), the Brief Psychiatric Rating Scale, the Multilingual Aphasia Examination (MAE), the Token Test, and subtests from the Neurosensory Centre Comprehensive Examination for Aphasia (Spreen & Benton, 1969). They found that anomia was the most prominent expressive disturbance one year post-injury, and that only one-third of the subjects made a "good" recovery on the GOS, with only 22% of the subjects returning to work one year post-injury. It was noted that subjects' conversation frequently drifted to irrelevant topics, and that they were socially withdrawn one year post-injury. Although difficulty with communication would appear to be logically related to loss of social contact and failure to assume previous work status, this assumption has not been explicitly examined to date. There has been some criticism of the research designs in the area of psychosocial adjustment to TBI, including a reliance on data from small samples, inconsistency in definitions of TBI and of psychosocial adjustment, a failure to use adequate control groups, and a reliance on retrospective self-report data that may introduce confounding characteristics such as socially desirable responding (Antonak, Livneh, & Antonak, 1993). Nonetheless, it appears crucial to take psychosocial adjustment into account in the management of communication problems following TBI. In Chapter 6 (Body and Parker) the issues of how to best measure psychosocial adjustment from a disability and handicap perspective are discussed. The authors suggest that to capture the complexity of the impact of a TBI, it is necessary to use multiple assessments and informants, including the person with the TBI, their family, carers and friends, the speech pathologist, and other health professionals. They also provide an overview of the rating scales and questionnaires currently available, and factors that should be taken into account when these assessment tools are administered by professionals other than speech pathologists and carers.

Social skills. Evaluation of social skills provides another way of assessing disability following TBI (Godfrey, Knight, Marsh, Moroney, & Bishara, 1989; Marsh & Knight, 1991). Social skills involve the elements of competency and performance, which both assume a subset of underlying cognitive and linguistic competencies (Malkmus, 1989). Poor social skills following TBI have included sudden topic shifts, overly familiar disinhibited remarks and advances, repetition, literal thinking, difficulty with irony, sarcasm or abstract references, and difficulty generating a variety of topics (McDonald, 1992; Prigatano, 1986). Given that competent management of social interactions demands a combination of a number of component skills, the study of the breakdown of these components in the TBI population presents a significant challenge.

The relationship between one aspect of cognitive functioning, the speed of visual information processing, and social competence was investigated by Godfrey et al. (1989) with 18 TBI subjects and 18 matched controls. This was a first attempt at assessing the association between a cognitive process and global ratings of social competence. Results indicated that while the TBI subjects were found to be less socially skilled, and were slower on the visual information-processing tasks, there was no relationship between these two parameters. It was suggested that this lack of a relationship may have been due to the nature of the information-processing tasks. That is, the reaction time tasks these subjects were asked to complete required quick, simple, and discrete decisions, unlike the "sustained and complex information handling which is required in social interactions" (p.181). These results suggested that some of the current methods used to assess the neuropsychological impairments following TBI may not reflect the complexity of what is required to maintain a socially acceptable interaction.

The assessment and treatment of social skill impairments following TBI is described in Chapter 7 (Marsh). This chapter gives an overview of the conceptual issues relating to the assessment of social skills, the behavioural changes that have been observed in TBI patients plus two broad sections encompassing assessments currently available to evaluate social skills, and treatment approaches that have been used. Finally, Marsh provides some direction on issues that need to be taken into account when assessing social skills, including the importance of demonstrating change and the role of cognitive impairments.

Dysarthria and traumatic brain injury. In addition to the social communication difficulties that have been described, TBI can result in physical impairments that may interfere with speech production mechanisms. The resulting speech disorder, named dysarthria, may leave the TBI patient with a mild articulation difficulty so that occasional words need to be repeated or a listener needs to strain to understand, or, in its severest case, the person may be completely unable to communicate orally. Given the heterogeneous nature of TBI, a single pattern of dysarthric impairments has not been reported. The assessment and treatment of dysarthric impairments therefore provides the clinician with the challenge of identifying the nature of the disorder by taking into account its perceptual, acoustic, and physiological features. Discussion of dysarthric impairments and their treatment following TBI is given in Chapter 8 (Murdoch & Theodoros).

Paediatric traumatic injury. Severe TBI is not only found in the adult population. Children also sustain TBIs, with often profound consequences for their communication skills. Until recently, the unique communication problems of children with TBI were assessed and treated in a similar manner to children with specific language impairments (Chapman et al., 1992). Given the significant differences between these types of communication impairment, the management of communication in children with TBI was often inappropriate and ineffective. Chapter 9 (Chapman, Levin, and Lawyer) provides a comprehensive overview of the prevalence and nature of the communication problems that may occur in children following TBI. They also describe the importance of using discourse analysis with this population and relate discourse function to cognitive abilities. The factors that contribute to communicative disability (e.g. severity and neuropathophysiologic aspects) are delineated and, finally, treatment implications are discussed.

Rehabilitation. One of the great challenges in rehabilitation is what to do about communication problems following TBI. With the array of assessment approaches available to us, it is often difficult to isolate practical goals for therapy that are objective and from which we can demonstrate change. The ability to communicate is obviously crucial to maintaining intact social and vocational networks, and therefore communication impairments will significantly affect a TBI individual's ability to reintegrate into these networks after their injury. Identifying appropriate treatment methodologies to facilitate this process is intricately linked with successful return to these networks. Treatment usually commences very soon after the occurrence of the injury and may extend for many years. There are many issues that must be considered when designing treatment. Chapter 10 (Snow & Douglas) provides a description of a conceptual and philosophical framework for intervention that incorporates issues such as the importance of describing the speech pathologist's role to the TBI patient and his or her family; problems with giving and receiving feedback on performance in treatment given the impaired insight of some TBI patients; the debate regarding whether treatment should be based on restitution of language functions or compensation for their loss; the importance of goal setting; the role of cooperative teamwork in rehabilitation; the role and limitations of group vs. individual therapy; and, finally, the important issue of evaluation of treatment efficacy.

The importance of assessing TBI patients on discourse tasks—including narrative, procedural, and conversational tasks—is echoed throughout a number of chapters in this book. It is therefore fitting that in the final chapter, Snow and Douglas spend some time describing specific approaches to treating discourse impairments. They conclude their chapter with a case study that illustrates many of the issues inherent in the rehabilitation of communication problems following TBI.

It is well recognised that a TBI results in significant long-term disability encompassing personal, social, and vocational prospects (Levin, Grossman, Rose, & Teasdale, 1979; Tate et al., 1989; Willer, Rosenthal, Kreutzer, Gordon, & Rempel, 1993). The occurrence of a TBI may result in a range of cognitive, communication, physical, and psychosocial problems, such as loss of friends, reduction in work options, and break-up of the family unit with resulting social isolation. Cognitive impairments can include difficulty with memory, attention, concentration, information processing, reasoning and integration, and impaired mental shifting (Hagan, 1984; Levin, Benton, & Grossman, 1982; Lezak, 1979; Prigatano, 1986). The ability to communicate is obviously crucial to maintaining intact social and vocational networks, and therefore communication impairments will significantly affect a TBI individual's ability to reintegrate into these networks after their injury. These issues are the central focus of this book.

REFERENCES

Adamovich, B.L.B., & Henderson, J.A. (1984). Can we learn more from word fluency measures with aphasic, right brain-injured and closed head trauma patients? In R.H. Brookshire (Ed.), *Clinical aphasiology conference proceedings* (Vol. 14, pp.124–131). Minneapolis, MN: BRK Publishers.

Antonak, R.F., Livneh, H., & Antonak, C. (1993). A review of research on psychosocial adjustment to impairment in persons with traumatic brain injury. *Journal of Head Trauma Rehabilitation, 8*, 87–100.

Armstrong, E.M. (1993). Aphasia rehabilitation: A sociolinguistic perspective. In A.L. Holland & M.M. Forbes (Eds.), *Aphasia treatment: World perspectives* (pp.263–290). San Diego, CA: Singular.

Benton, A.L. (1967). Problems of test construction in the field of aphasia. *Cortex*, *3*, 32–58.

Benton, A.L. (1968). Differential behavioural effects in frontal lobe disease. *Neuropsychologia*, *6*, 53–60.

Benton, A.L., & Hamsher, K. de S. (1983). *Multilingual aphasia examination*. Iowa City, IA: AJA Associates.

Bishop, D.V.M. (1983). *Test for reception of grammar*. Cambridge, UK: Medical Research Council.

Bond, F., & Godfrey, H.P.D. (1997). Conversation with traumatically brain-injured individuals: a controlled study of behavioural changes and their impact. *Brain Injury*, *11(5)*, 319–329.

Bond, M.R. (1976). Assessment of the psychosocial outcome of severe head injury. *Acta Neurochirurgica*, *34*, 57–70.

Bottenberg, D.E., Lemme, M.L., & Hedberg, N.L. (1985). Analysis of oral narratives of normal and aphasic adults. In R.H. Brookshire (Ed.), *Clinical aphasiology conference proceedings* (pp.241–247). Minneapolis, MN: BRK Publishers.

Braun, C.M.J., & Baribeau, J.M.C. (1987). Subclinical aphasia following closed head injury: A response to Sarno, Buonagaro, and Levita. In R.H. Brookshire (Ed.), *Clinical aphasiology conference proceedings* (pp.326–333). Minneapolis, MN: BRK Publishers.

Bryan, K.L. (1989). *The right hemisphere language battery*. London: Whurr.

Burton, L.A., & Volpe, B. (1993). Social adjustment scale assessments in traumatic brain injury. *Journal of Rehabilitation*, Oct–Dec, 4–7.

Chapman, S.B., Culhane, K.A., Levin, H.S., Harward, H., Mendelsohn, D., Ewing-Cobbs, L., Fletcher, J.M., & Bruce, D. (1992). Narrative discourse after closed head injury in children and adolescents. *Brain and Language*, *43*, 42–65.

Code, C. (1991). Symptoms, syndromes, models: The nature of aphasia. In C. Code (Ed.), *The characteristics of aphasia* (pp.1–22). Hove, UK: Lawrence Erlbaum Associates Ltd.

Coelho, C.A., Liles, B.Z., & Duffy, R.J. (1991). Analysis of conversational discourse in head-injured clients. *Journal of Head Trauma Rehabilitation*, *6 (2)*, 92–99.

Coltheart, M. (1987). Functional architecture of the language processing system. In M. Coltheart, G. Sartori, & R. Job (Eds.), *The cognitive neuropsychology of language* (pp.1–26). Hove, UK: Lawrence Erlbaum Associates Ltd.

Crisp, R., & Medulla, V. (1991). The perceptions of persons with head injury concerning their psychosocial adjustment. *Australian Disability Review*, *1-91*, 37–41.

Ehrlich, J., & Barry, P. (1989). Rating communication behaviours in the head-injured adult. *Brain Injury*, *3 (2)*, 193–198.

Glosser, G., & Deser, T. (1990). Patterns of discourse production among neurological patients with fluent language disorders. *Brain and Language*, *40*, 67–88.

Godfrey, H.P.D., Knight, R.G., Marsh, N.V., Moroney, B., & Bishara, S.N. (1989). Social interaction and speed of information processing following very severe head injury. *Psychological Medicine*, *19*, 175–182.

Goldstein, K. (1942). *After-effects of brain injuries in war*. New York: Grune & Stratton.

Goodglass, H., & Kaplan, E. (1972). *The assessment of aphasia and related disorders*. Philadelphia: Lea & Kaplan.

Grafman, J., & Salazar, A.M. (1987). Methodological considerations relevant to the comparison of recovery from penetrating and closed head injuries. In H.S. Levin, J. Grafman, & H.M. Eisenberg (Eds.), *Neurobehavioural recovery from head injury*. New York: Oxford University Press.

Grimes, J. (1975). *The thread of discourse*. The Hague: Mouton.

Groher, M. (1977). Language and memory disorders following closed head trauma. *Journal of Speech and Hearing Research*, *20*, 212–223.

Hagan, C. (1982). Language-cognitive disorganization following closed head injury: A conceptualization. In L. Trexler (Ed.), *Cognitive rehabilitation conceptualization and intervention* (pp.131–151). New York: Plenum Press.

Hagan, C. (1984). Language disorders in head trauma. In A. Holland (Ed.), *Language disorders in adults* (pp.245–281). San Diego, CA: College Hill Press.

Halliday, M.A.K. (1985). *An introduction to functional grammar*. London: Edward Arnold.

Halpern, H., Darley, F.L., & Brown, J.R. (1973). Differential language and neurologic characteristics in cerebral involvement. *Journal of Speech and Hearing Disorders*, *38 (2)*, 162–173.

Hartley, L.L. (1995). *Cognitive-communicative abilities following brain injury: A functional approach*. San Diego, CA: Singular.

Hartley, L.L., & Jensen, P.J. (1991). Narrative and procedural discourse after closed head injury. *Brain Injury*, *5 (3)*, 267–285.

Heilman, K.M., Safran, A., Geschwind, N. (1971). Closed head trauma and aphasia. *Journal of Neurology, Neurosurgery and Psychiatry*, *34*, 265–269.

Hillis, A. (1991). Effects of separate treatment for distinct impairments within the naming process. In T. Prescott (Ed.), *Clinical aphasiology* (Vol. 19, pp.255–276). Austin, TX: Pro-Ed.

Holland, A.L. (1982). When is aphasia aphasia? The problem of closed head injury. In R.H. Brookshire (Ed.), *Clinical aphasiology conference proceedings* (pp.345–349). Minneapolis, MN: BRK Publishers.

Hymes, D. (1986). Models of the interaction of language and social life. In J.J. Gumperz &

D. Hymes (Eds.), *Directions in sociolinguistics: The ethnography of communication* (pp.35–71). Oxford: Blackwell.

Jordan, F.M., Cannon, A., & Murdoch, B.E. (1992). Language abilities of mildly closed head injured (CHI) children 10 years post-injury. *Brain Injury, 6 (1)*, 39–44.

Jordan, F.M., Ozanne, A.E., & Murdoch, B.E. (1990). Performance of closed head injured children on a naming task. *Brain Injury, 4*, 27-32.

Kaplan, E., Goodglass, H., Weintraub, S., & Segal, O. (1983). *Boston naming test*. Philadelphia, PA: Lea & Febiger.

Kay, J., Lesser, R., & Coltheart, M. (1992). *PALPA: Psycholinguistic assessments of language processing in aphasia*. Hove, UK: Lawrence Erlbaum Associates Ltd.

Kennedy, M.R.T., & DeRuyter, F. (1991). Cognitive and language bases for communication disorders. In D.R. Beukelman & K.M. Yorkston (Eds.), *Communication disorders following traumatic brain injury: Management of cognitive, language and motor impairments* (pp.123–190). Austin, TX: Pro-Ed.

Kerr, C. (1995). Dysnomia following traumatic brain injury: An information-processing approach to assessment. *Brain Injury, 9 (8)*, 777–796.

Kertesz, A. (1982). *Western aphasia battery*. New York: Grune & Stratton.

Labov, W. (1970). The study of language in its social context. *Studium Generale, 23*, 30–87.

Levin, H.S., Benton, A.L., & Grossman, R.G. (1982). *Neurobehavioural consequences of closed head injury*. New York: Oxford University Press.

Levin, H.S., Grossman, R.G., & Kelly, P.J. (1976). Aphasic disorder in patients with closed head injury. *Journal of Neurology, Neurosurgery and Psychiatry, 39*, 1062–1070.

Levin, H.S., Grossman, R.G., Rose, J.E., & Teasdale, G. (1979). Long-term neuropsychological outcome of closed head injury. *Journal of Neurosurgery, 50*, 412–422.

Levin, H.S., Grossman, R.G., Sarwar, M., & Meyers, C.A. (1981). Linguistic recovery after closed head injury. *Brain and Language, 12*, 360–374.

Levinson, S.C. (1983). *Pragmatics*. London: Cambridge University Press.

Lezak, M.D. (1979). Recovery of memory and learning functions following traumatic brain injury. *Cortex, 15*, 63–72.

Lezak, M.D. (1993). Newer contributions to the neuropsychological assessment of executive functions. *Journal of Head Trauma Rehabilitation, 8 (1)*, 24–31.

Liles, B.Z., Coelho, C.A., Duffy, R.J., & Zalagens, M.R. (1989). Effects of elicitation procedures on the narratives of normal and closed head-injured adults. *Journal of Speech and Hearing Disorders, 54*, 356–366.

Livingston, M.G., & Livingston, H.M. (1985). The Glasgow Assessment Schedule: Clinical and research assessment of head injury outcome. *International Rehabilitation Medicine, 7*, 145–149.

Livingston, M.G., & McCabe, R.J.R. (1990). Psychosocial consequences of head injury in children and adolescents: Implications for rehabilitation. *Pediatrician, 17*, 255–261.

Lohman, T., Ziggas, D., & Pierce, R.S. (1989). Word fluency performance on common categories by subjects with closed head injuries. *Aphasiology, 3 (8)*, 685–693.

Luria, A.R. (1970). *Traumatic aphasia*. The Hague: Mouton.

Malkmus, D.D. (1989). Community re-entry: Cognitive-communicative intervention within a social skill context. *Topics in Language Disorders, 9*, 50–66.

Mandler, J.A., & Johnson, N.S. (1977). Remembrance of things parsed: Story structure and recall. *Cognitive Psychology, 9*, 111–151.

Marsh, N.V., & Knight, R.G. (1991). Behavioural assessment of social competence following severe head injury. *Journal of Clinical and Experimental Neuropsychology, 13 (5)*, 729–740.

McDonald, S. (1992). Communication disorders following closed head injury: new approaches to assessment and rehabilitation. *Brain Injury, 6*, 283–292.

McDonald, S. (1993). Pragmatic skills after closed head injury: Ability to meet the informational needs of the listener. *Brain and Language*, *44 (1)*, 28–46.

McNeil, M.R., & Prescott, T.E. (1978). *Revised Token Test*. Baltimore, MD: University Park Press.

Mentis, M., & Prutting, C.A. (1987). Cohesion in the discourse of normal and head-injured adults. *Journal of Speech and Hearing Research*, *30*, 88–98.

Mentis, M., & Prutting, C.A. (1991). Analysis of topic as illustrated in a head-injured and a normal adult. *Journal of Speech and Hearing Research*, *34*, 583–595.

Milton, S.B., Prutting, C.A., & Binder, G.M. (1984). Appraisal of communicative competence in head injured adults. In R.H.Brookshire (Ed.), *Clinical aphasiology conference proceedings* (pp.114–123). Minneapolis, MN: BRK Publishers.

Newton, A., & Johnson, D. (1985). Social adjustment and interaction after severe head injury. *British Journal of Clinical Psychology*, *24*, 225–234.

Penn, C., & Cleary, J. (1988). Compensatory strategies in the language of closed head-injured patients. *Brain Injury*, *2 (1)*, 3-17.

Porch, B.E. (1967). *Porch Index of Communicative Ability*. Palo Alto, CA: Consulting Psychologists Press.

Prigatano, G.P. (1986). *Neuropsychological rehabilitation after brain injury*. Baltimore, MD: Johns Hopkins University Press.

Prigatano, G.P., Roueche, J.R., & Fordyce, D.J. (1985). Non-aphasic language disturbances after closed head injury. *Language Sciences*, *7*, 217–229.

Russell, W.R., & Espir, M.L.E. (1961) *Traumatic aphasia*. Oxford: Oxford University Press.

Salazar, A.M., Grafman, J., Vance, S.C., Weingarter, H., Dillon, J.D., & Ludlow, C. (1986). Consciousness and amnesia after penetrating head injury: Neurology and anatomy. *Neurology*, *36*, 178–187.

Sarno, M.T. (1980). The nature of verbal impairment after closed head injury. *The Journal of Nervous and Mental Disease*, *168 (11)*, 685–692.

Sarno, M.T., & Levita, E. (1986). Characteristics of verbal impairment in closed head-injured patients. *Archives of Physical Medicine Rehabilitation*, *67*, 400–405.

Schank, R., & Abelson, R. (1977). *Scripts, plans, goals and understanding*. Hillsdale, NJ: Lawrence Erlbaum Associates Inc.

Shallice, T. (1987). Impairments of semantic processing: Multiple dissociations. In M. Coltheart, G. Sartori, & R. Job (Eds.), *The cognitive neuropsychology of language* (pp.111–127). Hove, UK: Lawrence Erlbaum Associates Ltd.

Spreen, O., & Benton, A.L. (1969). *Neurosensory center comprehensive examination for aphasia*. Victoria: BC: Neuropsychology Laboratory, University of Victoria.

Tate, R.L., Broe, G.A., & Lulham, J.M. (1989). Impairment after severe blunt head injury: The results from a consecutive series of 100 patients. *Acta Neurology Scandinavia*, *79*, 97–107.

Thomsen, I.V. (1975). Evaluation and outcome of aphasia in patients with severe closed head trauma. *Journal of Neurology, Neurosurgery and Psychiatry*, *38*, 713–718.

Ulatowska, H.K., & Bond Chapman, S. (1989). Discourse considerations for aphasia management. In R.S. Pierce & M.J. Wilcox (Eds.), *Seminars in speech and language: Aphasia and pragmatics*, *10 (4)* (pp.293–314). New York: Thieme Medical Publishers.

Ulatowska, H.K., North, A.J., & Macaluso-Haynes, S. (1981a). Production of discourse and communicative competence in aphasia. In R.H. Brookshire (Ed.), *Clinical aphasiology* (Vol. 11, pp.75–82). Minneapolis, MN: BRK Publishers.

Ulatowska, H.K., North, A.J., & Macaluso-Haynes, S. (1981b). Production of narrative and procedural discourse in aphasia. *Brain and Language*, *13*, 345–371.

van Dijk, T.A. (1977). *Text and context: Explorations in the semantics and pragmatics of discourse*. London: Longman.

Wechsler, D. (1981). *Wechsler Adult Intelligence Scale: Revised*. San Antonio, TX: Psychological Corporation.

Wiig, E.H., & Secord, W. (1989). *Test of language competence: Expanded edition*. San Antonio, TX: Psychological Corporation.

Wiig, E.H., & Semel, E.M. (1976). *Language disabilities in children and adults*. Columbus, OH: Merrill.

Willer, B., Rosenthal, M., Kreutzer, J.S., Gordon, W.A., & Rempel, R. (1993). Assessment of community integration following rehabilitation for traumatic brain injury. *Journal of Head Trauma Rehabilitation*, *8*, 75–87.

Ylvisaker, M., & Szekeres, S.F. (1994). Communication disorders associated with closed head injury. In R. Chapey (Ed.), *Language intervention strategies in adult aphasia* (3rd ed., pp.546–568). Baltimore, MD: Williams.

CHAPTER TWO

The nature of traumatic brain injury: Basic features and neuropsychological consequences

Skye McDonald
School of Psychology, University of New South Wales, Australia

Leanne Togher
Brain Damage and Communication Research, School of Communication Sciences and Disorders, University of Sydney, Australia, and Liverpool Brain Injury Rehabilitation Unit, Australia

Chris Code
Brain Damage and Communication Research, School of Communication Sciences and Disorders, University of Sydney, Australia, and Department of Psychology, Exeter University, UK

As described in Chapter 1, communication disorders following traumatic brain injury are complex and heterogeneous, reflecting the influences of a variety of neurophysical and neuropsychological impairments. In order to appreciate the spectrum of these disorders and to understand the different assessment and remediation approaches discussed in this book, it is necessary to be familiar with the basic features of TBI. The first section of this chapter provides a general overview, including classification of the severity, incidence, neuropathology, clinical course, and outcome of TBI. Following this, an overview of the neuropsychological impairments seen in this population is provided in order to equip the reader with information about cognitive and psychosocial factors that influence communication as well as some common neuropsychological assessment techniques that are referred to in subsequent chapters.

BASIC FEATURES OF TRAUMATIC BRAIN INJURY

Classification

A patient is normally classified as having a mild, moderate, or severe TBI. An indication of severity is given by the extent of altered consciousness experienced immediately following the head injury. This may vary from transient disorientation to deep coma. In the latter cases the patient may remain in coma for hours, days, weeks, or longer, and in very severe cases may never resume full consciousness. In such a case a persistent vegetative state is diagnosed. The majority of patients do, however, gradually regain consciousness, whereupon they are normally disorientated and confused. This period of confusion immediately following coma is known as post-traumatic amnesia (PTA) because it is defined as the failure to lay down new memories for ongoing events (Russell & Smith, 1961).

Opinions differ regarding how best to measure altered consciousness to classify the severity of TBI. In one approach, blunt head injuries are categorised according to the depth of initial coma, which, in turn, is usually quantified by giving the patient a score between 3 and 15 on the Glasgow Coma Scale (Teasdale & Jennett, 1976). On this widely used scale, points are gained in three categories: eye opening (ranging from four points for spontaneous eye opening to one point for nil); best motor response (ranging from six points for obeying commands through to one point for nil); and best verbal response (ranging from five points for oriented through to one point for nil). An alternative estimate is provided by the duration of altered consciousness. This is defined as actual loss of consciousness or coma as well as any subsequent period of confusion (PTA). Classifications of different degrees of severity of head injury are provided in Table 2.1. Mild head injuries are those that result in an initial score on the Glasgow Coma Scale of 13–15, or a period of altered consciousness (coma plus subsequent PTA) of less than one hour; moderate head injuries have a score of 9–12 or a period of altered consciousness of 1 to 24 hours; and severe injuries have a score of 3–8 and altered consciousness of 24 hours or more.

TABLE 2.1
Classification of severity of head injury according to depth of coma or length of period of altered consciousness

Severity	*Glasgow Coma Scale*	*Period of altered consciousness*
Mild	13–15	less than 1 hour
Moderate	9–12	1–24 hours
Severe	3–8	more than 24 hours

Incidence

The general incidence of head injury has been estimated at 180–200/100,000 population per annum, with males outnumbering females 2:1 and the highest incidence occurring in the 15–24 year age group (Kalsbeek, McLaurin, Harris, & Miller, 1980; Kraus, Black, Hessol, Ley, Rokaw, Sullivan, Bowers, Knowlton, & Marshall, 1984). Not all head injuries are serious, cause brain injury, or result in long-lasting impairment. It has been estimated that 82% of cases presenting to hospitals with head injuries were actually mild and either resulted in no brain injury per se or at most very mild brain injury (Kraus et al., 1984). The figures for moderate or severe TBI are much fewer and have been estimated between 12–14/100,000 and 15–20/100,000 population per annum respectively (Kraus et al., 1984; Tate, McDonald, & Lulham, 1998).

Motor vehicle accidents are by far the most common cause of TBI in general and specifically in the peak (18–25) age group (Kalsbeek et al., 1980; Kraus et al., 1984; Selecki, Ring, Simpson, Vanderfield, & Sewell, 1981). Falls are a common cause in the elderly (aged 75 or over) and the very young (0–4) while sporting accidents account for a significant proportion of injuries in the 5–14 age group (Tate et al., 1998). There is variation in the relative proportion of different causal factors that relate to the cultures examined. For example, there is a high incidence of brain injury as a result of violence and falls in the Bronx (Cooper, Tabaddor, Hauser, Shulman, Feiner, & Factor, 1983) and as a result of bicycle accidents in China (Wang, Schoenberg, Li, Yang, Cheng, & Bolis, 1986).

Neuropathology

The high velocity of the impact causing TBI produces a range of immediate neuropathological changes. First, the fibres constituting the white matter of the cerebrum are often stretched and rotated by the force of the injury leading to diffuse axonal damage. Secondly, small (and sometimes large) blood vessels are ruptured leading to multiple, often microscopic, areas of haemorrhage throughout the cerebrum. In addition, there are the classical coup injuries where the brain is bruised and lacerated at the point of impact and also contracoup injuries at distant points due to the brain ricocheting against the bony protuberances of the skull (see Fig. 2.1). The orbital and lateral surfaces of the frontal and temporal lobes are particularly vulnerable to such injury due to their proximity to the bony shelves of the anterior and middle fossae (see Fig. 2.2). A TBI may be either closed where the skull and/or the dura, the membrane covering the brain, remain intact, or open, in which case additional injury may occur because the skull is fractured and the cerebrum is penetrated by bony fragments.

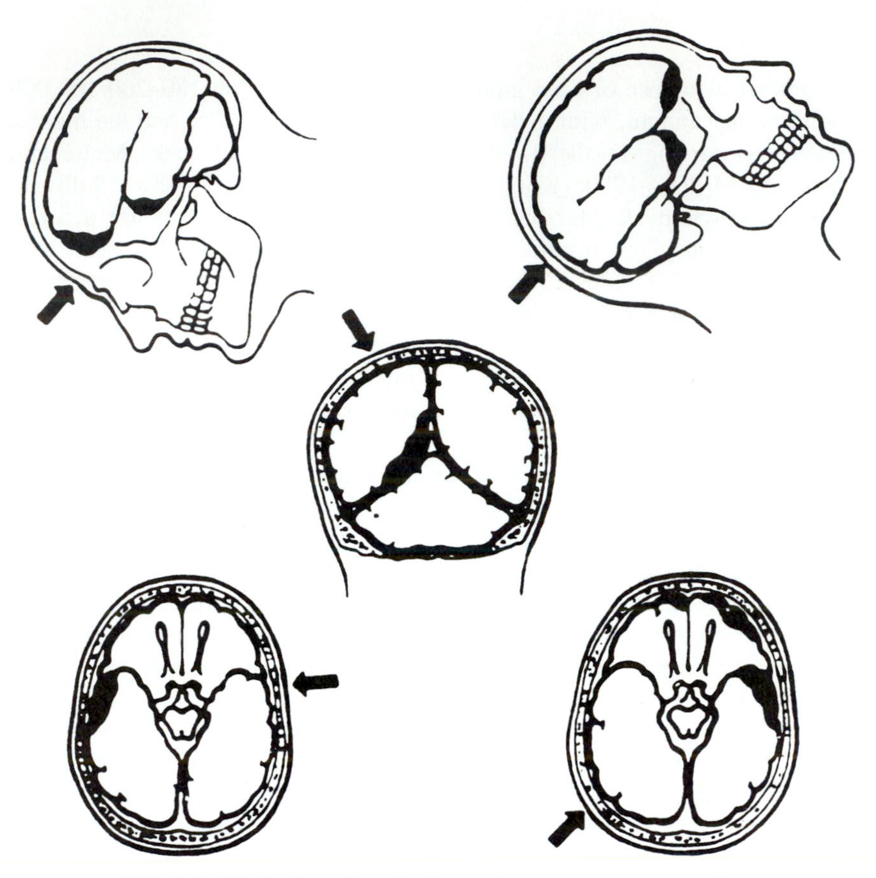

FIG. 2.1 Mechanism of cerebral contusion: From Courville (1945).

Secondary effects further complicate the injury and include odema, which rapidly causes generalised compression of the brain. Subdural haematoma, intracerebral haemorrhage and localised infarction can occur, as can more widespread hypoxia secondary to changes in cerebral blood flow, or chest and airway injuries. Infection where the brain has become exposed due to skull fracture or neurosurgical intervention is also a frequent consequence. Finally, metabolic changes and air or fat emboli from other injuries may further complicate the condition (Levin, Benton, & Grossman, 1982).

Clinical events

Management of a patient immediately following the TBI requires establishment of an adequate oxygen supply (by intubation if necessary) and stabilisation of other injuries. Neurosurgery may be necessary to debride

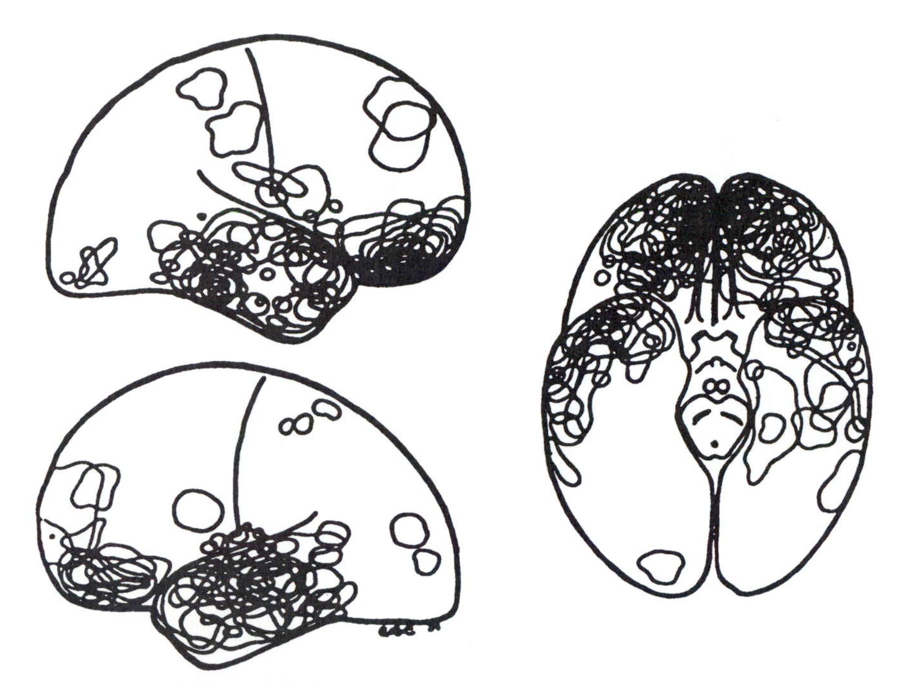

FIG. 2.2 Sites of cerebral contusion: From Courville (1945).

brain tissue of bone and other debris, stop bleeding, or relieve intracranial pressure. Once stabilised, the cardiorespiratory function and intracranial pressure of the unconscious patient are carefully monitored.

When the patient emerges from coma he or she enters into the state of post-traumatic amnesia (PTA), which requires quite different management techniques. While PTA is so named because of the characteristic amnesia for ongoing events, there are additional behavioural changes. There may be inappropriate and disturbed behaviour ranging from restless agitation to noisy shouting, verbal aggression, and occasionally assaultive behaviour (Eames, Haffey, & Cope, 1990). During this time the patient may be mobile and restless requiring special attention and supervision to prevent him or her coming to any harm. Emergence from PTA is usually gradual, characterised by increasing periods of lucidity, until the patient is noted to be consistently oriented in time and place and laying down memories of daily events. In modern head injury units, PTA is monitored via some form of PTA scale that provides probes for assessing orientation and simple new learning (e.g. Shores, Marosszeky, Sandanan & Batchelor, 1986). Prior to the systematic use of such scales, the duration of PTA was often estimated retrospectively by detailed questioning of the patient to determine when ongoing memories commenced.

In the weeks and months following PTA the patient usually demonstrates significant spontaneous improvement in physical and cognitive functions but this levels off within the second year of injury (Lezak, 1995). Active rehabilitation programmes for TBI sufferers usually commence once the patient has emerged from PTA. Severe TBI patients may require many months of in-patient therapy followed, in many cases, by additional therapy as out-patients. Despite improvements in rehabilitation services for the TBI population in recent years, long-term outcome studies have shown that the majority of severely injured patients continue to experience debilitating impairments, especially in cognitive function and behaviour, years after their injury (Brooks, McKinlay, Symington, Beattie, & Campsie, 1987; Conzen, Ebel, Swart, Skreczek, Dette, & Oppel, 1992; Kaplan, 1993; Levin, Coughlan, Tyerman, & Jenkins, 1985; Oddy, Grossman, Rose, & Teasdale, 1979; Thomsen, 1984).

Outcome of traumatic brain injury

Presence of impairment

Mild TBI rarely leads to ongoing disability (Tate et al., 1998), although a "post-concussional syndrome" of poor attention, slowed information processing, dizziness, headaches, and fatigue has been reported in a small proportion of such injuries (Bohnen, Jolles, Twijnstra, Mellink, & Wijnen, 1995; Leininger, Gramling, Farrell, Kreutzer, & Peck, 1990) which usually dissipates over the ensuing months (Gentilini, Nichelli, Schoenhuber, Bortolotti, Tonelli, Falasca, & Merli, 1985; Gronwall & Wrightson, 1981)[1]. Moderate injuries too are infrequently associated with lasting impairment (Tate et al., 1998). On the other hand, severe head injuries are almost always associated with some form of lasting impairment.

It has been estimated that 75% of patients with severe TBI have ongoing neurophysical impairments (Jennett, Snoek, Bond, & Brooks, 1981; Thomsen, 1984) although in 40% of cases these are mild and not apparent to the casual observer (Tate, Broe, & Lulham, 1989a). Similarly, approximately 67% of patients have ongoing neuropsychological problems defined as impairment on a range of tasks tapping cognitive abilities (e.g. memory, concept formation) and psychosocial parameters (e.g. loss of drive, loss of control) (Tate et al., 1989a). Only 8% of patients escape clinically significant deficits in either neurophysical or neuropsychological functioning and even these cases may have subtle impairments as a result of the TBI (Tate et al., 1989a). It is members of this severe group that have come under scrutiny for their poor communication skills.

Psychosocial outcome

There have been a number of studies that have followed up survivors of severe TBI in order to determine the level of functional outcome. It has been generally found that the majority of such patients examined had achieved independence in terms of activities of daily living (Tate, Lulham, Broe, Strettles, & Pfaff, 1989b; Ponsford, Olver, & Curran, 1995a) but had much poorer outcomes in terms of psychosocial function. For example, almost 50% of patients suffering a severe TBI have been found to have limited or no social contacts and few leisure interests one year or more later (Tate et al., 1989b; Wedell, Oddy, & Jenkins, 1980), while 64–68% were found to rely more on their parents or spouse for emotional support than prior to the injury (Ponsford et al., 1995a) and to have substantial difficulty forming new social relationships (Tate et al., 1989b). Only 30% or less of TBI patients previously employed find themselves in full-time employment (Brooks et al., 1987; McMordie, Barker, & Paolo, 1990; Ponsford, Olver, Curran, & Ng, 1995b; Tate et al., 1989b) and the majority of these either have a drop in occupational status or maintain their previous level only with difficulty (Tate et al., 1989b).

Psychosocial outcome is related to, but not synonymous with, degree of brain damage. In general terms, the severity and breadth of impairments experienced will have direct consequences for the capacity of the patient to resume his or her previous lifestyle. But the nature and constellation of these impairments have a complex relationship to outcome, with some kinds of impairment having greater consequence than others. Despite the fact that neurophysical and neuropsychological impairments occur at similar frequencies in the TBI population, it is the neuropsychological aspects, particularly those affecting personality and behaviour, that are most strongly related to poor social outcome (Bond, 1975, 1976; Tate, 1991) and relative stress (Brooks, Campsie, Symington, Beattie, & McKinlay, 1986; Kinsella, Packer, & Olver, 1991; Thomsen, 1984).

Incidence of dysarthria

Dysarthria refers to a group of speech disorders resulting from disturbances in muscular control that may be characterised by weakness, slowness, or incoordination of the speech mechanism due to damage to the central or peripheral nervous system or both. The term encompasses coexisting neurogenic disorders of several or all of the basic processes of speech; respiration, phonation, resonance, articulation, and prosody (Wertz, 1985). The incidence of dysarthria has been reported to occur in 8% (Thomsen, 1984) to 100% of TBI patients (Ylvisaker, 1986). Dysarthria following TBI has been reported to be one of the most persistent of communication impairments, resulting in a significant impact on the TBI victim's ability to regain functional independence (Beukelman & Yorkston, 1991). Dysarthric impairments following TBI vary widely in terms of type (e.g. ataxic, spastic, and mixed dysarthria) and severity (e.g. mild through to severe). The perceptual, acoustic, and physiological features associated with dysarthria following TBI are described in detail in Chapter 8. Although there is a paucity of research examining dysarthria treatment for people with TBI, there have been recent moves advocating the use of instrumentation in assessment and treatment (Theodoros & Murdoch, 1994) and awareness that recovery of dysarthric impairments may be possible over the period of several years (Enderby & Crow, 1990).

Incidence of aphasia

As discussed in Chapter 1, the actual incidence of aphasia has been estimated at between 2% (750 cases—Heilman, Safran, & Geschwind, 1971) and roughly 30% (56–125 patients—Sarno, 1980, 1984, 1988; Sarno, Buonaguo, & Levita, 1986). Anomic aphasia is reported to be the most prevalent in adults (Heilman et al., 1971; Levin, Grossman, & Kelly, 1976; Thomsen, 1975), whereas non-fluent aphasias (Global and Broca-like) are more prevalent in children and adolescents (Basso & Scarpa, 1990). For a proportion of these patients such aphasic deficits resolve over the ensuing months (Grosswasser, Mendelson, Stern, Schecter, & Najenson, 1977; Thomsen, 1975, 1984), although few completely regain premorbid language abilities (Basso & Scarpa, 1990; Thomsen, 1984).

Although not classified as aphasic, many other TBI patients perform lower than expected on aphasia battery subtests—e.g. confrontation naming, word-finding or verbal associative tasks, as well as structured tests of comprehension (Coppens, 1995; Gruen, Frankle, & Schwartz, 1990; Levin et al., 1976, 1979; Sarno, 1988). As we canvassed in Chapter 1, opinion has differed as to whether such deficits reflect a "subclinical aphasia" not apparent in casual conversation (Sarno, 1988) or other cognitive deficits including attention and memory disorders rather than linguistic impairment per se (Holland, 1984; Sohlberg & Mateer, 1989).

Incidence of neuropsychological sequelae

Non-linguistic cognitive impairments may or may not be responsible for poor performance on aphasia battery subtests. There can be no doubt, however, that effective communication skills rely upon the integrity of a range of cognitive and psychosocial abilities and that this integrity is frequently disrupted in the severe TBI population. Given the complexity of neuropathology associated with severe TBI, it is not surprising that the population is heterogeneous with respect to both nature and severity of neuropsychological impairments. Nevertheless, certain deficits are more common than others. In a consecutive series of severe TBI patients assessed 6 years post-injury (Tate, Fenelon, Manning, & Hunter, 1991) it was found that 56.5% suffered a disorder of memory and learning, 34% having a material specific learning problem (either verbal or non-verbal), while 22% had generalised learning difficulties. Slowed information processing was apparent in 34%, while in this study basic neuropsychological functions such as orientation, visual perception, ideomotor apraxia, constructional apraxia, and aphasic disorders accounted for only 16% of the deficits seen. Finally, executive disorders of either drive (inflexibility) or control (disinhibition) were seen in 40%. These latter deficits were apparent upon formal neuropsychological tests but also have implications for psychosocial function (Tate et al., 1991).

COGNITIVE DEFICITS AND PSYCHOSOCIAL FUNCTION FOLLOWING TBI

In the following sections we discuss the nature of specific cognitive impairments that are common in TBI and that are potentially important contributors to loss of communicative competence. In particular, we will focus on disorders of attention, memory, and executive function. In each section, the impairments will be described in detail, the neuroanatomical and cognitive implications considered, and common methods of assessment outlined. Following this, we will discuss psychosocial factors that have implications for communication skills. Organic personality change will be explored as well as other factors contributing to post-traumatic psychosocial function.

Attention and information processing speed

Clinical features

Poor attention and concentration are common complaints throughout the spectrum of severity of TBI, although notably more frequent and persistent after severe TBI (McKinlay, Brooks, Bond, Martinage, & Marshall, 1981; McKinlay, Brooks, & Bond, 1983; Oddy et al., 1985; Oddy, Humphrey, & Uttley, 1978; van Zomeren & van den Burg, 1985). Poor attention is manifested in a variety of ways. First, many severe TBI patients have difficulty dealing with complex information or tasks that are routine in everyday life. For example, it may be necessary to break down the planning of a bus trip into the component parts (getting a timetable, determining the fare, working out travel time, etc.) in order for the patient to complete this task successfully. Secondly, severe TBI patients are frequently extremely distractible. They may, for example, drop the task at hand in order to engage in conversation with a stranger who enters the therapy area or may cease responding to an instruction in physiotherapy in order to pick up a trivial object from the floor. The tendency to abandon one task for another also highlights an incapacity to attend to more than one thing at a time. In addition, therapists frequently complain that patients make mistakes due to lapses of attention (Ponsford & Kinsella, 1991).

Attention for demanding tasks

In an effort to examine the nature of attentional problems after TBI, researchers have turned to the cognitive psychology literature for a framework with which to explore different facets of attentional processes[2]. One model of cognitive processes describes attentional phenomena using the concept of working memory (Baddeley, 1990). This model is particularly useful as a perspective from which to consider problems attending to complex information following TBI.

Working memory theory. According to this approach, conscious attention, or working memory, is required whenever the task at hand is novel or demanding. Many quite complex tasks (e.g. driving a car) can be dealt with at a semi-automatic level and thus require little conscious attentional resources, with certain cues strongly prompting the habitual response. Such tasks can often be performed simultaneously with other more (attention) demanding tasks with little interference between the two (Schneider & Shiffrin, 1977). On the other hand, novel tasks require working memory in order to (1) juggle cognitive resources in order to perform more than one task simultaneously, (2) suppress habitual responses that might interfere with the generation of new ways of responding, and (3) guide cognitive activity in a goal-directed fashion. In working memory the "central executive" (Baddeley, 1990) or "supervisory attentional system" (Norman & Shallice, 1986) utilises information that is temporarily stored in an unspecified number of subsystems, including a "phonological loop" and "visuospatial scratch pad".

The central executive is limited in its capacity both in terms of the amount of information it can process at one time and also the speed with which this occurs. If its limits are exceeded, for example by increasing the amount of information it has to process, then the rate with which tasks are performed decreases accordingly (Baddeley, 1986; Baddeley & Hitch, 1974). If the demands are increased further errors begin to occur, and these typically reflect failure to inhibit habitual or stereotyped responses that are not appropriate in the given context (Baddeley, 1966). This model of attention and the roles that it plays fits well with clinical descriptions of TBI subjects who are slow to respond and inaccurate in their performance on demanding tasks.

Empirical evidence for impaired working memory. A variety of tasks that challenge working memory capacity in TBI patients in different ways have been conducted and, interestingly, these have demonstrated a loss of efficiency in quantitative rather than qualitative terms. For example, severe TBI subjects, while as accurate on the Stroop Test as matched controls, were slow under neutral conditions as well as conditions requiring the suppression of competing responses (Ponsford & Kinsella, 1992; Stuss, Ely, Hugenholtz, Richard, Larochelle, Poirier, & Bell, 1985). Divided attention tasks, including choice reaction time tasks have repeatedly demonstrated that severe TBI subjects are no less accurate than their matched controls although, once again, they are significantly slower (van Zomeren, 1981; Ponsford & Kinsella, 1992; Shum, McFarland, Bain, & Humphreys, 1990; Stuss, Stethem, Hugenholtz, Picton, Pivik, & Richard, 1989) with a disproportionate increase in reaction time, relative to controls, as the complexity of the task increases (Ponsford & Kinsella, 1992; van Zomeren, 1981; van Zomeren & Brouwer, 1987). Severe TBI subjects were also significantly slower than controls, although again, no less accurate on the Tower of London, a complex problem-solving task (Ponsford & Kinsella, 1992).

Problems of accuracy do, however, emerge when such patients are faced with tasks requiring divided attention that are paced in a manner that they cannot control—e.g. the Paced Auditory Serial Addition Test (Gronwall & Sampson, 1974). In such cases, severe TBI subjects have been reported to be significantly less accurate than controls (Ponsford & Kinsella, 1992). Ponsford and Kinsella (1992) concluded from their series of experiments that TBI subjects perform less efficiently on a variety of attentional tasks than non-brain damaged controls because their speed of information processing is reduced. Where possible they trade off speed in order to maintain accuracy but when this cannot occur errors emerge. Slowed information processing thus appears to have a significant impact upon working memory and therefore attentional capacity.

Neuroanatomical correlates of working memory. Van Zomeren and Brouwer (1987) have argued that slowed information processing has been demonstrated to be a non-specific effect of any type of brain damage and, in the case of TBI, may represent the net effect of diffuse injury resulting from shearing of long nerve fibres that constitute the white matter. This explanation fits with modern animal, cerebral blood flow, and computer simulation studies, all of which favour an explanation of working memory as a parallel distributed network that is not centralised and therefore not strongly localised. Instead, such models describe working memory as a set of dynamic associations between representations of goals, environmental stimuli, and stored knowledge (Kimberg & Farah, 1993). In turn, these representations are mediated by a specific constellation of subsystems spread across the human cortex, the particular subsystems activated being dependent on the given task (Goldman-Rakic & Friedman, 1991). According to this formulation, slowed information processing will have an effect that is not specific to task, but is disruptive to all demands on working memory.

Maintenance of attention over time

An aspect of attentional control that is not directly incorporated in the working memory thesis is the ability to maintain arousal and attention over an extended period. This has been termed "tonic" arousal (van Zomeren, 1981) and related to the brain stem reticular formation and its connections to the frontal lobes (Gronwall, 1987). Given the propensity for damage to occur in these areas in TBI it might be expected that many TBI patients suffer from loss of tonic arousal and therefore ability to maintain arousal, particularly in the context of long and monotonous tasks. However, experimental studies of TBI subjects (of varying degrees of severity from mild to very severe) performing such vigilance tasks have produced no changes in performance over time in comparison with controls (Brouwer & van Wolffelaar, 1985; Ponsford & Kinsella, 1992; van Zomeren & Brouwer, 1987).

Attention to important or novel events

Finally, "phasic" arousal is defined as those transient states of arousal that are stimulated by significant environmental or internal events (van Zomeren, 1981). Impaired phasic arousal has been suggested to underlie impaired selective attention and concomitant distractibility (Trexler & Zappala, 1988). It has been suggested that this reflects a failure to inhibit the salience of irrelevant stimuli secondary to damage to the dorsolateral prefrontal cortex (Knight, 1991). Given that distractibility is commonly reported after TBI (Ponsford & Kinsella, 1991) and the prefrontal lobes are frequently implicated (Lezak, 1995) the possibility exists that phasic arousal is specifically disturbed in TBI. However, investigation of the ability of severe TBI patients to benefit from warnings in a reaction time task suggest that, as a group, their phasic awareness was unimpaired (Ponsford & Kinsella, 1992).

Overview of attentional deficits following TBI

In summary, attentional deficits are frequently reported following severe TBI but are unlikely to reflect uniform impairment. A common finding is that of slowed information processing that limits both the amount of information that can be attended to and the time taken to perform complex tasks. Where possible speed is traded for accuracy, but when this is not possible errors emerge. Slowed information processing has been attributed to diffuse axonal injury. In addition, TBI patients have been observed to suffer underarousal and lapses in attention on extended tasks and this has been attributed to loss of tonic arousal associated with frontomedial brain stem dysfunction. Experimental evidence has not, at this stage, confirmed these observations. Finally, distractible behaviour is commonly associated with TBI, and has been attributed to diminished phasic arousal secondary to dorsolateral frontal lesions, but this too awaits experimental verification.

It is interesting that, on the whole, TBI patients have performed better than expected in most experimental studies of attention. Nevertheless, it is important to recognise that complex unstructured situations as commonly occur in everyday life are more demanding of attention than the controlled experimental tasks described here (Ponsford, Sloan, & Snow, 1995). Failure to elicit impaired attention on experimental tasks cannot, therefore, be taken as evidence of an absence of attentional deficit, particularly in the light of such frequent clinical observation to the contrary. The challenge remains to produce measures that are sensitive to observed attentional deficits that clearly elucidate their nature, and that are able to characterise these in a way that can be meaningfully translated into everyday behaviour.

Assessment of attention and information processing

Attention and concentration problems may be patently apparent when the TBI patient is faced with any task that is complex, demanding or sustained, or that must be performed in a noisy or otherwise busy environment. Neuropsychological testing does not always capture such problems because it is usually conducted in a quiet room free from distractions. Where attentional problems are sufficiently severe to interfere with neuropsychological testing these can be seen on standard tests that are sensitive to the needs of working memory and information-processing speed. Thus, Digit Span, especially Digits Backwards, of the revised or the third edition of the Wechsler Adult Intelligence Scale (WAIS-R, Wechsler, 1981; WAIS-III, Wechsler, 1997) may be differentially poor along with Letter-Number Sequencing (WAIS-III only), Arithmetic, Digit Symbol, and Symbol Search (WAIS-III only) subtests. Other WAIS subtests that require problem-solving skills may also be affected in some cases. Other tests specifically designed to tap working memory type skills include the Paced Auditory Serial Addition Test (PASAT) (Gronwall, 1977), the Trail Making Test (TMT) (Reitan, 1958), the Stroop Test (Trenerry, Crosson, DeBoe, & Leber, 1989) and various measures of complex reaction time (e.g. van Zomeren & Brouwer, 1987). A more comprehensive, behavioural approach to the assessment of attention is also provided by the Test for Everyday Attention (TEA) (Robertson, Ward, Ridgeway, & Nimmo-Smith, 1994).

Memory

Clinical features

Severe TBI is always associated with some period of amnesia comprising the period of post-traumatic amnesia (PTA). In addition, many TBI patients experience limited problems recalling events from the immediate past prior to the injury. There is inevitably a loss of recall for the moments immediately prior to the injury but in addition there may be a substantial loss of important autobiographical information such as all events in the weeks before, the last birthday prior to the accident, a wedding, or the birth of a child. In addition, there is commonly more substantive difficulties recalling ongoing events. Thus such patients may be forgetful of instructions, messages, and telephone calls while on the ward. They may get lost returning from the bathroom to their bed or when attempting to find their way to therapy. They may be unreliable in attending therapy without prompting and may fail to carry through information from one session to the next. Once at home, such memory problems can be extremely disabling. Shopping may be impossible without a list and driving may be seriously impeded by frequent wrong turns and episodes of disorientation. Appointments may be remembered only with the assistance of a diary. Work may be disrupted due to failure to recall names, information or new procedures, and the capacity to pass school or university tests may be severely impaired regardless of the amount of study and preparation. It is also difficult for a patient with poor ongoing memory to engage in social conversation and chat that often revolves around "gossip" or "small talk" involving free exchange of a copious number of details concerning recent events. Retrograde amnesia and ongoing new learning difficulties appear to represent distinct phenomena and will be discussed separately.

Retrograde amnesia

Retrograde amnesia—i.e. loss of memory for events preceding the trauma—can range from seconds to days, weeks or even months prior to the injury, and often shrinks as the patient recovers, although some brief period of permanent amnesia usually remains (Squire, 1987; Baddeley, 1990). The pervasiveness of retrograde amnesia varies in the TBI population as it does in other clinical groups (see Squire, 1987; Baddeley, 1990, for review). In some patients, particularly those still in PTA, retrograde amnesia may extend for decades with relative preservation of early, personally salient, memories (Levin, High, Meyers, von Laufen, Hayden, & Eisenberg, 1985). Once out of PTA, retrograde amnesia does tend to shrink to a time-limited period immediately preceding the injury (e.g. Barbizet, 1970) although it can also continue to operate across decades (Hunkin, Parkin, Bradley, Burrows, Aldrich, Jansari, & Burdon Cooper, 1995; Levin et al., 1985). Patients with severe TBI may also demonstrate faulty autobiographical knowledge that appears to be due to intrusions and confabulation (Baddeley, 1990; Baddeley, Harris, Sunderland, Watts, & Wilson, 1987).

New learning

Ongoing impairment in the capacity to lay down new memories is a salient feature of severe TBI. As noted above, this may present as a specific learning disorder for either verbal learning, reflecting damage to the left hemisphere, non-verbal learning implicating the right hemisphere, or, in fewer cases, a non-specific learning disorder reflecting bilateral cerebral pathology. Deficits in the ability to recall new memories can range from mild and inconvenient to severe and debilitating. There is also variability in the type of learning process affected.

Pure forgetting. For some, there is a problem of acquisition of new information—i.e. the memory is not stored or consolidated and therefore can neither be recalled nor recognised at a later stage. Such memory disorders are similar to those seen following damage to the hippocampus and associated structures (Lezak, 1995) and have therefore been attributed to damage to the medial temporal lobes—right in the case of visuospatial learning impairment, left in the case of verbal learning impairment, and both in the case of generalised learning impairment.

Imperfect learning. In many cases, the TBI patient may have faulty or imperfect learning. Information may be inadequately stored due to disorganised or passive learning strategies (Blachstein, Valkil, & Hoofien, 1993; Millis & Ricker, 1994). Alternatively, accurate recall may be diminished and contaminated by irrelevant intrusions (Haut & Shutty, 1992; Millis & Ricker, 1994). In many such cases the TBI patient may have difficulty spontaneously retrieving information but have adequate recall when provided with specific cues. Thus recognition of material previously encountered far outweighs spontaneous recall (Wilde, Boake, & Sherer, 1995). In addition to problems recalling isolated facts, severe TBI patients have been found to have additional difficulty recalling the temporal sequence of the information (Cooke & Kausler, 1995).

As regards the neuroanatomical correlates of imperfect learning, these same characteristics—i.e. impaired use of organisational strategies, susceptibility to interference, and poor temporal and contextual memory—have been reported following frontal lobe lesions from other aetiologies (e.g. della Rochetta & Milner, 1993; Janowsky, Shimamura, & Squire, 1989; Milner, 1971; Petrides, 1991; Shimamura, Janowsky, & Squire, 1990; Stuss, Alexander, Palumbo, Buckle, Sayer, & Pogue, 1994), as well as diencephalic lesions in Korsakoff's disease (Squire, 1987) and damage to the basal forebrain and striate secondary to anterior communicating artery aneurysm (DeLuca and Diamond, 1995). Given the propensity for damage to be sustained in the orbitomedial frontal areas in TBI it is likely that these features of learning impairment in TBI also arise from damage to frontal cortex and adjacent subcortical systems.

It has been suggested that learning impairments secondary to frontal lobe lesions reflect disturbance to a qualitatively distinct learning process in which context is systematically used to facilitate encoding and retrieval (Squire, 1987; Lezak, 1995). However, there is argument whether a dichotomy exists between the "classic" amnesias secondary to medial temporal lesions and "frontal" amnesias, or whether indeed these reflect degrees of severity in combination with other cognitive impairment (Baddeley et al., 1987; DeLuca & Diamond, 1995). Although the role of general executive impairment in producing frontal lobe learning deficits has been stressed in the past (Stuss & Benson, 1986; Walsh, 1987), empirical exploration has failed to confirm this relationship in TBI using standard tests of memory and executive function (Vanderploeg, Schinka, & Retzlaff, 1994). On the other hand, an association between general measures of impaired verbal learning, susceptibility to interference, and impaired working memory has been reported in TBI (Vanderploeg et al., 1994), implicating impaired working memory in some manifestations of imperfect learning in TBI.

Procedural learning. In some cases it has also been demonstrated that TBI patients are impaired in the acquisition of skills and procedures (Baddeley et al., 1987). Poor procedural learning has been associated with lesions specifically to the basal ganglia and is thought to reflect a quite distinct kind of memory problem (Mishkin & Appenzellar, 1987).

Assessment of memory

Assessment of retrograde memory loss has frequently been performed via interview and questioning of the patient on autobiographical details with collaboration from family members and friends. More recently, new tests of autobiographical memory have been developed—e.g. the Autobiographical Memory Interview (Kopelman, Wilson, & Baddeley, 1991).

In contrast, numerous tests and procedures have been developed to assess ongoing memory and learning. This is a complex procedure that takes into account modality, level of complexity, structure available when encoding, and availability of cues in recall. Commonly used tests include the original Wechsler Memory Scale (WMS) (Wechsler, 1974), the revised version (Wechsler, 1987), and the third edition (Wechsler, 1997). In addition there is the Rey Auditory Verbal Learning Test (Taylor, 1959), the more recent Californian Verbal Learning Test (Delis, Kramer, Kaplan, & Ober, 1987), the Rey Osterrieth Complex Figure (Osterrieth, 1944), and the Benton Visual Retention Test (Benton, 1974). The Rivermead Behavioural Memory Test (Wilson, Cockburn, & Baddeley, 1985) provides a simple, practical assessment of everyday memory function that is particularly useful for more severe memory impairments.

Executive impairment

Executive functions are those that mediate and regulate other cognitive activities and behaviour in a purposeful and goal-directed fashion. Loss of executive control thus results in failure to problem solve effectively and to adapt to changing circumstances. Executive deficits have been considered the most disruptive to successful rehabilitation (Lezak, 1995). Unfortunately, of all neuropsychological sequelae of TBI, executive impairment has also been estimated to be, on average, the most severely disturbed of cognitive functions when premorbid intelligence is controlled for (Johnstone, Hexum, & Ashkanazi, 1995).

Clinical features

Having said this, the severity and degree to which executive impairment manifests from one individual to the next varies enormously, influenced not only by the severity of the injury but also premorbid intelligence, motivation, and the nature of the task (Shallice & Burgess, 1991; Sloan & Ponsford, 1995). In less severe cases, routine behaviour previously learnt may be carried out normally and basic skills retained. However, there may be a disruption of the capacity to focus attention voluntarily and to deal with novel situations adaptively. When deficits are more pervasive all behaviour may be disrupted.

Many aspects of executive impairment can be described as representing either a loss of drive or a loss of control. Impaired drive will result in an uncontrolled apathy or inertia, rigidity, inflexibility, and perseveration. Such patients may have difficulty initiating any behaviour unprompted, or in less severe cases may be restricted to behaviour that is stereotypic, repetitive, and stimulus bound. A disorder of control is characterised by poor response inhibition. These patients are impulsive, disinhibited, and distractible. Disorders of drive and control are dissociable, representing distinct pathological processes, as evidenced by the finding that they manifest both separately and in coexistence in a significant minority of severe TBI patients (Tate et al., 1991).

Problem-solving behaviour may be disrupted by either kind of impairment. Patients may be unable to anticipate a situation, or analyse it critically. They may focus on concrete or superficial aspects of their environment, failing to assume a more abstract attitude or be disorganised and fragmented when formulating a plan of action, and have difficulty maintaining a stable intention when carrying it out. Executive impairment may result in failure to regulate behaviour with an internal command producing the curious dissociation between "knowing" and "doing" whereby the patient can verbalise an instruction or intention while being unable to use that intention to guide behaviour (Walsh, 1985). Error utilisation may also be affected, preventing the patient from evaluating his or her progress critically and modifying it in the light of feedback. In other words, such patients may fail to learn from experience.

Neuroanatomical correlates of executive function

Executive function has been associated with the frontal lobes, in particular the prefrontal regions that have been attributed with the activation, programming, regulation, and verification of other cognitive activity (Luria, 1973, 1976). It has been suggested that the dorsolateral aspects of the prefrontal lobes with their rich connections to sensory and motor functional systems mediate the intellectual regulation of behaviour and cognition, while the orbitomedial and basal aspects with their rich limbic connections have been associated with control and regulation of internal drives and emotion (Alexander, Benson, & Stuss, 1989).

The particular manifestation of executive impairment will depend on the size and locus of the pathology. It has been shown experimentally that the severity and pervasiveness of intellectual disturbance ascribed to frontal lobe pathology is often a result of frontal lobe pathology in association with more global cerebral dysfunction (Canavan, Janota, & Schurr, 1985). Patients with more circumscribed lesions may escape many of the deficits described (Drewe, 1975). In the case of TBI, there is strong argument that many features of the "frontal lobe syndrome" are, in fact, produced by diffuse pathology (Anderson, Bigler, & Blatter, 1995). To account for this observation in TBI and other diffuse or multi-focal pathologies it has been argued that "frontal lobe" deficits may not necessarily reflect disruption to a "centre" in the frontal lobes but, rather, result from lesions to frontal distributed networks and/or subcortical relay stations and associated connections (Mesulam, 1990).

Cognitive explanations of executive dysfunction

Because the underlying neuropathology associated with loss of regulation of behaviour and thought is thus difficult to localise, it has been argued that the syndrome should not be described in terms of neuroanatomy, but rather in terms of its cognitive effects—i.e. as a "dysexecutive syndrome" (Baddeley, 1990). The focus of contemporary cognitive models of executive function has been on the development of a unified account for the mechanisms underlying executive *control*. According to such models, executive control is mediated by a diffuse network of operations that fits with the neuroanatomical evidence for more diffuse pathology underlying executive dysfunction in TBI. For example, according to the influential model proposed by Shallice (1988) the symptoms seen in the dysexecutive syndrome are thought to reflect the impairment of a "supervisory attentional system" (Norman & Shallice, 1986) which has access to all other cognitive processes, and which overrides routine and habitual responses to enable novel responses to occur. This conceptualisation suggests that behaviour such as perseveration, stimulus-bound responding, and distractibility are reflections of habitual responses triggered automatically and in an uncontrolled manner by internal or external events (Duncan, 1986; Shallice, 1988). This type of explanation also places working memory as central to executive control (Baddeley, 1990; Daigneault, Braun, & Whitaker, 1992; Fuster, 1991; Goldman-Rakic & Friedman, 1991; Kimberg & Farah, 1993) because it is here that representations of perceptual information, memory, actions, and goals are activated and maintained and irrelevant associations inhibited so that purposeful plans can be formed and behaviour monitored to ensure the desired goal is achieved.

Disruption of working memory as an explanation for impaired executive function in TBI is consistent with observation of impaired working memory on other kinds of tasks as described in our discussion of attentional disorders. Whether all attributes of executive impairment in TBI can be usefully described using this rubric has, however, been questioned (e.g. van Zomeren & Brouwer, 1987). Certainly the model is useful for addressing the regulation of ongoing behaviour and the control of cognitive processes engaged in goal-directed behaviour. However, the role of emotion and personality change following TBI must also be considered when describing the full spectrum of the "dysexecutive" syndrome/s.

Assessment of executive dysfunction

It has been frequently observed that patients with frontal lobe impairment do not demonstrate deficit on standardised tests of intelligence such as the WAIS-R (e.g. Shallice & Burgess, 1991) or other tests that rely on well-learned or familiar routines.

There is, however, enormous variability in the severity and pervasiveness of executive dysfunction exhibited and, in severe cases, performance on even the most basic tasks can be disrupted due to disorganised, concrete, or perseverative responding. For example, patients who are confined to extremely concrete responses may perform abnormally on the Wechsler Vocabulary Subtest because they interpret part of the word without reference to its entirety—e.g. interpreting "fortitude" as referring to a fort (Walsh, 1987). In less severe cases, standard tests that rely on well-learned knowledge (such as vocabulary) may be performed adequately by patients with executive disorders, whereas tasks that require novel inference or simple problem solving may be below premorbid expectations. Thus, using the WAIS-R (or WAIS III), it is not uncommon to see subtests such as Block Design, Object Assembly, and Similarities performed poorly by frontally damaged patients compared with subtests tapping general knowledge such as Vocabulary and Information (Lezak, 1995). There is, of course, enormous normal variation in the capacity to perform on such tests and interpretation of abnormal performance needs to be made with care, taking into consideration the psychometric properties of the tests as well as the appropriate normative data.

Where the TBI patient is well educated, highly intelligent and/or has relatively subtle executive impairments there may be no evidence of difficulty on such tasks, and problems will only be apparent on more difficult and taxing tests. Thus the Controlled Oral Word Association Test (COWAT) (Benton, 1973), the Wisconsin Card Sorting Test (WCST) (Heaton, Chelune, Talley, Kay, & Curtiss, 1993), the Rey-Osterrieth Complex Figure (Osterrieth, 1944), the Halstead Category Test (DeFilippis, McCampbell, & Rogers, 1979), and the Tower of London (Shallice, 1982) have each become known as "frontal lobe tests". This term is misleading because such tests can be failed for a variety of reasons and are therefore susceptible to the effects of many types of cognitive impairment as well as generalised cerebral dysfunction. Only in cases where there is no evidence of basic cognitive disturbance can impaired performance on such tests be reasonably attributed to executive dysfunction. In such cases quantitative scores are frequently in the abnormal range. In addition there may be qualitative features of test performance that point to executive disturbance. For example, perseveration, rule breaking and failure to maintain attentional set are often observed and are indicative of disorders of drive and control respectively. The WCST actually enables such behaviour to be scored and compared with available normative data (Heaton et al., 1993). New tests directly designed to assess a variety of aspects of dysexecutive function are also beginning to emerge, like the Behavioural Assessment of the Executive Syndrome (BADS) (Wilson, Alderman, Burgess, Emslie, & Evans, 1996).

Finally, there is a significant proportion of TBI patients who appear to suffer executive dysfunction, and may indeed have demonstrable pathology on CT scan, who do not exhibit deficits at all on standardised tests (e.g. Shallice & Burgess, 1991). In such cases impairment of frontal control systems is mainly apparent in behaviour in everyday life. For example, despite normal or even superior ability on most neuropsychological tests, frontal lobe dysfunction has been associated with a profound disorganisation of daily activities, irresponsibility, and indecision on the most trivial matters, sometimes of sufficient severity to prohibit return to work and independent living (e.g. Saver & Damasio, 1991; Shallice & Burgess, 1991).

Personality change

Personality change is extremely common following severe TBI, occurring in 60–80% of the population (Brooks et al., 1986; Jennett et al., 1981; McKinlay et al., 1981; Thomsen, 1975). It is also a problem that persists in the majority of these patients as indicated by similar prevalence figures many years later (Brooks et al., 1986; Oddy et al., 1985; Thomsen, 1984) and must be considered a significant contributing factor to reduction of psychosocial functioning observed in this group.

Organic changes to emotional behaviour

There have been a number of studies that have attempted to categorise the nature of personality change using questionnaires and interviews completed by the TBI patient or their relatives. According to this research, irritability and fatigue are the most common complaints (Brooks et al., 1986; Dikmen, Machamer, & Tomkin, 1993; Kaitaro, Koskinen, & Kaipo, 1995; Kinsella, Packer, & Olver, 1991; Thomsen, 1984; Weddell, Oddy, & Jenkins, 1980). These features have been thought to reflect quite different underlying pathologies. In parallel to explanations of cognitive changes following executive impairment it appears that personality change can also be characterised as a loss of emotional control and loss of motivation (arousal) respectively (Kinsella et al., 1991), each encompassing a range of behavioural changes. Short temper, quarrelsomeness, aggression, emotional lability, self-centredness, and impulsiveness have been associated with loss of emotional control (Kinsella et al., 1991). In addition, childishness and sexually disinhibited behaviour have been frequently reported (Brooks et al., 1986; Lezak, 1978;

Thomsen, 1984); Thomsen, 1984; Lezak, 1978) and would seem to belong to this constellation of problems. On the other hand, decreased initiative, loss of spontaneity, disinterest, socially inappropriate behaviour, and talkativeness have also been frequently observed (Kaitaro et al., 1995; Kinsella et al., 1991; Thomsen, 1984) and have been associated with lowered arousal or motivation (Kinsella et al., 1991). In support of these observations of behavioural changes, direct assessment of personality provided by relatives completing the Eysenck Personality Questionnaire has supported the notion that TBI subjects become increasingly withdrawn and emotionally unstable relative to their premorbid nature after the injury (Tate, 1995).

Contribution of cognitive deficits to personality change

Lezak, in her oft cited description of the characterologically altered person following TBI (Lezak, 1978), includes aspects of cognitive functioning in her description of personality change. Thus she suggests that stimulus-bound behaviour, rigidity, poor planning and organisational skills, and a failure to profit from experience characterise many TBI patients. Translated into the psychosocial sphere these deficits have major ramifications for adequate social function. First, stimulus-bound behaviour and rigidity may result in poor judgement, the tendency to be "black and white" in the appraisal of social information, and perseverative, rigid, and uncompromising when responding in social contexts. Such patients may also have difficulty perceiving the viewpoint of others. The notion that there is a loss of empathy has been empirically supported by the finding that a group of TBI patients were incapable of filling out a personality questionnaire "as though they were someone else" (Spiers, Pouk, & Santoro, 1994) and also by the related finding that loss of flexibility is associated with measures of empathy (Eslinger & Grattan, 1993) and more general estimates of social skill (Marsh & Knight, 1991).

Secondly, poor planning, organisation, and self-regulation results in a failure to successfully plan, initiate and complete projects, often despite proclaimed schemes and assurances to the contrary. This kind of behaviour was perhaps most vividly described by Dr. Harlow of his celebrated patient Phineas Gage (as cited in Walsh, 1987, p.117): "impatient of restraint and advice when it conflicts with his desires, at times perniciously obstinate yet capricious and vacillating, devising many schemes for future operation which no sooner are arranged than they are abandoned in turn for others seeming more feasible". In less extreme cases, projects may be commenced only to be abandoned before completion, or the patient may experience difficulty juggling priorities in order to maximise the use of time and resources (Shallice & Burgess, 1991).

Lack of insight

Finally, an important and frequent observation is that many TBI patients are unrealistic in self-appraisal and suffer from a lack of insight (Flanagan, McDonald, & Togher, 1995; Levin, Goldstein, Williams, & Eisenberg, 1991; Lezak, 1978; Lishman, 1990;). Thus, plans for the future may be unrealistically optimistic as patients continually fail to take their newly acquired deficits into account. For example, a young man with severe TBI seen by these authors was insistent that he could return to his trade as an electrician despite massive damage to his eyes and consequent total blindness. Even when this was pointed out, he insisted that he could return, relying on a workmate to tell him the colours of the wires. Empirical studies have demonstrated that a proportion of severe TBI subjects consistently underestimate memory impairments (Boake, Freelands, Ringholz, Nance, & Edwards, 1995), their ability to do a variety of simple and complex tasks (Fordyce & Roueche, 1986; Prigatano & Altman, 1990), and their intellectual and behavioural limitations (Godfrey, Partridge, Knight, & Bishara, 1993).

Lack of insight is a complex phenomenon and may encompass organic deficit culminating in a loss of self-reflection (Lezak, 1978), combined with the acute effects of adjustment to altered physical and mental abilities (e.g. denial and anger) (Crosson, 1987). Insight improves over time (Bond, 1984; Fordyce, Roueche, & Prigatano, 1983; Godfrey et al., 1993) perhaps as continual exposure to the consequences of his or her impairments provides the patient with feedback concerning these. Furthermore, there is some evidence that insight is not uniformly diminished. For example, while concern about lack of insight has resulted in the avoidance of self-report measures in earlier studies of emotional and behavioural consequences of TBI (e.g. Brooks & McKinlay, 1983; Oddy & Humphrey, 1980; Thomsen, 1975, 1984), it has been demonstrated more recently that TBI patients are capable of reliably reporting emotional changes both in the short and longer term—i.e. six months or less and five years or more respectively (Elsass & Kinsella, 1987; Kinsella, Moran, Ford, & Ponsford, 1988). Not only this, but there is reasonable correlation between self-report of emotional responses and ratings provided by a "close other" (Elsass & Kinsella, 1987; Fordyce et al., 1983; Kinsella et al., 1988) providing additional validation for the stability of head-injured self-report of their emotional state. The extent to which such self-ratings of emotion reflect accurate self-appraisal in a broader sense is unclear. For example, such patients, while able to report that they had fewer opportunities for social contact than premorbidly, were not less satisfied with this state of affairs (Elsass & Kinsella, 1987).

Neuroanatomical correlates of personality change

To some extent, personality change can be attributed to loss of regulation of emotional behaviour similar to the dysexecutive syndrome affecting intellectual processes. Damage to the orbitomedial and orbitobasal aspects of the prefrontal lobes, thought to mediate emotional control, is particularly prevalent in TBI and has been associated with descriptions of personality change in TBI (Levin et al., 1991) and frontal lobe injury from other aetiologies (DeLuca and Diamond, 1995; Girgis, 1971; Lishman, 1990; Saver & Damasio, 1991). Further specification of emotional changes in terms of intrafrontal organisation follows suggestion that damage to the orbitomedial cortex and connections will produce lower arousal while lesions to the orbitobasal cortex will produce impaired impulse control (Lezak, 1995). The inability to critically self-reflect with concomitant lack of insight has also been attributed to the prefrontal systems of the brain (Alexander, Benson, & Stuss, 1989; Stuss & Benson, 1986) and has been associated with relatively more extensive lesions in TBI, particularly affecting the frontal and parietal lobes (Prigatano & Altman, 1990). Finally, it has been suggested that explosive outbursts of anger may reflect temporal lobe abnormalities (Eames, 1990).

Psychological reactions

In addition to organic personality change there are normal psychological reactions to acute disablement and its chronic effects. Denial and anger may masquerade as, or else exacerbate, lack of insight and loss of emotional control in the acute stages (Crosson, 1987). In the longer term depression is common, being estimated at between 33% (Kinsella et al., 1988) and 60% (Tyerman & Humphrey, 1984), as is anxiety, occurring in 26% to 44% of TBI patients sampled, as reported by these same researchers. Furthermore, there is reason to believe that these conditions become more prevalent in the early years following the injury (Fordyce et al., 1983) as insight improves (Godfrey et al., 1993), and particularly in subjects who do not have any close confidantes (Kinsella et al., 1988).

Premorbid personality

The premorbid personality of patients with TBI will obviously influence the manner in which they present post-trauma. Pre-existing psychiatric conditions, personality difficulties, or lack of social skills will create additional obstacles to successful rehabilitation and reintegration. Nevertheless, it is important not to overstate the extent to which premorbid factors account for post-traumatic personality problems. For example, it has been argued that youth at risk of TBI tend to have poor social adjustment premorbidly, as evidenced by learning difficulties, criminal behaviour, and drug and alcohol abuse (Bond, 1984; Brooks, 1984; Levin et al., 1982). However, systematic and controlled study of the incidence of premorbid personality problems in TBI relative to other members of their cohort is generally unavailable. Where incidence estimates have been obtained for selected groups of TBI subjects, these have revealed that poor social adjustment is only apparent in the minority. For example, it has been estimated that between 18% and 44% of young male patients with head injuries had a history of alcohol abuse (Hall, Karzmark, Stevens, Englander, O'Hare, & Wright, 1994; Rimel, Giorani, Barth, & Jane, 1982), which is commensurate with the incidence seen in the general population of young American males (Cahalan & Cisin, 1968). Between 10% and 36% of head-injured subjects have used illicit drugs pre-injury (Kreutzer, Wehman, Harris, Burns, & Young, 1991; Tate, 1995), and between 15% and 30% have had criminal convictions (Hall et al., 1994; Kreutzer, Marwitz, & Witol, 1995, Tate, 1995). The incidence of these behaviours in the comparable cohort for these patients have not been reported, but risk-taking behaviour is generally high in this particular age group as evidenced by the finding that two-thirds of the general population with criminal convictions are under the age of 30 (Zawitz, 1988, as cited in Kreutzer et al., 1995). Finally, about 30% of patients presenting with severe TBI have been judged to have pre-existing educational difficulties (Tate, 1995) and 30% overall appeared to have definitely poor social adjustment premorbidly as evidenced by multiple areas of difficulty but, even so, none were defined as psychopathic on standard personality measures (Tate, 1995).

Thus it can be safely stated that while a minority of TBI subjects have definite premorbid social adjustment difficulties, this is not necessarily related to gross personality disturbance and is unlikely to account for the extent of personality problems seen post-morbidly. Indeed, attempts to establish a relationship between premorbid personality variables and psychosocial outcome have been unsuccessful (Tate, 1998). In addition, efforts to dismiss post-morbid personality change on the basis of premorbid characteristics are greatly diminished by the finding that when appropriate matched control groups are used—e.g. sibling controls (Tate et al., 1991); orthopaedic controls (Snow, 1994); or vocation and education matched controls (McDonald, 1992, 1993; McDonald & van Sommers, 1993)—group differences in facets of personality and social communicative behaviour emerge strongly.

As another slant on the role of premorbid personality in the post-traumatic picture, it has been suggested that post-traumatic personality change, particularly the less severe forms, reflects an exaggeration of premorbid personality (e.g. Crosson, 1987; Jarvie, 1954; Lishman, 1990) but, once again, there is no systematic study to substantiate this claim. Indeed, the preliminary results of an investigation into post-traumatic personality change indicates qualitative rather than quantitative differences (Tate, 1995).

Children and traumatic brain injury

This chapter has focused on the nature and sequelae of TBI as it affects the adult population, with particular emphasis on young adults because these represent the group with the highest prevalence for this kind of injury. Children too, however, are frequent victims of TBI as a result of similar causes to those seen in adults as well as a higher preponderance of falls and domestic abuse. The sequelae for children is, however, different for a variety of reasons. Depending on age, the cranium may not yet be fully developed and rigid, leading to a different constellation of forces impacting upon the cerebrum. The pattern of deficits too will differ depending on the age of the child. Impairments in executive skills may not be manifest in the younger child due to their relatively late maturation in normal development. Such problems, however, may become apparent as the child grows older. The cognitive sequelae of the TBI are also quite different in children compared with adults because the injury is incurred at a time when the child is actively developing and gaining relevant cognitive abilities and skills. The injury will therefore curtail the extent to which the child can benefit normally from this developmental process. Finally, the psychosocial implications are different for children, who are still dependent on their families for most of life's activities and are still actively learning, usually within the school system. Rehabilitation of children with TBI thus concentrates on educational reintegration.

Communication disorders

Although aphasia is infrequent in severe TBI, loss of communication skills is not. Unlike many aphasic patients who are observed to communicate better than they can talk, TBI patients appear to have problems in the reverse (Holland, 1984). Many of the characteristics of communication disorders after TBI have been introduced in Chapter 1 and these will be explored in much finer detail in the chapters to come. A summarised account of the clinical descriptions of these disorders is as follows.

First, they have been described as overtalkative (Hagan, 1984; Milton, Prutting, & Binder, 1984; Milton & Wertz, 1986) but inefficient (Hartley & Jensen, 1992), drifting from topic to topic (Snow, Lambier, Parsons, Mooney, Couch, & Russell, 1986), and making tangential and irrelevant comments (Prigatano, Roueche, & Fordyce, 1986). Alternatively, some patients are impoverished in the amount and variety of language produced (Chapman, Culhane, Levin, Harward, Mendelsohn, Ewing-Cobbs, Fletcher,

& Bruce, 1992; Ehrlich, 1988; Hartley & Jenson, 1991, 1992) and their conversational style is characterised by slow, frequently incomplete responses, numerous pauses, and a reliance on set expressions (Thomsen, 1975). Comprehension of conversational language may also be affected, particularly long or complex utterances (Thomsen, 1975) or conversational inference and innuendo (McDonald, 1992, 1993; McDonald & Pearce, 1995, 1996, 1998; McDonald & van Sommers, 1993). Conversational style may fail to acknowledge important social requirements as suggested by insensitivity to others, self-focused conversation without interest in other people, immature or inappropriate humour, frequent interruptions, blunt manner, overly familiar and disinhibited remarks or advances, and inappropriate levels of self-disclosure (Crosson, 1987; Flanagan et al., 1995; Milton & Wertz, 1986; Prigatano, 1986). Presumably, cognitive and psychosocial sequelae of TBI play a major role in the manifestation of these disorders and are implicated in their remediation. Having reviewed the nature of these neuropsychological and psychosocial parameters we are now well placed to examine different approaches to the assessment and management of communication disorders after TBI.

NOTES

1. There is some controversy about the outcome of mild head injury, possibly due to variation in subject population and test selection. While some ascertain that the symptomatic mild head-injured patient recovers completely within a few months of the injury, others have found persisting impairments. See Lezak (1995) for a review.
2. For those interested in this topic, a comprehensive account of experimental approaches to attentional processes can be found in Baddeley (1990) and, specifically as this relates to head injury, in van Zomeren and Brouwer (1987) and Ponsford and Kinsella (1992).

REFERENCES

Alexander, M.P., Benson, D.F., & Stuss, D.T. (1989). Frontal lobes and language. *Brain and Language*, *37*, 656–691.

Anderson, C.V., Bigler, E.D., & Blatter, D.D. (1995). Frontal lobe lesions, diffuse damage and neuropsychological functioning in traumatic brain-injured patients. *Journal of Clinical and Experimental Neuropsychology*, *17*, 900–908.

Baddeley, A. (1966). The capacity for generating information by randomisation. *Quarterly Journal of Experimental Psychology*, *18*, 119–129.

Baddeley, A. (1986). *Working memory*, Oxford: Oxford University Press.

Baddeley, A. (1990). *Human memory: Theory and practice*. Hove, UK: Lawrence Erlbaum Associates Ltd.

Baddeley, A., Harris, J., Sunderland, A., Watts, K.P., & Wilson, B.A. (1987). Closed head injury and memory. In H.S. Levin, J. Grafman, & H.M. Eisenberg (Eds.), *Neurobehavioural recovery from head injury*. New York: Oxford University Press.

Baddeley, A., & Hitch, G. (1974). Working memory. In G.A. Bower (Ed.), *Recent advances in learning and motivation* (Vol. 8). New York: Academic Press.

Barbizet, J. (1970). *Human memory and its pathology*. San Francisco, CA: Freeman.

Basso, A., & Scarpa, M.T. (1990). Traumatic aphasia in children and adults: A comparison of clinical features and evolution. *Cortex*, *26*, 502–514.

Benton, A.L. (1973). The measurement of aphasic disorders. In A. Caceres Velasquez (Ed.), *Aspectos patologicos del lengage*. Lima: Centro Neuropsicologico.

Benton, A.L. (1974). *The Revised Visual Retention Test* (4th ed.). New York: Psychological Corporation.

Beukelman, D.R., & Yorkston, K.M. (1991). Traumatic brain injury changes the way we live. In D.R. Beukelman & K.M. Yorkston (Eds.), *Communication disorders following traumatic brain injury* (pp.1–13) Austin, TX: Pro-Ed.

Blachstein, H., Valkil, E., & Hoofien, D. (1993). Impaired learning in patients with closed head injuries: An analysis of components of the acquisition process. *Neuropsychology*, *7*, 530–535.

Boake, C., Freelands, J.C., Ringholz, G.M., Nance, M.L., & Edwards, K.E. (1995). Awareness of memory loss after severe closed head injury. *Brain Injury*, *9*, 273–283.

Bohnen, N.I., Jolles, J., Twijnstra, A., Mellink, R., & Wijnen, G. (1995). Late neurobehavioural symptoms after mild head injury. *Brain Injury*, *9*, 27–33.

Bond, M.R. (1975). Assessment of the psychosocial outcome after severe head injury. In R. Porter & D.W. Fitzsimmons (Eds.), *Outcome of severe damage to the CNS* (pp.141–155). Ciba Foundation Symposium 34 (new series). Amsterdam: Elselvier.

Bond M.R. (1976). Assessment of the psychosocial outcome of severe head injury. *Acta Neurochirurgica*, *34*, 57–70.

Bond, M.R. (1984). The psychiatry of closed head injury. In N. Brooks (Ed.), *Closed head injury*. Oxford: Oxford University Press.

Brooks, D.N. (1994). *Closed head injury: Psychological, social and family consequences.* Oxford: Oxford University Press.

Brooks, D.N., & McKinlay, W. (1983). Personality and behavioural change after severe blunt head injury: A relative's view. *Journal of Neurology, Neurosurgery, and Psychiatry, 46,* 336–344.

Brooks, N., Campsie, L., Symington, C., Beattie, A., & McKinlay, W. (1986). The five-year outcome of severe blunt head injury: A relative's view. *Journal of Neurology, Neurosurgery and Psychiatry*, 49, 764–770.

Brooks, N., McKinlay, W., Symington, C., Beattie, A., & Campsie, L. (1987). Return to work within the first seven years of severe head injury. *Brain Injury*, *1*, 5–19.

Brouwer, W.H., & van Wolffelaar, P.C. (1985). Sustained attention and sustained effort after closed head injury. *Cortex*, *21*, 111–119.

Cahalan, D., & Cisin, I. (1968). American drinking practices: Summary of findings from a national probability sample: I. Extent of drinking by population subgroups. *Quarterly Journal of Studies on Alcohol*, *29*, 130–151.

Canavan, A., Janota, I., & Schurr, P.H. (1985). Luria's frontal lobe syndrome: Psychological and anatomical considerations. *Journal of Neurology, Neurosurgery and Psychiatry*, *48*, 1049–1053.

Chapman, S.B., Culhane, K.A., Levin, H.S., Harward, H., Mendelsohn, D., Ewing-Cobbs, L., Fletcher, J.M., & Bruce, D. (1992). Narrative discourse after closed head injury in children and adolescents. *Brain and Language*, *43*, 42–65.

Conzen, M., Ebel, H., Swart, E., Skreczek, W., Dette, M., & Oppel, F. (1992). Long-term neuropsychological outcome after severe head injury with good recovery. *Brain Injury*, *6*, 45–52.

Cooke, D.L., & Kausler, D.H. (1995). Content memory and temporal memory for actions in survivors of traumatic brain injury. *Journal of Clinical and Experimental Neuropsychology*, *17*, 90–99.

Cooper, K.D., Tabaddor, K., Hauser, A., Shulman, K., Feiner, C., & Factor, P.R. (1983). The epidemiology of head injury in the Bronx. *Neuroepidemiology*, *2*, 70–88.

Coppens, P. (1995). Subpopulations in closed head injury: Preliminary results. *Brain Injury*, *9*, 195–208.

Courville, C.B. (1945). *Pathology of the nervous system* (2nd ed.). Mountain View, CA: Calfornia Pacific Press.

Crosson, B. (1987). Treatment of interpersonal deficits for head-trauma patients in inpatient rehabilitation settings. *The Clinical Neuropsychologist*, *1*, 335–352.

Daigneault, S., Braun, C.M.J., & Whitaker, H.A. (1992). An empirical test of two opposing theoretical models of prefrontal lobe function. *Brain and Cognition*, *19*, 48–71.

DeFilippis, N.A., McCampbell, E., & Rogers, P. (1979). Development of a booklet form of a category test: Normative and validity data. *Journal of Experimental and Clinical Neuropsychology*, *1*, 339–342.

Delis, D.C., Kramer, J.H., Kaplan, E., & Ober, B.A. (1987). *Californian verbal learning test: Adult version*. San Antonia, TX: Psychological Corporation.

della Rochetta, A.I., & Milner, B. (1993). Strategic search and retrieval inhibition: The role of the frontal lobes. *Neuropsychologia*, *31*, 503–524.

DeLuca, J., & Diamond, B.J. (1995). Aneurysm of the anterior communicating artery: A review of neuroanatomical and neuropsychological sequelae. *Journal of Clinical and Experimental Neuropsychology*, *17*, 100–121.

Dikmen, S., Machamer, J., & Tomkin, N. (1993). Psychosocial outcome of patients with moderate–severe head injury: Two-year follow-up. *Brain Injury*, *7*, 113–124.

Drewe, E.A. (1975). An experimental investigation of Luria's theory on the effects of frontal lobe lesions in man. *Neuropsychologia, 13,* 421–429.

Duncan, J. (1986). Disorganisation of behaviour after frontal lobe damage. *Cognitive Neuropsychology*, 3, 271–290.

Eames, P. (1990). Organic bases of behavioural disorders after traumatic brain injury. In R.L. Wood (Ed.), *Neurobehavioural sequelae of traumatic brain injury*. Hove, UK: Psychology Press.

Eames, P., Haffey, W.J., & Cope, D.N. (1990). Treatment of behavioral disorders. In M. Rosenthal, M.R. Bond, E.R. Griffith, & J.D. Miller (Eds.), *Rehabilitation of the adult and child with traumatic brain injury* (2nd ed.). Philadelphia, PA: F.A. Davis.

Ehrlich, J.S. (1988). Selective characteristics of narrative discourse in head-injured and normal adults. *Journal of Communication Disorders*, *21*, 1–9.

Elsass, L., & Kinsella, G. (1987). Social interaction following severe closed head injury. *Psychological Medicine*, *17*, 67–78.

Enderby, P., & Crow, E. (1990). Long-term recovery patterns of severe dysarthria following head injury. *British Journal of Disorders of Communication*, *25*, 341–354.

Eslinger, P.J., & Grattan, L.M. (1993). Frontal lobe and frontal-striatal substrates for different forms of human cognitive flexibility. *Neuropsychologia*, *31*, 17–28.

Flanagan, S., McDonald, S., & Togher, L. (1995). Evaluation of the BRISS as a measure of social skills in the traumatically brain injured. *Brain Injury*, *9(4)*, 321–338.

Fordyce, D.J., & Roueche, J.R. (1986). Changes in perspectives of disability among patients, staff, and relatives during rehabilitation of brain injury. *Rehabilitation Psychology*, *31*, 217–219.

Fordyce, D.J., Roueche, J.R., & Prigatano, G.P. (1983). Enhanced emotional reactions in chronic head trauma patients. *Journal of Neurology, Neurosurgery and Psychiatry*, *46*, 620–624.

Fuster, J.M. (1991). Role of prefrontal cortex in delay tasks: Evidence from reversible lesion and unit recording in the monkey. In H.S. Levin, H.M. Eisenberg, & A.L. Benton (Eds.), *Frontal lobe function and dysfunction* (pp.59–71). New York: Oxford University Press.

Gentilini, N., Nichelli, P., Schoenhuber, R., Bortolotti, P., Tonelli, L., Falasca, A., & Merli, G.A. (1985). Neuropsychological evaluation of mild head injury. *Journal of Neurology, Neurosurgery and Psychiatry*, *48*, 137–140.

Girgis, M. (1971). The orbital surface of the frontal lobe of the brain. *Acta Psychiatrica Scandinavica, Supplementum*, *222*, 1–58.

Godfrey, H.P., Partridge, F.M., Knight, R.G., & Bishara, S. (1993). Course of insight disorder and emotional dysfunction following closed head injury: A controlled cross-sectional follow-up study. *Journal of Clinical and Experimental Clinical Neuropsychology*, 15, 503–515.

Goldman-Rakic, P.S., & Friedman, H.R. (1991). The circuitry of working memory revealed by anatomy and metabolic imaging. In H.S. Levin, H.M. Eisenberg, & A.L. Benton (Eds.), *Frontal lobe function and dysfunction* (pp.72–91). New York: Oxford University Press.

Gronwall, D.M.A. (1977). Paced Auditory Serial-Addition Task: A measure of recovery from concussion. *Perceptual and Motor Skills*, *44*, 367–373.

Gronwall, D.M.A. (1987). Advances in the assessment of attention and information processing after head injury. In H.S. Levin, J. Grafman, & H.M. Eisenberg (Eds.), *Neurobehavioural recovery from head injury* (pp.355–371). Oxford: Oxford University Press.

Gronwall, D.M.A., & Sampson, H. (1974). *The psychological effects of concussion.* Auckland: University Press/Oxford University Press.

Gronwall, D.M.A., & Wrightson, P. (1981). Memory and information-processing capacity after closed head injury. *Journal of Neurology, Neurosurgery and Psychiatry*, *44*, 889–895.

Grosswasser, Z., Mendelson, L., Stern, M.J., Schecter, I., & Najenson, T. (1997), Re-evaluation of prognostic factors in rehabilitation after head injury, *Scandinavian Journal of Rehabilitation Medicine, 9,* 147–149.

Gruen, A.K., Frankle, B.C., & Schwartz, R. (1990). Word fluency generation skills of head-injured patients in an acute trauma center. *Journal of Communication Disorders, 23,* 163–170.

Hagan, C. (1984). Language disorders in head trauma. In Holland, A. (Ed.), *Language Disorders in Adults*. San Diego, CA: College Hill Press.

Hall, K., Karzmark, P., Stevens, M., Englander, J., O'Hare, P., & Wright, J. (1994). Family stressors in traumatic brain injury: A two-year follow-up. *Archives of Physical Medicine and Rehabilitation, 75*, 876–884.

Hartley, L.L., & Jensen, P.J. (1991). Narrative and procedural discourse after closed head injury. *Brain Injury, 5*, 267–285.

Hartley, L.L., & Jensen, P.J. (1992). Three discourse profiles of closed head-injured speakers: Theoretical and clinical implications. *Brain Injury, 6*, 271–382.

Haut, M.W., & Shutty, M.S. (1992). Patterns of verbal learning after closed head injury. *Neuropsychology, 6*, 51–58.

Heaton, R.K., Chelune, G.J., Talley, J.L., Kay, G., & Curtiss, G. (1993). *The Wisconsin Card Sorting Test manual: Revised and expanded.* Odessa, FL: Psychological Assessment Resources.

Heilman, K.M., Safran, A., & Geschwind, N. (1971). Closed head trauma and aphasia. *Journal of Neurology, Neurosurgery, and Psychiatry*, *34*, 265–269.

Holland, A.L. (1984). When is aphasia aphasia? The problem of closed head injury. In R.W. Brookshire (Ed.), *Clinical aphasiology* (Vol. 14, pp.345–349). Minneapolis, MN: BRK Publishers.

Hunkin, N.M., Parkin, A.J., Bradley, V.A., Burrows, E.H., Aldrich, F.K., Jansari, A., & Burdon Cooper, C. (1995). Focal retrograde amnesia following closed head injury: A case study and theoretical account. *Neuropsychologia, 33*, 509–523.

Janowsky, J.S., Shimamura, A.P., & Squire, L.R. (1989). Source memory impairment in patients with frontal lobe lesions. *Neuropsychologia, 27*, 1043–1056.

Jarvie, H.F. (1954). Frontal lobe wounds causing disinhibition. A study of six cases. *Journal of Neurology, Neurosurgery and Psychiatry, 17*, 14–32.

Jennett, B., Snoek, J., Bond, M.R., & Brooks, N. (1981). Disability after severe head injury:

Observations on the use of the Glasgow Outcome Scale. *Journal of Neurology, Neurosurgery and Psychiatry, 44*, 285–293.

Johnstone, B., Hexum, C.L., & Ashkanazi, G. (1995). Extent of cognitive decline in traumatic brain injury based on an estimate of premorbid intelligence. *Brain Injury, 9*, 377–384.

Kaitaro, T., Koskinen, S., & Kaipo, M.L. (1995). Neuropsychological problems in everyday life: A five-year follow-up study of young, severely closed head-injured patients. *Brain Injury, 9*, 713–727.

Kalsbeek, W.D., McLaurin, R.L., Harris, B.S.H., & Miller, J.D. (1980). The national head and spine cord injury survey: Major findings. *Journal of Neurosurgery, 53*, S19–S31.

Kaplan, S.P. (1993). Tracking psychosocial changes in people with severe traumatic brain injury over a five-year period using the Portland Adaptability Inventory. *Rehabilitation Counselling Bulletin, 36*, 151–159.

Kimberg, D.Y., & Farah, M.J. (1993). A unified account of cognitive impairment following frontal lobe damage: The role of working memory in complex, organised behaviour. *Journal of Experimental Psychology: General, 122*, 411–428.

Kinsella, G., Moran, C., Ford, B., & Ponsford, J. (1988). Emotional disorder and its assessment within the severe head-injured population. *Psychological Medicine, 18*, 57–63.

Kinsella, G., Packer, S., & Olver, J. (1991). Maternal reporting of behaviour following very severe blunt head injury: two-year follow-up. *Journal of Neurology, Neurosurgery and Psychiatry, 54*, 422–426

Knight, R.T. (1991). Evoked potential studies of attention capacity in human frontal lobe lesions. In H.S. Levin, H.M. Eisenberg, & A.L. Benton (Eds.), *Frontal lobe function and dysfunction* (pp.139–156). New York: Oxford University Press.

Kopelman, M., Wilson, B., & Baddeley, A. (1991). *The Autobiographical Memory Interview*. Suffolk, UK: Thames Valley Test Company.

Kraus, J.F., Black, M.A., Hessol, N., Ley, P., Rokaw, W., Sullivan, C., Bowers, S., Knowlton, S., & Marshall, L. (1984). The incidence of acute brain injury and serious impairment in a defined population. *American Journal of Epidemiology, 119*, 186–201.

Kreutzer, J.S., Marwitz J.H., & Witol, D. (1995). Inter-relationships between crime, substance abuse and aggressive behaviours among persons with traumatic brain injury. *Brain Injury, 9*, 757–768.

Kreutzer, J.S., Wehman, P.H., Harris, J.A., Burns, C.T., & Young, H.F. (1991). Substance abuse and crime patterns among persons with traumatic brain injury referred for supported employment. *Brain Injury, 5*, 177–187.

Leininger, B.E., Gramling, S.E., Farrell, A.D., Kreutzer, J.S., & Peck, E.A. (1990). Neuropsychological deficits in symptomatic minor head injury patients after concussion and mild concussion. *Journal of Neurology, Neurosurgery and Psychiatry, 53*, 293–296.

Levin, H.S., Benton, A.L., & Grossman, R.G. (1982). *Neurobehavioural consequences of closed head trauma*. New York: Oxford University Press.

Levin, H.S., Goldstein, F.C., Williams, D.H., & Eisenberg, H.M. (1991). The contribution of frontal lobe lesions to the neurobehavioural outcome of closed head injury. In H.S. Levin, H.M. Eisenberg, & A.L. Benton (Eds.), *Frontal lobe function and dysfunction* (pp.318–338). New York: Oxford University Press.

Levin, H.S., Grossman, R.G., & Kelly, P.J. (1976). Aphasic disorders in patients with closed head injury. *Journal of Neurology, Neurosurgery and Psychiatry, 39*, 1062–1070.

Levin, H.S., Grossman, R.G., Rose, S.E., & Teasdale, G. (1979). Long-term neuropsychological outcome of closed head injury. *Journal of Neurosurgery, 50*, 412–422.

Levin, H.S., High, W.M., Meyers, C.A., von Laufen, A., Hayden, M.E., & Eisenberg, H.M. (1985). Impairment of remote memory after closed head injury. *Journal of Neurology, Neurosurgery and Psychiatry, 48*, 556–563.

Lezak, M.D. (1978). Living with the characterologically altered brain-injured patient. *Journal of Clinical Psychology, 39*, 592–598.

Lezak, M.D. (1995). *Neuropsychological assessment* (3rd ed.). New York: Oxford University Press.

Lishman, W.A. (1990). *Organic psychiatry* (2nd ed.). Oxford: Blackwell Scientific Publications.

Luria, A.R. (1973). *The working brain*. London: Penguin.

Luria, A.R. (1976). *Higher cortical functions in man*. London: Basic Books.

Marsh, N., & Knight, R.G. (1991). Relationship between cognitive deficits and social skill after head injury. *Neuropsychology, 5*, 107–117.

McDonald, S. (1992). Differential pragmatic language loss following closed head injury: Ability to comprehend conversational implicature. *Applied Psycholinguistics, 13(3)*, 295–312.

McDonald, S. (1993). Pragmatic language loss following closed head injury: Inability to meet the informational needs of the listener. *Brain and Language, 44*, 28–46.

McDonald, S., & Pearce, S. (1995). The Dice Game: A new test of organisational skills in language. *Brain Injury, 9(3)*, 255–271.

McDonald, S., & Pearce, S. (1996). Clinical insights into pragmatic language theory: The case of sarcasm. *Brain and Language, 53*, 81–104.

McDonald, S., & Pearce, S. (1998). Requests that overcome listener reluctance: Impairment associated with executive dysfunction in brain injury. *Brain and Language, 61*, 88–104.

McDonald, S., & van Sommers, P. (1993). Differential pragmatic language loss following closed head injury: Ability to negotiate requests. *Cognitive Neuropsychology, 10(4)*, 297–315.

McKinlay, W.W., Brooks, D.N., & Bond, M.R. (1983). Post-concussional symptoms, financial compensation, and outcome of severe blunt head injury. *Journal of Neurology, Neurosurgery and Psychiatry, 46*, 1083–1091.

McKinlay, W.W., Brooks, D.N., Bond, M.R., Martinage, D.P., & Marshall, M.M. (1981). The short-term outcome of severe blunt head injury as reported by relatives of the injured persons. *Journal of Neurology, Neurosurgery and Psychiatry, 44*, 527.

McMordie, W.R., Barker, S.L., & Paolo, T.M. (1990). Return to work (RTW) after head injury. *Brain Injury, 4*, 57–99.

Mesulam, M.M. (1990). Large-scale neurocognitive networks and distributed processing for attention, language and memory. *Annals of Neurology, 28*, 597–613.

Millis, S.R., & Ricker, J.H. (1994). Verbal learning patterns in moderate and severe traumatic brain injury. *Journal of Clinical and Experimental Neuropsychology. 16*, 498–507.

Milner, B. (1971). Interhemispheric differences in the localisation of psychological processes in man. *British Medical Bulletin, 27*, 272–277.

Milton, S.B., Prutting, C.A., & Binder, G.M. (1984). Appraisal of communication in head-injured adults. In R.W. Brookshire (Ed.), *Clinical aphasiology* (Vol. 14, pp.114–123). Minneapolis, MN: BRK Publishers.

Milton, S.B., & Wertz, R.T. (1986). Management of persisting communication deficits in patients with traumatic brain injury. In B.P. Uzzell & Y. Gross (Eds.), *Clinical neuropsychology of intervention*. Boston, MA: Martinus Nijhoff Publishing.

Mishkin, M., & Appenzellar, T. (1987). The anatomy of memory. *Scientific American, 256*, 62–71.

Norman, D.A., & Shallice, T. (1986). Attention to action: Willed and automatic control of behaviour. In R.J. Davidson, G.E. Schwartz, & D. Shapiro (Eds.), *Consciousness and self-regulation: Advances in research and theory* (Vol. 4. pp.1–18). New York: Plenum Press.

Oddy, M., Coughlan, T., Tyerman, A., & Jenkins, D. (1985). Social adjustment after closed head injury: A further follow-up seven years after injury. *Journal of Neurology, Neurosurgery and Psychiatry, 48*, 564–568.

Oddy, M., & Humphrey, M. (1980). Social recovery during the year following severe head injury. *Journal of Neurology, Neurosurgery, and Psychiatry*, *43*, 798–802.

Oddy, M., Humphrey, M., & Uttley, D. (1978). Subjective impairment and social recovery after closed head injury. *Journal of Neurology, Neurosurgery, and Psychiatry, 41*, 611–616.

Osterrieth, P. (1944). Le test de copie d'une figure complexe. *Archives de Psychologie, 30*, 206–356.

Petrides, M. (1991). Learning impairments following excisions of the primate frontal cortex. In H.S. Levin, H.M. Eisenberg, & A.L. Benton (Eds.), *Frontal lobe function and dysfunction* (pp.256–274). New York: Oxford University Press.

Ponsford, J.L., & Kinsella, G. (1991). The use of a rating scale of attentional behaviour. *Neuropsychological Rehabilitation, 1*, 241–257.

Ponsford, J.L., & Kinsella, G. (1992). Attentional deficits following closed head injury. *Journal of Clinical and Experimental Neuropsychology, 14*, 822–838.

Ponsford, J.L.. Olver, J.H., & Curran, C. (1995a). A profile of outcome two years following traumatic brain injury. *Brain Injury, 9*, 1–10.

Ponsford, J.L., Olver, J.H., Curran, C., & Ng, K. (1995b). Prediction of employment status two years after traumatic brain injury. *Brain Injury, 9*, 11–20.

Ponsford, J.L., Sloan, S., & Snow, P. (1995). *Traumatic brain injury: Rehabilitation for everyday adaptive living*. Hove, UK: Lawrence Erlbaum Associates Ltd.

Prigatano, G.P. (1986). Personality and psychosocial consequences of brain injury. In G.P. Prigatano, D.J. Fordyce, H.K. Zeiner, J.R. Roueche, M. Pepping, & B. Casewood (Eds.), *Neuropsychological rehabilitation after brain injury*. Baltimore, MD: Johns Hopkins University Press.

Prigatano, G.P., & Altman, I.W. (1990). Impaired awareness of behavioural limitations after traumatic brain injury. *Archives of Physical Medicine and Rehabilitation, 71*, 1058-1064.

Prigatano, G.P., Roueche, J.R., & Fordyce, D.J. (1986). Nonaphasic language disturbances after brain injury. In G.P. Prigatano, D.J. Fordyce, H.K. Zeiner, J.R. Roueche, M. Pepping, & B. Casewood (Eds.), *Neuropsychological rehabilitation after brain injury* (pp.18–28). Baltimore, MD: Johns Hopkins University Press.

Reitan, R.M. (1958). Validity of the Trail Making Test as an indicator of organic brain damage. *Perceptual and Motor Skills, 8*, 271–276.

Rimel, R., Giordani, B., Barth, J., & Jane, J.A. (1982). Moderate head injury: Completing the clinical spectrum of brain trauma. *Neurosurgery, 11*, 344–351.

Robertson, I.H., Ward, T., Ridgeway, V., & Nimmo-Smith, I. (1994). *The Test of Everyday Attention*. Suffolk, UK: The Thames Valley Test Company.

Russell, W.R., & Smith, A. (1961). A post-traumatic amnesia in head injury. *Archives of Neurology, 5*, 16–29.

Sarno, M.T. (1980). The nature of verbal impairment after closed head injury. *Journal of Nervous and Mental Diseases, 168*, 685–692.

Sarno, M.T. (1984). Verbal impairment after closed head injury: Report of a replication study. *Journal of Nervous and Mental Diseases, 172*, 475–479.

Sarno, M.T. (1988). Head Injury: Language and speech defects. *Scandinavian Journal of Rehabilitation. (Medical Supplement), 17*, 55–64.

Sarno, M.T., Buonaguo, A., & Levita, E. (1986). Characteristics of verbal impairment in closed head injury patients. *Archives of Physical Medicine and Rehabilitation, 67*, 400–405.

Saver, J.L., & Damasio, A.R. (1991). Preserved access and processing of social knowledge in a patient with acquired sociopathy due to ventromedial frontal damage. *Neuropsychologia, 29*, 1241–1249.

Schneider, R., & Shiffrin, R.M. (1977). Controlled and automatic information processing. I: Detection, search and detection. *Psychological Review, 84*, 1–66.

Selecki, B.R., Ring, I.T., Simpson, D.A., Vanderfield, G.K., & Sewell, M.F. (1981).

Injuries to the head, spine and peripheral nerves. Sydney: Sydney Health Commission of New South Wales.

Shallice, T. (1982). Specific impairments of planning. *Philosophical Transactions of the Royal Society of London, 298*, 199–209.

Shallice, T. (1988). *From neuropsychology to mental structure*. New York: Cambridge University Press.

Shallice, T., & Burgess, P.W. (1991). Deficits in strategy application following frontal lobe damage in man. *Brain, 114*, 727–741.

Shimamura, A.P., Janowsky, J.S., & Squire, L.R. (1990). Memory for the temporal order of events in patients with frontal lobe lesions and amnesic patients. *Neuropsychology, 28*, 803–813.

Shores, A., Marosszeky, J., Sandanam, J., & Batchelor, J. (1986). Preliminary validation of a clinical scale for measuring the duration of post-traumatic amnesia. *Medical Journal of Australia, 144*, 569–582.

Shum, D., McFarland, K., Bain, J.D., & Humphreys, M.S. (1990). Effects of closed head injury on attentional processes: An information-processing stage model. *Journal of Clinical and Experimental Neuropsychology, 12*, 247–264.

Sloan, S., & Ponsford, J. (1995). Assessment of cognitive difficulties following TBI. In J.L. Ponsford, S. Sloan, & P. Snow (Eds.), *Traumatic brain injury: Rehabilitation for everyday adaptive living*. Hove, UK: Lawrence Erlbaum Associates Ltd.

Snow, P. (1994). Discourse assessment following traumatic brain injury. In J. Fourez & N. Page (Eds.), *Treatment issues and long-term outcomes: Proceedings of the 18th Annual Conference of the Australian Society for the Study of Brain Impairment*. Bowen Hills: Australian Academic Press.

Snow, P., Lambier, J., Parsons, C., Mooney, L., Couch, D., & Russell, J. (1986). Conversational skills following closed head injury: Some preliminary findings. In C. Field, A. Kneebone, & M.W. Reid (Eds.), *Brain impairment: Proceedings of the 11th Annual Conference of the Australian Society for the Study of Brain Impairment*. Richmond, Victoria: Australian Society for the Study of Brain Impairment, Bethesda Hospital.

Sohlberg, M.M., & Mateer, C.A. (1989). *Introduction to cognitive rehabilitation: Theory and practice*. New York: Guildford Press.

Spiers, M.V., Pouk, J.A., Santoro, J.M. (1994). Examining perspective taking in the severely head injured. *Brain Injury, 8*, 463–473.

Squire, L.R. (1987). *Memory and brain*. New York: Oxford University Press.

Stuss, D.T., Alexander, M.P., Palumbo, C.L., Buckle, L., Sayer, L., & Pogue, J. (1994). Organisational strategies of patients with unilateral and bilateral frontal lobe injury in word list learning tasks. *Neuropsychology, 8*, 355–373.

Stuss, D.T., & Benson, D.F. (1986). *The frontal lobes*. New York: Raven Press.

Stuss, D.T., Ely, P., Hugenholtz, H., Richard, M.T., Larochelle, S., Poirier, C.A., & Bell, I. (1985). Subtle neuropsychological deficits in patients with good recovery after closed head injury. *Neurosurgery, 17*, 41–47.

Stuss, D.T., Stethem, L.L., Hugenholtz, H., Picton, T., Pivik, J., & Richard, M.T. (1989). Reaction time after head injury: Fatigue, divided and focused attention, and consistency of performance. *Journal of Neurology, Neurosurgery and Psychiatry, 52*, 742–748.

Tate, R.L. (1991). Impairments after severe blunt head injury: Their consequences for rehabilitation and psychosocial reintegration. In W.R. Levick, B.G. Frost, M. Watson, & H.P. Pfister (Eds.), *Brain impairment: Advances in applied research. Proceedings of the 15th Annual Conference of the Australian Society for the Study of Brain Impairment* (pp.219–227). Newcastle, UK: University of Newcastle.

Tate, R.L. (1995). A prospective study of personality change after traumatic brain injury: A preliminary report. In J. Fourez & N. Page (Eds.), *Treatment issues and long-term outcomes: Proceedings of the 18th Annual Conference of the Australian Society for the Study of Brain Impairment*. Bowen Hills: Australian Academic Press.

Tate, R.L. (1998). "It is not only the kind of injury that matters but the kind of head": The contributions of premorbid psychosocial factors to rehabilitation outcomes after severe traumatic brain injury. *Neuropsychological Rehabilitation, 8*, 1–18.

Tate, R.L., Broe, G.A., & Lulham, J.M. (1989a). Impairment after severe head injury: the results from a consecutive series of 100 patients. *Acta Neurologica Scandinavia, 79*, 97–107.

Tate, R.L., Fenelon, B., Manning, M.L., & Hunter M. (1991). Patterns of neuropsychological impairment after severe blunt head injury. *Journal of Nervous and Mental Disease, 179*, 117–126.

Tate, R.L., Lulham, J.M., Broe, G.A., Strettles, B., & Pfaff, A. (1989b). Psychosocial outcome for the survivors of severe blunt head injury: The results from a consecutive series of 100 patients. *Journal of Neurology, Neurosurgery and Psychiatry, 52*, 1128–1134.

Tate, R.L., McDonald, S., & Lulham, J.L. (1998). Traumatic brain injury: Severity of injury and outcome in an Australian population. *Journal of Australian and New Zealand Public Health, 22*, 11–15.

Taylor, E.M. (1959). *Psychological appraisal of children with cerebral defects*. Harvard, MA: Harvard University Press.

Teasdale, G., & Jennett, B. (1976). Assessment and prognosis of coma after head injury. *Acta Neurochirurgica, 34*, 45–55.

Theodoros, D.G., & and Murdoch, B.E. (1994). Laryngeal dysfunction in dysarthric speakers following severe closed head injury. *Brain Injury, 8(8)*, 667–684.

Thomsen, I.V. (1975). Evaluation and outcome of aphasia in patients with severe closed head trauma. *Journal of Neurology, Neurosurgery and Psychiatry, 38*, 713–718.

Thomsen, I.V. (1984). Late outcome of very severe blunt head trauma: A 10–15 second follow-up. *Journal of Neurology, Neurosurgery and Psychiatry, 47*, 260–268.

Trenerry, M.R., Crosson, B., DeBoe, J., & Leber, W.R. (1989). *Stroop Neuropsychological Screening Test*. Odessa, FL: Psychological Assessment Resources.

Trexler, L.E., & Zappala, G. (1988). Neuropathological determinants of acquired attention disorders in traumatic brain injury. *Brain and Cognition, 8*, 291–302.

Tyerman, A., & Humphrey, M. (1984). Changes in self-concept following severe head injury. *International Journal of Rehabilitation Research, 7*, 11–23.

Vanderploeg, R.D., Schinka, J.A., & Retzlaff, P. (1994). Relationship between measures of auditory verbal learning and executive functioning. *Journal of Clinical and Experimental Neuropsychology, 16*, 243–252.

van Zomeren, A.H. (1981). *Reaction time and attention after closed head injury*. Lisse, The Netherlands: Swets Publishing Services.

van Zomeren, A.H., & Brouwer, W.H. (1987). Head injury and concepts of attention. In H.S. Levin, J. Grafman, & H.M. Eisenberg (Eds.), *Neurobehavioural recovery from head injury* (pp.398–415). Oxford: Oxford University Press.

van Zomeren, A.H., & van den Burg, W. (1985). Residual complaints of patients two years after severe head injury. *Journal of Neurology, Neurosurgery and Psychiatry, 48*, 21–28.

Walsh, K.W. (1985). *Understanding brain damage: A primer of neuropsychological evaluation*. Edinburgh: Churchill Livingstone.

Walsh, K.W. (1987). *Neuropsychology: A clinical approach* (2nd ed.). Edinburgh: Churchill Livingstone.

Wang, C-C., Schoenberg, B.S., Li, S-C, Yang, Y-C.; Cheng, X-M., & Bolis, L. (1986). Brain injury due to head trauma. Epidemiology in urban areas of the People's Republic of China. *Archives of Neurology, 43*, 570–572.

Wechsler, D. (1974). *The Wechsler Memory Scale*. San Antonio, TX: Psychological Corporation.

Wechsler, D. (1981). *Wechsler Adult Intelligence Scale - Revised*. New York: Psychological Corporation.

Wechsler, D. (1987). *Wechsler Memory Scale - Revised*. San Antonio, TX: Psychological Corporation.

Wechsler, D. (1997). *Wechsler Adult Intelligence Scale* (3rd ed.). San Antonio, TX: Psychological Corporation.

Weddell, R., Oddy, M., & Jenkins, D. (1980). Social adjustment after rehabilitation: A two-year follow-up of patients with severe head injury. *Psychological Medicine, 10*, 257–263.

Wertz, R.T. (1985). Neuropathologies of speech and language: An introduction to patient management. In D.F. Johns (Ed.), *Clinical management of neurogenic communicative disorders* (2nd ed., pp.1–96). Boston, MA: Little, Brown & Company.

Wilde, M.C., Boake, C., & Sherer, M. (1995). Do recognition-free recall discrepancies detect retrieval deficits in closed head injury? An exploratory analysis with the Californian Verbal Learning Test. *Journal of Clinical and Experimental Neuropsychology, 17*, 849–855.

Wilson, B.A., Alderman, N., Burgess, P., Emslie, H., & Evans, J. (1996). *The Behavioural Assessment of the Dysexecutive Syndrome*. Suffolk, UK: Thames Valley Test Company.

Wilson, B.A., Cockburn, J., & Baddeley, A. (1985). *The Rivermead Behavioural Memory Test*. Suffolk, UK: Thames Valley Test Company.

Ylvisaker, M. (1986). Language and communication disorders following pediatric head injury. *Journal of Head Trauma Rehabilitation, 1*, 48–56.

CHAPTER THREE

Discourse analysis in traumatic brain injury

Carl A. Coelho
Department of Communication Sciences, University of Connecticut, Storrs, USA

The purpose of this chapter is to discuss the application of discourse analyses to the assessment of oral verbal communicative behaviour of traumatically brain injured adults. Just as predominant impairments of language caused by focal lesions may mask subtle cognitive disturbances, predominant cognitive disturbances resulting from diffuse brain damage, as in TBI, may mask subtle language deficits (Adamovich, 1991). Such deficits in higher functioning TBI adults—i.e. rated at Level VII (Automatic-Appropriate) or Level VIII (Purposeful and Appropriate) on the Rancho Los Amigos Levels of Cognitive Functioning (Hagan, Malkmus, & Durham, 1979) are frequently difficult to delineate. Performance on aphasia batteries may reflect only minimal problems on the most complex tasks, giving the impression that communicative skills are functionally intact. However, interactions with these same individuals leave the listener with the impression that they are off-target, tangential, or disorganised. The overestimated communicative performance of such individuals is clearly a function of the ceiling effect of aphasia batteries that were never intended to assess the subtle types of deficits many TBI individuals demonstrate. Further, by their very nature, most aphasia batteries assess language at the single word or sentence level with which most of these TBI individuals have little difficulty. Although the administration of a standardised language battery is often a reasonable first step in the evaluation process, as Sohlberg and Mateer (1989) caution, it is rarely sufficient for diagnosing and describing the communicative deficits associated with TBI.

Discourse is a unit of language that conveys a message. It does not have a specific set of rules that defines it grammaticality as is the case with sentences (Ulatowska, Allard, & Chapman, 1990). Although discourse is usually described as a series of related sentences, it may be of any length (e.g. single word, phrase, sentence, or a combination of these forms), with the length determined by its communicative function. Normal discourse production involves both macro- and microprocesses organised in a hierarchical fashion (Levelt, 1989; van Dijk & Kintsch, 1983). Message development precedes linguistic formulation. During the development of a message, cognitive and emotional information as well as communicative intentions are coded into both macro- and micropropositions (Huber, 1990). For example, in describing a cartoon story, a speaker will first need to recognise the general theme of the cartoon before the description is planned and formulated. The end result will be a pragmatically and semantically coherent text in which the individual actions and events depicted in the stimulus pictures are ordered in a logical fashion with minimal comments on irrelevant details.

Accurate production and/or comprehension of a narrative requires a complex interaction of linguistic, cognitive, and social abilities (i.e. language use) that would seem to be sensitive to the particular communicative deficits demonstrated by TBI individuals. Several recent studies have demonstrated the clinical utility of various narrative discourse analyses for detecting subtle non-aphasic communicative impairments in TBI individuals (e.g. Chapman, Culhane, Levin, Harward, Mendelsohn, Ewing-Cobbs, Fletcher, & Bruce, 1992; Coelho, Liles, & Duffy, 1991a; Hartley & Jensen, 1991; Liles, Coelho, Duffy, & Zalagens, 1989; Mentis & Prutting, 1987). The following discussion will review several studies pertaining to the application of discourse analyses with individuals who have survived severe TBI—specifically, discourse analysis procedures and findings, and potential interpretations of the discourse deficits.

DISCOURSE ANALYSIS PROCEDURES AND FINDINGS

The discourse analysis procedure begins with the elicitation of a discourse sample, ideally five sentences or more in length. Nicholas and Brookshire (1993) have noted that a valid discourse sample should consist of a minimum of 200 words. Many elicitation tasks have been described in the literature and are related to different discourse types or genres. There is a variety of discourse genres, with differing cognitive and linguistic requirements, which are distinguishable on the basis of the function that each serves. Discourse types include:

- *descriptive*, involving the listing of static concepts, attributes, and relations;
- *narrative*, which conveys actions and events unfolding over time;
- *procedural*, providing instructions or directions specified in a particular order;
- *persuasive*, which provides reasons or facts to support an opinion;

- *expository*, in which factual and interpretative information is provided about a topic; and
- *conversational*, communicating thoughts, ideas, and feelings to others in a cooperative interaction.

The discourse samples are typically audiotaped or videotaped and later transcribed verbatim. Once transcribed the discourse sample(s) may be distributed into more basic units for analysis, such as T-units. A T-unit, as described by Hunt (1970), is more reliably identified than sentences and is defined as an independent clause plus any dependent clauses associated with it. Depending on the elicitation task and the focus of the analysis, the actual discourse analysis may take place at a variety of levels, including within sentences, across sentences, and, in the case of stories, across the entire story text. Although a variety of analysis procedures will be described in the sections that follow, it is important to note that there are numerous other discourse analyses more consistent with qualitative research methods employed throughout the social sciences (see Chapters 4 and 5 of this text for examples of such approaches).

Microlinguistic analyses

Phonologic and/or lexical production

Campbell and Dollaghan (1990) longitudinally monitored the recovery of discourse abilities in children and adolescents with TBI, and noted that accuracy of consonant production remained a problem for three of nine subjects up to 13 months post-injury. The number of different words produced in discourse was also judged to be still impaired in two of the nine subjects after the same period. When phonological and lexical production has been addressed in other studies it has not been noted to be problematic (Milton, Prutting, & Binder, 1984; Penn & Cleary, 1988). Glosser and Deser (1990) reported that their TBI subjects produced significantly more verbal paraphasias, but no more indefinite terms than their normal controls. Conversational fluency and naming were the most impaired areas on the language testing reported by Hartley and Jensen (1991) for their TBI subjects.

The findings of phonological and lexical production deficits in TBI individuals are consistent with much of the existing literature on language proficiency in this population, specifically the presence of problems with word retrieval. However, it is important to note that the presence of aphasia or dysarthria has not been ruled out in several of these studies (e.g. Campbell & Dollaghan, 1990; Glosser & Deser, 1990; Hartley & Jensen, 1991) and therefore application of these findings to the TBI population as a whole should be undertaken with caution.

Syntax

There are numerous measures that can be generated at the sentence level once the transcribed discourse sample has been distributed into a basic unit such as T-units. Total number of T-units per sample might be used as a measure of a subject's verbal output or productivity for a given task. The total number of subordinate clauses might be tallied for each discourse sample as a measure of the complexity of sentence-level grammar. Various measures may also be combined to generate additional measures, such as the number of subordinate clauses in each sample divided by the total number of T-units. Such a ratio could be obtained in order to permit comparisons across samples that vary in length. An additional measure is the number or ratio of agrammatical sentences per sample. Such a ratio could be obtained in order to establish sentence-level grammatical competence.

Grammatical aspects of discourse have been studied in several recent investigations. Syntactic complexity—as measured by percentage of T-units containing dependent clauses (Chapman et al., 1992), embeddedness of subordinate clauses (Glosser & Deser, 1990), and subordinate clauses per T-unit (Liles et al., 1989)—was found comparable to that of normal controls and not judged as a primary deficit when rated on various pragmatic scales (Ehrlich & Barry, 1989; Milton et al., 1984; Penn & Cleary, 1988). Campbell and Dollaghan (1990), however, noted that syntactic complexity measured by percentage of utterances containing two or more verbs remained a problem for six of their nine subjects at 13 months post-onset. These researchers noted that previous investigations of language abilities following TBI emphasised persistent problems in lexical retrieval and discourse organisation. The finding of problems with syntactic complexity in their TBI subjects suggests that syntax production skills are not immune to long-term disruption. Consistent with these findings, the TBI subjects studied by Glosser and Deser made significantly more grammatical errors than the normal subjects (e.g. omissions of the subject, main verb, and other required grammatical morphemes) in spite of demonstrating an adequate range of grammatical constructions in their spontaneous speech. Once again, these findings must be interpreted cautiously in as much as aphasia was not ruled out in the TBI subjects studied in either investigation.

Macrolinguistic analyses

Cohesion

According to Halliday and Hasan (1976), "Cohesion occurs when the interpretation of some element in the discourse is dependent on that of another" (p.4). Sentences are linked by various kinds of meaning relations referred to as cohesive ties. A word is identified as a cohesive marker (i.e.

tie) if its meaning cannot be adequately interpreted by the listener and if the listener must "search" outside of that sentence for the completed meaning. In addition, a word may be judged as a cohesive element if it is used as a linguistic marker that leads the listener to expect that its interpretation is outside the sentence (e.g. definite articles). The type of tie used varies depending on the communicative function of the text, as well as the style and ability of the speaker. A speaker's relative frequency of use of the various types of cohesive tie is referred to as cohesive style (Liles et al., 1989). Each of the different types of discourse (e.g. procedural, descriptive, story narratives, etc.) is distinct and therefore requires a different pattern of cohesive use. Speakers normally shift their patterns of cohesive use across types of discourse.

The analysis of cohesion involves three tasks: the first is the identification of words that are used as cohesive ties; the second is the classification of those ties as linguistically structured categories; and the third is the determination of the "adequacy" of the cohesive tie's function in a given text. Identification of words used as cohesive ties is critical. If cohesive ties cannot be identified reliably, analysis of linguistic function and adequacy will not provide an accurate description of an individual's performance. Consistent with Halliday and Hasan's criteria, no item is described as "cohesive" unless its use consistently prompts the listener to go outside the sentence for the correct and complete interpretation of meaning.

The second task is based on the assertion that a speaker's use of a particular linguistic form cues the listener to expect that the information resides outside the sentence. It is through the use of these linguistic structures that a speaker achieves cohesive organisation and displays various styles of language use. According to Halliday and Hasan, each instance of a cohesive tie can be classified according to one of the following linguistic categories of meaning relations:

1. reference (personal, demonstrative, or comparative);
2. conjunction (causal, adversative, temporal, or additive);
3. lexical (reiteration, collocation);
4. ellipsis; or
5. substitution.

Definitions of these types of cohesive markers are presented in Table 3.1.

Cohesive adequacy. The third task in the analysis of cohesion procedure involves the "adequacy" of the speaker's use of cohesion. Because speakers cannot be expected to be perfect in the realisation of their narrative organisation, this aspect of the analysis describes how an individual departs from complete clarity and accuracy in indicating the meaning relation between the

TABLE 3.1
Definitions of types of linguistic markers (Halliday & Hasan, 1976)

Cohesive marker	*Definition*
1. Reference	The information to be retrieved is the identity of the thing or class of things being referred to in the preceding (anaphora) or following text (cataphora).
a. Personal	Personal pronouns, possessive determiners, and possessive pronouns that represent a single system of persons, referring to the identity of relevant persons, objects, and events (e.g. ***he, mine, it, one***). Example: *I dropped the glass on the floor.* ***It*** *shattered into pieces.*
b. Demonstrative	A form of verbal pointing, identifying the referent by location in place or time (e.g. ***this, that, there, those***). Example: *Ted was at Bill's Steakhouse last night. I had never seen him* ***there*** *before.*
c. Comparative	Comparison refers to whether two things are similar or different. Example: *Tim bought a* ***lemon yellow*** *car. All the* ***other*** *cars he looked at were too drab.*
2. Conjunction	Specification of the way sentence meaning (i.e. content) that has gone before is to cohere with content of the sentence to follow. The following types of conjunctive cohesion are listed from most to least complex.
a. Causal	Sentence meanings that cohere via the expression of a relationship that specifies result, reason, and purpose (e.g. ***because, for this reason, to this end, otherwise***). Example: *I didn't receive your message.* ***Otherwise,*** *I would have been happy to help you.*
b. Adversative	Sentence meanings that cohere via the expression of a relation that is contrary to expectation (e.g. ***yet, though, only, but, instead***). Example: *We won't be leaving tonight.* ***Instead,*** *we'll head out early in the morning.*
c. Temporal	Sentence meanings that cohere via the expression of a relation that specifies time (e.g. ***simultaneously, then, afterwards, subsequently***). Example: *We cleaned the house and bought some groceries.* ***Afterwards*** *we relaxed and had some supper.*
d. Additive	Sentence meanings that cohere simply by denoting added information, similarity of meaning, alternative meanings, and de-emphatic afterthought (e.g. ***and, furthermore, likewise, by contrast, incidentally***). Example: *Helen and Bill had known each other for years.* ***By contrast,*** *Chris and Betsy had just met.*

(continued)

Table 3.1 continued

3. Lexical	Lexical cohesion is achieved by selection of vocabulary. Lexical cohesion may take either the form of reiteration (i.e. where both the cohesive item and that to which it refers have a common referent) or collocation (i.e.where cohesion is achieved through association of lexical items that regularly co-occur).
a. Reiteration	
i. Same word	Example: *You can drive to the house on the back road. Drive slowly because it's a treacherous **road**.*
ii. Synonym	Example: *We all rode in the back of the van. It's a very comfortable **vehicle**.*
iii. Superordinate	Example: *You can eat all the apples you want. **Fruit** is a healthy snack.*
iv. General word	Example: *We had to pay Fred full-price for the sofa. I know that **robber** got it for half-price.*
b. Collocation	Example: *The teacher sent Colleen to the nurse. She had complained of a **headache.***
4. Ellipsis	Ellipsis refers to sentences or clauses the structure of which is such as to presuppose some preceding item, which then serves as the source of the missing information. Ellipsis is simply "substitution by zero". Ellipsis consists of three categories:
a. Nominal	Example: *What kind of shoes are you looking for? **Adidas** (shoes).*
b. Verbal	Example: *Who's coming along? **They are** (coming).*
c. Nominal	Example: *Has she painted the bedroom? **She has** (painted the bedroom).*
5. Substitution	In substitution, the cohesive link is established through the use of a substitute linguistic item of the same grammatical class as the item necessary for interpretation. The substitute item has the same structural function as that for which it is substituted.
a. Nominal	one, ones; same Example: *I've been looking for large brackets. Where did you find the big **ones**?*
b. Verbal	do Example: *I have no ideas where they hid the money, and I don't think you **do** either.*
c. Nominal	so, not Example: *Then the Jazz beat the Bulls? I'm afraid **so**.*

cohesive items. This procedure describes to what extent subjects are successful at presenting the listener with "complete" (i.e. unambiguous or non-erroneous) semantic relationships. Three categories of adequacy are used—complete, incomplete, and erroneous. Descriptions of these categories are provided in Table 3.2.

Studies using cohesion analyses. Cohesion analyses, as described by Halliday and Hasan (1976), have been described in a variety of studies of TBI subjects, most of whom were severely injured but had recovered a high

TABLE 3.2
Categories of cohesive adequacy

Cohesive adequacy category	*Definition*
Complete tie	A tie is complete if the information referred to by the cohesive tie is easily found and defined with no ambiguity. Example: *The young girl was very tired.* ***She*** *went to bed early and slept until 10 o'clock.*
Incomplete tie	A tie is judged to be incomplete if the information referred to by the cohesive marker is not provided in the text. Example: *The men worked until dark. On the way home they stopped at* ***his*** *house for a beer.*
Erroneous tie	A tie is judged to be an error if the listener is guided to ambiguous information. Example: *Alex and Chris went to the concert.* ***He*** *bought a compact disc on the way out.*

level of functional language—that is, they had achieved fluent conversation. Hartley and Jensen (1991) noted their TBI subjects used significantly fewer cohesive ties per communication unit than the normal controls in both narrative and procedural discourse tasks. This finding was felt to provide evidence that the TBI subjects' discourse lacked continuity. Mentis and Prutting (1987) also noted that their TBI subjects used fewer cohesive ties than the normal subjects in narrative tasks. Liles et al. (1989), however, reported that the number of cohesive ties (per T-unit) produced by their TBI subjects was the same as the normal subjects for both story generation and story retelling. These findings are consistent with those of Glosser and Deser (1990) and McDonald (1993), who noted that their TBI subjects did not differ from the normal subjects on any of their cohesion measures. It is important to note that there were TBI subjects in both the Hartley and Jensen and Mentis and Prutting studies who were aphasic; therefore the problems with cohesion must be interpreted accordingly.

Differences in the proportional use of types of cohesive tie across discourse tasks were reported in the studies by both Mentis and Prutting (1987) and Liles et al. (1989). Mentis and Prutting (1987) stated that the use of different cohesion patterns by their TBI subjects appeared to be related to their reduced linguistic processing abilities, their limited pragmatic abilities, as well as their attempts at compensating for the linguistic deficits. Liles et al. (1989) noted that, in a story retelling task (in which subjects watched a picture story on a filmstrip and were then asked to retell the story), similar proportions of referential, lexical, and conjunctive markers occurred in TBI and normal groups. However, in a story generation task (in which subjects were asked to tell a story about what was happening in a picture) a major difference between the groups appeared, in which the TBI subjects showed a reversal of the pattern of the normal subjects, as well as a reversal of their own cohesive pattern used in the story retelling task. In story generation, all of the TBI subjects decreased the proportional use of reference and increased the proportion of lexical ties. The differences in the proportional use of types of cohesive tie across story tasks were attributed by Liles et al. (1989) to their TBI subjects' apparent direct reference to the stimulus picture. These direct references were characterised as interjected descriptors of the picture that were unrelated to the rest of the text. The authors state that the TBI subjects rarely integrated these lexical items into the text structure, and they consequently were often judged to be incomplete ties. The TBI subjects' rather marked tendency to refer outside their texts suggested that they were unable to detach themselves from the perceptual salience of the picture in order to organise their language for story development.

Mentis and Prutting (1987) also noted that their TBI subjects used incomplete ties, which was not characteristic of the normal subjects. Liles et al. (1989) observed that, like the normal subjects, the TBI subjects showed greater cohesive adequacy in the story retelling task, in which they demonstrated a higher percentage of complete ties and a lower percentage of incomplete ties than in the story generation task. However, in story generation, half of the TBI subjects exhibited a much lower percentage of complete ties than the normal subjects. Error ties were rare in both groups of subjects.

Finally, Coelho, Liles, and Duffy (1991a) examined cohesion in discourse samples from a story generation task gathered longitudinally from two TBI subjects. One subject's stories were characterised by poorly organised sentences and cohesive adequacy. The number of complete ties per T-unit was consistently below the mean of the normal subjects in the story generation task. In spite of this subject's poorly organised narratives, the content was task-appropriate. Over time the number of complete episodes approached and eventually surpassed the mean of the normal subjects for this task. The second subject, whose discourse performance was assessed with the same measures and task, demonstrated a very different pattern of deficits. This subject's stories were well organised—that is, meaning was tied across sentences. The number of complete ties per T-unit for the story generation task was below the normal subjects' mean performance, but her score improved with time. As reflected in the number of complete episodes, the content of the second subject's stories was poor. She never produced a complete episode in the story generation task. These findings emphasise the clinical utility of monitoring discourse abilities longitudinally and of employing a multi-level analysis procedure.

Story structure

Story structure knowledge refers to the purported regularities in the internal structure of stories that guide an individual's comprehension and production of the logical relationships between people and events (e.g. temporal and causal). Descriptions of story grammars differ, but the episode unit is central to virtually all models proposed by many investigators (e.g. see Stein & Glenn, 1979). Analysis at the story grammar level generally consists of looking at the number of "complete" episodes in each story. An episode (as described by Stein & Glenn) is judged to be complete only if it contains all three components:

1. an initiating event that causes a character to formulate a goal-directed behavioural sequence;
2. an action; and
3. a direct consequence marking attainment or non-attainment of the goal.

In addition, these three components must be logically related.

Analysis of story structure has been undertaken in a few recent investigations of the discourse of TBI individuals. Chapman et al. (1992) observed that their group of severe TBI children and adolescent subjects showed a reduction in essential story components, failing to signal new episodes with setting information, and often omitted essential action information in a story retelling task. These authors noted that the finding of disrupted story structure in their TBI subjects was unexpected, in that it is developed relatively early, and is more resistant to disruption than intersentential structures in aphasic individuals. They further observed that it is unclear whether this difficulty was a reflection of an underlying impairment in internal story schema or difficulty implementing story schema during discourse production.

TBI and normal subjects produced a comparable number of episodes in story retelling (presented via filmstrip), as reported by Liles et al. (1989). In story generation (generating a story depicted in a single picture), however, three of the four TBI subjects produced no episodes. The greater difficulty with story structure in the generation task demonstrated by Liles et al.'s (1989) subjects, was related to Blank, Rose, and Berlin's (1978) notion of cognitive reordering. Adequate story development requires a speaker to transpose a static representation of the depicted events (in a picture) to a dynamic representation (a story). Blank et al. (1978) refer to such a disparity between the context and required language use as cognitive reordering. The TBI subjects' apparent inability to use episode structure in the story generation task, in spite of having been able to produce complete episodes in the story retelling task, suggested that the story generation task required an interaction of cognition and language use in which the TBI subjects could not consistently engage. Further, the interactions among sentential grammar, intersentential cohesion, and story structure required to produce a story may place a communicative load on TBI individuals' performance, which may reveal problems not observable in other forms of discourse.

The multi-level analysis employed by Coelho et al. (1991a), which examined both cohesion and story structure, facilitated the identification of distinct discourse patterns in two TBI subjects. The first presented with poor cohesion but relatively good story structure and the second good cohesion with poor story structure. Use of a single-component analysis procedure (either cohesion or story structure) would have failed to identify these patterns.

Coherence

Whereas cohesion refers to the syntactic, morphological, and lexical means of connecting sentences within a text, coherence refers to their semantic and pragmatic connectedness (de Beaugrande & Dressler, 1981). Coherence may be considered as either "local", addressing the relationship between the content of a verbalisation with that of the immediately preceding utterance, or "global", addressing the relationship between the content of a verbalisation with that of the general topic of conversation (Glosser & Deser, 1990). Judgements of coherence are typically based on raters' impressions of the meaning of a speaker's whole verbalisation with respect to meaning in the adjoining discourse, regardless of lexical or syntactic errors (Glosser & Deser, 1990) or rating spontaneous communication for such things as inclusion of adequate detailing, word reference, plausibility, and conclusiveness of the narrative (Ehrlich & Barry, 1989). Ehrlich and Barry rated coherence as part of their pragmatic scale. Coherence was one aspect of overall improvement that Giles, Fussey, and Burgess (1988) rated and monitored in a treatment study aimed at increasing a TBI individual's response succinctness in conversation.

Similarly, Glosser and Deser (1990) noted that their TBI subjects were rated as significantly impaired relative to normal subjects in both local and global coherence. A greater impairment, however, was noted for global coherence. These authors state that their TBI subjects' difficulties with coherence greatly compromised their performance on descriptive tasks. They suggested that coherence depends on intact access to semantic memory representations of real-world knowledge, as well as the perceptual and conceptual integration necessary to maintain the plan and overall organisation of discourse. Finally, an intact ability for simultaneous attention and mental manipulation of several bits of information is required for coordinating and integrating the speaker's plan and the listener's perspective in order to produce discourse that is perceived as coherent. The TBI subjects' greater impairment in maintaining global, as opposed to local, coherence suggests that their disordered discourse results from impaired macro-organisational abilities more than from disrupted meaning relationships between contiguous concepts.

Finally, McDonald (1993) examined various dimensions of coherence in a procedural narrative task using three different analyses: (a) a set of five rating scales based on Grice's maxims of quantity and manner; (b) cohesion; and (c) information. The author observed a wide range of performance in two TBI subjects. One subject produced fewer propositions than any of the 12 matched control subjects, and several of the propositions were inferred or ambiguous. Another subject produced several more propositions than any control subject. One subject adhered to a temporal logic in introducing steps of a procedure, while the other subject generated a sequence very different from the real order of events. Both TBI subjects produced irrelevant propositions, many of which preceded information that would have put them in context. McDonald notes that, with the exception that the TBI subjects used unexplained references, overall their texts were linguistically as coherent as those of the normal subjects. The major problem with their performance on this referential communication task appeared to be information content and its organisation.

Miscellaneous analyses

Productivity

Productivity measures typically involve quantifying some aspect of speaking time and amount of discourse produced. A variety of productivity measures have been applied to TBI speakers and may be categorised into three groups: total output; speaking time; and mazes (i.e. false starts, revisions, repetitions, etc.). Measures classified in the total output category included total number of syllables (Ehrlich, 1988), words, T-units, sentences (Mentis & Prutting, 1987), utterances (Campbell & Dollaghan, 1990), content units (Ehrlich, 1988), communication units (Hartley & Jensen, 1991), mean number of words per T-unit and number of words divided by the number of information units (Chapman et al., 1992), and number of words per communication unit (Hartley & Jensen, 1991). The speaking time category included total speaking time and syllables per second (Hartley & Jensen, 1991), syllables and content units (Ehrlich, 1988), and words (Giles et al., 1988) per minute. Finally, percentage of syllables in mazes (i.e. false starts, revisions, filled pauses, and hesitations in putting thoughts into words) and number of words in communication units after mazes were removed were also tallied (Hartley & Jensen, 1991) as well as the number of repetitions and revisions per T-unit (Chapman et al., 1992).

As was the case with phonological and lexical production, interpretations regarding productivity problems must be considered with the presence of dysarthria and aphasia in mind. Campbell and Dollaghan (1990) noted that many of their subjects' output remained limited at 13 months post-onset, as measured by number of utterances, words, mean length of utterance in morphemes, and percentage of utterances in mazes. Chapman et al. (1992) reported that their severe TBI group produced less language (i.e. number of words and sentences) than either the mild to moderate TBI group or the normal subjects. Similarly, Hartley and Jensen's (1991) TBI subjects produced significantly fewer meaningful words and shorter communication units, spoke at a slower rate of speech, and produced a larger percentage of syllables in mazes. The authors concluded that these problems may have been attributable to dysarthria, word retrieval problems, or decreased psychomotor speed. The authors speculated that maze production may have been due to problems with verbal planning and word fluency, whereas the decrease in meaningful words may have been attributable to memory problems.

In Ehrlich's (1988) study the TBI subjects were similar to the normal subjects in the amount of pertinent content expressed, narrative length, and rate of speech in a narrative task, but were found to be significantly slower in rate of information produced. Ehrlich commented that, while the TBI subjects produced texts that were comparable to the normal subjects in terms of completeness and inclusion of essential information, communicative efficiency was compromised. Presuming that there is no trade-off between the amount and rate of information produced in discourse, the TBI subjects appeared to "talk past the point of diminishing returns" in terms of communicative efficiency (p.6). Their oral narratives were lengthier and slower relative to the amount of content provided. Liles et al. (1989) and Mentis and Prutting (1987) observed similar performance on productivity measures such as the number of T-units produced in story retelling and generation, and total number of sentences respectively between the TBI and normal subjects. Giles et al. (1988) used a different measure of productivity in their treatment study, targeting a decrease in the number of words per minute that was achieved with treatment.

Rating scales

A number of studies have reported on the use of various scales to rate dimensions of discourse. Ehrlich and Barry (1989) reported that preliminary data on their rating scale suggested that selected communicative behaviours (e.g. intelligibility, eye gaze, sentence formulation, coherence, topic management, initiation) could be reliably evaluated, and provided descriptive information concerning communicative function in TBI adults. McDonald (1993) observed that TBI subjects had substantial difficulty meeting informational needs of their listeners on the basis of ratings of repetitiveness, detail, clarity, organisation, and effectiveness. Using the Pragmatic Profile (Prutting & Kirchner, 1987), Milton, Prutting, and Binder (1984) noted that all of their TBI subjects demonstrated some inappropriate behaviour. The highest proportion fell into the areas of illocutionary/perlocutionary acts (e.g. topic maintenance and turn-taking) and propositional acts (e.g. lexical selection and use). Their findings suggested that communicative breakdown occurred most frequently in the way TBI adults functioned as discourse partners. The rating scale utilised by Parsons, Snow, Couch, and Mooney (1989)—(Damico, 1985)—indicated that linguistic nonfluency, revision behaviours, and inability to structure discourse, accounted for approximately 90% of all conversational errors for their TBI group. Parsons et al. noted that, although there was a great deal of individual variability, when the errors of their TBI subjects were analysed as group data there was a trend for conversational errors to vary according to task requirements. Fewer errors were noted during tasks that involved the sharing of the conversational load, than in tasks that required the speaker to take responsibility for initiating, organising, and maintaining the conversation.

Response appropriateness/relevance

Coelho, Liles, and Duffy (1991b) evaluated the appropriateness of TBI subjects' utterances within conversations. Utilising procedures described by Blank and Franklin (1980), each utterance produced within the conversational dyad was categorised either as a speaker initiation or a speaker response. Speaker initiations were classified as obliges or comments. Obliges were utterances containing explicit requirements for a response from the listener—e.g. "How long have you worked for that company?". Comments were utterances not containing an explicit demand for a response—e.g. "We had sunny weather all week". Speaker responses were classified in terms of adequacy—that is adequate-plus (i.e. providing more information than was requested), adequate, inadequate, or ambiguous. The authors noted that the TBI subjects had a greater number of turns per conversation than the normal subjects. In addition, the TBI subjects had decreased response adequacy resulting in utterances that were at times disjointed and seemingly irrelevant to conversation. Coelho et al. (1991b) reported that the greater number of turns by the TBI subjects resulted from their shorter length of utterance per turn and their conversational partner's higher percentage of oblige production. The TBI subjects had more difficulty initiating and sustaining conversation, which resulted in a higher incidence of oblige production (i.e. questions) by the conversational partner. Many utterances produced by the TBI subjects required interpretation and clarification by the examiner, resulting in additional obliges. The normal subjects were more apt to develop and extend dialogue on specific topics than were TBI subjects.

TBI subjects' responses in conversation during group interactions were examined by Gajar, Schloss, Schloss, and Thompson (1984) throughout the course of a treatment study. Desirable responses were those in which a subject contributed relevant statements to the group's conversation, agreed or disagreed with another participant's statement and provided a rationale, or asked a related question. Gajar et al. reported that the results of their study indicated that feedback and self-monitoring had positive effects on the conversational behaviours of their two subjects. Rates of positive social interactions were higher in all treatment phases.

In a third study, Peter (1995) investigated the conversational skills of a TBI individual who was engaged in separate conversations with her mother and an examiner. Results indicated that the quality and effectiveness of the conversations were significantly different across the two normal partners. The TBI individual was more adequate with her mother who frequently provided feedback, which structured topics under discussion as well as stopping digressions. The examiner's feedback consisted primarily of confirmation, and consequently tangential utterances were not curtailed. Peter noted that the TBI individual's conversational proficiency was affected not only by her brain injury, but by the ability of the conversational partner to meet her conversational needs during the interaction (i.e. by structuring the interaction to decrease tangential responses).

Compensatory strategies

Penn and Cleary (1988) developed a taxonomy for evaluating the effectiveness of TBI subjects' self-initiated compensatory strategies. Strategies were divided into seven broad categories: simplification; elaboration; repetition; fluency (e.g. filled pauses or stalling); sociolinguistic (e.g. turn-taking, self-corrections, topic shifts); non-verbal (e.g. gesture, intonation); and interlocutor (e.g. modification of speed of input or cueing). Results indicated that all subjects used a wide range of strategies to compensate for cognitive and language deficits with varying degrees of success. The authors noted that it was unclear why certain subjects adopted certain strategies, but compensation following brain injury was viewed as a process involving both neurological and subject variables, including such factors as severity of deficits, age, time post-onset, as well as the influence of therapy and environmental context.

Analysis of topic

Mentis and Prutting (1991) employed an elaborate multi-dimensional classification system for studying topic management in their study of conversational and monologue samples of a TBI subject. In this procedure the basic unit for analysing topic and subtopic maintenance was the intonation unit as described by Chafe (1987). Chafe defines an intonation unit as "a sequence of words combined under a single, coherent intonation contour, usually preceded by a pause" (p.22). According to Chafe, each intonation unit expresses only one new concept at a time. Therefore, the intonation unit may be used as a measure of the amount of information conveyed within a single topic as well as the individual contributions to topic maintenance of each of the participants in a conversation. Mentis and Prutting categorised intonation units as ideational (i.e. which carry propositional, ideational information), and textual or interpersonal (i.e. which serve a primarily textual or interpersonal function in a conversation). The ideational units were further classified into four categories based on the extent to which each participant contributes to the development of a conversation by adding novel or relevant information: (1) new information; (2) no new information; (3) side sequence units; and (4) problematic.

Findings indicated that topic management abilities of Mentis and Prutting's (1991) TBI subject were impaired. Specific difficulties included non-coherent topic changes as well as the production of ambiguous, unrelated, and incomplete ideational units. These resulted in a decrease in continuity of topic development. Reduction in the TBI subject's topic management abilities were evident in his production of fewer new information units than the normal control. In addition, the TBI subject did not maintain discourse topics through the addition of novel information to the same extent as the normal subject also studied. According to Mentis and Prutting (1991), in order for discourse to be coherent, topic changes and all ideational units need to be structured so as to reveal thematic relevance and informational salience. The TBI subject's failure to structure discourse was evident in his production of non-coherent topic changes and his ambiguous, unrelated and incomplete ideational units. Ambiguity of the TBI subject's ideational units was primarily the result of his reference to items that were absent from the text and not identifiable from the context. Given that this TBI subject was also aphasic, the observed problems with topic management cannot be attributed to cognitive deficits alone.

Content analysis

Content or informational analysis examines whether an individual's utterance is relevant, truthful, non-redundant, and plausible (Shadden, 1998). Most analyses look at an individual's communication from the perspectives of amount of information, quality of information (i.e. irrelevant, redundant, off-target, overly personalised, etc.), and efficiency or conciseness. Ehrlich (1988) noted that TBI subjects were comparable to normal subjects in terms of the amount of salient and critical information produced in narratives. TBI subjects' decreased communicative efficiency was noted to be a result of lengthier and slower spoken language. Ehrlich concluded that it may require more words and time to convey the important information through spoken language for TBI individuals. Hartley and Jensen (1991) reported that their TBI subjects produced only one-half to two-thirds the amount of accurate content produced by the normal speakers. Unlike the control subjects, the TBI subjects introduced inaccurate content into their narratives. These findings were attributed to the TBI subjects' failure to interpret the visual stimulus correctly, or to determine the most relevant aspects of the pictures, as well as to reduced auditory verbal memory during the story retelling task. Neither aphasia or dysarthria were ruled out in either of these studies.

SUMMARY OF DISCOURSE DEFICITS FOLLOWING TBI

After reviewing several studies with a primary focus of discourse production deficits following TBI the following conclusions are offered. Findings are somewhat unclear regarding phonological and/or lexical production deficits, due primarily to the fact that the presence of aphasia or dysarthria has not been accounted for in the interpretation of the findings. There is general agreement that word retrieval problems are often present following TBI, which would certainly impact upon discourse production. Syntactic complexity was judged to be comparable to that of the normal control subjects in the majority of the studies in which it was addressed. In those studies that described problems with syntax in the discourse of children or adults, aphasia was again a potentially coexisting condition. Cohesion was noted to be an area of inconsistent impairment. The variability of the findings of the studies that examined cohesion highlighted the importance of using multiple-discourse elicitation tasks; for example, the cohesive adequacy of TBI subjects was noted to be comparable to that of normal subjects in story retelling, but was impaired for story generation. Similarly, the proportion of types of cohesive ties used by the TBI subjects changed from story retelling to story generation, which was not the case for normal subjects. Overall, analysis of cohesion is useful for detecting subtle discourse organisation deficits in TBI individuals; however, performance may vary considerably depending on the discourse elicitation task presented. In addition, the issue of individual differences, even among normal subjects, is not well understood.

The reviewed studies also indicated consensus regarding impairments in story structure abilities following TBI. As was the case with cohesion, TBI subjects' ability to generate complete episodes was frequently affected by the nature of the task, with story retelling being easier than story generation.

Story generation requires a complex interaction of language and various cognitive abilities that was difficult for even mildly impaired TBI subjects. Analysis of story structure in conjunction with cohesion enables discourse samples to be examined at multiple levels, allowing for the delineation of distinct discourse patterns. The issue of coherence was addressed in a number of the studies reviewed. Coherence was noted to be impaired in TBI subjects, with global coherence more impaired than local coherence.

Results of various pragmatic rating scales, and analyses of response appropriateness and topic management, all suggest that TBI individuals experience difficulty when called upon to function as a discourse partner, whether in conversation or referential communication. These individuals demonstrate problems initiating and sustaining topics in conversation, and frequently rely on their discourse partner to assume a greater proportion of the communicative burden to ensure a successful interchange of information. Finally, TBI individuals appear to implement a variety of compensatory strategies for their discourse deficits with varying success.

DISCOURSE DEFICITS AS EVIDENCE OF IMPAIRMENT IN EXECUTIVE FUNCTIONS

In this section discourse deficits are interpreted as a potential reflection of a disruption of executive functions. Executive functioning is briefly defined here, but was discussed in detail in Chapter 2. According to Lezak (1982), "executive functions comprise those mental capacities necessary for formulating goals, planning how to achieve them, and carrying out the plans effectively" (p.281). Executive function does not represent a discrete process but rather an umbrella function that comes into play with all realms of cognitive processing. When executive function is impaired, all other cognitive systems (e.g. attention, memory, reasoning, etc.) have the potential to be affected, even though they may individually remain intact (Sohlberg & Mateer, 1989). Sohlberg and Mateer have noted that damage to the frontal lobes may result in behavioural and emotional deficits as well as cognitive deficits, particularly decreased executive functioning. According to Stuss and Benson (1986) the frontal lobes coordinate input from all other regions of the brain and therefore are important for coordinating and actualising activities involved in cognitive processing. However, Goldberg and Bilder (1987) argued that prefrontal pathology is not necessary to produce "executive syndrome" and that this syndrome may be relatively common in any diffuse brain dysfunction.

Ylvisaker and Szekeres (1989) noted that following severe TBI most individuals demonstrate communicative deficits directly attributable to disruption of executive functions. They list seven broad dimensions of executive function in which this dysfunction may occur:

1. *Self-awareness and goal setting*, involving decreased insight of cognitive and verbal deficits as well as the implications of such deficits.
2. *Planning*, involving decreased knowledge of the appropriate steps to complete a task and/or the ability to sequence and organise these steps.
3. *Self-directing/initiating*, involving a decreased ability to initiate an activity, despite having all the necessary resources, without prompting from another individual.
4. *Self-inhibiting*, involving an impaired ability to inhibit verbal behaviour that may be impulsive, tangential, perseverative, or socially inappropriate.
5. *Self-monitoring*, involving decreased monitoring of the context (social or otherwise) that a behaviour occurs in.
6. *Self-evaluation*, involving a decreased ability to evaluate performance objectively.
7. *Flexible problem solving*, involving an impaired ability to revise a plan and consider alternative solutions when presented with new information.

As summarised earlier, individuals with TBI demonstrate an array of discourse deficits. Such deficits are demonstrated in a variety of discourse forms and analyses and may be best explained from a cognitive rather than linguistic framework. Coelho, Liles, Duffy, Clarkson, and Elia (1994) using a story retelling task, monitored discourse performance in a mildly aphasic individual (secondary to a single unilateral left thrombo-embolic cerebrovascular accident) over a period of 12 months and noted that as severity of aphasia decreased (as measured by the Porch Index of Communicative Ability—Porch, 1981) sentence formulation and cohesion abilities improved. Story structure abilities, however, remained relatively impaired. This finding would appear to be inconsistent with those of previous investigators who noted that, even in moderately impaired aphasic individuals, essential elements of superstructure (defined as categories of story structure-setting, action, resolution, and evaluation, or as steps of instrumental scripts—e.g. steps required for changing a light bulb) are well preserved (Ulatowska, Freedman-Stern, Weiss-Doyel, Macaluso-Haynes, & North, 1983; Ulatowska, North, & Macaluso-Haynes, 1981; Ulatowska, Weiss-Doyel, Freedman-Stern, Macaluso-Haynes, & North, 1983). However, it should be noted that these studies employed elicitation tasks requiring descriptions of action sequences or procedures that may not have tapped story structure abilities. Further, the mildly aphasic subject studied by Coelho et al. did exhibit rudimentary story structures in all of his story retellings, but over the 12-month period that his discourse performance was monitored, story structure ability did not improve or recover to the degree that his sentence formulation and cohesion abilities did. This discrepancy suggests that story structure ability may be more cognitively based than linguistic. The authors further noted that story structure dysfunction may be a result of brain injury in general versus simply aphasia.

This notion is consistent with the clinical observation that in the face of functional performance on standardised language batteries and good sentence-level grammar, the communicative abilities of adults with TBI are frequently judged to be inadequate (Coelho, Liles, & Duffy, 1991a; Holland, 1982; Liles et al., 1989). The discourse deficits reviewed here serve as a partial explanation for the observed pragmatic-communicative deficiencies. However, many of these impairments in discourse performance may be considered secondary deficits and a reflection of a more global deficit of executive function. Lezak (1983) observed that the executive function system can "break down at any stage in the behavioural sequence that makes up planned or intentional activity" (p.508). Applying Ylvisaker and Szekeres' (1989) framework of communicative deficits attributable to disruption of executive function, findings from several of the studies of discourse performances in TBI individuals reviewed earlier are interpreted in terms of impaired executive function. It should be noted that this is by no means the only interpretation of such discourse deficits, and Chapter 4 includes a discussion of alternative interpretations such as working memory and information-processing speed.

Story structure

Adequate production and comprehension of a story depends on the logical sequence of cognitively based story structures. These structures guide an individual's interpretations, expectations, and inferences about the possible relationships between people and events in a story. The very nature of an episode implies the involvement of executive functions. Episodes form a framework for stories organising content as behavioural sequences consisting of three parts: (a) an initiating event causing a character to formulate a goal-directed sequence; (b) an action; and (c) a direct consequence marking attainment or non-attainment of the goal. Episode generation requires identification of goals, recognition of an intended plan, and evaluation of the success or failure of this plan with regard to attainment of the goal. For example, the TBI subjects studied by Liles et al. (1989) demonstrated difficulty formulating episodes in the story generation task. Although they were able to recall complete episodes from the pictorial stimuli used in various story retelling tasks they were unable to use episode structure for story generation. This disparity in the subjects' performance across the retelling and generation tasks may be interpreted to mean that executive planning was not required in the retelling task to the same extent as in the generation task because of the structured presentation of the pictured story in the retelling task. In contrast, the story generation task required the subjects to internalise, or enter into the world of the story in space and time, and reorganise the pictured scene into a logical and coherent structure.

Cohesion and cohesive adequacy

The notion of cohesiveness refers to the organisation and clarity of a narrative text. Cohesive ties conjoin sentences by various kinds of meaning relations. Adequate cohesion may require an individual to analyse the content of a proposed narrative and to select a structure or format of organisation (cohesive pattern) to best communicate the intended meaning. More specifically, the individual is required to make choices about what kinds of linguistic devices should be used to coordinate the meaning across sentences. These choices are made in the light of the text's function (e.g. procedures, story, etc.) and structure (e.g. causal and temporal organisation of content). This process would implicate goal formulation, planning (i.e. sequencing and organisation), self-monitoring, and problem solving (to monitor the relationship between task requirements and content and to be able to make the appropriate adjustments in the cohesive pattern). Clearly, dimensions of executive function are critical for adequate use of cohesion as are other cognitive processes such as working memory capacity discussed in the next chapter.

The principal findings related to cohesion and cohesive adequacy were that the TBI subjects produced a lower percentage of complete ties in their narratives on certain tasks. In addition, there were differences noted in the proportional use of certain types of cohesive ties across tasks. Specifically, in story generation because the TBI subjects were apparently unable to detach themselves from the perceptual salience of the stimulus picture they were unable to integrate language for story development. Therefore, a decrease in the proportional use of reference and an increase in the use of lexical ties was noted (Liles et al., 1989; Mentis & Prutting, 1987). Although cohesion interacts with episode organisation, because both episodes and local sentences' coherence must be considered, the systems can be distinguished. A speaker can, under some circumstances, produce a coherent rendition if the content is very simple or overlearned (e.g. the story retelling task). One may propose then at some level of an overlearned task, intersentential cohesion would require little executive planning, whereas episode organisation will always require such input.

Conversation

Brinton and Fujiki (1989) observed that "the ability to participate in conversation is basic to getting along from day to day in society" (p.1). Conversation is a dynamic and complex activity that requires participants to adhere to certain rules as they interact. Management of these rules for turn-taking, topic initiation, and maintenance, as well as conversational repair determines both the quality and success of a conversation. Meaningful participation in conversations requires that each participant has an ongoing awareness of his or her partner's perspective or needs, is able to initiate and change topics throughout the interaction, to inhibit comments and other behaviours that are inappropriate to the exchange, and to continually monitor the overall flow of the conversation and make necessary adjustments as needed. Executive functions are obviously critical to successful conversational performance.

TBI subjects have demonstrated difficulty initiating and sustaining conversations as illustrated by their shorter turns, the limited number of topics they introduced in conversations, and the shorter less elaborated discussions that occurred in their conversations (Coelho et al., 1991b; Mentis & Prutting, 1991). Further, the TBI subjects were reliant on their conversational partner to maintain the flow of the conversation as seen in part in the high proportion of question (i.e. obliges) production by the partner (Coelho et al., 1994). When TBI subjects did introduce topics it was at times at the expense of textual coherence and continuity of overall topic development (Mentis & Prutting, 1991). Finally, although TBI subjects attempted to compensate for difficulty in conversational interactions, the strategies employed were not always effective (Penn & Cleary, 1988).

IMPLICATIONS

Although the interpretation of discourse deficits as an impairment of executive functions is logically very appealing, a great deal of research remains to be done to assist development of this explanation. Development of a model depicting the hypothesised relationship of discourse abilities to executive function should also be undertaken and tested. Investigation of the potential relationships between measures of cognitive abilities (e.g. attention and memory) and measures of discourse performance (e.g. story structure, cohesion, and topic maintenance) would be an important beginning. However, the task of delineating the relationship between discourse performance and cognitive abilities may be far more complex than simply correlating measures of various cognitive abilities with measures of discourse performance. A recent investigation attempted to do just that. Discourse performance of 55 TBI adults was correlated with measures of attention, memory, and executive functions (Coelho, Liles, & Duffy, 1996). Results revealed few significant or even modest correlations between these variables. The authors offered several potential explanations for their findings:

1. Although attention, memory, and executive functions may be related to

discourse production, other measures of these cognitive processes (other than those employed in this study) more closely aligned with the prerequisite abilities of the discourse tasks need to be identified.
2. Considering cognitive abilities such as attention, memory, and executive functions as discrete processes is undoubtedly elementalistic. The cognitive deficits after TBI are more likely to be the result of disruption of a complex network of cognitive processes including attention, memory, and executive functions, as well as other processes not investigated. The question is then what other processes need to be studied and how they can be measured?
3. Perhaps the processes that need to be investigated in order to better understand the nature of discourse deficits in TBI are cognitive-linguistic in nature versus purely cognitive.
4. Finally, the TBI subjects studied were a purposefully selected group of relatively higher functioning individuals that should not be considered as representative of all TBI individuals. Different findings may have been noted had more severely impaired patients been investigated.

In any event, this line of inquiry has great potential with regard to its clinical implications. From the perspective of assessing executive functions, which is frequently difficult because the nature of formal testing often compensates for many of the dimensions of executive functions examiners seek to measure (Lezak, 1982), discourse measures may provide a means of objectifying deficits of executive function in natural, everyday communicative behaviours and environments. From the perspective of assessing and treating discourse impairments, this explanation provides a better understanding of the functional consequences of such deficits. In other words, discourse deficits may be indicative of significant, and functionally more compromising, impairments than simply an inability to tell a story. Finally, the study of the relationship between executive function, as well as other cognitive processes, and discourse abilities may shed light on the nature of the cognitive and language impairments of individuals with TBI.

REFERENCES

Adamovich, B.L.B. (1991). Cognition, language, attention, and information processing following closed head injury. In J.S. Kreutzer & P.H. Wehman (Eds), *Cognitive rehabilitation for persons with traumatic brain injury*. Baltimore, MD: Paul H. Brookes.

Blank, M., & Franklin, E. (1980). Dialogue with preschoolers: A cognitively-based system of assessment. *Applied Psycholinguistics 1*, 127–150.

Blank, M., Rose, S.A., & Berlin, L.J. (1978). *Preschool language assessment instrument: The assessment of learning in practice*. New York: Grune and Stratton.

Brinton, B., & Fujiki, M. (1989). *Conversational management with language-impaired children*. Rockville, MD: Aspen.

Campbell, T.F., & Dollaghan, C.A. (1990). Expressive language recovery in severely brain-injured children and adolescents. *Journal of Speech and Hearing Disorders*, *55*, 567–581.

Chafe, W. (1987). Cognitive constraints on information flow. In R.S. Tomlin (Ed.), *Coherence and grounding in discourse* (Typological Studies in Language, Vol. 11, pp.21–51). Philadelphia, PA: John Benjamins.

Chapman, S.B., Culhane, K.A., Levin, H.S., Harward, H., Mendelsohn, D., Ewing-Cobbs, L., Fletcher, J.M., & Bruce, D. (1992). Narrative discourse after closed head injury in children and adolescents. *Brain and Language*, *43*, 42–65.

Coelho, C.A., Liles, B.Z., & Duffy, R.J. (1991a). Discourse analyses with closed head injured adults: Evidence for differing patterns of deficits. *Archives of Physical Medicine and Rehabilitation*, *72*, 465–468.

Coelho, C.A., Liles, B.Z., & Duffy, R.J. (1991b). Analysis of conversational discourse in head-injured adults. *Journal of Head Trauma Rehabilitation*, *6*, 92–99.

Coelho, C.A., Liles, B.Z., & Duffy, R.J. (1996). *Relationship between cognitive variables and narrative discourse in closed head injury*. Paper presented at the Clinical Aphasiology Conference, Newport, RI, USA.

Coelho, C.A., Liles, B.Z., Duffy, R.J., Clarkson, J.V., & Elia, D. (1994). Conversational patterns of aphasic, closed head injured and normal speakers. *Clinical Aphasiology*, *21*, 183–191.

Damico, J. (1985). Clinical discourse analysis: A functional approach to language assessment. In C.S. Simon (Ed.), *Communication skills and classroom success*. London: Taylor & Francis.

de Beaugrande, R.A., & Dressler, W.U. (1981). *Introduction to text linguistics*. London: Longman.

Ehrlich, J.S. (1988). Selective characteristics of narrative discourse in head-injured and normal adults. *Journal of Communication Disorders*, *21*, 1–9.

Ehrlich, J.S., & Barry, P. (1989). Rating communication behaviours in the head-injured adult. *Brain Injury*, *3*, 193–198.

Gajar, A., Schloss, P.J., Schloss, C.N., & Thompson, C.K. (1984). Effects of feedback and self-monitoring on head trauma youths' conversational skills. *Journal of Applied Behaviour Analysis*, *17*, 353–358.

Giles, G.M., Fussey, I., & Burgess, P. (1988). The behavioural treatment of verbal interaction skills following severe head injury: A single case study. *Brain Injury*, *2*, 75–79.

Glosser, G., & Deser, T. (1990). Patterns of discourse production among neurological patients with fluent language disorders. *Brain and Language*, *40*, 67–88.

Goldberg, E., & Bilder, R.M. (1987). The frontal lobes and hierarchical organization of cognitive control. In E. Perecman (Ed.), *The frontal lobes revisited* (pp.159–187). New York: IRBN Press.

Hagan, C., Malkmus, D., & Durham, P. (1979). Levels of cognitive functioning. In *Rehabilitation of the head-injured adult: Comprehensive physical management*. Downey, CA: Professional Staff Association of Rancho Los Amigos Hospital.

Halliday, M.A.K., & Hasan, R. (1976). *Cohesion in English*. London: Longman.

Hartley, L.L., & Jensen, P. (1991). Narrative and procedural discourse after closed head injury. *Brain Injury*, *5*, 267–285.

Holland, A. (1982). When is aphasia aphasia? The problem with closed head injury. *Clinical Aphasiology*, *12*, 345–349, Minneapolis, MN: BRK Publishers.

Huber, W. (1990). Text comprehension and production in aphasia. In Y. Joanette & H.H. Brownell (Eds.), *Discourse ability and brain damage*. New York: Springer-Verlag.

Hunt, K. (1970). Syntactic maturity in school children and adults. *Monographs of the Society for Research in Child Development*, *35*: (Serial No. 134).

Levelt, W.J.M. (1989). *Language production*. Cambridge, MA: MIT Press.

Lezak, M. (1982). The problem of assessing executive functions. *International Journal of Psychology*, *17*, 281–297.

Lezak, M. (1983). *Neuropsychological assessment*. New York: Oxford University Press.

Liles, B.Z., Coelho, C.A., Duffy, R.J., & Zalagens, M.R. (1989). Effects of elicitation procedures on the narratives of normal and closed head-injured adults. *Journal of Speech and Hearing Disorders*, *54*, 356–366.

McDonald, S. (1993). Pragmatic language skills after closed head injury: Ability to meet the informational needs of the listener. *Brain and Language*, *44*, 28–46.

Mentis, M., & Prutting, C.A. (1987). Cohesion in the discourse of normal and head-injured adults. *Journal of Speech and Hearing Research*, *30*, 583–595.

Mentis, M., & Prutting, C.A. (1991). Analysis of topic as illustrated in a head-injured adult and a normal adult. *Journal of Speech and Hearing Research*, *34*, 583–595.

Milton, S.B., Prutting, C.A., & Binder, G.M. (1984). Appraisal of communicative competence in head injured adults. *Clinical Aphasiology*, *14*, 114–123.

Nicholas, L.E., & Brookshire, R.H. (1993). A system for quantifying the informativeness and efficiency of the connected speech of adults with aphasia. *Journal of Speech and Hearing Research*, *36*, 338–350.

Parsons, C.L., Snow, P., Couch, D., & Mooney, L. (1989). Conversational skills in closed head injury: Part 1. *Australian Journal of Human Communication Disorders*, *17*, 37–46.

Penn, C., & Cleary, J. (1988). Compensatory strategies in the language of closed head-injured patients. *Brain Injury*, *2*, 3–17.

Peter, C. (1995). Conversations avec une patiente souffrant de lésions traumatiques bifrontales: Adjustements mutuels. *Revue de Neuropsychologie*, *5*, 53–85.

Porch, B.E. (1981). *Porch Index of Communicative Ability*. Palo Alto, CA: Consulting Psychologists Press.

Prutting, C.A., & Kirchner, D.M. (1987). A clinical appraisal of the pragmatic aspects of language. *Journal of Speech and Hearing Disorders*, *52*, 105–119.

Shadden, B.B. (1998). Informational analyses. In L. Cherney, B.B. Shadden, & C.A. Coelho (Eds.), *Analyzing discourse in communicatively impaired adults*. Gaithersburg, MD: Aspen.

Sohlberg, M.M., & Mateer, C.A. (1989). *Introduction to cognitive rehabilitation theory and practice*. New York: Guilford Press.

Stein, N.L., & Glenn, C.G. (1979). An analysis of story comprehension in elementary school children. In R.O. Freedle (Ed.), *New directions in discourse processing* (pp.53–120). Norwood, NJ: Ablex.

Stuss, D., & Benson, F. (1986). *The frontal lobes*. New York: Raven Press.

Ulatowska, H.K., Allard, L., & Chapman, S.B. (1990). Narrative and procedural discourse in aphasia. In Y. Joanette & H.H. Brownell (Eds.), *Discourse ability and brain damage*. New York: Springer-Verlag.

Ulatowska, H.K., Freedman-Stern, R., Weiss-Doyel, A., Macaluso-Haynes, S., & North, A.J. (1983). Production of narrative discourse in aphasia. *Brain and Language*, *19*, 317–334.

Ulatowska, H.K., North, A.J., Macaluso-Haynes, S. (1981). Production of narrative and procedural discourse in aphasia. *Brain and Language*, *13*, 345–371.

Ulatowska, H.K., Weiss-Doyel, A., Freedman-Stern, R., Macaluso-Haynes, S.M., & North, A.J. (1983). Production of procedural discourse in aphasia. *Brain and Language*, *18*, 315–341.

van Dijk, T.A., & Kintsch, W. (1983). *Strategies of discourse comprehension*. New York: Academic Press.

Ylvisaker, M., & Szekeres, S.F. (1989). Metacognitive and executive impairments in head-injured children and adults. *Topics in Language Disorders,* 9, 34–42.

CHAPTER FOUR

Pragmatics, cognition, and communication in traumatic brain injury

Richard Body
Community Brain Injury Rehabilitation Team, St. George's Community Health Centre, Sheffield, UK

Michael Perkins
Department of Human Communication Sciences, University of Sheffield, UK

Skye McDonald
School of Psychology, University of New South Wales, Australia

As evident from the preceding chapters, one of the characteristics of recent literature on communication after traumatic brain injury (TBI) is the recognition that analyses of lexis, syntax, and semantics do not give sufficient focus to some of the complexities of language use. A primary consequence of this recognition has been an increasing appreciation of pragmatics, which has been paralleled by the decrease in the use of terms such as "subclinical aphasia" (Sarno, 1980) and "non-aphasic language disturbances" (Prigatano, Roueche, & Fordyce, 1985).

References to the need for assessment of pragmatic ability in some form are increasingly common in the TBI literature, both from the perspective of clinical practice and in terms of research. Miller, Halper, and Cherney (1991), for example, state that the effectiveness of the patient's pragmatic skills should be assessed through conversation in different situations. Similarly, the perspective of pragmatics is seen as extremely relevant to the nature of communication in TBI, in that pragmatic theory focuses on dynamic aspects of communication, which are seen to be vulnerable to TBI (McDonald, 1992a).

This general acceptance of pragmatics as a potentially fruitful area of study in TBI is countered by some cautionary notes. Snow, Douglas, and Ponsford (1995), writing on the subject of communication and interpersonal skills following TBI, list a number of limitations of pragmatic assessment. These include the lack of information about the range of normal pragmatic behaviours seen in different community groups and the difficulty of establishing validity and reliability. Similarly, McGann and Werven (1995) cite the lack of published normative data and the enormous diversity of normal performance as serious limitations to quantification of pragmatic deficits in TBI.

This chapter focuses on the nature of pragmatics and its potential clinical applicability to communication after TBI, contrasting this with an alternative framework based on cognition.

PRAGMATICS

Pragmatics is broadly concerned with the way language is used, both in terms of the linguistic choices made by its users and the way such choices are affected by contextual and sociocultural considerations. It contrasts, therefore, with areas of language study such as syntax and semantics that focus on the structure and meaning of language independently of use. The single term "pragmatics" (Morris, 1938) belies a bewildering range of approaches that have their roots in disciplines as different as linguistics, philosophy, psychology, sociology, and anthropology, and the boundary between pragmatics and other areas is not always clear. We will restrict ourselves here to outlining some of the major concepts and theoretical frameworks of pragmatics in current use. A review of the ways in which pragmatics has been applied to TBI is given in the section on "Pragmatics and TBI". For more extensive introductory treatments of pragmatics the reader is referred to Blakemore (1992), Green (1989), Grundy (1995), Leech (1983), Levinson (1983), Mey (1993), Thomas (1995), and Yule (1996).

Semantic and pragmatic meaning

When we interpret what is said to us we are rarely aware that only part of the meaning we derive is explicitly provided. Much of the meaning we typically have to work out for ourselves is based on the context of utterance, what we know about the speaker, and our knowledge of the world in general. Explicit, or literal, meaning is known as "semantic" meaning and inferred meaning is known as "pragmatic" meaning. The distinction can be seen in the use of words like I, here and now (i.e. "deictic expressions"). Although their semantic meaning is the same whenever they are used (i.e. they refer to the speaker and the place and time of the speaker's utterance), in order to identify the specific individual, location, and time on any given occasion of use, a hearer will in addition need to correctly identify specific aspects of the context in which the utterance occurs—i.e. their pragmatic meaning. The distinction is an important one for speakers as well as hearers. We can only get the balance right between what we decide to say and what we leave to be inferred if we have an accurate idea of what the hearer already knows and even what kind of person they are. For example, there is no point in saying "Charming!" if our addressee does not know we are referring to something he has just done and does not have the wit to realise that we are being ironic. It will be apparent even from a simple example like this that pragmatics is a complex phenomenon that involves a widely disparate set of factors ranging from social skills and sociocultural awareness to inferential ability and general knowledge. The following theoretical approaches—Speech Act Theory, Conversational Implicature, and Relevance Theory—offer three contrasting perspectives.

Speech act theory

One way of characterising pragmatic meaning is to regard language use as the performance of speech acts designed to achieve a particular goal (Austin, 1962; Searle, 1969). In order for a speech act to succeed, the speaker must indicate—and the hearer identify—its purpose, or "illocutionary force". For example, we use statements to show that we believe something to be true. We issue commands and requests in order to get other people to perform an action. We make promises to commit ourselves to a future course of action. When we deplore or apologise we indicate our attitudes or feelings towards some state of affairs. If we are being sincere in performing a particular speech act then our statements and explanations require us to *believe* what we are saying, our commands and requests require us to *want* what we are asking, our promises and threats require our *intention* to carry out what we are committing ourselves to, and our congratulations and welcomes require us to feel *pleasure*. Illocutionary force and the speaker's state of mind, however, are rarely stated explicitly (i.e. they are not part of the semantic meaning of an utterance). A sentence such as *You're standing on my foot*, which is ostensibly a statement, will often be used to mean "Please get off my foot". Similarly, we may be sincere but not indicate this in a straightforward way, as in the case of irony. In other words, illocutionary force is not always predictable from the form of an utterance alone, and many speech acts are in this sense "indirect".

Conversational implicature

An alternative approach to explaining how we may not "mean what we say" is to argue that all conversants follow a "Cooperative Principle" (Grice, 1975). This means that we generally assume that what is said to us is said in good faith, and furthermore is at some level truthful, relevant, and as explicit and clear as it needs to be. These latter conditions are described as a set of "maxims of conversation" which may be glossed as: "Don't say any more or less than you need to" (maxim of quantity); "Don't say anything you believe to be false or for which you lack adequate evidence" (maxim of quality); "Be relevant" (maxim of relevance); and "Don't be obscure or ambiguous, but be brief and orderly" (Maxim of Manner). The Cooperative Principle is not some kind of moral code—it is simply a device that helps to explain how we infer meanings from what is said. Part of what enables us to derive the implied meaning (or "implicature") "Get off my foot" from *You're standing on my foot* is the assumption that the speaker is following the four maxims.

It may appear that maxims are frequently broken, as in the following exchange—A: "I'll pay you back before the weekend"; B: "Yeah, and my mother is Genghis Khan!" If B's utterance is taken literally it appears to break both the maxim of quality (i.e. it is untrue) and the maxim of relevance. However, if we assume that B is implicating "I don't believe you" by saying something he believes to be equally false, then we can derive an interpretation that is clearly not breaking these maxims at all.

Relevance theory

Why do we not make communication more straightforward by being literal all the time and avoiding implicatures? One explanation is provided by Sperber and Wilson's (1995) Relevance Theory, which explains pragmatics in terms of cognitive processing rather than principles of usage. They propose that an utterance is "relevant" to the extent that it guarantees enough effects to be worth the hearer's attention and at the same time puts the hearer to no gratuitous effort in achieving those effects. This is known as the Principle of Relevance. In other words, we assume that any utterance addressed to us takes the particular form it does for a good reason, and that any extra effort required to process it (for example, as a result of its not being intended literally) brings a pay-off. For example, one effect of saying *You're standing on my foot* rather than *Get off my foot* is an increase in politeness. Often, the reward for extra inferential processing is simply that it is more *interesting* to say things in an indirect way. Speaker B, in the above exchange, could have simply said *I don't believe you* but its increase in clarity is offset by its decrease in humour and interest.

The theoretical frameworks outlined above do not by any means represent the entirety of what is taken to constitute pragmatics. Indeed, the breadth of potential aspects of behaviour that could come under the rubric of pragmatics leads to a lack of clarity within the subject itself, demonstrated by the difficulty of arriving at exact definitions of terms. One instance is the overlap between pragmatics and discourse (see Chapter 3), which are to some extent interdefinable. For example, if one adopts loose definitions such as "pragmatics = contextualised language use" and "discourse = a sequence of utterances" then part of the context of use will consist of preceding and following utterances (i.e. pragmatics includes discourse), and the coherence of a given sequence of utterances will be partly determined by their context of use (i.e. discourse includes pragmatics). The difference, therefore, is largely a matter of focus and emphasis.

Despite this, a number of attempts have been made to apply theoretical approaches to pragmatics to the description and analysis of communication disorders in general, and to TBI in particular. These are described in the following section.

PRAGMATICS AND TBI

The terminological variation existing within theoretical pragmatics is also evident in the work on pragmatics and TBI that has been carried out so far, making approaches difficult to compare. For many researchers the term "pragmatics" is used as a way of signifying communication skills that are more complex than those assessed in aphasia batteries and appears to be largely interchangeable with terms such as "functional", "everyday", and "high(er) level" (e.g. Perkins, Body, & Parker, 1995). Others may give a definition in fairly broad terms. Milton, Prutting, and Binder (1984), for example, in one of the first studies of pragmatics in TBI, refer to pragmatics as "how language is used in interpersonal situations" and slightly more specifically as "behaviours which have the potential, if used inappropriately, to disrupt or penalize conversational interchanges" (p.114).

A further complication arises from the fact that many of the behaviours that are described by some authors as "pragmatic" may also appear as part of different frameworks employing different terminology, exemplified by the use of terms associated with the notion of "topic". For example, "topic change" is one of four topic parameters on the Pragmatic Protocol (Prutting & Kirchner, 1983) used by Milton et al. (1984) with TBI subjects. The same term on the Behaviorally Referenced Rating System of Intermediate Social Skills (BRISS) used by Flanagan, McDonald, and Togher (1995) in their study of TBI adults is part of a description employing social skills terminology rather than pragmatics. Moreover, Galski, Tompkins, and Johnston (1998), in a study of narrative skills after TBI, specifically contrast "topic management" and "pragmatic behaviours" as separate categories. Similar terminological variation arises under the heading of "discourse", with Ehrlich and Barry (1989) including "topic" as one of the parameters of their study of discourse in adults with TBI with no use of the term pragmatics. In addition, broad concepts such as "appropriateness" and "adequacy", which find expression in many theories of pragmatics and which are central to overtly pragmatic profiles such as Prutting and Kirchner's, also feature in studies of, for example, conversational skills in TBI (e.g. Coelho, Liles, &

Duffy, 1991) without the term pragmatics being employed. Penn and Cleary (1988) complete the picture by employing Prutting and Kirchner's Pragmatic Protocol in a study of "conversational discourse".

In spite of the terminological variation, two main approaches can be discerned in the literature on pragmatic skills in TBI. The first has generally applied a pragmatic framework taken from the broader literature on language use to the *totality* of TBI subjects' communication. This approach typically employs some form of profile or checklist of abilities (e.g. Milton et al., 1984; Snow et al., 1995; Snow, Douglas, & Ponsford, 1997, 1998; Snow, Lambier, Parsons, Mooney, Couch, & Russell, 1987). The second approach, exemplified by the work of McDonald and colleagues (McDonald, 1992b, 1993b; McDonald & Pearce, 1996, 1998; Pearce, McDonald, & Coltheart, 1998; Turkstra, McDonald, & Kaufmann, 1996) addresses a specific aspect of interpersonal communication from a pragmatic perspective.

Grice's (1975) writings on pragmatic theory, especially the Cooperative Principle and more specifically the four conversational maxims, have served as the theoretical basis for much of the profile approach to pragmatics in TBI. Since Grice's work is not presented in the form of assessment materials, the first task facing researchers has been to devise assessments based on the descriptions of linguistic theory. In some cases the work of Damico (1985) has provided a halfway point in the interpretation of Grice's work. Damico's Clinical Discourse Analysis (CDA) provides a list of behaviours that are said to contravene Grice's maxims of quantity, quality, relation, and manner, and allows the assessor to count occurrences of these behaviours in a variety of interactive contexts.

CDA has been used either in its original form or with slight modifications in a number of studies of TBI conversation (Benjamin, Debinski, Fletcher, Hedger, Mealings, & Stewart-Scott, 1989; Jordan & Murdoch, 1990; Snow et al., 1987, 1995, 1997, 1998). For example, Snow et al. (1995), in a study focusing partly on the influence of demographic variables on the interpretation of communication, studied the conversation of three TBI subjects and three matched controls. The interactions were based around a set of seven questions ranging in complexity from "How long have you been coming in as an out-patient?" to "How successful do you think the government has been in reducing the road toll?". They found that the total number of discourse errors (as categorised on the CDA) ranged from 48 to 158 (with both ends of that range being produced by control subjects). Further analysis to subcategorise the errors revealed that the quantity and manner categories accounted for the bulk of the discourse errors produced by both groups of subjects.

In the same study Snow et al. used a further modification of Damico's (and hence Grice's) work in the form of a Communication Questionnaire

(CQ)—subsequently expanded and renamed as the La Trobe Communication Questionnaire (Douglas, O'Flaherty, & Snow, in press). This consisted of 17 questions, each based on a parameter of the Damico profile, which were asked of each subject and of the subject's "nominated close other". The authors give as examples of questions on the CQ, "When talking to others, do you say or do things which others might see as rude?" and "When talking to others do you use lots of 'empty' words such as, 'you know what I mean'?". In addition to the presence or absence of such behaviours, the study focused on whether the behaviours had changed since injury (made possible by the use of controls who had been involved in road traffic accidents but who had not sustained TBI). On the basis of this questionnaire it appeared that brain-injured subjects and their close others might be more likely to report a change in communication style post-injury as compared with pre-injury.

Grice's work has also seen other modifications that have resulted in assessments of TBI communication. For example, Linscott, Knight, and Godfrey (1996) describe the development and implementation of a Profile of Functional Impairment in Communication (PFIC), stating that they elaborated upon Grice's pragmatic model of conversation in order to develop the measure. They derived a set of 10 "communication rules" from Grice's maxims, covering aspects such as logical content, social style, and aesthetics. The rule for aesthetics, for example, states that a "certain level of quantitative and qualitative aesthetic variation is used to add meaning, emphasis, or variety to the contribution made by the subject" (p.399). Furthermore, a subscale of specific behaviour items for each communication rule was derived from a review of the literature documenting communication skill deficits following TBI together with other literature, the extension of Grice's conversational model, and anecdotal reports from previous research. This broad spectrum of factors suggests that the influence of Grice's theories is likely to have been somewhat diluted. Again using aesthetics as the example, the specific behaviour items include animation, expressed affect, humour, loudness, pauses, pitch, and word play, though it is not entirely clear how this set of behaviours relates to the original pragmatic theory. A total of 84 specific behaviour items was isolated in this way.

The concept of rating TBI communicative behaviours by means of adaptations of Grice's maxims has also been used to allow comparison of specific linguistic or logical behaviours with global impressions of dimensions such as communicative effectiveness. For example, McDonald (1993b) developed a set of five seven-point subjective rating scales based on the conversational maxims described by Grice. The scales covered repetitiveness, detail (focusing on the attribute of quantity), clarity, organisation, and effectiveness (focusing on manner) and were used by nine judges. As well as giving a picture of performance by two TBI subjects and twelve controls on the "dice game" (a task involving explanation of the procedures of a game to an uninformed third party), the rating scores were compared with the pattern of propositions produced by subjects. One of McDonald's conclusions (relating to the TBI subjects) was that the sequence characteristics of the propositional content were revealing in terms of the source of the raters' perceptions concerning the disorganised, confusing quality of the texts. The work originating in this study has since been extended to other studies using the dice game (McDonald & Pearce, 1995; Turkstra et al., 1996).

Speech Act Theory has also provided some of the theoretical underpinning to both approaches to pragmatic skills in TBI. Milton, Prutting, and Binder (1984) describe the foundation of Prutting and Kirchner's (1983) Pragmatic Profile in terms of three speech act categories—namely the utterance act, the propositional act and the illocutionary/perlocutionary act. Group results from their study of 5 TBI adults and 5 controls found that for the TBI subjects 76% of behaviours examined were judged appropriate whereas the control group had a mean percentage of 99.4% appropriate behaviours. The same subjects were also rated in this study on the Communicative Abilities of Daily Living (Holland, 1980). The Pragmatic Protocol is also employed in Penn and Cleary's (1988) study of six TBI subjects.

In addition to studies involving the dice game (above), McDonald has investigated specific aspects of pragmatic ability in TBI subjects. In 1992 she studied the ability to comprehend conversational implicature in two TBI subjects compared with twelve controls (McDonald, 1992b). The study used two sets of materials; the first related to understanding direct speech acts and the second to comprehending indirect speech acts in the form of sarcasm. Although McDonald acknowledged conflicting arguments regarding the processes underlying these skills, she suggested that there is good reason to believe that TBI with concomitant cognitive impairment will result in an inability to process the pragmatic non-literal implicature. On the basis of the results, one of McDonald's broad conclusions was that certain non-linguistic cognitive deficits lead to impairments in the comprehension of pragmatic inferences.

In a further study, McDonald and Pearce (1996) investigated the role of the frontal lobes in the interpretation of sarcasm. They suggested that subjects (including TBI) with executive deficits commonly associated with frontal lobe (FL) damage, can potentially offer insight into different models of irony that make different claims regarding the status of the literal meaning of a sarcastic remark. The study demonstrated that on the written version the FL subjects had relatively greater difficulty reconciling inconsistent pairs of conversational remarks in order to interpret them as sarcastic. Additionally, the FL subjects' performance was in general not significantly improved by prosodic cues on an auditory version of the same task. Among their conclusions was a suggestion that the Gricean model of sarcasm was consistent with the performance of the FL patients, though it was recognised that the results do not imply that the processes of understanding sarcasm are as straightforward as Grice's model describes them.

McDonald has also studied the ability of people with TBI to formulate requests that overcome listener reluctance (McDonald & Pearce, 1998) and to understand ambiguous advertisements (Pearce, McDonald, & Coltheart, 1998).

The studies of TBI that take an aspect of pragmatics as a starting point have provided valuable insights into the complex communication patterns of this group. However, we would suggest that there is a need to re-examine the background to pragmatics and to inform the clinical application of pragmatic theories from the perspective of cognition.

PRAGMATICS AND COGNITION

There are two related reasons for re-examining the background to pragmatics. First, although none of the various theories proposed to date were developed with communication impairment in mind, they have been imported wholesale into the clinical domain and remain largely unmodified. Secondly, their rationale and area of focus have been guided by the concerns of their parent disciplines—principally philosophy, sociology, and linguistics—with the result that the relationship between pragmatics and areas such as cognition and neurology, both crucial in understanding communication pathologies, have been relatively little explored.

Some authors on pragmatics have assumed rather simplistically that pragmatics constitutes a single separate cognitive "module"[1], on a par with (though distinct from) syntax, morphology, and phonology (see, for example, the discussion in Craig, 1995). Kasher (1991, 1994), on the other hand, argues that pragmatics covers too wide a range of phenomena to be a single cognitive module. He does, however, suggest that certain pragmatic phenomena such as specific types of speech act are modular, but that others like conversational implicature are not, in that they are instances of more general principles that are not restricted to language alone. It is interesting to note, though, that the various pragmatic phenomena Kasher entertains as possible candidates for pragmatic modules are invariably defined using the terminology of standard pragmatic theory which is not cognitively oriented. Wilson and Sperber (1991), whose Relevance Theory is a serious attempt to ground pragmatics in cognition, also eschew the single module view but their description of pragmatics as "the domain in which grammar, logic, and memory interact" (p.583) is very non-specific and includes no reference to various areas that neuropsychologists would regard as being essential to any discussion of cognition.

What we have, then, are two distinct sets of theoretical constructs, provided by pragmatic theory and cognitive theory respectively, but so far virtually no mutual influence and certainly no superordinate framework to integrate the two. Some preliminary progress has been made in work on TBI by mapping between specific areas of cognitive deficit and pragmatic performance couched in terms of Speech Act Theory (McDonald, 1993b) and Conversational Implicature (McDonald, 1992b). However, it can be argued that there are good reasons for taking a less balanced approach and for *grounding* pragmatic theory in cognition.

Perkins (1998) suggests that pragmatic ability is most usefully seen as a consequence of the way in which linguistic and non-linguistic cognitive systems interact. In other words, phenomena such as speech acts, conversational maxims, and so on, are not primary entities themselves but are instead the secondary consequences of interactions between more fundamental cognitive systems. The reason why we have come to regard such abstract constructs as primary entities, worthy of consideration as cognitive modules, is simply that they have been deemed such by pragmatic theorists who have not been particularly interested in, and therefore constrained by, the way human cognition operates. In support of this view, Perkins et al. (1995) in a case study of a man with TBI show that the notion of topic, for which pragmatic theorists have been unable to provide an adequate definition, can be seen partially as an effect of interaction between memory and executive function. A cognitive approach to pragmatics also makes it possible to distinguish between instances of communicative behaviour such as repetitiveness that may appear similar in pragmatic terms (e.g. breaking Grice's maxim of quantity) but in fact have different cognitive causes such as (a) executive dysfunction or (b) a strategy for compensating for poor lexical access. In this example, (a) is a result of a primary cognitive deficit, whereas (b) is an indirect consequence of a linguistic deficit (Perkins, in press).

McDonald (1992a) argued that there was greater scope to become more specific regarding the impact of different forms of cognitive impairment on communication. With this in mind, we first review what has been done so far in this field and then explore the relationship between pragmatics, cognition, and communication in a case study of a head-injured woman.

COGNITION, COMMUNICATION, AND TBI

TBI commonly (but not universally) results in diffuse damage and multifocal lesions concentrated in the temporal and frontomedial lobes of the brain. Consistent with this, deficits in attention, memory, and executive function are by far the most common cognitive disorders seen following TBI (Tate, Fenelon, Manning, & Hunter, 1991), although a minority suffer impairment of more basic functions such as language, praxis, and perception (Heilman, Safran, & Geschwind, 1971; Sarno, 1980, 1984, 1988; Sarno, Buonaguro, & Levita, 1986; Tate et al., 1991).

While the general picture is well established, it is also clear that there is enormous individual variation in the particular profile of cognitive impairment seen. This is exemplified in a study by Tate et al. (1991) in which a consecutive series of 82 severe TBI subjects was assessed 6 years post-trauma. It was evident that few subjects demonstrated generalised impairment, while roughly a third had impairment restricted to one of the three areas—information processing, memory, or executive function. The remainder had various combinations of deficits, although no particular combination was more prevalent than any other. Furthermore, individual variability also characterised performance within these functional areas, each of which encompasses a broad range of symptoms and severity.

How then can such diverse cognitive disorders be reflected in the communicative abilities of TBI subjects? During the 1980s and 1990s interest in this relationship was developed on the basis of case descriptions and discussion of the similarity between perceived language disturbances and coexisting patterns of cognitive impairment. For example, as described in Chapter 1, Hagan (1982, 1984) argued that common cognitive impairments after TBI affecting attention, memory, and associative abilities result in a reduction in the organisation of one's thoughts and a concomitant disorganisation of language processes, including non-sensible, irrelevant utterances, word-finding problems, and impaired sequencing of language output at the word level, propositional level, or both. Impaired capacity to comprehend auditory or written information, particularly when such material was complex or otherwise demanding, would also implicate such disorganisation.

Prigatano, Roueche, and Fordyce (1986) likewise attributed tangential language, poor word selection, and impaired abstraction to general cognitive disorganisation—i.e. "a fragmented thought process, the intrusion of ideas, and the confusion of the melting together of concepts and feelings in the patient's mind" (p.22). Interestingly, Prigatano et al. also discussed the phenomenon of overtalkativeness which was, in their studies, demonstrated to be prevalent in those with disturbed emotions such as heightened belligerence, negativism, and anxiety. This highlights the role of post-traumatic personality change and emotional reaction to the injury as additional important variables to consider when analysing the nature and cause of post-traumatic communication deficits. In each case the picture may be further complicated by the presence of true linguistic as well as neurophysical impairments.

Finally, Ylvisaker (1993) argued that, similar to adults, there were characteristic changes in communication competence in children and adolescents with TBI that were suggestive of frontal lobe dysfunction. In particular, he suggested that socially unskilled behaviour, disorganised discourse, and poor verbal abstraction skills were common in children with TBI, mirrored similar deficits seen in adults with frontal lobe damage, and were independent of "psychometric intelligence" and linguistic skill.

These general descriptions of the relationship between cognition and communication leave the impression that the net effect of cognitive dysfunction is relatively uniform—i.e. disorganisation of thought processes, and that communication disturbance reflects this. However, it is clear that TBI does not produce homogeneous deficits; rather the population is characterised by heterogeneity and individuals commonly experience a variety of specific cognitive impairments in the context of otherwise intact abilities. The question must therefore be addressed as to whether communication disturbances vary systematically according to the nature of the underlying cognitive disturbance(s).

Interestingly, descriptions in the literature do suggest that subcategories of communicative ability exist, although there is substantial individual variation. Hartley and Jensen (1992) described three discourse profiles. The first they characterised as an over-abundance of talk that is inefficient and tangential in its delivery. This manifestation of expressive language has also been frequently reported by others (e.g. Hagan, 1984; Milton et al., 1984; Milton & Wertz, 1986; Prigatano et al., 1986; Snow, Lambier, Parsons, Mooney, Couch, & Russell, 1986). A second subtype encompasses those patients who are impoverished in the amount, rate, and variety of language produced, and this has also been described elsewhere (Chapman, Culhane, Levin, Harward, Mendelsohn, Ewing-Cobbs, Fletcher, & Bruce, 1992; Ehrlich, 1988; Thomsen, 1975). The third category of discourse was characterised by confused, inaccurate, and confabulatory verbal behaviour. In addition, these authors stress that other combinations of these features occur in individual patients and this, also, has been substantiated elsewhere (McDonald, 1992a).

So, we have evidence that cognitive impairment following TBI varies widely in severity and nature, although attention, memory, and executive functions are commonly impaired in various combinations and manifestations. We have evidence that communication disturbances, too, are highly variable with some characteristic patterns as well as individual variation. It is reasonable to predict, therefore, that particular constellations of cognitive impairment underlie particular patterns of communication disturbance. However, attempts to link empirically particular cognitive profiles with specific subtypes of communication disturbance have, thus far, been speculative at best (e.g. Coppens, 1995; Hartley & Jensen, 1992). This approach is limited by both the demonstrated heterogeneity of this population and the complexity of the measures required. What might potentially be a more plausible approach is the demonstration of a systematic relationship between particular types of cognitive impairment and specific measures of communicative disturbance.

Information-processing deficits and communication

In principle, attentional problems, slowed information processing with an associated reduction in working memory, and verbal retrieval difficulties each have implications for communication. Certainly, such deficits will impair the speed and efficiency with which TBI patients can comprehend communication, particularly complex utterances or conversation in distracting environments, and observations of this type of difficulty are frequently made (e.g. Thomsen, 1975 and Chapter 6 this volume). But in addition, it is reasonable to suggest that such deficits will impede the efficiency and general coherence of language production in TBI. In the previous chapter discourse analysis was discussed as a means to characterise extended discourse and this approach has proven fruitful for investigating problems in both the efficiency and coherence of TBI language production.

As detailed in Chapter 3, compared with non-brain-damaged control subjects, adult and adolescent TBI patients have been found to speak more slowly (Hartley & Jensen, 1991), produce fewer meaningful words overall (Chapman et al., 1992; Hartley & Jensen, 1991), more incomplete or ambiguous utterances (Hartley & Jensen, 1991), as well as shorter informational units (C-units) (Hartley & Jensen, 1991), and less information per minute (Ehrlich, 1988). Studies linking such inefficiency to reduced information-processing capacity are, however, few in number. Immediate memory span—digits forward, from the Wechsler Memory Scale–Revised (Wechsler, 1987)—reflecting basic attentional capacity has been associated with some efficiency measures (Hartley & Jensen, 1991) although, surprisingly, information-processing speed has not been found to be related (Godfrey, Knight, Marsh, Moroney, & Bishara, 1989).

Secondly, the connectedness, or coherence, of TBI discourse, indexed by appropriate semantic and grammatical relationships between propositions (see Chapter 3), has been found to vary from that of non-brain-damaged control subjects (e.g. Hartley & Jensen, 1991; Liles, Coelho, Duffy, & Zalagens, 1989; McDonald, 1993b; Mentis & Prutting, 1987). The achievement of lexicogrammatical cohesion in extended discourse—e.g. by ensuring that each pronominal reference used has an unambiguous source—requires on-line processing and continuous monitoring of verbal output and is clearly a working memory task. It is therefore reasonable to suggest that this type of cohesion is likely to be reduced in TBI patients who suffer impaired attentional processing. Thus far, one study has used independent measures of working memory capacity—repetition from the Western Aphasia Battery (Kertesz, 1982), and digits backward from the Wechsler Memory Scale—and has demonstrated an association between these indices and linguistic measures of cohesion in TBI (Hartley & Jensen, 1991) corroborating this relationship. It has also been queried whether verbal retrieval deficits underlie reduced cohesion (Mentis & Prutting, 1987), but an attempt to establish this empirically has been unsuccessful (Hartley & Jensen, 1991).

Executive dysfunction and communication

In addition to attentional problems, executive dysfunction must be considered a potentially disruptive influence upon communication skills. The successful management of communication is a dynamic task that requires adapting to changing needs, the ability to interpret inference and innuendo, and the capacity to control verbal behaviour in the light of contextual constraints. Chapter 3 provided a detailed exploration of dimensions of executive function and their implications for communication. Furthermore, it has been independently established that frontal lobe damage disrupts communication abilities and, indeed, there is a striking resemblance between descriptions of language after TBI and descriptions of non-aphasic language impairment following focal lesions to the frontal lobes (see Alexander, Benson, & Stuss, 1989; McDonald, 1993a for a review). It might be predicted, therefore, that a systematic relationship between different measures of executive dysfunction and communication behaviour can be substantiated.

Planning and monitoring

In the first instance, it is worth considering the importance of regulatory mechanisms in language production. In particular, failure to plan and monitor verbal output has been discussed in Chapter 3 as the potential source of difficulty for TBI subjects attempting to follow conventional discourse structures when asked to relate a simple narrative. Specifically, they had difficulty providing all the information necessary to complete each sequence of events in the story. Such problems were associated with perseverative errors on the Wisconsin Card Sorting Test (Coelho, Liles, & Duffy, 1995) suggesting that perseveration led to a pathological failure to terminate each episode when developing the narrative.

Similarly, problems in regulating behaviour appear to disrupt the capacity to deliver a clear and effective procedural explanation. In an intense investigation of two TBI subjects carried out by McDonald (1993b), independent raters characterised both subjects as producing disorganised, ineffective, and confusing descriptions when asked to explain how to play a simple board game (transgressing Grice's maxims of quantity and manner—see the section earlier in this chapter on "Pragmatics and TBI"). Interestingly, the two subjects differed in the nature of problems they experienced in their procedural explanations, reflecting underlying differences in the type of executive dysfunction they displayed. The first subject had poor impulse control on neuropsychological testing and, consistent with this, produced a disorganised, overly brief, and tangential explanation. Conversely, the second TBI subject suffered predominantly from inertia and perseveration on formal tests and his explanation was also reflective of this, being laborious and contaminated with concrete detours and multiple repetitions. Despite these qualitative similarities between neuropsychological indices of executive impairment and discourse characteristics, the relationship between specific measures of executive dysfunction and a failure to develop and adhere to a discourse plan has not yet been established empirically (McDonald & Pearce, 1995).

Impaired abstraction skills

Stimulus-bound behaviour and poor conceptual ability are hallmarks of executive dysfunction that affect problem-solving skills on formal neuropsychological evaluation as well as in daily life. Much of everyday communication is indirect, relying upon inference and innuendo in the service of politeness and other cultural conventions (Brown & Levinson, 1987). Therefore the loss of abstraction skills will presumably impact upon the successful interpretation and utilisation of such conversational inference. Indeed, TBI patients have been found to have difficulty both comprehending and producing conversational inference. For example, in one study it was found that conventional indirect speech acts (e.g. "Can you pass the salt") were understood with varying degrees of success (McDonald & van Sommers, 1993), while in another, non-conventional indirect speech acts in the form of sarcastic comments were more poorly comprehended (McDonald, 1992b; McDonald & Pearce, 1996). In addition, the production of non-conventional indirect requests in the form of hints has been demonstrated to be severely impaired (McDonald & van Sommers, 1993).

The relationship between the incapacity to understand conversational inference and other measures of concept formation has been supported by the finding that some TBI subjects who were poor on the language tasks described were also poor on standard neuropsychological measures of concept formation (McDonald & Pearce, 1996; McDonald & van Sommers, 1993) although not all efforts to find such correlations have proven successful (Turkstra et al., 1996). Using discourse analysis it has also been speculated that patients who over-rely upon lexical items in their narratives have a pathological fixation with the concrete, visible attributes of the stimuli used to generate stories (Liles et al., 1989). This interpretation is feasible but awaits empirical confirmation. Interestingly, the capacity to generate inferences from stories has also been associated with working memory performance in TBI patients (Dennis & Barnes, 1990). This may indicate that working memory has a critical role in the ability to form concepts in general and pragmatic inference in particular.

Disinhibition

A third aspect of executive impairment, that of disinhibition, has further ramifications for the production of socially appropriate communication. Performance on the hinting task mentioned earlier is an example of this. The TBI patients studied, who had executive dysfunction and concomitant communication problems, were unable to produce effective hints that only alluded to the actual request by subtle innuendo. This was not only because they found the use of inference difficult, but because they were also unable to refrain from stating their true intention, thus failing in their attempt to be indirect (McDonald & van Sommers, 1993). Direct requests likewise suffered, but in this case because the subjects failed to inhibit tangential remarks that were not conducive to listener compliance. For example, when asked how he might convince a fellow worker to swap a night shift with him, one TBI subject provided detailed descriptions of all the catastrophes that could occur on night shift, including the possibility of being raped. In the latter study such behaviours appeared to be associated with neuropsychological measures of disinhibition (McDonald & Pearce, 1998).

Finally, poor abstract reasoning, poor inferential skills, and poor planning and monitoring of verbal behaviour are likely to impact upon the ability to converse in an interactive manner that is sensitive to the needs of a conversational partner. In one of the few attempts to relate general conversational skills to neuropsychological deficits it has been verified that poor performance on a verbal fluency task, taken as a measure of inflexibility, was positively correlated to broad ratings of social competence in spontaneous conversation (Marsh & Knight, 1991).

Memory impairments and communication

Interestingly, in one of the very few studies that attempted to establish a link between memory and communication, numerous measures of new learning and memory were not correlated to estimates of social competence (Marsh & Knight, 1991). Thus, even though memory impairments are as common following TBI as executive impairments (Tate et al., 1991), these have not yet been shown to have a direct impact on social communication, though descriptive accounts such as that by Perkins et al. (1995) suggest that they might at least have some role.

Although further work is required, the likelihood that many communication disturbances after TBI are a manifestation of coexisting deficits in attention, information processing, and executive control is supported by the emergence of these few correlational studies. The empirical and clinical evidence is at least sufficiently compelling to make the case that communication disturbances following TBI should be seen in the context of coexisting cognitive impairments and to some extent can be explained by these. Future models of language function after TBI will therefore benefit from a cognitive-communication perspective and in the case study that follows we will attempt to demonstrate the utility of such an approach.

CASE STUDY

This case is based on assessment for admission to a rehabilitation unit. It is set out in terms of brief background details, illustrative conversational extracts, supplemental material from cognitive test scores, and observations of performance in other circumstances. These are followed by discussion of the mechanisms that are at work and tentative hypotheses regarding cause.

The description of this subject represents a situation with which many clinicians are familiar—a short period of assessment that produces a great deal of information that then needs to be ordered into some sort of working hypothesis. The assessment process consisted of a home visit by two members of staff (including an interview with a carer) and then two full days of assessment at the rehabilitation unit. This was conducted by all disciplines, incorporating administration of formal assessments, interview, and observation of the client both inside the unit and in local community facilities.

Pat was 47 years old at the time of the injury, which she sustained as the driver of a van in a road traffic accident. At the time of the injury she was working as a vet in a rural area. Immediately after the injury she was admitted to hospital with a Glasgow Coma Scale score of 3/15. CT scan showed a diffuse head injury with swelling, a left temporoparietal extradural haematoma, and base of skull fractures. She underwent a left craniotomy and an anterior cranial fossa repair. She was transferred to a subacute rehabilitation ward two months after the injury and remained there for a further six months. On admission to the subacute rehabilitation ward she was described as disorientated and showing few specific responses. Over the next few months she moved into a phase in which she was said to be aggressive, anxious, repetitive, and frustrated.

Extracts

The following extracts are all taken from interactions that took place on the first day of assessment and serve to give a general impression of Pat's style of communication. Pat had not previously met the member of staff (T =

therapist) in Extracts 1 and 2 but had met the staff member in Extract 3 during the interview at home. The first extract took place at the beginning of the first scheduled assessment session, before any assessment had occurred. Preliminary discussion of the extracts focuses on the most obvious features of the communication, though some of the behaviours will be revisited in later discussion.

Extract 1

1. T: *sets up video camera*
2. P: *waves to camera, smiles*
3. P: Hi
4. P: *rummages in handbag*
5. P: Do you mind if I use your telephone, please? I want to telephone my daughter at home
6. to tell her I haven't got a house key.
7. T: Do you need to do that straight away?
8. P: If you don't mind.
9. T: Will she not be . . . what's she going to do today?
10. P: She'll be ironing.
11. T: So isn't she likely . . .
12. P: *stands up, starts to leave room*
13. T: . . . to be at home anyway?
14. P: Yes, but not for much longer.
15. P: *leaves room*

This extract highlights a relatively minor disruption (particularly in comparison with later extracts) to the conversational flow. It centres on Pat's response (line 10) to the question "What's she going to do today?". In the context of the missing house key and a potential difficulty for Pat of getting into the house later, this question was intended to elicit a response as to whether Pat's daughter was likely to be at home. Pat's response of "She'll be ironing" appears to either miss the underlying intention of the question or, if it *is* a response at this level, to be in conflict with her action of leaving the room, because her daughter would presumably be available to let Pat in if she is ironing. The second extract is taken from the same interview approximately one hour later.

Extract 2

1. T: Where did you ... where did you go to school?
2. P: Fairfax.
3. T: Fairfax?

4. P: Yes. I hated school.
5. T: Did you? Why was that?
6. P: Because it was shit ...
7. T: Why was that?
8. P: ... but not half as shit as hospital.
9. T: What was wrong with school?
10. P: *wipes mouth with tissue*
11. P: It was boring. Do I look presentable?
12. T: You look fine.
13. P: Good. I hate to look a mess.
14. T: Why didn't you like hospital?
15. P: Because it was shit.
16. T: Well, what does that mean?
17. P: It was pony and trap, crap.
18. T: It was a long time to be in hospital.
19. P: *belches*
20. P: Sorry about burping.

The use of the terms "shit" (lines 6, 8, and 15) and "crap" (line 17) in this extract is in marked contrast to the tenor of the other parts of the extracts and, indeed, most of Pat's conversation. She showed no awareness of the potential inappropriateness of the terms and her facial expression did not change from the previous statements. It is interesting to compare this with her apology (line 20) "Sorry about burping", which strikes as odd partly because of the phraseology (selected in preference to the more usual "Excuse me") and partly because she has not shown any awareness of the impact of the term "shit".

Extract 3

In Extract 3, in the afternoon of the same day, the staff member is explaining part of the Rivermead Behavioural Memory Test (Wilson, Cockburn, & Baddeley, 1985).

1. T: I'm going to set this alarm to go off in 20 minutes. When it rings I want you to ask me
2. about your next appointment ...
3. P: It's on Wednesday.
4. T: Right. I want you to ask me when you're going to see me again.
5. P: On Wednesday probably.
6. T: OK. So when the alarm rings you need to ask me when you're going to see me again.
7. P: Will it be Wednesday? Will I see you on Wednesday?

8. T: Mmhm.
9. P: Good, because I like you very much.

In this extract Pat gives an unexpected response (line 3) to the therapist's initial instruction and subsequently not only fails to repair the breakdown but compounds the difficulty by repeating the response. She also finishes the exchange with an inappropriate phrase (line 9).

Assessment of verbal abilities

In terms of assessments that focus predominantly on verbal abilities, Pat was formally tested on the Graded Naming Test (McKenna & Warrington, 1983), the Test for Reception of Grammar (Bishop, 1983), and the Inference and Metaphor subtests of the Right Hemisphere Language Battery (Bryan, 1989). Although the Test for Reception of Grammar is designed primarily for use with children, the broad coverage of syntactic structures means that performance by adults can still serve as a useful indicator of grammatical knowledge.

Graded Naming Test

Pat scored 15/30 correct on the Graded Naming Test, which placed her in the average range. She was able to name some of the later items, such as "tutu" and "yashmak" but misnamed earlier items such as "sundial" (clock) and "periscope" (submarine).

Test for Reception Of Grammar (TROG)

Pat managed the early parts of the TROG (dealing with pronoun use, comparative clauses, and a variety of subject-verb-object structures) without error. She only began to have difficulty with the passive constructions, of which she got none correct (choosing the "active" interpretation in each case). This was followed by 3/4 errors on the constructions involving location (selecting, for example, "the circle is above the star" rather than "the circle is in the star"). She made intermittent errors on other items, particularly the most complex subordinate constructions such as "the square is in the star that is blue" and "the book the pencil is on is red".

Right Hemisphere Language Battery (RHLB)

Pat scored 8/10 on the Metaphor Picture Test. She chose the literal interpretation of "head in the clouds" and added the literal interpretation of "under the weather" to her first correct (metaphorical) response. On the item involving the phrase "keep it under your hat" she selected the control picture of a diver under water.

Pat scored similarly (7/10) on the Metaphor Written Test (claiming not to recognise the phrase "a dead duck"). She chose "The fat man was in the competition" as the interpretation of "He had a fat chance of winning the competition" and "You could get shot if you don't make friends with that chap" as an interpretation of "Make sure you stay friendly with that chap as he's a big shot in the service".

Assessment of cognition

Intelligence quotient

Pat was tested on the National Adult Reading Test (NART) (Nelson, 1982) as a retrospective measure of premorbid IQ. She made 19 errors, placing her in the normal average range. This equates to an estimated full scale IQ of 107 on the Wechsler Adult Intelligence Scale—Revised (WAIS-R) (Wechsler, 1981). In fact, her full scale IQ score on the WAIS-R was 72, a discrepancy of −35.

Attention

Though much of the information regarding Pat's attentional skills came from observation, she was formally assessed on a variety of assessments that offer insight into attention, including subtests of the Test of Everyday Attention (TEA) (Robertson, Ward, Ridgeway, & Nimmo-Smith, 1994), the WAIS-R and the Adult Memory and Information Processing Battery (AMIPB) (Coughlan & Hollows, 1985), together with the Stroop (Trenerry, Crossen, DeBoe, & Leber, 1989) and the Trail Making Test (Reitan, 1958).

Pat engaged attention to many tasks, often before the instructions were completed, but she also required prompting in some cases. Similarly, whereas she disengaged from some tasks without difficulty, she had to be dissuaded from continuing with others.

Focused attention. Pat's ability to direct attention to specific stimuli while ignoring others was tested on the Elevator Counting with Distraction subtest of the TEA (which involves counting one set of auditory tones and ignoring another) where she managed only one correct response before the test was terminated on the fifth item. Her performance on the Stroop Colour/Word test placed her below the sixth percentile. However, in more functional circumstances—for example, the assessment of physical function in the gym—she appeared oblivious to the presence of two other people in the same room.

Sustained attention. Pat was judged to be incapable of sustaining attention sufficiently to undertake the 10-minute Lottery subtest of the TEA, and in fact her basic level of arousal appeared to drop intermittently during several tasks. However, with careful management (i.e. where opportunities for self-distraction were kept to a minimum) she was able to sustain attention over periods of approximately 30 minutes.

Divided attention. Pat was able to switch between two simple attentional sets adequately (on the Trail Making Test) although her performance speed at the 25th percentile is probably lower than expected premorbidly. Her performance deteriorated substantially, however, when the competing demands of simultaneous tasks were increased. Thus the dual task element of the Telephone Search While Counting (from the TEA), in which subjects must count tones on a tape while identifying specific symbols in a telephone directory, appeared to cause her great difficulty and, although she responded to the prompt for responses on the tape, she got only 1/6 correct, in spite of the fact that she had previously been able to undertake this task in isolation (Elevator Counting).

Information-processing speed. Pat's performance on the information-processing subtest of the AMIPB was characteristic of much of her style generally. The task involves cancellation of specific items from a visual array, taking into account the effect of motor speed as well as cognitive processing. Her speed score fell between the 50th and 75th percentiles, but combined with a very poor error score dropped to below the 10th percentile. In other words she was able to maintain speed on simple processing tasks but at considerable cost to her accuracy.

Verbal learning and memory

Pat's performance on verbal learning and memory tasks was extremely variable and appeared to indicate a "shutter" mechanism in her approach to tasks. For example, on the Auditory Verbal Learning Test (Taylor, 1959), in which subjects are required to attempt to recall as many items as they can from a 15-word list on 5 repeated trials, she registered consecutive scores of 5, 5, 6, 5, and 7. The total score of 29 was well below the cut-off score (for her age) of 42. Conversely, her score of 49/56 items of information on the AMIPB Immediate Story Recall placed her around the 75th percentile and her delayed recall placed her between the 50th and 75th percentiles. These scores can be interpreted as indicating that Pat was able to learn simple, meaningful, semantically redundant information, but was impaired in her capacity to initiate strategies to assist in learning more complex and unstructured material.

Non-verbal learning and memory

The primary source of information on Pat's non-verbal learning and memory was the Rey-Osterrieth Complex Figure (Osterrieth, 1944). This produced an impaired immediate recall (16/36) which deteriorated to unscorable after a delay.

Perception

Pat had a primary visual difficulty of the left eye. This was evident in some of her behaviours—for example, tilting her head to look at her watch, which she did frequently. However, she scored above cut-off on the screening test of the Visual Object and Space Perception Battery (VOSP) so the assessment was continued.

Of the eight subtests on the VOSP, Pat scored above cut-off on six and equalled the cut-off score on the remaining two, namely Object Recognition in which the subject has to select the only real object from an array of four shapes, and Dot Counting, which involves simple spatial scanning. On several of the Object Decision items Pat gave two responses, even though the instructions specify that only one of the array is a real object. These results were taken to show that Pat did not show any object agnosias or constructional apraxia as such, but that her performances were detrimentally affected by impulsive, concrete, and ill-considered responses.

Problem solving

Pat's generally impaired approach to problem solving was evident during the course of many tasks, but the Key Search Test from the Behavioural Assessment of the Dysexecutive Syndrome (BADS) (Wilson, Alderman, Burgess, Emslie, & Evans, 1996) demonstrated a particularly unusual response. This test features a piece of paper with a 100 mm square drawn on it and a small black dot 50 mm below the square. The subject is told to imagine that the square represents a field in which they have lost their key. Starting from the dot outside the square the subject is required to trace their entry point in the field and their search pattern around it. Pat first drew a stick figure next to the dot and then drew a key in the field. Following this she drew a straight line from the figure to the key and put the pen down. At this point the examiner said, "But what if you didn't know where the key was?" in response to which Pat drew a longer, curved, line from the stick figure round to the back of the key and put the pen down again.

Qualitative features of test performance

As with tests of various skills, a number of features that emerged from the assessment process were not themselves the focus of the specific tests. The following aspects of Pat's skills and behaviour were particularly notable.

Impulsiveness

Pat responded to many situations with behaviours that appeared to indicate that she was taking action before making an adequate judgement of the requirements of that particular situation. This was felt to be the case, for example, on the block design subtest of the WAIS-R, where her failure was felt to represent speed of rushing into a judgement rather than a perceptual difficulty as such.

Perseveration

Pat used several phrases repeatedly during the assessment—for example the question "Is/Was that right?" during formal testing. A count of this latter phrase revealed that, for example, during the administration of the Visual Object and Space Perception Battery (Warrington & James, 1991), which took just under 20 minutes, she used the phrase 72 times, despite the fact that only six of these elicited a response from the examiner.

Pat also demonstrated perseverative actions in different forms of activity. During testing on the Action Program Test from the BADS (where subjects must solve the problem of getting a cork to the top of a tube) she became stuck in the action of scooping water with a beaker, in what appeared to represent an involuntary continuation of an inappropriate behaviour. This was terminated only by a strong emotional reaction when she announced she was fed up.

On more than one test involving selecting a target from an array by pointing, Pat was observed to demonstrate a response that increased in force for no clear reason. Thus, on the TROG and subtests of the RHLB and the VOSP her initial pointing response gradually increased to a forceful (repeated) finger tapping and subsequently developed into a repeated slap of the hand on to the chosen picture, this latter response itself increasing in force as the test went on.

This perseverative behaviour was also observed outside formal testing. For example, during a break in the assessment session that gave rise to Extracts 1 and 2 Pat made herself a cup of tea and poured milk in while she was making it. As the therapist and Pat settled themselves after the break Pat got up, saying "I'm going to put some milk in my tea" and returned after a minute. Two minutes later she repeated this, using the same phrase.

Throughout two days of varied assessment Pat repeatedly absented herself to go for a drink, sometimes only minutes after having already done so. There was no indication that this represented a physiological rather than a psychological or cognitively driven need.

Discussion

Pragmatic analysis

Overall, Pat's communicative behaviour showed a strong tendency to not take sufficient account of her interlocutor's perspective in conversational interaction. In all three extracts Pat gave the impression that she had her own agenda and perspective, which it was hard to shift her from. She arrived at an interpretation consistent with her agenda and perspective (but not necessarily those of her interlocutor) and ignored aspects of subsequent utterances that did not fit with this interpretation. Her resulting conversational behaviour may be perceived either as rudeness or naivety, depending on the circumstances. Some examples of this include:

- In Extracts 1 and 3 she interprets T's utterances in the light of her own agenda, which results in a lack of compliance with the requests (direct in Extract 3, indirect in Extract 1).
- In Extract 2 she uses swear words that are not appropriate in England in a conversation with a previously unknown professional interlocutor at their first meeting.
- In Extract 3 to say the over-familiar "I like you very much" in the same circumstances shows a similar disregard for social conventions.

In pragmatic terms, these behaviours may be described differently depending on what theoretical framework we use.

From the perspective of Speech Act Theory, Pat could be said to be sometimes unable to identify the intended illocutionary force of T's utterances. For example, in Extract 3 (lines 1–3) she interprets "When it rings I want you to ask me about your next appointment" as a request to immediately state the time of her next appointment, and so answers "It's on Wednesday". A similar misinterpretation is also made in lines 5 and 7. One contributory factor here that is not pragmatic may be a difficulty with processing complex syntactic and semantic constructions (cf., for example, her performance on the TROG), but the consequence—namely the misconstrual of the illocutionary force of speech acts—is clearly pragmatic.

In Gricean terms, we could describe these same cases as a failure by Pat to derive from T's utterances the conversational implicatures he had intended. If we assume that both parties are following the Cooperative

Principle, Pat will take it that T is being as truthful, explicit, clear, and to the point as he needs to be, and will work out implicatures accordingly. Her failure to do so successfully presumably results from distortions in this inferential process resulting from the various factors already stated. We can see the same distortions at work in cases where her utterances allow for an incorrect implicature to be derived by T. In Extract 2, for example, her use of swear words might be interpreted as implicating "Pat is being aggressive/ overly familiar/impolite", though T's awareness of Pat's case history will presumably lead him instead to infer the overriding implicature "Pat is head-injured", and also that these potential and actual implicatures are not intended by Pat. This could also be construed as Pat's apparent, though once again unintentional, contravention of the maxim of manner ("Don't be obscure or ambiguous").

In terms of Relevance Theory, Pat's occasional inappropriateness may be described as resulting from the fact that the unexpectedness of utterances like "I like you very much" in Extract 3 would normally guarantee that the extra effort required to process them is worthwhile for the speaker. But because the apparent effect (i.e. that Pat is being overly familiar) is not intended, the extra processing effort by the hearer has no obvious reward. However, if one includes in one's general background assumptions the fact that Pat has a brain injury and therefore does not always communicate appropriately, one can readjust the weighting of the equation between processing effort and communicative effects to allow for this. What this effectively means is that conversations with Pat—as with anyone who is communication-impaired—are going to require more compensatory effort on the interlocutor's part for less reward than conversations with unimpaired speakers.

Do the accounts of Pat's communicative behaviour afforded by these three different pragmatic theories offer us anything more than a convenient set of alternative descriptive labels? The differences stem from seeing communication as involving either a set of acts (Speech Act Theory), a set of cooperative conventions (Conversational Implicature), or a cognitive balancing act (Relevance Theory). Each account provides a convenient way of describing Pat's conversational inappropriateness in behavioural terms, though none provides much of a sense of explanation of what underlies or causes the inappropriate behaviour. This is where we must turn to cognitive accounts. Although pragmatics gives us a means of characterising and assessing some of the behavioural results of TBI, in order to achieve an understanding of what leads to such behaviour and to target areas for remediation we must supplement pragmatic description with cognitive explanation. In the case of Pat, it is possible to see how her pragmatic inappropriateness is a direct consequence of the range of cognitive deficits described above.

Cognitive analysis

According to her performance on neuropsychological tests, Pat was relatively unimpaired in terms of basic cognitive functions such as praxis, perception, simple learning, and basic linguistic abilities. While she had some difficulty with certain aspects of these tasks, there was no evidence that her difficulties were specific to a particular cognitive domain. For example, her poor performance in picture selection on the Right Hemisphere Language Battery, a language task, mirrored similar behaviour (exemplified by two responses where one was required) on the Visual Object and Space Perception Battery, a perceptual task. However, in the presence of intact basic cognitive functions, and as commonly observed after TBI, she had significant deficits in executive function disrupting both drive and control and affecting her ability to perform all kinds of activities. Thus, on the one hand, she was inert and often experienced difficulty with the spontaneous initiation of an activity, the sustaining of that activity, or its appropriate termination. Consistent with this, it was apparent from her behaviour that she was perseverative and had difficulty switching from one activity to another. On the other hand, Pat was impulsive and frequently responded to the most immediate and salient aspects of a situation without consideration or forethought. Her ability to focus and sustain attention reflected these same executive problems, as she was both distractible and dependent on external assistance to maintain appropriate levels of arousal.

This loss of superordinate control of cognitive activity has direct implications for her capacity to use language in a pragmatically appropriate manner. First, in many instances it was apparent that Pat was as perseverative in her verbal responses as she was in other behaviour. This translated into repetitive conversation and an apparent inappropriate preoccupation with particular topics. Secondly, her verbal behaviour indicated frequent failure to comprehend what was being said to her, reacting, instead, to the most immediate or salient aspect of the information provided. This may explain her tendency to respond to key words rather than the complete semantic and grammatical information imparted in complex utterances in formal assessment (e.g. the TROG) and conversation (Extract 3). It would certainly account for her failure to detect pragmatic inference (e.g. failing to appreciate the therapist's implication that if her daughter is at home she will not need a key in Extract 1) and the illocutionary force of the message (misinterpreting an instruction as a question in Extract 3). Thirdly, the use of socially inappropriate language and abrupt changes in topic (e.g. Extract 2) are consistent with poor impulse control and failure to monitor her (verbal) behaviour. In sum, Pat's difficulties with pragmatic language use mirrored more general behavioural disturbances and are consistent with her neuropsychological deficits as revealed on formal assessment.

SUMMARY

The search for theoretical frameworks and clinical analyses that accurately characterise communication after TBI has prompted, among other things, investigation of pragmatics as a potential source of insight and materials. While pragmatics offers some useful broad theories and a number of descriptive labels, it is limited in its ability to shed light on the mechanisms underlying disorders of communication.

The recognition of the need to make more explicit the mechanisms underlying communication in TBI has parallels in other fields of language pathology. It is illustrative to note for example that Kay, Byng, Edmundson, and Scott (1990), writing on a related field of study, namely the cognitive neuropsychological assessment of aphasia, refer to "a coherent framework within which to *interpret* aphasic disorders" (p.117: their italics). The same group of authors in a previous article on the same topic (Byng, Kay, Edmundson, & Scott, 1990) also discuss the aim of elucidating the underlying nature of the language disorder because it is possible that "the underlying impairment for the same surface symptom is different" (p.72). Despite the differences in clinical focus and conceptual structure, the descriptive terminology used by these authors is relevant to the assessment of communication after TBI.

So, there is little disagreement within the speech pathology field on the need to pinpoint mechanisms that might be addressed in rehabilitation, added to which the role of cognitive skills other than language as instrumental in communication after TBI is not in dispute. What seems to be lacking is the description of communication after TBI *in terms of* cognition. It is of note that within Pat's previous clinical notes was a description of her as having "problems with communication where it interfaces with cognition". One of the key arguments underlying this chapter is that it is incumbent upon professionals within speech pathology, psychology, and related fields to describe the interface between communication and cognition in more detailed terms in order to lay the trail to more effective rehabilitation.

NOTE

1. "Module" is being used here in the sense of Fodor (1983)—i.e. a self-contained cognitive system that is domain specific, informationally encapsulated, possesses a dedicated neural architecture, and manifests characteristic patterns of breakdown. This is the way it tends to be used by pragmatic theorists, as well as by cognitive neuropsychologists.

REFERENCES

Alexander, M.P., Benson, D.F., & Stuss, D.T. (1989). Frontal lobes and language. *Brain and Language*, *37*, 656–691.

Austin, J.L. (1962). *How to do things with words*. Oxford: Clarendon Press.

Benjamin, L., Debinski, A., Fletcher, D., Hedger, C., Mealings, M., & Stewart-Scott, A. (1989). The use of the Bethesda Conversational Skills Profile in closed head injury. In V. Anderson & M. Bailey (Eds.), *Theory and function: Bridging the gap. Proceedings of the 14th Annual Brain Impairment Conference*. Melbourne: Australian Society for the Study of Brain Impairment.

Bishop, D.V.M. (1983). *Test for Reception of Grammar*. Cambridge: Medical Research Council.

Blakemore, D. (1992). *Understanding utterances: An introduction to pragmatics*. Oxford: Blackwell.

Brown, P., & Levinson, S. (1987). *Politeness: Some universals in language use*. Cambridge: Cambridge University Press.

Bryan, K.L. (1989). *The Right Hemisphere Language Battery*. Kibworth, UK: Far Communications.

Byng, S., Kay, J., Edmundson, A., & Scott, C. (1990). Aphasia tests reconsidered. *Aphasiology*, *4*, 67–92.

Chapman, S.B., Culhane, K.A., Levin, H.S., Harward, H., Mendelsohn, D., Ewing-Cobbs, L., Fletcher, J.M., & Bruce, D. (1992). Narrative discourse after closed head injury in children and adolescents. *Brain and Language*, *43*, 42–65.

Coelho, C.A., Liles, B.Z., & Duffy, R.J. (1991). The use of discourse analyses for the evaluation of higher level traumatically brain-injured adults. *Brain Injury*, *5*, 382–392.

Coelho, C.A., Liles, B.Z., & Duffy, R.J. (1995). Impairments of discourse abilities and executive functions in traumatically brain-injured adults. *Brain Injury*, *9*, 471–477.

Coppens, P. (1995). Subpopulations in closed head injury: Preliminary results. *Brain Injury*, *9*, 195–208.

Coughlan, A.K., & Hollows, S.E. (1985). *The Adult Memory and Information Processing Battery*. Leeds: A.K. Coughlan, St James's University Hospital.

Craig, H.K. (1995). Pragmatic impairments. In P. Fletcher & B. MacWhinney (Eds.), *The handbook of child language* (pp.623–640). Oxford: Blackwell.

Damico, J.S. (1985). Clinical discourse analysis: A functional approach to language assessment. In C.S. Simon (Ed.), *Communication skills and classroom success* (pp.165–204). London: Taylor & Francis.

Dennis, M., & Barnes, M.A. (1990). Knowing the meaning, getting the point, bridging the gap, and carrying the message: Aspects of discourse following closed head injury in childhood and adolescence. *Brain and Language*, *39*, 428–446.

Douglas, J., O'Flaherty, C., & Snow, P. (in press). Measuring perception of communicative ability: The development and evaluation of the La Trobe Communication Questionnaire. *Aphasiology*.

Ehrlich, J.S. (1988). Selective characteristics of narrative discourse in head-injured and normal adults. *Journal of Communication Disorders*, *21*, 1–9.

Ehrlich, J.S., & Barry, P. (1989). Rating communication behaviours in the head-injured adult. *Brain Injury*, *3*, 193–198.

Flanagan, S., McDonald, S., & Togher, L. (1995). Evaluating social skills following traumatic brain injury: The BRISS as a clinical tool. *Brain Injury*, *9*, 321–338.

Fodor, J.A. (1983). *The modularity of mind*. Cambridge, MA: MIT Press.

Godfrey, H.P.D., Knight, R.G., Marsh, N.V., Moroney, B., & Bishara, S.M. (1989). Social interaction and speed of information processing following severe head injury. *Psychological Medicine*, *19*, 175–182.

Green, G.M. (1989). *Pragmatics and natural language understanding*. Hillsdale, NJ: Lawrence Erlbaum Associates Inc.

Grice, H.P. (1975). Logic and conversation. In F. Cole & J.L. Morgan (Eds.), *Syntax and semantics 3: Speech acts* (pp.41–58). New York: Academic Press.

Grundy, P. (1995). *Doing pragmatics*. London: Edward Arnold.

Hagan, C. (1982). Language-cognitive disorganisation following closed head injury: A conceptualisation. In L. Trexler (Ed.), *Cognitive rehabilitation: Conceptualisation and intervention*. New York: Plenum Press.

Hagan, C. (1984). Language disorders in head trauma. In A. Holland (Ed.), *Language disorders in adults*. San Diego, CA: College Hill Press.

Hartley, L.L., & Jensen, P.J. (1991). Narrative and procedural discourse after closed head injury. *Brain Injury*, *5*, 267–285.

Hartley, L.L., & Jensen, P.J. (1992). Three discourse profiles of closed head injury speakers: Theoretical and clinical implications. *Brain Injury*, *6*, 271–282.

Heilman, K.M., Safran, A., & Geschwind, N. (1971). Closed head trauma and aphasia. *Journal of Neurology, Neurosurgery and Psychiatry*, *34*, 265–269.

Holland, A. (1980). *Communicative abilities of daily living: A test of functional communication for aphasic adults*. Baltimore, MD: University Park Press.

Jordan, F.M., & Murdoch, B. (1990). A comparison of the conversational skills of closed head-injured children and normal adults. *Australian Journal of Communication Disorders*, *18*, 69–92.

Kasher, A. (1991). On the pragmatic modules: A lecture. *Journal of Pragmatics*, *16*, 381–397.

Kasher, A. (1994). Modular pragmatics. In R.E. Asher (Ed.), *The encyclopedia of language and linguistics* (pp.3279–3280). Oxford: Pergamon.

Kay, J., Byng, S., Edmundson, A., & Scott, C. (1990). Missing the wood *and* the trees: A reply to David, Kertesz, Goodglass, and Weniger. *Aphasiology*, *4*, 115–122.

Kertesz, A. (1982). *Western Aphasia Battery*. London: Harcourt Brace and Jovanovich.

Leech, G.N. (1983). *Principles of pragmatics*. London: Longman.

Levinson, S.C. (1983). *Pragmatics*. Cambridge: Cambridge University Press.

Liles, B.Z., Coelho, C.A., Duffy, R., & Zalagens, M.R. (1989). Effects of elicitation procedures on the narratives of normal and closed head-injured adults. *Journal of Speech and Hearing Disorders*, *54*, 356–366.

Linscott, R.J., Knight, R.G., & Godfrey, H.P.D. (1996). The Profile of Functional Impairment in Communication (PFIC): A measure of communication for clinical use. *Brain Injury*, *10*, 397–412.

Marsh, N.V., & Knight, R.G. (1991). Relationships between cognitive deficits and social skill after closed head injury. *Neuropsychology*, *5*, 107–117.

McDonald, S. (1992a). Communication disorders following closed head injury: New approaches to assessment and rehabilitation. *Brain Injury*, *6*, 283–292.

McDonald, S. (1992b). Differential pragmatic language loss after closed head injury: Ability to comprehend conversational implicature. *Applied Psycholinguistics*, *13*, 295–312.

McDonald, S. (1993a). Viewing the brain sideways? Frontal versus right hemisphere explanations of non-aphasic language disorders. *Aphasiology*, *7*, 535–549.

McDonald, S. (1993b). Pragmatic language loss after closed head injury: Inability to meet the informational needs of the listener. *Brain and Language*, *44*, 28–46.

McDonald, S., & Pearce, S. (1995). The "dice" game: A new test of pragmatic language skills after closed head injury. *Brain Injury*, *9*, 255–271.

McDonald, S., & Pearce, S. (1996). Clinical insights into pragmatic theory: Frontal lobe deficits and sarcasm. *Brain and Language*, *53*, 81–104.

McDonald, S., & Pearce, S. (1998). Requests that overcome listener reluctance: Impairment associated with executive dysfunction in brain injury. *Brain and Language*, *61*, 88–104.

McDonald, S., & van Sommers, P. (1993). Differential pragmatic language loss following closed head injury: Ability to negotiate requests. *Cognitive Neuropsychology*, *10*, 297–315.

McGann, W., & Werven, G. (1995). Social competence and head injury: A new emphasis. *Brain Injury*, *9*, 93–102.

McKenna, P., & Warrington, E.K. (1983). *Graded Naming Test*. Windsor, UK: NFER-Nelson.

Mentis, M., & Prutting, C.A. (1987). Cohesion in the discourse of normal and head-injured adults. *Journal of Speech and Hearing Research*, *30*, 88–98.

Mey, J.L. (1993). *Pragmatics: An introduction*. Oxford: Blackwell.

Miller, T.K., Halper, A.S., & Cherney, L.R. (1991). Evaluation of communication problems in the traumatic brain injured adult. In A.S. Halper, L.R. Cherney, & T.K. Miller (Eds.), *Clinical management of communication problems in adults with traumatic brain injury* (pp.27–56). Gaithersburg: Aspen.

Milton, S.B., Prutting, C.A., & Binder, G.M. (1984). Appraisal of communicative competence in head-injured adults. In R.H. Brookshire (Ed.), *Clinical aphasiology conference proceedings* (pp.114–123). Minneapolis, MN: BRK Publishers.

Milton, S.B., & Wertz, R.T. (1986). Management of persisting communication deficits in patients with traumatic brain injury. In B.P. Uzzell & Y. Gross (Eds.), *Clinical neuropsychology of intervention* (pp.223–256). Boston, MA: Martinus Nijhoff Publishing.

Morris, C.W. (1938). Foundations of the theory of signs. In O. Neurath, R. Carnap, & C. Morris (Eds.), *International encyclopedia of unified science* (pp.77–138). Chicago: University of Chicago Press.

Nelson, H.E. (1982). *The National Adult Reading Test (NART): Test manual*. Windsor, UK: NFER-Nelson.

Osterrieth, P. (1944). Le test de copie d'une figure complexe. *Archives de Psychologie, 30*, 206–356.

Pearce, S., McDonald, S., & Coltheart, M. (1998), Ability to process ambiguous advertisements after frontal lobe damage. *Brain and Cognition, 38*, 150–164.

Penn, C., & Cleary, J. (1988). Compensatory strategies in the language of closed head injured patients. *Brain Injury*, *2*, 3–17.

Perkins, M.R. (1998). Is pragmatics epiphenomenal? Evidence from communication disorders. *Journal of Pragmatics*, *29*, 291–311.

Perkins, M.R. (in press). The scope of pragmatic disability: A cognitive approach. In N. Muller (Ed.), *Pragmatics and clinical applications*. Amsterdam: John Benjamins.

Perkins, M.R., Body, R., & Parker, M. (1995). Closed head injury: Assessment and remediation of topic bias and repetitiveness. In M.R. Perkins & S.J. Howard (Eds.), *Case studies in clinical linguistics* (pp.293–320). London: Whurr.

Prigatano, G.P., Roueche, J.R., & Fordyce, D.J. (1985). Non-aphasic language disturbances after closed head injury. *Language Sciences*, *7*, 217–229.

Prigatano, G.P., Roueche, J.R., & Fordyce, D.J. (1986). *Neuropsychological rehabilitation after brain injury*. Baltimore, MD: Johns Hopkins University Press.

Prutting, C.A., & Kirchner, D.M. (1983). Applied pragmatics. In T.M. Gallagher & C.A. Prutting (Eds.), *Pragmatic assessment and intervention issues in language* (pp.29–64). San Diego, CA: College Hill Press.

Reitan, R.M. (1958). Validity of the Trail Making Test as an indicator of organic brain damage. *Perceptual and Motor Skills, 8*, 271–276.

Robertson, I.H., Ward, T., Ridgeway, V., & Nimmo-Smith, I. (1994). *The Test of Everyday Attention*. Suffolk, UK: Thames Valley Test Company.

Sarno, M.T. (1980). The nature of verbal impairment after closed head injury. *Journal of Nervous and Mental Disease*, *168*, 685–692.

Sarno, M.T. (1984). Verbal impairment after closed head injury: report of a replication study. *Journal of Nervous and Mental Disease*, *172*, 475–479.

Sarno, M.T. (1988). 1. Head injury: Language and speech defects. *Scandinavian Journal of Rehabilitation (Med. Suppl.)*, *17*, 55–64.

Sarno, M.T., Buonaguro, A., & Levita, E. (1986). Characteristics of verbal impairment in closed head injury patients. *Archives of Physical Medicine and Rehabilitation*, *67*, 400–405.

Searle, J.R. (1969). *Speech Acts*. Cambridge: Cambridge University Press.

Snow, P., Douglas, J., & Ponsford, J. (1995). Discourse assessment following traumatic brain injury: A pilot study examining some demographic and methodological issues. *Aphasiology*, *9*, 365–380.

Snow, P., Douglas, J., & Ponsford, J. (1997). Conversational assessment following traumatic brain injury: A comparison across two control groups. *Brain Injury, 11*, 409–429.

Snow, P., Douglas, J., & Ponsford, J. (1998). Conversational discourse abilities following severe traumatic brain injury: A follow-up study. *Brain Injury, 12*, 911–935.

Snow, P., Lambier, J., Parsons, C., Mooney, L., Couch, D., & Russell, J. (1986). Conversational skills following closed head injury: Some preliminary findings. In C. Field, A. Kneebone, & M.W. Reid (Eds.), *Brain impairment: Proceedings of the 11th Annual Brain Impairment Conference*. Melbourne: Australian Society for the Study of Brain Impairment.

Snow, P., Lambier, J., Parsons, C., Mooney, L., Couch, D., & Russell, J. (1987). *Conversational skills following head injury: Some preliminary findings*. Paper presented at the Australian Society for the Study of Brain Impairment Conference, Adelaide.

Sperber, D., & Wilson, D. (1995). *Relevance: Communication and cognition* (2nd ed.). Oxford: Blackwell.

Tate, R.L., Fenelon, B., Manning, M.L., & Hunter, M. (1991). Patterns of neuropsychological impairment after severe blunt head injury. *Journal of Nervous and Mental Disease*, *179*, 117–126.

Taylor, E.M. (1959). *Psychological appraisal of children with cerebral deficits*. Cambridge, MA: Harvard University Press.

Thomas, J. (1995). *Meaning in interaction: An introduction to pragmatics*. London: Longman.

Thomsen, I.V. (1975). Evaluation and outcome of aphasia in patients with severe closed head trauma. *Journal of Neurology, Neurosurgery and Psychiatry*, *38*, 713–718.

Trenerry, M.R., Crosson, B., DeBoe, J., & Leber, W.R. (1989). *Stroop Neuropsychological Screening Test*. Odessa, FL: PAR.

Turkstra, L.S., McDonald, S., & Kaufmann, P.M. (1996). Assessment of pragmatic communication skills in adolescents after traumatic brain injury. *Brain Injury*, *10*, 329–345.

Warrington, E.K., & James, M. (1991). *Visual Object and Space Perception Battery*. Suffolk, UK: Thames Valley Test Company.

Wechsler, D. (1981). *WAIS-R manual*. New York: Psychological Corporation.

Wechsler, D. (1987). *Wechsler Memory Scale: Revised manual*. San Antonio, TX: Psychological Corporation.

Wilson, B.A., Alderman, N., Burgess, P.W., Emslie, H., & Evans, J.J. (1996). *The Behavioural Assessment of the Dysexecutive Syndrome*. Suffolk, UK: Thames Valley Test Company.

Wilson, B.A., Cockburn, J., & Baddeley, A. (1985). *Rivermead Behavioural Memory Test*. Suffolk, UK: Thames Valley Test Company.

Wilson, D., & Sperber, D. (1991). Pragmatics and modularity. In S. Davis (Ed.), *Pragmatics: A Reader* (pp.583–595). Oxford: Oxford University Press.

Ylvisaker, M. (1993). Communication outcome in children and adolescents with traumatic brain injury. *Neuropsychological Rehabilitation*, *3*, 367–387.

Yule, G. (1996). *Pragmatics*. Oxford: Oxford University Press.

CHAPTER FIVE

Exchanges of information in the talk of people with traumatic brain injury

Leanne Togher
Brain Damage and Communication Research, School of Communication Sciences and Disorders, University of Sydney, Australia, and Liverpool Brain Injury Rehabilitation Unit, Australia

Linda Hand
Brain Damage and Communication Research, School of Communication Sciences and Disorders, University of Sydney, Australia

Chris Code
Brain Damage and Communication Research, School of Communication Sciences and Disorders, Faculty of Health Sciences, University of Sydney, Australia

Traditionally, communication impairment following traumatic brain injury (TBI) has been viewed as a range of deficits that are identified from assessments administered in clinical settings. Deficits have been described in terms of phonological, lexical, syntactic, and other more global impairments. Frequently, the testing process fails to include interlocutors other than the therapist and the person with TBI. Tasks are often monologic (i.e. the person with TBI is evaluated on their performance during tasks such as telling a story or describing the procedure underlying simple everyday activities). Procedural and narrative tasks provide valuable information regarding particular linguistic parameters such as story structure or cohesion, but they cannot be extrapolated to the wider strata of everyday interactions. The ability of the person with TBI to converse is typically judged on their interactions with the clinician or at best with a family member who might be present at the time of the assessment. What does this type of an assessment tell us about how the person with TBI manages once they leave the clinic environment? How representative are such "discourse" samples? The way a person interacts is determined by a number of complex factors that vary immensely from one interaction to the next. Such factors include the relationship between the interactants, the situation, the purpose of the interactions, and the way language is used during the interaction. This chapter will discuss the importance of approaching communication following TBI as a two-way process and will describe the use of Systemic Functional Linguistics as a framework for examining two-way language use following TBI.

ANALYSING CONVERSATIONAL DISCOURSE IN TBI

Traditionally, studies have aimed to describe verbal deficits following TBI focusing on assessment at semantic, syntactic, and phonological levels. Results have indicated that there is recovery at these linguistic levels (Sarno, 1980; Sarno & Levita, 1986). That is, it would appear that the majority of people with TBI have intact linguistic processing at the clause level. However, assessment above the level of the clause shows communication breaks down. In particular, it is clear that people with TBI do not manage in conversations (Groher, 1977; Halpern, Darley, & Brown, 1973; Levin, Grossman, Rose, & Teasdale, 1979). Nonetheless, conversation has not been examined extensively as a genre in TBI in its own right.

More recent studies have attempted to analyse language skills above the level of the sentence in the person with TBI. For example, discourse genres have been examined including narrative and procedural texts (as discussed in Chapter 3). So far, however, the number of studies is quite small, and they have used different theoretical perspectives, making comparison difficult.

Rating scales and checklists

With the pragmatics revolution of the early 1980s (Levinson, 1983) came the introduction of a number of rating scales using items that served to encapsulate particular pragmatic behaviours, such as turn-taking and topic maintenance (e.g. Ehrlich, 1988; Penn & Cleary, 1988; Prutting & Kirchner, 1987). The clinical utility of these scales has made them an essential part of most clinicians' assessment repertoire. Rating scales are clinically useful. They are quick to administer and highlight areas that may need further investigation. However, they are based on loose and eclectic theoretical foundations. The eclectic basis to rating scale development emerges from the need to assess the wide variety of aberrant behaviours that can follow TBI. Rating scales have been used with a range of discourse types including procedural discourse (McDonald, 1993), narrative (Ehrlich & Barry, 1989; Parsons, Snow, Couch, & Mooney, 1989), and clinical interviews between the person with TBI and a therapist (Ehrlich & Barry, 1989; Milton, Prutting, & Binder, 1984; Parsons et al., 1989; Penn, 1988). Deficiencies with discourse were found in the interactions of TBI subjects in all cited studies.

Milton, Prutting, and Binder (1984) were the first researchers to describe the pragmatic deficits of patients with TBI using an early version of the Pragmatic Protocol (Prutting & Kirchner, 1983) to compare five people with TBI with five normal subjects in unstructured conversation with a speech-language pathologist. The Pragmatic Protocol is described as a screening tool designed to isolate specific areas for further investigation. Conversational topics are not specified; however, a range of topics are suggested prior to the sampling. Results indicated that every subject with TBI exhibited some inappropriate behaviours. All subjects had difficulty with prosody, while four of the five subjects had difficulty with topic selection, topic maintenance, turn-taking initiation, turn-taking pause time, and turn-taking contingency. Three of the five were judged to have problems with quantity/conciseness and two of the five were judged to have poor intelligibility and fluency.

The eclectic nature of the Pragmatic Protocol raises questions about its theoretical foundations. Prutting and Kirchner (1983, 1987) incorporated items taken from a range of linguistic theories including Ethnomethodology (Sacks, Schegloff, & Jefferson, 1974), Speech Act Theory (Austin, 1962; Searle, 1969, 1975), Sociolinguistics (Keenan & Schieffelin, 1976), and Systemic Functional Linguistics (Halliday & Hasan, 1976) into three broad behavioural categories. These were *verbal* behaviours (such as speech act analysis and turn-taking), *paralinguistic* behaviours (such as intelligibility and prosody), and *non-verbal* behaviours (such as gesture and facial expression). It is worth noting at this point that the terminology Prutting and Kirchner use is not necessarily the same as that used by other linguists, and that they collapsed and grouped units to suit their own purposes. For example, the term "speech act" is not equivalent to Austin's (1962), Searle's (1969) or Grice's (1975) use of the term. Austin (1962) first based the idea of speech acts on the notion of speaker intention, which was expanded in considerable detail by Searle (1969, 1975). Their central argument is that language performs social acts. When we say "I warn you" or "I promise you", those words themselves are the warning or the promise. The speech *act* is doing something by saying it. Often what the words do is not contained in the surface of the message, such as a typical polite request "Can you open the door?". In this case the surface message is a question but the intended meaning is a request. Searle made a distinction between direct speech acts such as "Pass me the salt" and indirect acts, where the intention of the speaker is not comprehensively encoded in the words of the utterance as in the examples, "Could you pass me the salt?" or "Do you want to pass the salt?".

The Pragmatic Protocol includes a wide range of speech acts and encompasses a great deal more than envisaged by the original speech act theorists, as indicated by the definition provided by the authors: "The ability to take both speaker and listener roles appropriate to the context" (p.118). Thus for example, if an interlocutor can take a speaker and listener role, but is unable to respond or give indirect requests, then marking this particular item could present the judge with difficulty because the subject is initiating direct statements and answering questions but fails to detect an indirect request.

Although inter-judge and intra-judge reliability on the Pragmatic Protocol is high (Milton, Prutting, & Binder, 1984) it is still difficult to determine exactly what is being measured, apart from a global impression of a particular category. For example, to rate "cohesion" (Halliday & Hasan, 1976) as being "appropriate" or "inappropriate" is inadequate, given Armstrong's (1987) finding that listeners' perception of cohesion as rated on a four-point scale correlated poorly with the Cohesive Harmony Index (Hasan, 1985), a technically derived measure of linguistic cohesion. Therefore, a single binary judgement of appropriate/inappropriate may provide little insight into the language structures being judged.

Ehrlich and Barry (1989) found that the selected communication behaviours (e.g. intelligibility, eye gaze, sentence formation, coherence, topic management, and initiation) could be reliably rated and provided descriptive information concerning the communicative functioning of TBI adults. The items are described as being "behaviourally anchored" but there does not appear to be a unifying linguistic or behavioural underpinning to these rating scales. Rather, the items merely represent "selected features of discourse" (p.194) without theoretical rationale for their "selection".

In contrast, McDonald (1993) based the items in her rating scales (repetitiveness, detail, clarity, organisation, and effectiveness) on the Gricean maxims of quantity and manner. Use of these scales demonstrated that TBI subjects have difficulty meeting the informational needs of the listener. Although linguistic skills were relatively normal, informational content and the sequence of delivery were aberrant in TBI subjects compared with controls. These issues are discussed in greater detail in Chapter 4.

Another approach to the assessment of conversation with TBI subjects was suggested by Penn (1988) who developed a taxonomy of "compensatory strategies" that she used to classify communication behaviours that had the apparent purpose of facilitating conversation. These comprised seven broad types of compensation including simplification, elaboration, repetition, fluency, sociolinguistic, non-verbal, and interlocutor strategies. This taxonomy was used to describe TBI subjects' use of compensatory behaviours during interactions with a therapist who was known to them. In Penn's study, all subjects were found to use compensatory behaviours, which Penn explained as direct attempts to compensate for underlying cognitive and memory problems. Some of these included the use of simplification strategies such as having short conversational turns, elaboration strategies such as the use of circumlocution, and sociolinguistic strategies like self-correction and requests for clarification. Communication partners of TBI subjects were also judged according to the taxonomy of compensatory strategies and in this case the most commonly used strategies were probe and yes/no questions.

This study was one of the first to analyse the discourse of the therapist in interactive language samples and it demonstrated the heterogeneity of communication disorders following TBI, as all six subjects demonstrated different patterns of compensation. Viewing communicative behaviours that are often seen as problematic in terms of compensatory strategies was a valuable insight. However, the underlying theoretical construct of Penn's Profile remains fragmented, with its roots also coming from the field of pragmatics.

Such hybrid approaches are common in the field of pragmatics generally. Speech-language pathologists and communication researchers have been attracted to the field because it provides a way of studying communicative events holistically, rather than dividing them into their component parts. But, as Penn (1988) reminds us, pragmatics has a "mixed academic heritage including contributions of philosophy, sociology, linguistics, and anthropology" (p.180). Such a mosaic approach to language in context, using different parts of the expanse of pragmatics theory, makes comparison between studies difficult, and a clear description of the communication problems following TBI almost impossible. As Lesser and Milroy (1993) state: "The absence of an agreed descriptive and theoretical framework makes the task of pragmatic analysis difficult and contentious" (p. 45). This leads to terminological proliferation and confusion, and a blurring of the distinctions between behaviour identification and explanation (Gallagher, 1991). Clearly there are significant challenges ahead while the description of communication disorders in context continues to draw on the heterogeneous field of pragmatics. Some of the questions posited by Gallagher (1991) summarise these concerns: "Will pragmatic analyses clarify long-standing enigmas of language disorder, such as language structural inconsistencies? Are the interactional difficulties exhibited by individuals with language disorders the consequence of limited structural skills or are they related to broader non-linguistic impairments that may be cognitive or social in nature? Finally, can the boundaries of pragmatics be made sufficiently clear and delimited enough to support reliable clinical predictions?" (p.7).

Problems with the definition of conversation

Compounding the difficulties arising from the variegated field of pragmatics is the problem of defining the nature of conversation. A definition must recognise that it is a two-way process, where information sharing takes place as an interactionally negotiated achievement (McTear & King, 1991). Conversation is one type of discourse genre. Other types of genre include procedural discourse (i.e. describing the steps on how to carry out an activity) and narrative discourse (i.e. recounting a story about an event or retelling a story). The term "conversation" has been used with abandon, with some studies examining any kind of connected speech above the level of the sentence, and terming these tasks "conversational" (Ehrlich, 1988; Parsons et al., 1989). Some of these tasks include picture description and describing routine activities, such as changing a tyre. Describing the steps one needs to take to change a tyre cannot be considered a conversational task because it is a procedural discourse task. It is monologic (rather than dialogic) and therefore does not involve the communication partner in the same way that a conversation would. Unfortunately, some studies have made assumptions regarding conversational skills of people with TBI from results that involved completion of tasks that were in no sense interactional (Ehrlich, 1985; Parsons et al., 1989). Such assumptions are falsely based and conclusions from these studies need to be carefully considered.

To characterise conversation or social interactions in a meaningful way, and to contrast them with other discourse types (such as narrative and procedural) requires a coherent model that captures the complexity of the genre. What has been lacking in the literature describing discourse following TBI is a theoretical model that can account for the changing communicative environments that we are faced with when conversing on a daily basis. The concept of context has been taken up as a starting point to describe the characteristics of a communicative situation. Hartley (1990) identified three categories of context: (a) participants; (b) setting; and (c) medium or code. "Speakers select words, sentence structures, and modes of communication based on their knowledge of the cognitive and social status of the communication partner, of the physical context or setting of the communication, and of the linguistic and non-linguistic context" (Hartley, 1992, p.265). This way of viewing communication was driven by the pragmatics literature and, while valuable, it fails to elaborate on how different contextual variables may influence the way the words, sentences, and modes of communication are selected. The pragmatic categories that are described vary according to context and are not part of a cohesive theory.

So although recent research is starting to recognise the importance of viewing communication in a dialogic interactive setting (Hartley, 1992, Ylvisaker, Urbanczyk, & Feeney, 1992), it would appear that a further conceptualisation of communication in context is necessary. This leads us to the theory of Systemic Functional Linguistics (SFL) (Halliday, 1985, 1994), which has been used to provide a more coherent model of language function in TBI. The remainder of this chapter examines a range of genres in TBI using SFL, providing short examples of each.

SYSTEMIC FUNCTIONAL LINGUISTICS

Systemic Functional Linguistics (SFL) is a theory of language use developed by Halliday (1985, 1994), who was concerned with the practical use of language which he described as a system of choices. Each time we speak we make a choice (which is usually unconscious) about what we are going to say and how we are going to say it, which is influenced by whom we are speaking to and the situation we are in. All language characteristics are described in terms of the functions they perform in conveying meanings. Halliday (1985) described three primary functions of language that reflect three different types of meanings. These meanings are understood to occur simultaneously and in brief are as follows:

1. *Ideational meanings* that express processes, events, actions, states, and/or ideas. Analyses within this area of meaning examine the types of words used to express processes (or verbs) and participants (or what the text is about). These analyses investigate how speakers choose to represent their experiences through the types of processes and participants they use.
2. *Textual meanings* that ensure that what is said is relevant and relates to its context. Analyses of textual meaning examine how clauses are structured in relation to each other. One of the analyses used here is cohesion analysis, which describes the connections between words in a piece of discourse. It is discussed in greater detail in Chapter 3.
3. *Interpersonal meanings* are concerned with the interaction and how this is achieved. Analyses therefore focus on the speaker and the hearer and how they negotiate the interaction (e.g. who initiates an interaction and how this occurs). Interpersonal meanings are very useful to analyse the discourse of TBI subjects as they capture the problems people experience within their interactions. Being able to provide information credibly, asking for clarification of information given by others, and adhering to the appropriate sequence of events during a telephone enquiry all require an ability to manipulate interpersonal meanings. People with TBI, however, have difficulty with these "interactional" skills. We have used some of the analyses from within the interpersonal function to describe the difficulties that occur during interactions between TBI subjects and a range of communication partners.

Context

SFL explores the dimensions of, and the manner in which, context influences language use. Eggins (1994), building on Halliday's notion of context, suggests that systemics has attempted to describe: "(1) exactly what dimensions of context have an impact on language use. Since clearly not every aspect of context makes a difference to language use ... just what bits of the context do get 'into' the text? And (2), which aspects of language use appear to be affected by particular dimensions of the context. For example, if we contrast texts in which the interactants are friends with texts where the interactants are strangers, can we specify where in the language they use this contextual difference will by expressed?" (p.9).

Halliday (1985) conceptualised context as a combination of three important dimensions termed field, mode, and tenor. Field refers to what is happening, to the nature of the social interaction that is taking place—e.g. a lecture or a casual conversation. The ideational function relates to the field. The mode of the discourse refers to the part that the language is playing in the interaction in terms of the channel through which it is being transmitted (e.g. oral versus written). The textual function relates to the mode of discourse. The tenor refers to who is taking part, to the nature of the participants, their status and roles—e.g. lecturer–student, two friends, salesperson–customer. The interpersonal metafunction relates to the tenor. These three dimensions have a significant and predictable impact on language use. Taking an example of this thinking, if you were phoning to find out some information about bus timetables, the context could be described as shown in Table 5.1.

TABLE 5.1
A bus timetable telephone enquiry example of the three dimensions of context

Contextual variable	*Description*
Field	A verbal service encounter over the telephone.
Tenor	Unfamiliar participants, unequal status between participants, customers–superordinate, information provider–subordinate.
Mode	Spoken, but may refer to written material.

Genre

The concept of genre describes the impact of the context of culture on language by identifying the staged, step-by-step structure that cultures institutionalise as ways of achieving goals (Eggins, 1994). That is, our day-to-day activities are composed of a series of different generic structures that are made up of a series of goal-oriented steps that unfold according to the situation we are in. If, for example, you were telling a funny story to a friend on the way to work, you would probably follow a sequence of steps, such as providing the setting information, the time, the place, who told the story in the first place, the introduction to the story, the complicating action, the punch line, and the summary. These steps fall into what is generally known as the structure of a narrative. The important difference when viewing this structure from the SFL standpoint is that the language choices made are intertwined with the generic structure as well as the context (i.e. the field, tenor, and mode).

Ideology

A more recent development in the theory of SFL emphasises the importance of ideology (Martin, 1992). As well as the genre and the context of a situation, language choices also depend on our ideological positions—i.e. our biases or personal perspectives. Some of these influences may be quite unconscious or inherent in the speaker's make-up (e.g. gender, ethnicity, class, and generation).

SFL differs from traditional grammar in that it conceptualises function as driving the form of language rather than the form of language determining the functions. Language is not viewed as a set of rules, but rather as a set of linguistic resources. Each utterance we produce actualises all three metafunctions concurrently. That is, we don't just produce an utterance with interpersonal meanings or textual meanings or ideational meanings.

As mentioned earlier, our area of interest is the interpersonal function of language in TBI interactions. The interpersonal function analyses focus on the interaction between the speaker and the hearer by examining which language structures are used to establish and maintain interactions. In this chapter, we will be briefly outlining three interpersonal analyses from SFL that we have used to describe the discourse of people with TBI. In order to illustrate these, let us take the earlier example of an interaction where someone is making a request for information to the bus timetable information service on the telephone. This is an example of the service encounter genre. The interpersonal analysis of genre is "generic structure potential analysis", which outlines the overall structure of the interaction. Another level of discourse analysis that has been of interest to TBI researchers is the way people with TBI exchange information (e.g. Coelho et al., 1991a). In SFL, the exchange of information is examined using "exchange structure analysis", which addresses who has the knowledge in an interaction and how that knowledge is transferred. The way in which people with TBI and their communication partners word their utterances is also of interest. For example, the way people make requests or give instructions will vary according to with whom they are interacting. In SFL, "mood and modality analysis" provides some indication of the wording used to make the request and the politeness markers used by interlocutors.

The context of the situation (i.e. field, mode, and tenor) has an impact on the way requests for information are made. This impact can be seen across all analyses. For example, the type of request made between two people of equal status will be very different to one made by a superior to a subordinate. Example 5.1 shows a request for information between two people of equal status.

EXAMPLE 5.1
Request for information between communication partners of equal status

Customer:	What time would I need to be at Strathfield Station to catch a bus to Macquarie Shopping Centre and be there by 12.30?
Bus timetable person:	We don't have a service that does that

Using this example we can now illustrate each of the types of analysis. Starting with the genre level, this request would form part of the Service Request (SR) element in the generic structure potential (GSP) analysis. The SR element is one of the obligatory elements in the GSP analysis. It is usually followed by a Service Compliance (SC) where the answer to the SR is provided. At the discourse semantics level, exchange structure analysis would enable us to code the customer as a secondary knower (K2)—i.e. someone who doesn't have some information and who is requesting it from the bus timetable person who is the primary knower (K1). The degree to which a person is a primary knower has been associated with the degree of power they have in an interaction. At the lexicogrammar level we could code this request as a WH-interrogative. At the tone level the request would be characterised by rising intonation. This request is said to be "congruently formed"—i.e. it conforms with all the features one would expect when fulfilling the task of requesting information. Sometimes, however, requests are not congruently formed. This can be seen in Example 5.2.

EXAMPLE 5.2
Request for information from superior to subordinate

Superior:	Show me where the timetables are
Employee:	They're over on the table (pointing)

In this example the superior is requesting information from a subordinate. This is no longer a service encounter at the genre level and would more likely be part of a different generic structure potential such as workplace procedural discourse text. The superior's request for information would be marked in exchange structure analysis terms as a request for action. When requesting someone to do an action, you are said to be a secondary actor (A2) who requests an action from the primary actor (A1). Thus this request for information has now become a request for action. At the lexicogrammar level this request is therefore actualised as a command (or an imperative). At the tonal level there is a falling intonation pattern. Thus at all levels the different status of the participants is reflected in the language structures used. If people are in a position of unequal status their language use will reflect this from the tone they use through to the way information is requested and received, and all these levels relate to the activity that is occurring at the time. This brief example demonstrates the depth and complexity of some of the analyses within the SFL framework. It shows promise as a way of analysing communicative interactions between TBI subjects and a range of communication partners. The following section describes a series of studies we have completed to examine TBI interactions using exchange structure analysis, generic structure analysis and mood and modality analysis.

EXCHANGE STRUCTURE OF TBI INTERACTIONS

We used exchange structure analysis to measure the performance of people with TBI on a functional day-to-day task, to establish how their communication impairments influence their ability to assume the social roles of patient, son, and enquirer in service encounters with members of the public (Togher, Hand, & Code, 1996a, 1997a, 1997b). We looked at whether people with TBI and matched controls change their communication behaviour with different conversational partners, who vary according to familiarity (i.e. social distance) and power relationships. Exchange structure analysis examines who has the knowledge in an interaction and how this knowledge is conveyed from one communication partner to another. If the participants are of unequal power (e.g. in a doctor–patient interaction), the dominant communication partner is said to be more likely to be a primary knower (K1) or the person who has the information. The subordinate is more likely to be a secondary knower (K2) or the one who does not have the information and is wanting to gain it from the primary knower. Using this analysis, it is possible to examine how often a person is given the opportunity to be a primary knower in different interactions. This will vary according to the communicative task (field) and the people involved (tenor).

The field or activity was the same across conditions (i.e. an enquiry on the telephone). The mode, which was spoken with reference to some written material, was also held constant across conditions. The tenor was the variable of interest and was therefore varied systematically to enable us to investigate the interpersonal function of the exchanges.

Subjects were asked to request information over the telephone from four different communication partners. These included the bus timetable information service, the police, their mothers, and a therapist. A scenario was set up prior to each data collection to facilitate the ecological validity of the call. The scenario and purpose of each call is summarised in Table 5.2. Fuller details can be found in Togher et al. (1997a).

Subjects were five TBI adults and five normal adults matched for age

TABLE 5.2
Scenario and purpose of each interaction

Condition	*Scenario*	*Purpose of call*
Bus timetable	Researcher is organising an outing (for day centre group, or hospital group, depending on subjects), which focuses on facilitating public transport skills by catching trains and buses around Sydney: TBI and control subjects are asked to assist by finding out information.	To find out which bus goes from Strathfield Station to Macquarie Shopping Centre, to arrive by 12.30 for lunch outing, and costs involved.
Police	Researcher is currently preparing a talk about returning to driving after a head injury. TBI and control subjects are prompted to call police to find out how to procure a driver's licence following suspension as a result of TBI.	To find out how to obtain a licence after it has been suspended following a severe head injury.
Mother	Researcher introduces a discussion regarding subjects' current weekly programme and asks TBI and control subject for details. When subjects are unable to recall all details, they are prompted to contact their mothers to find out.	To find out the TBI subject's weekly programme.
Therapist	Researcher is currently writing a report for the insurance company, and would like to include information about goals and progress in other areas. TBI subjects are asked about their goals and, if unable to remember, they are cued to contact the therapist involved. Controls are asked whether they know about the areas that their relative/friends is working on, and cued to call the appropriate therapist to find out.	To find out from the therapist (O.T., P.T., psychologist etc.) what goals are being pursued, and current progress.

(mean = 29 years), sex, and education. Subjects were selected on the basis of evidence of inappropriate pragmatic behaviours, based on ratings by two independent speech-language pathologists, as assessed on the Pragmatic Protocol (Prutting & Kirchner, 1987). These included paralinguistic factors such as difficulty with prosody, which occurred with all subjects and reduced intelligibility and difficulty with topic change (4/5 subjects). Verbal problems with topic introduction and selection and quantity/conciseness were found in three subjects. Difficulty with topic maintenance, reduced vocal intensity, specificity/accuracy problems, and flat facial expression were found in two subjects.

Our studies have used control subjects who were socioeconomically closely matched to the TBI subjects. Control subjects were aged 24–36 years (mean = 30 years). Four of the five control subjects were brothers of the

TBI subjects. The fifth control subject was a volunteer worker matched for age and education.

The analyses

Two analyses are described in this chapter—exchange structure analysis and generic structure potential analysis. Exchange structure analysis taps into how information and goods and services are exchanged. All interactions are based around the demanding and giving of information or goods and services. These are typically realised by the speech functions of statements, questions, offers, and commands. Berry (1981) and Ventola (1987) developed this basic system further by examining who in the interaction has the information (or goods and services) and how this is conveyed.

The exchange is made up of moves, which are the basic units of analysis. A move is a unit of information and an exchange is composed of a sequence of moves. When involved in an exchange, one is either (a) requesting or providing information, or (b) requesting or providing action. Exchange analysis has two types of moves—"synoptic" moves and "dynamic" moves. When analysing conversational exchanges the abbreviations K1 and K2 are used to refer to the exchange of this information. Exchanges can be initiated by either interlocutor. Therefore, subjects and their communication partners can be both primary (K1) and secondary knowers (K2) in different exchanges. Synoptic moves are denoted by brackets and dynamic moves are marked with arrows. The following example shows an exchange consisting of a request for information (K2) by the control subject and provision of information (K1) by the bus timetable person, ending with a follow-up move (K2f).

EXAMPLE 5.3
Control subject 3: Bus timetable condition (moves 117–119: S=Subject B=Bus timetable person)

117	┌ K2	S: So I really suppose it wouldn't be more than two dollars?
118	├ K1	B: Well your bus is going to cost them a dollar twenty each way
119	└ K2f	S: Right

Exchanges of information are rarely this smooth, so to facilitate the exchange speakers use dynamic moves that perform the function of negotiating meanings such as checking or clarification. In Example 5.4 we have two exchanges of information that are made up of an information giving exchange (moves 19–22) and an information requesting exchange (moves 23–29). Dynamic moves of confirmation (cf) and responses to confirmation (rcf) are also used, possibly to assist the subject to remember the information being given to him or her, as well as backchannelling (bch), which is

EXAMPLE 5.4
Control subject 4: Police condition (moves 19–29: S=Subject P=Policeman)

19	K1	P: I mean if you contact their head office at Rosebery
20	cf	S: Head office at Rosebery, yeah
21	rcf	P: Yeah mate
22	K1	P: They'd be able to give you all the info you'd need
23	K2	S: Alright could I get that phone number?
24	K1	P: Mate I haven't got it unfortunately
25	cf	S: Oh you haven't got it
26	K1	P: If you look them up under the Roads and Traffic Authority, you'll come up their head office mate down at Rosebery
27	bch	S: Yeah
28	K1	P: And they'll be able to give you a hand from there
29	K2f	S: Alright then

another kind of dynamic move that is important for the flow of information during telephone calls.

Synoptic moves consist of K1, K2, K1f, and K2f moves during exchanges of information. If the request or receipt of action is occurring, the exchanges are made up of the synoptic moves of A1, A2, A1f, and A2f (see Table 5.3 for examples). The interactions that were the subject of interest in this study were primarily exchanges of information, and therefore K1, K2 and the follow up moves of K1f and K2f were the primary synoptic units of analysis.

K1 moves

The K1 move serves to provide information to the other person. When making a K1 move one is termed the "primary knower". The primary knower is "someone who already knows the information" (Berry, 1981). The tasks in this study required the communication partner in the interaction (e.g. the bus timetable person or the therapist) to assume this role, as they were being asked for information. Being the primary knower frequently during an interaction has been associated with being in a more powerful position in that interaction (Poynton, 1985). The primary knower must make a contribution (i.e., it is an obligatory element of the exchange structure) if an exchange is to occur (Berry, 1981). Thus, the K1 slot is where the primary knower indicates that they know the information and where they confer the information with a "kind of a stamp of authority" (Berry, 1981).

K2 moves

The "secondary knower" (i.e. K2) in an interaction is "someone to whom the information is imparted" (Berry, 1981). Interactants are in the K2 role either because they are directly requesting information or because they are receiving information. It is the former K2 role that is of interest. The subjects (both TBI and normal) were required in the tasks set for them to

TABLE 5.3
Example of exchange types

Types of move		*Examples*	
Information requesting exchange			
K2	= secondary knower, who does not have the information	K2	How do I get my licence back?
K1	= primary knower, who already knows the information	K1	You go to the registry
K2f	= a follow up move by the secondary knower to finish the cxchange	K2f	Oh
The teaching exchange			
dK1	= primary knower asking a question to which they know the answer	dK1	Where did we go?
		K2	To the beach
		K1	That's right!
Information seeking exchange			
		K2	Do you know where the registry is
cfrq	= dynamic move that asks for confirmation	cfrq	Where?
rcfrq	= response to confirmation	rcfrq	The registry
		K1	Yeah it's at Rosebery
Information giving exchange			
		K1	I'm here with Leanne at the moment
bch	= backchannelling move	bch	Ah ha
		K1	At Lidcombe
		K2f	OK

assume the K2 role to request specific information. This provides a measure of success in requesting information. Being placed in the K2 role has been described as being in a less powerful position (Poynton, 1985); however, the ability to ask questions has also been described by others as a powerful conversational strategy (Cameron, McAlinden, & O'Leary, 1987; O'Barr & Atkins, 1987). Analysis of K2 moves therefore needs to take account of the context in which they occur.

The sequence in which K1 moves and K2 moves can occur has been developed into a formula that has been adapted by Ventola (1987). For an information exchange this formula is as follows:

((dK1) K2) K1 (K2f K1f))

where K1 is the only obligatory element for an exchange of information to occur. Each element, if it appears, must appear in the given order. The elements within the brackets are optional. So, for example, it is possible to have a K2 K1 exchange, or a K1 K2f exchange, but it is not possible to have a K2 move in isolation. dK1 represents a delaying move, where the person is asking a question that they already know the answer to. The "d" stands for a delayed K1 move, as the K1 move does not occur until the end of the exchange. This is typical of teaching interactions (see Example 5.5).

EXAMPLE 5.5
TBI subject 1: Mother condition (moves 15–17: M=Mother S=Subject)

15	dK1	M: and what did you do on Mondays?
16	K2	S: Wasn't that the day, that afternoon we went to the swimming pool?
17	K1	M: Yes ... That's right

Dynamic moves

Dynamic moves are used to facilitate the negotiation of meaning, either actively (such as clarification or checking), or by giving feedback that the information has been conveyed successfully (by confirmation or backchannelling). Dynamic moves are used when the information exchange process is challenged or when interactants misunderstand each other.

The analysis allows us to examine how interactants are using language during the information exchange process. The choices that are made depend on the context of situation and the context of culture surrounding that interaction. The language choices made can be interpreted in the light of interpersonal factors such as social distance and perceived authority. Table 5.3 provides some further examples of different types of exchanges.

As conditions were varied according to social distance and power imbalance, it was hypothesised that the person with TBI would be less able to adapt to this variation. This hypothesis was based on evidence regarding the impaired adaptive executive functions reported to follow TBI (Ylvisaker & Szekeres, 1994). It was also hypothesised that the person with TBI would be less able to request information and would ultimately receive less information. It has been suggested that TBI subjects have difficulty requesting information (Coelho, Liles, & Duffy, 1991a; Mentis & Prutting, 1991). By examining K1 moves, K2 moves, and dynamic moves, social distance and power imbalance could be investigated.

Inter-rater and intra-rater reliability was established on 25% of the data. Two raters independently classified 25% of the texts according to the exchange structure described. Intra-rater agreement ranged between 82% and 96% for type of move and 84% and 95% for division of exchanges. Inter-rater reliability on the type of move was 86%, and 95% for the division of exchanges.

Exchange structure analysis allowed for a detailed description of the four texts each subject produced with their communication partners. The analysis provided information about the subjects and the people with whom they were interacting that has not come from other research. For the sake of expediency, each group of speakers will be discussed separately, although this division is artificial because we examined the interaction rather than each speaker's contribution to it.

Exchange structure analysis

We looked at the exchange structure from the point of view of who had the information in each interaction and how this information was conveyed. Keep in mind that the K1 position was viewed as being a powerful one: If you are giving information, you have the floor. We wanted to know which group was the most successful at finding out information—i.e. who was given the most information. We were particularly interested in whether there was a difference in the amount of information the TBI and control subjects gave. Our analysis was divided broadly into two sections:

1. Communication partner responses to TBI versus controls; and
2. TBI versus controls' responses across four conditions.

1. Communication partners and their use of exchange structure: TBI versus control subjects

We examined the behaviour of communication partners by asking the following three questions: (a) Did the interactants give the same amount of information to TBI subjects when compared with controls? (b) Did the interactants ask TBI and control subjects for similar amounts of information? (c) Did interactants use similar amounts of dynamic moves with TBI when compared with control subjects? As well as comparing communication partners across TBI versus control subjects we also compared interactants with each other within each of the TBI and control interactions.

To answer our first question, we compared the amount of information the partners gave (as K1 moves per minute). Secondly, we looked at the frequency of K2 moves per minute to gauge how much of the time the interlocutors were either requesting information or were in a position where they were being given information. Finally, we examined the dynamic moves per minute to look at the amount of negotiation that was needed. Mothers, and to a lesser extent, police and therapists, interacted differently with TBI subjects when compared with control subjects.

Therapists gave more information to controls than to TBI subjects. Mothers provided more information to their normal sons when compared with their head-injured sons, but the difference only approached significance. There was no difference in the amount of information provided by the bus timetable information service or police to TBI and control subjects.

Therapists were more likely to ask questions of the control subjects than the TBI subjects. Police were never in the K2 role and therefore never asked questions of the control subjects, but made enquiries (sometimes of a personal nature) of the TBI subjects. They were therefore in the K2 role significantly more often with the TBI subjects when compared with controls. In three of the five interactions with TBI subjects, bus information service providers made no K2 responses. There was no difference between the frequency of K2 moves by the bus timetable information service providers or mothers in their interactions with TBI and control subjects.

Therapists produced significantly more dynamic moves with TBI subjects than with controls. There were no significant differences in the overall frequency of dynamic moves in other conditions, although the nature of dynamic moves varied across conditions. For example, therapists' responses to the TBI's requests for clarification, confirmation, and repetition formed the majority of their dynamic moves with three of the five TBI subjects. In contrast, as Example 5.6 shows, police tended to rely on dynamic moves that served to check that TBI subjects had taken in the information that was being provided to them. The policeman "checks" with the TBI subject after each piece of information has been given, and this sometimes occurs mid-sentence. With the control subjects (Example 5.7) this "checking" behaviour rarely occurs, indicating that the policeman is satisfied that the control subject is able to take in the information he is giving. This constant checking behaviour with the TBI subjects gave them little credit for being aware of organisations such as the Roads and Traffic Authority, or driving schools,

EXAMPLE 5.6

TBI subject 1: Police condition (moves 29–44: S=TBI subject P=Policeman RTA=Roads and Traffic Authority)

29	K1	P: Um what what what you have to do is if you can um if you have to go to the RTA
30	K1	P: They'll put your application in to get a licence
31	bch	S: Sure
32	**check**	**P: Right? If you can understand that**
33	rcheck	S: Yeah
34	K1-Fg	P: But prior to that, um what you have you have to go
35	**check**	**P: ah you know a driving school?**
36	rcheck	S: Yeah
37	K1	P: Right and they um have rehabilitation people that ah can ah put you through oh like your driving lessons,
38	bch	S: Sure
39	K1-Fg	P: and then they decide whether you know
40	cp	S: Whether you're capable
41	rcp	P: Yeah whether you're then capable to go and get your licence
42	bch	S: Sure
43	check	**P: Right?**
44	K2f	S: OK then

EXAMPLE 5.7

Control subject 1: Police condition (moves 39–42: S=Control subject P=Policeman)

39	K1	P: so you've still gotta make the application to the RTA of course
40	K1	P: um and that's once once that application's made
41	K1	P: of course then they've gotta go then they've through all the driving lessons and whatever
42	K2f	S: oh right

even though they were all familiar with these. Such behaviour has the effect of disempowering the TBI subject.

2. TBI versus controls across four conditions

We were also interested in how the TBI subjects performed across the four conditions when compared with controls.

K1 moves per minute. TBI subjects gave significantly more information to the police than the matched controls. Some of this information was inappropriate, as can be seen in Example 5.8. This provision of information was partly in response to police behaviour because police were more likely to ask TBI subjects questions and therefore they demanded significantly more information.

TBI subjects gave significantly more information to police than to therapists and the bus information service. They gave few K1s to their mothers, which probably was due to the fact that mothers produced relatively fewer K2s when conversing with their TBI sons compared with their normal sons. That is, mothers asked their control sons more questions than they did of their TBI sons. As a result, control subjects gave significantly more information to their mothers than the police.

EXAMPLE 5.8

TBI subject 5: Police condition (unrelated comment)

81	K1	P: But the main thing is R. is that it's just gotta go through the Commonwealth Rehab
82	cf	S: Commonwealth Rehab
83	rcf	P: Yeah,
84	K1	P: and ah you know they are, they [provide
85	K1	S: [I've got a lot of Aboriginal mates
86	bch	P: Yeah
87	K1	S: In the service
88	cf	P: Yeah, oh yeah
89	K1	S: Ah, they're older men
90	K1	P: Yeah and just go to Cumberland College for the test
91	K1	P: and [then you're right

Although the general trend was that mothers asked TBI subjects fewer questions than their brothers, this was not always the case. For example, one TBI subject (S3) gave more information to his mother than any other TBI subject by far. He also gave more information to his mother than to any other communication partner (i.e. 7.5 K1 moves/minute with mother compared with 2 K1 moves/minute with police, 1.9 K1 moves/minute with the therapist, and 1.3 K1 moves/minute with the bus timetable person). This subject was encouraged to give information by his mother who asked an increased proportion of K2 moves (5.2 K2 moves/minute, compared with 2 K2 moves/minute by police, 1.9 K2 moves/minute with the therapist, and 0.7 K2 moves/minute with the bus timetable person). The talk that occurred with his mother appeared to be the most "normal" of all his interactions (Example 5.9). However, there were two features that marked this interaction as being abnormal. TBI subject 3 introduced the topic of enquiring about his licence with the police, which turned into a teaching exchange led by his mother. These teaching exchanges frequently occurred in the

EXAMPLE 5.9
TBI subject 3: Mother condition (moves 12–38: S=Subject M=Mother)

12	K1	S: Yeah we may be later
13	K1	S: I just did make an enquiry about me licence
14	cfrq	M: Did you
15	rcfrq	S: Yes
16	K2	M: And what did they say?
17	K1	S: Well first I'll have to see a doctor first
18	bch	M: Mm
19	K1	S: To make sure me reflexes and that are OK
20	K2f	M: Yes that's right
21	dK1	M: And what about your sight
22	K2	S: And me sight—yeah I'll have to test that again
23	K1	M: Yes
24	K1	S: That is getting a lot better though
25	cfrq	M: Are your sure?
26	rcfrq	S: Yes
27	K2	M: That's up to you I s'pose
28	bch	S: Yeah
29	K2	M: Only you would be able to tell that
30	K1	S: Oh it is getting a lot better than what it was
31	K2f	M: Good
32	K1	S: It hasn't got any worse
33	cf	M: Oh well (laughs) that's one way of looking at it I s'pose(.)
34	K2	M: Alright—have you got anything else to tell me?
35	K1	S: Oh no (.)
36	K1	S: It's always nice to talk to you mum
37	K2f	M: Oh thank you R.
38	K2f	M: Nice to talk to you too

mother–TBI son interactions we analysed. The mother also queried whether S3 was sure about his information giving—another feature frequently observed when a TBI subject gave information. Therefore, even though speaking to his mother was the most productive condition for S3's information giving, it was still marked as unusual as a result of the communication behaviour by the mother.

TBI subjects were in the K2 role significantly more often than controls in the therapist condition. The K2 role in an exchange is realised in two ways. We may be requesting information, or we may be placed in this role when we make an utterance that reflects that we do not have the information. The latter frequently occurs in teaching interactions. TBI subjects were active in asking questions, but they were also in the latter category of K2 role, where they indicated they were being provided with information. Two of the five TBI subjects used K2 moves, which were not requesting information. In one case (TBI subject 4), 70% of his K2 responses were indicating that he did not have the information and was in the less powerful position in the interaction (Example 5.10). Note in this example that while S4 is giving information, the accuracy of this information is being determined by the therapist, who remains in the K1 role throughout. All control subjects' use of the K2 moves involved requests for information. They were never involved in a teaching interaction.

TBI subjects used significantly more dynamic moves than controls in the therapist condition. These were primarily requests for clarification, confirmation, and repetition of information. There were no other significant differences between TBI and control subjects in other conditions in the use of dynamic moves.

We compared TBI subjects and controls with each other in their interactions with different communication partners. TBI subjects used significantly more dynamic moves with police compared with mothers. They also used

EXAMPLE 5.10

TBI subject 4: Therapist condition (moves 22–32: T=Therapist S=Subject)

22	K1	T: I can tell you what your programme is but altogether it's up to you—
23	dK1	T: Why do you feel as if the programme's good for you?
24	**K2**	**S: Um I suppose it's helping me to realise my potential in life**
25	cf	T: Yeah, yeah I guess it's the same thing
26	**K2**	**S: And just helping me to gain acceptance into the community**
27	K1	T: Yeah sort of trying new things like
28	bch	S: Yeah
29	K1	T: the child care thing and
30	bch	S: Yeah
31	K1	T: and I think you're doing that in your programme
32	K2f	S: Yeah

more dynamic moves in the police condition than in the bus timetable condition. The increased use of dynamic moves by TBI subjects with police indicates the importance placed on the joint negotiation of the message, which was also reflected in the control subjects' use of dynamic moves. They produced significantly more dynamic moves with police than with their mothers and with therapists. Even though the police condition entailed the most simple enquiry, there was a greater amount of negotiation and checking of the accuracy of the transfer of the message by both TBI and control subjects. This confirms the importance of successfully establishing the interpersonal relationship where there is a power imbalance.

Generic structure potential (GSP) analysis

The theory of SFL allows a clear description of how the context is realised in the text. We completed a study that attempted to answer a small part of one of the questions posed by Eggins (1994): namely, which aspects of language use appear to be affected by particular dimensions of the context following TBI (Togher et al., 1997a). The richness of this approach is that, as well as analysing at the level of discourse semantics (i.e. exchange structure analysis), it is also possible to take the same data and analyse it at the level of genre (i.e. generic structure potential, or GSP) analysis and lexicogrammar (mood and modality).

GSP analysis examines oral texts as genre (Hasan, 1984; Martin, 1985, 1992; Ventola, 1987). Each social process is seen as unfolding step by step according to the context of the situation (i.e. field, tenor, and mode) and also according to the core structural elements that would be expected in that particular type of interaction. The bus and police telephone data were analysed using this approach as they both represented service encounters (Togher et al., 1997b). Normal service encounters have been previously well described (Hasan, 1985; Ventola, 1987). The texts were divided into key structural elements (see Table 5.4 and the Appendix to this chapter for further detail), which have been described as typifying a service encounter. An example of a simple service encounter is:

Greeting:	A: Hello Telstra Australia
	B: Hello
Service Request:	B: Could you tell me what the time is in London?
Service Enquiry:	A: Do you mean at the moment?
	B: Yes
Service Compliance:	A: Yes it's 5am
Close:	B: OK thanks very much
Goodbye:	A: Bye

TABLE 5.4
Elements of generic structure potential in service encounters

Element	*Description*
Greeting (GR)	Caller and information service provider greet each other.
Address (AD)	Caller and information service provider identify selves or ask for identification—e.g. "What's your name?"
Service Initiation (SI)	"Can I help you?"
Service Request (SR)	Makes primary request for information known to service provider.
Service Enquiry (SE)	Seeks further information or detail regarding initial SR. Can be made by either party.
Service Compliance (SC)	Response to request for information and invitation for further requests.
Close (CL)	Closing remarks—usually interpersonally oriented, e.g. "Is that OK?, Thanks very much".
Goodbye (GB)	Final goodbye: "Bye-Bye".
Call for Attention (Call)	Call for attention from either speaker, either due to lack of response, or because speaker was returning to the phone after suspending conversation.
Action (ACT)	Statements of action (e.g. "I'll just write that down").
Incomplete/ Inappropriate (*)	Inappropriate or incomplete elements either because of delayed responding or a lack of response.
Unrelated (UNR)	Comments or enquiries that are unrelated to the task at hand.
Personal Comments (Personal)	Comments of a personal nature that, while not directly relevant to the information-seeking task, appear to fulfil an interpersonal function (e.g. "You're not nervous about driving are you?").
Repetition (rpt)	Elements that are repeated due to misunderstanding; failure to take in information or forgetting of information.

A more thorough description of this analysis can be found in Togher et al. (1997b), but for the purpose of this chapter it is useful to look at one aspect of the analysis to demonstrate its value. GSP analysis showed that the generic structural elements in the TBI service encounters were of a different length and composition to those of the control interactions. There were difficulties with the opening sequences of TBI interactions, as well as with the main Service Request. Repeated and inappropriate elements were present in TBI samples, whereas they did not occur in the control samples. There were also significant differences between the bus timetable condition GSP and the police GSP. In the control–police interactions, the Greeting sequences were short and quickly followed by a clear succinct service request and the Close/Goodbye sequences were significantly longer than in the bus condition. In contrast, the TBI subject–police interactions evidenced long Greeting sequences and short Close/Goodbye elements. Opening and closing elements reflect the development of interpersonal relationships by initially establishing credibility and, finally, by confirming the success of the encounter, as well as encouraging future contact. In all control interactions, the police officer encouraged subjects to call again. The interpersonal relationship was therefore reinforced by a longer closure than in the TBI interactions.

This analysis allowed a description of the overall macrostructure of the interactions that was not available from other levels. Once a particular structural element, such as the service request, can be targeted as being problematic, it is then possible to look at the exchange structure (i.e. discourse semantics) as we have already described, and the mood and modality (i.e. lexicogrammar) with which the *meanings* are expressed.

Mood and modality analysis

Mood and modality analysis examines the interpersonal metafunction at the clause level (Halliday, 1985; Martin, 1992). It is described in greater detail in Togher, Hand, and Code (1996b) and Togher and Hand (1998). This analysis provides some insight into the language choices that are made at clause level by examining the degree of "definiteness" in an interlocutor's utterances. It also refers to the way requests are made and how the answers are phrased, by taking context into account (Halliday, 1985). SFL describes a system of choices that may be activated if either speaker is attempting to preserve the other's "face" in an interaction (Brown & Levinson, 1987). This may be realised in two major ways. First, the system of mood provides different speech function choices to express meanings. That is, clauses are analysed according to the types of speech function they represent (such as Yes/No tag questions, Wh-Interrogative questions, declaratives, imperatives). Secondly, the modality analysis provides different levels of "definiteness" in the ways ideas are expressed. For example, the analysis of mood can be used to examine the wording that is being used during a therapy session. If a therapist wanted to stop a patient with TBI from talking so that she could have a turn, she can use a range of speech functions to realise this. She could use a command, realised through the imperative speech function, such as "Stop talking now". This is a fairly abrupt way of achieving her aim so she might make another choice such as a question that is realised with an interrogative, such as "Would you stop talking now?" Note that this is not a real question as a response is not expected. Either the person stops talking or they continue, which would signal potential conflict. Another way to stop the person talking could be to make a statement that is usually realised by a declarative such as "I can't concentrate on what we're doing while you're talking". This grammatical structure is typically used for information giving, but in this case it is not used to give information but to stop the patient from talking. By using some of these non-typical structures to get meaning across, the therapist is able to express his or her meaning in "ways that can be highly sensitive to contextual constraints" (Eggins, 1994;

p.121). Halliday (1985) refers to these types of structures as grammatical metaphor.

The other way to use language to reflect the context interpersonally at the level of lexicogrammar is through the system of modality. This refers to the area between "yes" and "no". Sometimes, perhaps to be more polite, we may want to "modalise" our utterances. For example, as well as changing the speech functions our therapist above used to make a request, he or she may have also said "Could you possibly stop talking now?" or "I suppose this might be difficult for you but could you stop talking now?" In these utterances, the therapist is using finite modal verbs (could, might), a modal adjunct (possibly), and comment adjuncts (I suppose). These are some of the resources described in Halliday's system of mood and modality to lessen the degree between "do it!" and "don't do it!". This system is also used when we are not particularly sure about the information we are giving. Compare the following four utterances:

1. I can't do it.
2. I might possibly be able to do it.
3. I suppose I might possibly be able to do it.
4. I can do it.

These demonstrate the range between "yes" and "no" by using the resources of the mood and modality network. Note that the more modality used in an utterance the less certain it is (Halliday, 1985).

Thus, lexicogrammatical analysis of this kind can provide significant information about how people with a TBI use interpersonal resources at the level of the clause to indicate that they are aware of the relationships set up through the context. If they make requests for information inappropriately, or appear to be abrupt or overly familiar, this is reflected at this level of analysis. It can also be used to examine whether interlocutors are being overly "polite" because the person with TBI obviously has a disability, and the consequences of this overpoliteness. For example, if a therapist makes an overly modalised request for action, it is possible that the person with TBI will fail to detect the request, and therefore fail to comply. This may end in conflict because the therapist perceives that the patient is refusing to cooperate, whereas at the same time the patient may be confused because they don't know what is expected of them.

SUMMARY

So what can exchange structure analysis and the underlying theory of SFL tell us that other analyses cannot? First and importantly, it emphasises the person with TBI as a co-participant in interactions, that will vary according to the tenor relationships. The factors of familiarity (i.e. social distance) and status or power appear to have a powerful influence on the language choices made by both parties in the interactions. These varied language choices, we would suggest, are the result of the different roles the interlocutors assume as well as a response to disability. Exchange structure analysis is one of many analyses available to us to investigate interpersonal meanings that both we, our clients, and their respective families and communities are making. This approach has clear implications for assessment and therapy which we discuss next.

Implications for management

SFL requires us to take the surrounding context of the communicative act into account. This may appear similar to the description of factors to be aware of in the pragmatics literature, but there are critical differences between the two approaches. Most accounts from the pragmatics literature cite participants, setting, and mode of communication (Hartley, 1990) but there is no further elaboration as to what effects these factors can possibly have on the language that is used. SFL provides a series of detailed frameworks that delineate the rich nature of the language choices that are available according to the field, tenor, and mode, or the context. As well as this, it allows an appreciation of factors such as the gender, ethnicity, class, and generation of the participants, which is realised by the choices speakers make at all levels.

Our assessments are typically carried out in a clinic room, hospital room, nursing home, or even in the client's home. The tenor relationships involved during our assessments, regardless of their physical location, are of a therapist–patient/client relationship. This immediately places contextual restraints on all levels of the meanings that can be made because of the roles we are in. These constraints on the meanings that can be made are rarely fully taken into account during assessment. Frequently a patient's communicative status is determined by their "performance" during a speech-language pathology assessment. SFL would suggest that given the range of interlocutors with whom our patients interact, they will most likely have a much broader range of meanings available to be expressed than those they produce in our clinic rooms.

Our exchange structure analysis suggested that the clinical interaction may provide a very different picture of a patient's communicative ability. A frequent observation is that people with TBI have difficulty adapting from one context to another. They are described as having "difficult to describe subtle cognitive language impairments" (Kennedy & DeRuyter, 1991) that are manifested when they are placed in functional situations that demand high levels of integration (Milton, 1988). An impaired ability to adapt to new situations may potentially be reinforced *by* the clinical interaction. By assessing patients in the same context over time (i.e. the clinic room), we as therapists are fixing the tenor variable. Our challenge is to provide our patients with the opportunity to exercise language choices over a wide range of tenor relationships.

There are two main aspects to the phenomenon of tenor. One of these is social distance between the participants and the other is power imbalance (Martin, 1992). Social distance is concerned with how familiar you are with the person you are interacting with. Power relates to who has control in the interaction. The therapy interaction is an example of where familiarity may vary over time, but where there is always an inherent power imbalance (Green, 1984; Silvast, 1991). One way of challenging the power imbalance is to vary the typical therapy session. Silvast (1991) described the typical session with aphasic patients as "therapist makes a request for information, aphasic responds, often with an extended answer, and therapist follows ... with short answers" (p.388). This is also typical of "conversations" that occur in the clinic with a person with TBI.

One of the aims of our studies (Togher, Hand, & Code, 1997a, 1997b; Togher & Hand, 1998) was to manipulate the parameters of social distance and role in the interactions. In the case of the task the TBI subjects were asked to complete with the therapist, *they* were in the role of requesting information from the therapist. This provided a situation where the above "typical" therapist–patient interaction was turned around. It allowed the TBI subject the opportunity to use a wider range of strategies, such as requesting clarification and confirmation, than may have been normally available during a therapy interview situation.

One of the promising results of our research was that the TBI subjects demonstrated strengths in communicative contexts other than the therapeutic one. This was particularly so for the bus timetable condition. Why was this condition a seemingly easier one for the TBI subjects? The bus timetable person was completely unfamiliar with the TBI subjects, and in this case the power imbalance was in their favour as a *customer*. They were expected in that role to make a request for information, and the bus timetable person was expected to provide that information. Therefore the contextual configuration was preset so that they could be at their most successful when compared with other conditions. The issue of roles in the interactions is important here. The different roles they assumed in each interaction (e.g. customer, son, patient) also had a powerful influence on the way they made requests.

The way we approach the treatment of communication following TBI usually follows logically from the interpretation of the results derived from our assessment. The treatment implications from a SFL approach to assessment are wide-reaching and significant. If we view the therapy interaction as only one of many contextual configurations that our clients may be faced with it becomes clear that we need to be spending less time talking with them and more time facilitating their interactions with others. We need to be providing our clients with as many different genres, tenor relationships, fields, and modes of communication as is practical within the clinical setting. In our study the telephone appeared to be a useful way to access different types of genres and tenor relationships. Essentially, many clinicians see these types of activities as "carryover" or "facilitating generalisation". The difference with this approach is that these tasks are viewed as the therapy from the beginning. The different levels of meaning in the language can be explored *during* the "carryover" task. For example, if you have a sample of text produced during a telephone call where the subject was asking for a piece of information from an unfamiliar speaker with no authority, you might note that the request appeared abrupt and was incomplete. In such a case the therapy could involve work at a range of levels.

Genre level

The structural elements of a service encounter can be described and modelled: The TBI patient can identify the service request element, as well as the service compliance element, and determine whether the request for information was successful. Once they are able to identify these elements, they can then practise the service request element by producing a suggested script themselves and practising this with the clinician.

Exchange structure level

Communication can be described as giving and receiving information. Emphasis could be placed on the fact that the person is phoning to ask for information and therefore might expect to be given some information. Without giving enough information in their request they cannot expect to receive a suitable answer. The use of keywords to prompt all the main concepts in the request could be useful here. The notion of communication breakdown could be described with reference to the use of dynamic moves, especially asking for clarification and perhaps repeating information to confirm and help them to remember. The notion of backchannelling during the Service Compliance could also be addressed as an important interpersonal resource, to let the speaker know that they were listening.

Mood and modality

This is where the structure of the service request can be examined in more detail with the patient. The use of polite requesting forms could be suggested, particularly when the request was to someone completely unfamiliar, and especially if they were in authority. This could simply be the difference between asking "Could you tell me how much a large supreme pizza would cost?" (i.e. using grammatical metaphor) in contrast with "I wanna know the cost of a pizza".

Obviously all levels of analysis are important and each covers a different area of interpersonal meaning. By addressing all areas in a treatment regime, the complexity of language may start to be reflected. Some of the difficulty with treatments that arise from the use of rating scales and checklists is related to the problem of knowing where to go next. Treating topic maintenance or problems with speech act pairs may only be scratching at the surface of the problem. Using the SFL framework allows for practical functional tasks to be analysed in greater depth, as well as providing for a framework of choices that are available to speakers at any time. It is a flexible framework that takes into account the myriad of factors that we intuitively know impact on language production.

Finally, the interpersonal metafunction in particular appears to tap into the cognitive communication disorder (Kennedy & DeRuyter, 1991) that has been described previously, because it taps into what happens between the speaker and the hearer. Because it analyses both the speaker's and hearer's utterances, it encapsulates the entire interaction. It also allows us to focus on the possibility that some of the communication problems we describe in those who have a severe TBI may partly be the result of the environment they are in or the language choices that have been made available to them by their communication partners. This view is quite the opposite of the deficit-driven models of the past. The person with TBI will have some strengths, or in Halliday's terms, some intact language resources that can be inhibited by the language choices of their partner. Training communication partners to be aware of the impact that they may have on the person with TBI is an obvious implication from this line of reasoning. This has been discussed recently by Ylvisaker (1998) when he described the concept of the co-construction of narratives, where family members and teachers were trained to be aware of their own communicative style and behaviours in their attempts to communicate with the person with TBI. Family training and training community agencies has received increasing attention in recent years (DePompei, Zarski, & Hall, 1988; Ylvisaker, 1992; Ylvisaker, Feeney, & Urbanczyk, 1993; Ylvisaker, Urbanczyk & Feeney, 1992). This has been a promising development in the field of the rehabilitation of cognitive communication disorder. A possible next step is examining the finer details of communication in different contexts and working through these with the family or friends. By examining video or audio-taped feedback and making suggestions using the SFL framework, it may be possible to target the language that both the person with TBI and their communication partner are using that is both facilitative and non-facilitative. Ylvisaker's (1998) description of collaborative/non-collaborative style and elaborative/non-elaborative style fits well here. The underlying notion is that rather than the therapist "prescribing" ways to communicate with the person with TBI, the communication dyad works together with the therapist to analyse the discourse and make suggestions. The therapist has the tools to work with, but ideally these tools could be handed over to the person with the TBI and their communication partners. This is the essence of empowerment, and ultimately this is one of the primary goals of the treatment process.

ACKNOWLEDGEMENTS

The research described in this paper was funded through the Motor Accidents Research Scheme (MARS), which is an initiative of the Motor Accidents Authority of N.S.W. The authors would like to thank Alison Ferguson and the speech-language pathologists at the Bankstown-Lidcombe Hospital, the subjects, their families, the staff of the Lidcombe Head Injury Unit (now the Liverpool Brain Injury Unit), the Adult Development Programme, the N.S.W. Police Service, and the State Transit Sydney Buses Info Line.

REFERENCES

Armstrong, E. (1987). Cohesive harmony in aphasic discourse and its significance to listener perception of coherence. In R.H. Brookshire (Ed.), *Clinical aphasiology conference proceedings* (pp.210–215). Minneapolis, MN: BRK Publishers.

Austin, J.L. (1962). *How to do things with words*. Oxford: Clarendon Press.

Berry, M. (1981). Systemic linguistics and discourse analysis: A multi-layered approached to exchange structure. In C. Coulthard & M. Montgomery (Eds.), *Studies in discourse analysis* (pp.120–145). London: RKP.

Brown, P. & Levinson, S.C. (1987). *Politeness: Some universals in language usage*. Cambridge: Cambridge University Press.

Cameron, D., McAlinden, F., & O'Leary, K. (1987). Lakoff in context: The social and linguistic functions of tag questions. In J. Coates & D. Cameron (Eds.), *Women in their speech communities* (pp.74-93). London: Longman.

Coelho, C.A., Liles, B.Z., & Duffy, R.J. (1991a). Analysis of conversational discourse in head-injured clients. *Journal of Head Trauma Rehabilitation*, *6*, 92–99.

Coelho, C.A., Liles, B.Z., & Duffy, R.J. (1991b). Discourse analysis with closed head-injured adults: Evidence for differing patterns of deficits. *Archives of Physical Medicine Rehabilitation*, *72*, 465–468.

DePompei, R., Zarski, J.J., & Hall, D.E. (1988). Cognitive communication impairments: A family focused viewpoint. *Journal of Head Trauma Rehabilitation*, *3*, 13–22.

Eggins, S. (1994). *An introduction to systemic functional linguistics*. London: Pinter.

Ehrlich, J.S. (1988). Selective characteristics of narrative discourse in head-injured and normal adults. *Journal of Communication Disorders*, *21*, 1–9.

Ehrlich, J., & Barry, P. (1989). Rating communication behaviours in the head-injured adult. *Brain Injury*, *3*, 193–198.

Gallagher, T.M. (1991). A retrospective look at clinical pragmatics. In T.M. Gallagher (Ed.),

Pragmatics of language: Clinical practice issues (pp.1–9). San Diego, CA: Singular Publishing.

Green, G. (1984). Communication in aphasia therapy: Some of the procedures and issues involved. *British Journal of Disorders of Communication*, *19*, 35–46.

Grice, H.P. (1975). Logic and conversation. In P. Cole & J.L. Morgan (Eds.), *Syntax and semantics, Vol. 3: Speech acts* (pp.41–58). New York, NY: Academic Press.

Groher, M. (1977). Language and memory disorders following closed head trauma. *Journal of Speech and Hearing Research*, *20*, 212–223.

Halliday, M.A.K. (1985). *An introduction to functional grammar*. London: Edward Arnold.

Halliday, M.A.K. (1994). *An introduction to functional grammar* (2nd ed.). London: Edward Arnold.

Halliday, M.A.K., & Hasan, R. (1976). *Cohesion in English*. London: Longman.

Halpern, H., Darley, F.L., & Brown, J.R. (1973). Differential language and neurologic characteristics in cerebral involvement. *Journal of Speech and Hearing Disorders*, *38*, 162–173.

Hartley, L.L. (1990). Assessment of functional communication. In D.E. Tupper & K.D. Cicerone (Eds.), *The neuropsychology of everyday life: Assessment and basic competencies* (pp.135–168). Boston, MA: Kluwer Academic.

Hartley, L.L. (1992). Assessment of functional communication. *Seminars in Speech and Language 13*, 264–279.

Hasan, R. (1984). The nursery tale as a genre. *Nottingham Linguistic Circular*, *13,* (special issue on systemic linguistics), 71–102.

Hasan, R. (1985). *Language, context, and text: Aspects of language in a social-semiotic perspective*. Victoria, Australia: Deakin.

Keenan, E., & Schieffelin, B. (1976). Topic as a discourse notion. In C. Li (Ed.), *Subject and topic* (pp.337–384). New York: Academic Press.

Kennedy, M.R.T., & DeRuyter, F. (1991). Cognitive and language bases for communication disorders. In D.R. Beukelman & K.M. Yorkston (Eds.), *Communication disorders following traumatic brain injury: Management of cognitive, language and motor impairments* (pp.123–190). San Antonio, TX: Pro-Ed.

Lesser, R., & Milroy, L. (1993). *Linguistics and aphasia: Psycholinguistic and pragmatic aspects of intervention*. London: Longman.

Levin, H.S., Grossman, R.G., Rose, J.E., & Teasdale, G. (1979). Long-term neuropsychological outcome of closed head injury. *Journal of Neurosurgery*, *50*, 412–422.

Levinson, S.C. (1983). *Pragmatics*. London: Cambridge University Press.

Martin, J.R. (1985). *Factual writing: Exploring and challenging social reality*. Geelong, Victoria: Deakin University Press.

Martin, J.R. (1992). *English text. System and structure*. Amsterdam: Benjamins.

McDonald, S. (1993). Pragmatic skills after closed head injury: Ability to meet the informational needs of the listener. *Brain and Language*, *44*, 28–46.

McTear, M.F., & King, F. (1991). Miscommunication in clinical contexts: The speech therapy interview. In N. Coupland, H. Giles, & J.M. Wiemann (Eds.), *"Miscommunication" and problematic talk* (pp.195–214). Newbury Park, CA: Sage.

Mentis, M., & Prutting, C.A. (1991). Analysis of topic as illustrated in a head-injured and a normal adult. *Journal of Speech and Hearing Research*, 34, 583–595.

Milton, S.B. (1988). Management of subtle cognitive communication deficits. *Journal of Head Trauma Rehabilitation*, *3*, 1–11.

Milton, S.B., Prutting, C.A., & Binder, G.M. (1984). Appraisal of communicative competence in head injured adults. In R.H. Brookshire (Ed.), *Clinical aphasiology conference proceedings* (pp.114–123). Minneapolis, MN: BRK Publishers.

O'Barr, W.M., & Atkins, B.K. (1987). "Women's language" or "powerless language"? In B.M. Mayor & A.K. Pugh (Eds.), *Language, communication and education* (pp.205–217). London: Croom Helm.

Parsons, C.L., Snow, P., Couch, D., & Mooney, L. (1989). Conversational skills in closed head injury: Part 1. *Australian Journal of Human Communication Disorders*, *17*, 37–46.

Penn, C., & Cleary, J. (1988). Compensatory strategies in the language of closed head-injured patients. *Brain Injury, 2*, 3–17.

Poynton, C. (1985). *Language and gender: Making the difference*. Victoria, Australia: Deakin University Press.

Prutting, C.A., & Kirchner, D.M. (1983). Applied pragmatics. In T. Gallagher & C.A. Prutting (Eds.), *Pragmatic assessment and intervention issues in language*. San Diego, CA: College Hill Press.

Prutting, C.A., & Kirchner, D.M. (1987). A clinical appraisal of the pragmatic aspects of language. *Journal of Speech and Hearing Disorders*, *52*, 105–119.

Sacks, H., Schegloff, E.A., & Jefferson, G. (1974). A simplest systematics for the organization of turn-taking for conversation. *Language, 50*, 696–735.

Sarno, M.T. (1980). The nature of verbal impairment after closed head injury. *The Journal of Nervous and Mental Disease*, *168*, 685–692.

Sarno, M.T., & Levita, E. (1986). Characteristics of verbal impairment in closed head-injured patients. *Archives of Physical Medicine Rehabilitation*, *67*, 400–405.

Searle, J. (1969). *Speech acts*. Cambridge: Cambridge University Press.

Searle, J. (1975). Indirect speech acts. In P. Cole & J.L. Morgan (Eds.), *Syntax and semantics, Vol. 3: Speech acts* (pp.59–82). New York: Academic Press.

Silvast, M. (1991). Aphasia therapy dialogues. *Aphasiology*, *5*, 383–390.

Togher, L., & Hand, L. (1998). Use of politeness markers with different communication partners: An investigation of five subjects with traumatic brain injury. *Aphasiology*, *12(7/8)*, 755–770.

Togher, L., Hand, L., & Code, C. (1996a). Disability following head injury: A new perspective in the relationship between communication impairment and disempowerment. *Disability and Rehabilitation*, *18(11)*, 559–566.

Togher, L., Hand, L., & Code, C. (1996b). *Politeness and the traumatic brain injury population*. Paper presented at the International Systemic Functional Congress, Sydney, Australia.

Togher, L., Hand, L., & Code, C. (1997a). Analysing discourse in the traumatic brain injury population: Telephone interactions with different communication partners. *Brain Injury*, *11(3)*, 169–189.

Togher, L., Hand, L., & Code, C. (1997b). Measuring service encounters in the traumatic brain injury population. *Aphasiology*, *11(4/5)*, 491–504.

Ventola, E. (1987). *The structure of social interaction: A systemic approach to the semiotics of service encounters*. London: Pinter.

Ylvisaker, M. (1992). Communication outcome following traumatic brain injury. *Seminars in Speech and Language*, *13*, 239–250.

Ylvisaker, M. (1998). Socially co-constructed narratives: Competencies associated with an elaborative/collaborative interactive style. In M. Ylvisaker (Ed.), *Traumatic brain injury rehabilitation: Children and adolescents*. Newton, MA: Butterworth-Heinemann.

Ylvisaker, M., Feeney, T.J., & Urbanczyk, B. (1993). Developing a positive communication culture for rehabilitation: Communication training for staff and family members. In C.J. Durgin, N.D. Schmidt, & L.J. Fryer (Eds.), *Staff development and clinical intervention in brain injury rehabilitation*. Gaithersburg, MD: Aspen.

Ylvisaker, M., & Szekeres, S.F. (1994). Communication disorders associated with closed head injury. In R. Chapey (Ed.), *Language intervention strategies in adult aphasia* (3rd ed.) (pp.546–568). Baltimore, MD: Williams & Wilkins.

Ylvisaker, M., Urbanczyk, B., & Feeney, T.J. (1992). Social skills following traumatic brain injury. *Seminars in Speech and Language*, *13*, 308–311.

APPENDIX

Generic Structure Potential analysis

The elements that are scored in GSP analysis appear in Table 5.4. Hasan (1985) developed a formula whereby these elements may be recurring and optional. This allows for analysis of the dynamic nature of spontaneous interactions. Hasan's (1985) analysis has been adapted to account for a service encounter where information (rather than goods) is being exchanged so that:

[<GREETING> • (SERVICE INITIATION)$^{\Lambda}$] [(SERVICE ENQUIRY ←•)
{SERVICE REQUEST $^{\Lambda}$ SERVICE COMPLIANCE}]
$^{\Lambda}$ CLOSING $^{\Lambda}$ GOODBYE

( ) = Optionality
[ ] = Limitation for mobility
• = A mobile element
← = Recursiveness (Hasan, 1985; Martin, 1992)
{ } = Homogeneous recursion (Hasan, 1985)
$^{\Lambda}$ = Fixed sequence

For example, in the first bracket, the Greeting (GR) is obligatory, but may be preceded by a Service Initiation (SI) (e.g. "Can I help you?). The square brackets indicate that this sequence must precede the Service Enquiry. (GR) and (SI) cannot follow the elements to the right (SI). The carets ($^{\Lambda}$) indicate the sequence of structural elements. The dot and arrow next to Service Enquiry (SE) indicate: (a) that SE is optional; (b) SE can occur anywhere, as long as it does not precede GR or SI, or follow Closing (CL) or goodbye (GB). The braces {} indicate that the degree of repetition (or iteration/recursion as termed by Hasan, 1985) for elements within the braces is equal. For example if SR occurs twice, then SC must occur twice.

Thus, once the data have been marked for individual elements, the structure of that interaction can be described by placing the elements in the sequence in which they appear. The number and order of structural elements can then be evaluated according to the field and tenor configuration of that interaction.

CHAPTER SIX

The use of multiple informants in the assessment of communication after traumatic brain injury

Richard Body
Community Brain Injury Rehabilitation Team, Sheffield, UK

Mark Parker
Head Injury Rehabilitation Centre, Sheffield, UK

INTRODUCTION

The move away from aphasia testing in communication after traumatic brain injury (TBI) has been extensively documented (e.g. Hartley & Levin, 1990; Chapter 1, this volume). In part this move has been driven by recognition, originating in 1970s' studies of the performance of large TBI populations on aphasia batteries (e.g. Heilman, Safran, & Geschwind, 1971) that specific language disorders are relatively rare after TBI. At the same time there has been a parallel development of interest within TBI rehabilitation in handicap (in contrast to impairment), with a focus on the effects of changes in cognitive and psychosocial skills after TBI on social relationships (Godfrey, Knight, Marsh, Moroney, & Bishara, 1989), employment prospects (Gil, Cohen, Korn, & Groswasser, 1996; Macdonald & Johnson, 1996), and educational functioning (Knights, Ivan, Ventureyra, Bentivoglio, Stoddart, Winogron, et al., 1991).

The shift in focus away from specific linguistic deficits has also been accompanied by a recognition of the potential influence of other cognitive skills on language ability and particularly on the way that language is used. The interplay between attention, memory, reasoning, and executive skills and language has been described in broad theoretical terms (e.g. Hagan, 1981; Prigatano, Roueche, & Fordyce, 1985), with some recent moves towards a more specific delineation of patterns of skills (e.g. McDonald 1993; Hartley 1995; Chapters 3 and 4, this volume). There is, then, widespread support for the notion of language and other cognitive skills as an interwoven system that is vulnerable to the effects of TBI, together with a recognition that this system affects how the injured person will function in a range of personally relevant settings (Snow & Ponsford, 1995). What is less clear, however, is how the variables in such personally relevant settings interact with the cognitive-communicative system. In other words, if the language system is subject to the influence of other cognitive abilities, what are the factors in individuals' everyday interactions that influence the broader cognitive-communicative system? Moreover, how can the assessment of TBI individuals' communication skills take these factors into account?

Within the field of TBI rehabilitation in general there have been two primary responses to the breadth of potential issues to be dealt with. The first has been to recognise the need to cast the assessment net as widely as possible because a narrow focus on isolated skills within an artificial setting is seen as lacking applicability to the needs of brain-injured people in their everyday lives. According to Hartley (1995), input must be obtained from multiple sources and across a variety of situations and settings to generate an ecologically valid profile of an individual. The notion of ecological validity has permeated many fields of cognitive study including memory (Cohen, 1989), problem solving (Sinnott, 1989), and language (Body & Perkins, 1998; Hartley, 1990). As well as research based on this concept there has been a proliferation of assessment materials focusing on "everyday" performance; e.g. the Test of Everyday Attention (TEA) (Robertson, Ward, Ridgeway, & Nimmo-Smith, 1994) and the Rivermead Behavioural Memory Test (Wilson, Cockburn, & Baddeley, 1985).

A second response, recognising the size of this task, has been for assessment and management of brain-injured people in rehabilitation to become the joint responsibility of several professional disciplines. Thus, the concepts of multi-disciplinary or inter-disciplinary team involvement have become central to TBI rehabilitation (Powell, Partridge, Nicholls, Wright, Mould, Cook et al., 1994). Moreover, the inclusion of brain-injured people and their carers as part of the rehabilitation team is seen as fundamental if they are to contribute in an informed way to decision making and planning. However, although the principles of inter-disciplinary working and involvement of brain-injured people and carers are relatively well established, the tools and structures required to put these principles into operation have been less thoroughly debated. This is particularly the case in relation to specific areas of assessment (e.g. communication) where the principle of "joint responsibility" has been relatively slow to develop.

Body, Herbert, Campbell, Parker, and Usher (1996) describe a structure for the overall assessment of brain-injured peoples' preferred lifestyle and their ability to function within it. The structure facilitates comprehensive coverage of various aspects of functioning by providing a focus for the observations of multiple informants. Three principles underlying this structure are of particular relevance to the assessment of communication:

1. *Provide different perspectives on superficially similar areas.* This principle is intended to prevent simplistic conclusions about complex abilities. For example, the ability to interpret written instructions may appear to be (and certainly may be discussed as) a unitary phenomenon (in much the same way that a Yes/No response in severely disordered individuals is sometimes discussed in terms of presence or absence). In fact, written instructions come in a variety of forms and present a range of demands to each brain-injured individual.
2. *Cover areas that are not the core responsibility of a specific discipline.* Although the assessment of communication is often the core responsibility of speech and language professionals, it is important to recognise that communication in its widest sense is the responsibility of everybody involved with the brain-injured person, not least because all assessment and management is necessarily mediated via some form of communication. Therefore, professionals of all disciplines together with the brain-injured person and their carers share responsibility for contributing to discussion of a brain-injured person's communication skills, even if their primary focus is elsewhere.
3. *Ensure that account is taken of variation in function under different circumstances.* The ability to vary communication skills to meet contextual requirements is essential to successful interaction. Given the range of pressures on communication skills and the potential vulnerability of other influencing abilities, it is likely that a brain-injured person's success in manipulating such variations will itself vary under different circumstances. Therefore, the assessment process has to be carried out on the basis that a single observation of a particular skill is not sufficient to be able to draw firm conclusions about overall ability. This is an aspect of communication (in line with the discussion of superficially similar areas above) that often causes friction within families because a brain-injured person's ability to deal successfully with one conversational interaction but not with another (perceived by the family to be superficially similar) may be interpreted as obstructive when in fact the contextual circumstances may either support or undermine successful interaction.

The way that cognitive-communicative difficulties translate into brain-injured people's everyday lives can be illustrated by the two following examples.

Heather is a 45-year-old woman who, prior to her injury, held a senior administrative position and pursued an active sports life. Two years prior to referral for rehabilitation she suffered a severe head injury when she was hit by a falling object. A computerised tomography (CT) scan, x-ray, and neurological observations did not suggest any long-term problems and she was discharged from the acute hospital after 36 hours. Four months later she continued to complain of poor concentration and a slowing of thought processing. Heather's general practitioner referred her for a psychiatric opinion, where she was diagnosed as having post-concussion syndrome and prescribed anti-depressants. She received some support from the mental health services in her district but a gradual deterioration in the family's ability to cope led to a further neurological opinion. On this occasion, some two years post-injury, the neurologist suggested that a significant head injury had in fact occurred and recommended that anti-depressants should cease. Heather was then referred for rehabilitation.

The inter-disciplinary assessment conducted at that time identified key problem areas as being reduced speed of processing, perceptual difficulties, poor planning and organisation skills, reading difficulties, reduced balance, and altered tone on the right side. Psychometric testing demonstrated significant difficulties in dealing with external distractions and in alternating or dividing attention. These were accompanied by a severe reduction in the speed of information processing across all modalities. She had devised strategies such as subvocal rehearsal and counting on her fingers in an attempt to supplement her information-processing capacity. The assessment by the speech and language therapist included observations of a word-finding deficit and concluded that her reduced speed and capacity of information processing placed severe limitations on her auditory skills within conversation. Indeed, Heather's conversational skills were characterised by latencies in the region of 10–20 seconds before each response.

Prior to the injury Heather had been an exceptionally active person with a highly developed range of cognitive skills to balance the demands of work life, home life, a high profile in the running of a family business, and a role in organising sporting events. Chapter 4 (this volume) includes a discussion of the way in which certain constellations of cognitive impairments may be reflected in a deterioration in language abilities. Heather provides innumerable examples of how devastating this can be in practice. One such anecdotal report that led to rather dramatic consequences involved a trip on a friend's boat. On entering a stretch of water with strong currents, Heather's friend started to shout instructions. Although Heather was aware of the need to act quickly and was familiar with the operation, the speed at which linguistic information was being presented (coupled with the need for a rapid response to the commands) caused her to panic and led to her leaping overboard and being swept away. The situation was only resolved when air–sea rescue were called. Reflecting on this event later, Heather could describe the sequence of events, identify her reaction to the predicament as inappropriate, and construe what a more measured response might have been to the situation.

Heather was thus able to demonstrate the linguistic ability to understand the complexity of the information that was presented in that situation. She could, in hindsight, process the lexical items, the syntactic structures, and the pragmatic features involved. However, when all these factors occurred "on-line", there was a very dramatic breakdown in her ability to draw all the information together simultaneously.

The second case involves Trevor, a 40-year-old personnel manager who was injured as a pedestrian in a road traffic accident approximately nine months prior to assessment for rehabilitation. He was originally admitted to hospital with a Glasgow Coma Scale score of 5 (see Chapter 2 for discussion of GCS) and a CT scan revealed multiple cerebral contusions in the left hemisphere. After six weeks he was transferred to a residential rehabilitation unit where he remained for four months.

Interviews with various family members suggested that there had been a marked change in Trevor's personality and communication style. Following the injury he was described as gregarious with an overwhelming need to talk, whereas before he had been quiet and reserved in company. He was reported to be unable to plan and initiate simple household tasks or to integrate a simple chores list into an otherwise empty week. If left in the house on his own to complete a job (that he had identified as being necessary for him to complete), he would quickly leave the house to find someone to talk to. He had difficulty in attending to conversation that he had not initiated and often misconstrued what had been said to him. Sometimes this appeared to be an inability to actually understand the complexity of the information whereas at other times he appeared to interpret what was said to him in the light of what he had assumed the conversation was about. This often led to information being misrepresented to a third party if Trevor was reporting the conversation. Another characteristic that was reported by his family was that he would lose himself in a morass of tangential connections that would draw him away from the central topic so that he ended up losing the thread of what he was saying.

The reports by family and friends of Trevor's behaviour (including his interactive style) were supported by formal assessment, where the key areas of difficulty were identified as being memory problems, poor attention skills, planning and organisation problems, and a difficulty with initiation. Examples included difficulty dealing with external distractions and in alternating or dividing his attention between two competing stimuli (as evidenced by performance on the Test of Everyday Attention) and difficulty understanding instructions if too much information was given (as demonstrated on the Behavioural Assessment of the Dysexecutive Syndrome—Wilson, Alderman, Burgess, Emslie, & Evans, 1996).

With these illustrative examples in mind, the rest of this chapter follows the principle that the most comprehensive assessment of TBI communication will come from multiple sources of information, and discusses some of the issues associated with this approach. These include the characteristics of potential sources of information, some of the methods that have been devised for gathering information from people with TBI, carers, and other professionals, and factors that need to be considered in selecting appropriate methods of functional assessment.

INFORMATION FROM MULTIPLE INFORMANTS

In theory, the range of informants who might be able to shed light on an individual's communication is vast, though conceptualisation of this range is complicated by the number of overlapping parameters (e.g. familiarity, frequency of contact, social role). Any conceptualisation needs to centre on the person with TBI because their own perception of their communication is the starting point for describing and addressing any difficulties. At some distance in many respects is the speech and language therapist, working from a standpoint of professional, rather than personal, involvement but charged with the primary responsibility for overseeing the assessment and treatment process. Indeed, it is often the case that the speech and language therapist is the only professional with a direct focus on communication. It is, however, a basic tenet of the approach outlined in this chapter that other professionals involved in the assessment of a person with TBI can offer valuable insights into communication, even (and perhaps especially) where this is not their primary concern.

Somewhere between these may be family or friends living in the same accommodation, those who are in regular contact and others further away, together with work colleagues, fellow students, or whatever other contacts are relevant to the individual. In theory, a further grouping of people with whom a brain-injured person interacts may also include less frequent "community contacts" (e.g. shop workers, bus drivers, etc.), though the practical difficulties of collecting reliable information, coupled with the likely absence of personal interest in the welfare of the brain-injured person, renders them a generally poor source of information. Having said this, artificial restrictions to a brain-injured person's available contacts (e.g. acute hospital) can sometimes increase the potential usefulness of other groups such as ancillary workers.

A pertinent feature of this whole range of people is the potential discrepancy between the observational skills of the informant and the salience of the information (in terms of the assessment of communication skills) to which they have access. In other words, although the speech and language therapist should be the most highly trained observer of communication skills, he or she may not share the same lifestyle, views and expectations as the brain-injured person and will certainly not share the same circle of contacts or be present at many types of interaction. Conversely, a partner may be present at many types of interaction and will directly affect, and be affected by, the brain-injured person's communication style but it is unrealistic to expect all but a tiny minority to be able to make informed observations without being given a structure and/or training to base them on.

Another feature of the range of informants is the amount of time each can spend with the brain-injured person. There has been some discussion of this issue in the TBI literature that has implications for speech and language therapists. For example, Miller, Halper, and Cherney (1991) suggest that the effectiveness of the patient's pragmatic skills should be assessed through conversation in different situations, while Hartley (1995) states that observation in multiple settings with multiple partners is generally the best strategy. The notion is further supported by Snow and Ponsford (1995) who recommend that speech pathologists need to spend more time directly observing the injured person in real-world contexts. Although the basic principle underlying these statements is unchallengeable, the practicalities can sometimes present more of a problem. In many rehabilitation settings it is possible to take a brain-injured person on visits to local facilities that can provide valuable information. It can be significantly more difficult to observe people in settings that are familiar to them (work, pub, sports clubs) because of the time involved (particularly if account is taken of variation over time) and the potentially disruptive influence on communication of the presence of the speech and language therapist themselves. Thus, in practice, the most efficient use of therapists' time is likely to be achieved by matching the amount of time he or she spends in direct contact with the person with TBI (either in formal assessment or observation) with the amount of information gleaned from other sources. The logic of this is supported by the fact that family, friends, and other professionals already spend time with the brain-injured person, much of which will involve overt communicative interactions, with the result that potentially valuable information on communication skills is being gathered all the time.

Benefits of multiple informants

The use of multiple informants carries a number of benefits, the most obvious of which is that it ensures coverage of multiple interactional settings and raises the chances that the person with TBI will be observed fulfilling a number of different roles. In addition, multiple informants can provide a means of diluting "examiner bias" and can act to raise insight in the informant themselves.

Ensures multiple settings/contexts/roles

The collection of observations from multiple informants ensures that the brain-injured person's communication in a number of settings will contribute to the overall picture. Many authors have reflected on the artificiality of formal assessment in TBI in general, pointing to such factors as the imposition of external structure, the manipulation of environmental variables (e.g. noise level), and the effect of the examiner's interactive style reducing potential difficulties a brain-injured person might have with a task (Ylvisaker & Szekeres, 1986). Because multiple informants will, by definition, be in different places at different times discussing a variety of subjects, the problem of artificiality is likely to be reduced.

The use of multiple informants, with the resulting distribution of contexts, also goes some way to ensuring that the brain-injured person is observed fulfilling a variety of roles, and that the effect of these roles on communication is taken into account. McGann and Werven (1995) give as examples the facilitative role taken by a leader of a group therapy session, a passive role in a meeting of administrators, a symmetrical role at lunch with friends, and an authoritative role with one's own children. A brain-injured person's ability to adopt roles that are relevant to their circumstances and to adapt their communication to each role may play a significant part in the potential success of reintegration into their community. For example, many brain-injured parents find the resumption of suitably sensitive roles with their children a particularly difficult course to negotiate and their use of appropriate communication skills to fulfil shifting roles is crucial.

Dilutes examiner bias

A further benefit of using multiple informants in the assessment of communication is that it reduces the potential for "examiner bias". This is a topical issue in many fields of speech pathology as researchers grapple with the problems of defining normal behaviour in wide ranging skills. Leinonen and Smith (1993), for example, writing in relation to language disorders in children, assert that there are no "either-or" rules for much (or perhaps all) of pragmatic functioning, as a result of which the appropriacy of pragmatic behaviours is a matter likely to differ according to observers. Likewise, Armstrong (1987) is of the opinion that in measurement of coherence in aphasic discourse the ultimate test of a speaker's coherence is in listeners' reactions to that speaker.

A number of authors have discussed the importance of this issue in relation to TBI. Snow, Douglas, and Ponsford (1995), for example, report that discourse profiles do not take account of demographic characteristics, as a result of which speech pathologists are forced to make quite arbitrary distinctions between "normal" and "abnormal". They go on to highlight the potential influence of speech and language therapists' own subculture characteristics and summarise the situation in more forthright terms: "It may simply be the case that at least some of what middle-class speech pathologists see as impaired discourse reflects normal sociolinguistic variations within the population as a whole" (p. 374).

This point is further elaborated by McGann and Werven (1995), who express concern about the casual use of the terms "appropriate" and "inappropriate" to describe behaviour, which they say seems to be supported by no more than our personal standards. In addition, they describe the use of the concept of "central tendency" to define normal, whereby those behaviours that are far removed from a common standard will be perceived, or at least assessed, as disordered in some way. However, McGann and Werven point out that one of the difficulties inherent in this perspective lies in deciding how different a behaviour has to be before it is considered significant. A result of this dilemma is what Leinonen and Smith (1993) describe as the inevitable circularity involved in training professionals to regard certain features of behaviour as inappropriate and then defining such features as symptomatic of a disorder.

The need to be aware of the potential for examiner bias is underlined by the results of a recent study (Santos, Castro-Caldas, & De Sousa, 1998) that found that mothers of people with TBI tended to agree with their sons' perceptions of abilities and behaviours, whereas partners were more likely to report a higher incidence of problems than the brain-injured person. Having said this, Body and Perkins (1998), in a study based on ratings of narratives after TBI, found that speech and language therapists did share broad perceptions about the quality of TBI narratives with untrained raters, though the clinicians were more confident about identifying individual good performances.

It seems reasonable to assume that the involvement of multiple informants will at least increase the validity of conclusions reached during an assessment. A number of factors can be addressed in this way. For example, it is sometimes the case during assessment that people with TBI adopt markedly different styles of interaction with male and female members of staff, beyond the variation which might be expected in normal circumstances. Sometimes this can be as obvious as sexually inappropriate remarks addressed to one sex but not the other. In other cases, there may be only a vague feeling of discomfort expressed by staff of one sex. The point here is that the subjective nature of the staff responses suggests the need for multiple informants to either contradict or validate such observations.

The subjective nature of observations about communicative behaviour can often be seen in labels that brain-injured people acquire as they progress through different stages of care. For example, it is not uncommon for terms like "inappropriate", "disinhibited", "uncommunicative", and "verbose" (often based on the opinion of one member of staff) to accompany brain-injured people in their written notes from the acute stage. This seems to be particularly the case where patients are managed, for one reason or another (e.g. influence of other medical conditions), in non-specialist wards, where the label may arise out of the environment as much as from the individual themselves. Once written down, these become difficult to shift and it is only by means of multiple informants that the label can be either corroborated or contradicted.

Raises awareness, knowledge, and involvement

Perhaps the most important benefit of using multiple informants is the potential for raising the levels of awareness and understanding of the informants themselves, whether they have suffered the head injury, are carers, or are non-speech and language professionals. In addition, it is likely that such increases in understanding will themselves encourage and facilitate greater involvement on the part of the informant in the therapy process. Regardless of the views of speech and language therapists on the possible reliability or accuracy of information gained from sources other than themselves, there is general agreement that (a) the greater the level of awareness of all involved, the better and that (b) absence (or low levels) of awareness on the part of the person with TBI may block or hinder further intervention. For example, Snow and Ponsford (1995) feel that impaired self-evaluation may need to be the first priority in intervention. The principle that greater insight is a foundation for rehabilitation can also be applied to carers and to all the professionals involved with a brain-injured person. This is because the notion of teamwork encompassing these people often founders on discrepancies in knowledge levels between professionals from different disciplines and between professionals and families.

Person with TBI as informant

The literature on TBI, both in general and with reference to communication, shows evidence of a degree of uncertainty on the part of practitioners regarding the status of client self-report. Snow, Douglas, and Ponsford (1995), discussing the perceptions of patients and families, suggest that one or both parties may have limited insight into changes wrought by the injury. To some extent at least, the general lack of pre-injury familiarity with anything but the primary effects of TBI (and indeed the prevalence of misleading portrayals in the media) suggests that most lay informants start from a position of some disadvantage. Moreover, a number of authors (e.g. McKinlay & Brooks, 1984; Prigatano, Altman, & O'Brien, 1991) have suggested that the views of people with TBI and their carers (and sometimes rehabilitation staff) show discrepancies and possibly overestimation of abilities on the part of the brain-injured person.

However, the need for TBI individuals to have insight into (and be actively engaged in) their own programme means that the TBI individual has a potentially valuable role to play as informant despite difficulties involved in introspection and the psychological mechanisms associated with TBI. In addition, recent work suggests that the ability of TBI individuals to supply information on certain aspects of their lives may partly depend on asking them appropriate questions. For example, Elsass and Kinsella (1987), in a study of social interaction, reported that people with TBI were aware of the degree of behavioural change. At the very least it should be recognised that where a brain-injured person's insight is very different to that of those around them, this is the material with which the speech and language therapist and the brain-injured person have to work.

A primary reason for checking the brain-injured person's introspections regarding communication is that some of the information on influencing factors is not available by any other means. For example, McGann and Werven (1995) describe the concept of a speaker feeling "on-stage" (i.e. under pressure to perform in a particular way). This is discussed in relation to a person with apraxia who reported an improvement in her speech when she felt under pressure, in this case during her interactions with the therapist. McGann and Werven point out that unless a person is asked directly, it is difficult for an observer to determine when he or she is going to feel that pressure.

The potential usefulness of exploring the brain-injured person's thoughts on communication in detail is illustrated by Alan, a patient undergoing rehabilitation following an industrial injury. For a number of reasons Alan had not initially been referred on his discharge from an outlying acute hospital and had consequently spent several months experiencing post-TBI difficulties with no professional support, although his family provided what support they could. Prior to the injury Alan had worked in a supervisory capacity in heavy industry and by the time of his referral he had in fact already attempted to return to the job. He had lasted only a few weeks and at the time of assessment was in the process of taking retirement on medical grounds.

As with many people with TBI, Alan had no visible sign of injury and in fact looked fit and healthy. He was articulate, though somewhat hesitant, in his verbal output and appeared to be able to follow conversation without difficulty. However, he was described by his family as uncooperative and uninterested in conversation because he would frequently remove himself from interactions, particularly where the whole family was present. This type of behaviour also underpinned a degree of unspoken hostility in his community where he was seen as being capable of work but unwilling to undertake it.

Given time and encouragement, Alan was able to describe his experience using very graphic images. For example, he described the effort of trying to express himself as being "like wearing carpet slippers to walk up a slippery slope". In a discussion about following conversation he reported that it was like listening to a record being played at too slow a speed. A final image, which he used to describe the general difficulties he was experiencing, underlines the amount of effort he was having to apply to communication. This image was of his brain sitting comfortably in an armchair with a newspaper and a cup of tea, declining to get up and do anything that Alan suggested. Thus, although his overt communication skills were relatively good, the effort he was having to use, discernible only by asking him, was having a deleterious effect on many of his interactions.

Carers/friends as informants

The routine, structured use of sources of information close to the TBI individual remains limited. Snow et al. (1995) point out that the perceptions of patients and families are an untapped resource in the evaluation of discourse skills. On the other hand, the recognition that this is, theoretically at least, a rich resource is relatively well established. As outlined earlier, carers are often available (especially as observers of communication), willing to contribute (free of charge), and likely to be involved in some way in future care.

Moreover, there is increasing recognition that information is actually needed from sources close to the brain-injured person in order to shed light on the communication background. Snow et al. (1995) go on to recommend that speech and language therapists should acquire a greater understanding of the role of premorbid sociolinguistic and demographic characteristics in determining the clinical presentation of these patients. The relevance can be seen most clearly in relation to the notion of handicap (or the more recent term, "participation restriction"), since the World Health Organisation definition makes reference to age, sex, and social and cultural factors in determining appropriate roles (WHO, 1980, 1997).

An example illustrating some aspects of the carers' potential role in providing information on communication and incorporating their observations into a management programme is given in the case history of a brain-injured man described by Perkins, Body, and Parker (1995). Colin, who sustained a TBI in a fall from a roof about a year prior to the description, was found to have significant problems with selection of conversational topics that were appropriate to the context, one of his strategies being to revert to a relatively small set of subjects that many of his conversational partners had heard before. This was felt to be in large measure a consequence of problems with impaired ability to process information on-line and to hold an overall structure in memory. Colin's family were involved in the original description of his conversational behaviour and in the ongoing recording of the incidence of specific topics. They were particularly distressed by Colin's tendency to express very strong feelings of vengeance in the face of crime reports on the television, which also occurred whenever there were visitors to the house that Colin did not know. Both of these contextually dependent communicative behaviours were reported to be very different from his pre-injury personality and both would have been invisible to direct assessment of Colin's discourse skills within the rehabilitation facility. Discussion of these issues facilitated a means of recording the behaviours.

Following attempts to remediate the problems via direct discussion and recording with Colin and via a programme of external prompts within the rehabilitation unit, both of which met with little success, the family was asked to participate in a programme of behaviour management that included verbal reinforcement/contradiction, diverting Colin to another activity and terminating inappropriate interactions abruptly, all of which were successful to some degree. The authors of the programme describe (at p.318) the role of the jointly derived information on Colin's communication:

> From the clinical point of view, a particularly useful aspect of having a theoretical framework was in being able to deal productively with the variety of issues raised by Colin's family, along the lines of "Why does he keep saying that?" or "He's like a dog with a bone that won't let go". Furthermore, the fact that they could be given a framework by which to understand Colin's conversational style legitimised for them the adoption of a seemingly peculiar pattern of interaction, in which they were required to interrupt verbally, to reflect overtly on the content of Colin's conversation, to supply Colin with appropriate phrases, and to terminate conversations that were getting out of hand.

Other professionals as informants

The idea that TBI rehabilitation requires at least some level of teamwork has reached a degree of general acceptance across all disciplines involved in the process. However, Finset, Krogstad, Hansen, Berstad, Haarberg, Kristansen, et al. (1995) point out that in spite of the frequent declarations of how important teamwork is, little is published in terms of actual research on teamwork, in particular on the significance of team interaction for rehabilitation outcome. They go on to outline a programme designed to facilitate the practical application of better team cooperation patterns in the further development of one specific treatment programme. One of the central targets for improving team cooperation is described as joint responsibilities for conducting treatment. In other words, the authors are proposing that the whole process of team working should be enhanced by the effect of joint responsibility for specific tasks.

There is no reason why this principle cannot be applied as much to the process of assessment as to treatment. Indeed, on the assumption that accurate and comprehensive assessment is the foundation of good rehabilitation, there are grounds for concluding that joint responsibilities in assessment might have an even greater cohesive effect on a rehabilitation team. Body et al. (1996) state that the aim of inter-disciplinary assessment should be to provide a framework within which individual team members, regardless of discipline, can contribute to the overall picture of the client's needs, as well as contributing their specialist knowledge. Thus, although the speech and language therapist is likely to hold the primary responsibility for collating information about communication, there are a number of reasons why professionals of other disciplines are well placed to observe a brain-injured person's communication skills and feed those observations into wider team discussions.

Most rehabilitation professionals have been through training processes that place a strong emphasis on observation skills. This is not to say that individuals will not require training or structure to successfully observe areas of communication that are not their core responsibility, but they are at the very least familiar with the concepts of observing and reporting behaviour.

Although a brain-injured person's family members may well take part in meetings with rehabilitation team members, professionals are likely to have significantly more routine access to forums for exchanging information and seeking clarification of issues. In particular, most teams have some form of case conference following assessment, which can be structured to focus on areas of communication and draw out responses to specific questions. Moreover, professionals' familiarity with such processes and, to a large extent, with the terminology of communication assessment, should enhance their ability to contribute.

It is perhaps stating the obvious to say that all assessments entail communication. However, the point is worth making if only to underline the richness of this source of assessment material. In addition, the fact that the specific focus of an assessment is on something other than communication can take the pressure off a patient's sense of the need to "perform". To give an example, many assessment processes include an analysis of physical status and physical activity preferences, at least some of which is conducted within a gymnasium. During the time that the brain-injured person is being asked to carry out particular physical tasks there is an opportunity for observation of, among other things, many of the items listed by Hartley (1995) as important listening behaviours, including the ability to ignore distractions (especially of other people in the same room), to wait until instructions have been given before starting a task, and to ask for clarification when unsure of a message. In addition, the person with TBI may feel less constrained in their initiation of conversation and the selection of conversational topic than they would in a more formal one-to-one interview.

Over and above the observation of communication skills during assessment of non-verbal skills, many formal tests of other cognitive functions can shed light on communication skills in the course of manipulating composite skills that include communication. While tests of cognitive function which seek to isolate specific subskills (e.g. 3D construction) may by design not provide such opportunities, the use of more functional tests in TBI provides opportunities to observe a variety of skills. In addition, because the spotlight of attention is focused away from the communication skills themselves, a somewhat more naturalistic performance may be observable.

A good example of this comes from the Modified Six Elements subtest of the Behavioural Assessment of the Dysexecutive Syndrome (BADS) (Wilson et al., 1996). In this subtest subjects are required to undertake at least part of six subtasks (which consist of two dictation exercises, two written calculation exercises, and two written picture naming exercises) within 10 minutes. Subjects are informed that it is not possible to complete all six tasks and that this is not the point of the assessment. In addition, they have to organise their approach to the task in a way that avoids moving from one exercise directly to the paired exercise from the same category. In order to ensure that they have understood the task instructions, subjects must describe them to the examiner before starting.

Thus, the focus of this test is placed directly on the need for the subject to organise the distribution of effort across all the tasks. It is theoretically possible for subjects to complete the test in under a minute by allotting only enough time to touch on each task. In practice, this does not seem to happen. In fact, subjects appear to feel under pressure to complete as many items as possible from each task. What emerges from this is a picture of written naming and verbal description under the pressure of both time and organisational demands.

An example involves a businessman who had sustained a TBI two years before assessment for rehabilitation. Prior to the injury he had been actively involved in running a number of businesses and had an eye for new business opportunities. Since the injury he had managed to stay involved in one business but was putting in a minimum of effort and felt unmotivated. One of his own reported symptoms post-injury was word-finding difficulty. However, because he came across as extremely articulate and had a rapid delivery of speech it was difficult to delineate exactly what the problem was. He achieved normal scores on tests of confrontation naming and even under the more time-pressured circumstances of the Controlled Oral Word Association Test (Benton & Hamsher, 1989). When the assessment case discussion took place it transpired that he had found the Modified Six Elements subtest of the BADS very difficult, and despite spending a significant proportion of the available 10 minutes on the naming tasks had only managed to name a few items and had shown visible frustration during the task. This led to a later discussion with him about the influence of planning tasks (a major potential aspect of his employment) on his feelings of word-finding difficulty, and helped to isolate this as a key area of intervention.

Some of the elements to be found in the Modified Six Elements task are also found in conventional language tests. For example, tests that require subjects to name as many specific items as possible within a set amount of time—such as the Controlled Oral Word Association Test (Benton & Hamsher, 1989)—are a routine part of cognitive assessment. What is neater about the Modified Six Elements test is that it includes an element of self-direction that is not only central to many daily activities but is also potentially vulnerable to TBI. Moreover, other commonly used tests of, for example, naming, are carried out under different conditions. For example, word association tasks have time pressure but have a direct focus on the naming skill, whereas confrontation naming tasks usually do not set time limits, though they may recommend noting the time taken. What is perhaps most important about such tests as the Modified Six Elements is that they may well be carried out anyway to inform observations of broad organisational skills. In other words, the information on communication is often available without significant extra effort other than that of cross-referencing the findings.

METHODS OF GATHERING INFORMATION

The discussion in the previous section illustrates the range of sources of information on communication skills over and above that gained by formal assessment or direct observation of a brain-injured person. Given the amount of potential information and the diversity of potential sources, it stands to reason that speech and language therapists responsible for gathering and collating such information may need to employ assessment tools in the form of checklists and questionnaires to add structure to the process. This is not to say that a (relatively unstructured) clinical interview, in which a speech and language therapist may follow any number of informational leads based on their professional knowledge and experience, is not a vital part of assessment. Indeed, checklists and questionnaires themselves need to be implemented on the basis of, and supplemented by, clinical judgement. On the other hand, as well as aiding the therapist, such tools can serve as training materials for students and less experienced professionals, can potentially offer people with TBI and carers/friends a means to make sense of complex and often bewildering behaviours, and may also contribute to both treatment programmes and outcome measures.

The fields of both TBI and speech pathology (and indeed cognitive rehabilitation in general) have seen an increase in the design and dissemination of assessment tools aimed at investigating behaviour arising in "real-life" settings. Some of these are designed specifically to aid observation by rehabilitation professionals while others are intended to gather information from wider sources. Snow and Ponsford (1995) list a number of different areas in which questionnaires and checklists have been used to elicit the perceptions of brain-injured people and their close others, including attentional behaviour, cognitive functioning, and psychosocial adaptation.

Within speech pathology an interest in methods of both naturalistic observation and ways of incorporating the views of an individual's community into assessment can be seen in works from the 1960s onwards, with a recent upsurge in study and debate and a corresponding increase in materials to facilitate these processes. The assessment materials themselves come under a variety of headings, but can often be identified by such terms as "functional" (e.g. Functional Communication Profile—Sarno, 1969), "pragmatic" (e.g. Pragmatics Profile of Early Communication Skills—Dewart & Summers, 1988; Pragmatic Protocol—Prutting & Kirchner, 1987), and "appropriate" (Profile of Communicative Appropriateness—Penn, 1985). Many of these tools have in fact been specifically designed for use by speech and language therapists to assess interactive skills, with the result that their potential for use by other professionals and carers is limited, particularly by the inclusion of complex terminology (e.g. "speech act pair analysis", "turn-taking contingency").

The number of assessments of communication that have been either specifically designed for use in brain injury or standardised on a TBI population is still relatively small. However, before considering these in detail it is important to recognise the contribution of both ideas and materials to be made by related fields of study, because the drive towards development of assessments that are able to tap the perceptions of a range of professionals and/or patients/carers is by no means limited to either TBI or communication.

The following brief review will outline some assessment tools, the original design of which was based on (a) communication but not TBI and (b) TBI but not communication, in addition to materials produced specifically for assessment of communication in TBI. Consideration will then be given to some of the factors that need to be taken into account when selecting these materials for use.

Assessment tools from areas other than TBI

Recent work undertaken in a variety of areas of speech pathology highlights attempts to tap the perceptions of non-speech and language therapists. In the main these are targeted primarily at carers, which may to some extent reflect the difficulties inherent in using language-based materials to ascertain perceptions from language-disordered people. Not surprisingly, most of these materials contain some items that are specific to the client group in question and therefore of more limited use in TBI. However, many individual questions relate to a wide spectrum of communication disorders. Perhaps the most useful aspect of looking wider than just TBI is that these materials offer a variety of question formats, thereby increasing the chances that at least one form of words will elicit an informative response. The examples that follow are taken from the fields of aphasia and dementia.

A major recent contribution to this aspect of aphasia study comes from researchers at the University of Sydney (Oxenham, Sheard, & Adams, 1995; Manochiopinig, Sheard, Reed, & Choo, 1996) who developed a questionnaire based on communication characteristics commonly described in relation to aphasia and expressed in lay terms. This employed a seven-point interval scale with end descriptors of "minimal or no disruption to communication" (1) and "maximal disruption to communication" (7). Although a number of items (e.g. "Understands a variety of different words") are clearly more relevant to the communication experience of aphasic people than they are to those with TBI, the 18 items under the heading of "Conversation/Pragmatic conversational skill" could easily be used in TBI. These include such items as "Keeps a conversation going, encouraging the speaker to keep talking" and "Interrupts appropriately". Manochiopinig, Sheard, and Reed (1992) also include an overview of the use of questionnaires in a review of pragmatic assessments used in adult aphasia.[1]

The field of dementia has seen several attempts at eliciting the perceptions of carers (e.g. Ulatowska, Allard, Donnell, Bristow, Haynes, Flower, et al., 1988; Bayles & Tomoeda, 1991), although Powell, Hale, and Bayer (1995), having concluded that there is currently no fully comprehensive checklist of symptoms associated with communication breakdown in dementia, set about designing their own. This resulted in a set of 32 statements as part of a study of 79 subjects with dementia in which carers were asked to identify the absence/presence of each communication symptom and frequency of occurrence, the latter being rated as "Yes always", "Yes usually", "Yes fairly often", "Yes but rarely", and "No never". In fact, virtually all of the items (with the possible exception of "Talks to imaginary people or things") could be used in TBI. For example, it is likely that most clinicians working at the subacute/community end of rehabilitation would recognise the relevance of such items as "During the conversation, changes the subject inappropriately", "Difficulty following a conversation when a group of people are talking", and "Talks out loud in an inappropriate place".

General assessment tools that include communication

Predictably, given the widely documented interaction between communication and other skills, items relating to communication are often to be found within questionnaires that cover wider aspects, particularly those focusing on social behaviour and executive function. Since the principal focus of these questionnaires is on other aspects of behaviour, in most cases there will be only one or two items that are particularly relevant to communication. In addition, this raises the whole question of where the boundaries lie between communication, social skills, and behaviour, because some behaviours, such as repetition of conversational topic, are reflected in communication and social skills. However, on the assumption that brain-injured people's skills do not fall into neat categories, it is suggested that the relatively straightforward process of cross-referencing results may either add new findings to an assessment of communication or shed further light on abilities and deficits that have already been identified. Examples of tools that fall into this category include the Iowa Collateral Head Injury Interview (Varney, 1991; Varney & Menefee, 1993) and the Dex Questionnaire (from the Behavioural Assessment of the Dysexecutive Syndrome, described earlier).

The Iowa Collateral Head Injury Interview (Varney & Menefee, 1993) is a structured interview that assesses psychosocial symptoms commonly reported after TBI. The aim of the interview is to detect *change* in areas of behaviour such as "indecisiveness", "risk-seeking", and "self-centredness" (thereby avoiding the difficulty of comparison with behaviour in the non-brain damaged population) and the suggested wording for the interviewer reflects this (e.g. "Does your husband seem to initiate fewer behaviours on his own?"). Within the interview a question on Impolitic Speech ("Does your husband stick his foot in his mouth more often than he used to?") reflects directly on communication skills, while several items would be of significant interest to a speech and language therapist. Among these are Neutral/Flat Affect ("Is he inanimate, sort of like a piece of furniture is inanimate?") and Poor Empathy ("Does he have a harder time taking your perspective on things?"). The use of very plain language to render the questions accessible to non-professionals is of particular note.

The Dex Questionnaire from the BADS can be completed by the brain-injured person or a carer. It consists of 20 statements that are to be rated on a 0–4 scale representing "Never", "Occasionally", "Sometimes", "Fairly Often", and "Very Often". Again, many of the behaviours are not specific to communication but relevant items include "I have problems understanding what other people mean unless they keep things simple and straightforward", "I do or say embarrassing things when in the company of others", and "I find it hard to stop repeating, saying or doing things once they've started".

Questionnaires/checklists designed for communication in brain injury

As noted earlier, the number of measures that specifically target communication in TBI is still relatively small and as yet there is certainly no single measure that has reached a significant level of general acceptance within the TBI rehabilitation community. This is not to say that efforts are not being made in that direction, and the types of measure being produced are illustrated by the La Trobe Communication Questionnaire (Douglas, O'Flaherty, & Snow, in press), the Profile of Functional Impairment in Communication (Linscott, Knight, & Godfrey, 1996), and the Family Questionnaire: Communication Skills from the Measure of Cognitive-Linguistic Abilities (Ellmo, Graser, Krchnavek, Calabrese, & Hauck, 1995).

La Trobe Communication Questionnaire

The La Trobe Communication Questionnaire (LCQ) has been developed from Damico's (1985) Clinical Discourse Analysis and consists of 30 items rated on a 4-point scale ("Never or rarely", "Sometimes", "Often", and "Usually or always"). The LCQ has two forms—Form S for use with the primary subject and Form O for use with a nominated close other. There is also a variation of Form O that can be used with rehabilitation staff. In addition, a second response format focuses on the degree of change that has occurred in communication, with respondents being asked to specify whether behaviours have increased, decreased, or remained the same. Examples of the questions include "When talking to others do you leave out important information?" and "When talking to others, do you say or do things which others might see as rude?".

Profile of Functional Impairment in Communication

The origins of the Profile of Functional Impairment in Communication (PFIC) in pragmatic theory are described in Chapter 4. The profile consists of 10 communication rules (and derived feature summary scales) and a set of specific behaviour items (84 in total) associated with each subscale. For example, Rule 2 relates to "General Participation", perceptions about which are elicited by the question "... how would you rate the subject's ability to participate in social interaction in a manner which is organised and sensitive to the other's interests?". The response to this is rated on a six-point scale, ranging from "normal" to "very severely impaired". For this particular feature summary scale the specific behaviour items include "Boring: inability to engage another's interest" and "Effortful: conversing with the patient is tiring and demanding", these being rated on a four-point scale ranging from "not at all" to "always". According to the authors, the measure was intended to be practical for clinicians to use and, with slight modifications, for family members or other collateral informants.

Family Questionnaire: Communication Skills

The Family Questionnaire (FQ) is part of the Measure of Cognitive-Linguistic Abilities (MCLA) (Ellmo et al., 1995) designed to evaluate abilities in people who have mild to moderate impairments caused by TBI. The full assessment includes subtests of story recall, verbal abstract reasoning, narrative discourse analysis, a pragmatic rating scale and an interview schedule, plus the FQ. This consists of 13 items under the heading of "Speaking and Expressive Abilities" and 4 "Non-verbal Communication Skills" items. Each is rated on a five-point scale with descriptions at each end of the scale and a descriptive label for each overall item. Examples include "Expresses ideas randomly with no main theme or organisation of ideas" contrasted with "Expresses ideas completely in a well-organised way" and "Appears unaware of errors, makes no attempt to correct or repeat" compared with "Recognises errors, can revise message to be understood".

Factors in selecting assessment tools for use by non-speech and language therapists

The discussion and brief review above have touched on a number of factors that need to be taken into account if the perceptions of people with TBI, carers, and other professionals are to be incorporated in the assessment process. These factors, many of which are interdependent, are summarised in the following subsections.

Applicability to TBI

The need to consider applicability of individual items stems mainly from the suggested selection of materials from a variety of sources. Thus, sources from other areas of speech pathology and from general assessments of TBI may provide anything from single questions to coverage of whole areas of functioning. The question of applicability will also need to take into consideration the stage post-injury of the brain-injured person, the severity of the symptoms, and any concomitant restrictions on the person's communicative environment.

Type of respondent

For obvious reasons, it is generally accepted that severely brain-injured people make very poor respondents. Thus Giles and Clark-Wilson (1993) state that assessment by questionnaire is best directed towards the patient's family or friends and towards the brain-injured adult with mild to moderate impairments. Despite the fact that some questionnaires are designed specifically to be used by brain-injured people and carers, while others are more clearly targeted at non-brain-injured people, respondents are more likely to influence the selection of assessment tools by virtue of their individual characteristics than by membership of a particular group. Some brain-injured people may well be able to respond informatively to items involving abstract concepts and relatively esoteric terminology, while many carers, and indeed other professionals, may benefit from having questions phrased in straightforward language.

Method of administration

Consideration needs to be given to the intended method by which a profile or questionnaire is to be administered. Some tools may be specifically designed as semi-structured interviews in which a trained clinician uses initial direct questions to elicit responses that can act as leads to more detailed information; other materials (e.g. Conversational Skills Rating Scale—Spitzberg & Hurt, 1987) might lend themselves to joint observation by a speech and language therapist and a carer of a specific set of interactions; still others may be used with no direct supervision—i.e. where a questionnaire is sent out by post to otherwise inaccessible informants. Speech and language therapists may find themselves in situations where carers are accessible on one occasion but observation needs to be made over a period of time.

Format of items

Different question and response formats will naturally elicit different types of information, with a consequent effect on how that information can be used. Generally speaking, the more open the potential response, the more restricted the number of informants who can make use of the question format. In other words, questions such as "How does your partner converse?" are relatively unlikely to feature on questionnaires, while "Does your partner lose track of what they are saying?" will appear more often.

There is also a range of specificity to be considered in relation to direct questioning, with "Yes/No" responses likely to need supplementing with a more detailed description of the frequency with which a behaviour occurs (e.g. the "never"–"always" continuum, or percentage of time ratings) or the degree to which it has changed. Even with the more specific ratings, informants may find it challenging to reflect on behaviours that are difficult to isolate into discrete entities and that occur under changing circumstances over long periods of time. It can sometimes be helpful for informants to be "keyed in" by focusing on a particular time period—for example, "Has X misunderstood anything that someone has said to them this week?" or "Have you noticed any effect on X's conversation this week of (a) background distractions, (b) the number of people in the conversation, (c) X's level of tiredness, etc?".

Pre- or post-injury communication

There is some discussion in the TBI and speech pathology literature of the need to find out about the brain-injured person's communicative style prior to injury so that management can be targeted most appropriately. For example, the questionnaire designed by Swindell, Pashek, and Holland (1982) allows detailed investigation of the ways in which the injured person used verbal skills to negotiate a range of common communication tasks prior to injury (Snow & Ponsford, 1995). While it is clearly of importance that brain-injured people are not encouraged to aim for communication styles that would never have been comfortable for them or appropriate for their community, a number of cautions should be borne in mind in relation to this approach. The most obvious is that people find it extremely difficult to remember how they or their partner/friend communicated perhaps several years previously. Secondly, the notion of communicative style is itself very nebulous and consequently difficult to pin down. Thirdly, there may be a subconscious pressure to distort pre-injury capabilities. External factors may also influence this, as evidenced by the finding of a study that plaintiffs after TBI tended to rate their pre-injury functioning higher than did non-plaintiffs (Lees-Haley, Williams, Zasler, Marguilies, English, & Stevens, 1997). Finally, there is a danger that an emphasis on pre-injury abilities distracts from the need to try and adjust to the current situation and develop communication skills relevant to a new life.

Terminology

In her discussion of rating scales and checklists, Hartley (1995) describes a number of tools designed primarily for use by speech and language therapists and then states that simplified versions can be used with clients for self-rating and self-monitoring of social interactions. Clinical experience suggests that the process of simplification is itself anything but simple and that the presence of even small amounts of jargon in an otherwise straightforward assessment can restrict the ability of people who do not share that basic terminology to respond. This is not necessarily to criticise the use of formal terms by professionals who share a frame of reference, since this may enhance exact sharing of information. However, it is unusual to find carers familiar with the terminology of communication pathology.

As an example, on the basis of research using occupational therapy students the Profile of Functional Impairment in Communication (Linscott et al., 1996) was noted to have relatively high levels of inter-rater reliability and was judged by the authors to be a good measure of communication problems and quite practical. It therefore seems reasonable to conclude from this that the profile warrants consideration for use with professionals of varying disciplines in clinical settings. However, the language employed in the scales might require rather more than the recommended slight modification for use by families. For example, the question for the Subject Matter feature summary scale is worded in terms of "the subject's ability to adhere to socially, culturally, or morally appropriate subject matter in their conversations" (p.399), phraseology which does not immediately lend itself to widespread use.

Listening/speaking skills

The tendency for listening skills to be overlooked (or at least attributed less importance than speaking skills) in assessment of communication is emphasised by Hartley (1995), who states that despite the importance of listening skills and the likelihood of problems in this area after brain injury, clinicians often devote only limited attention to evaluating functional listening skills. In spite of this general trend, questions regarding listening skills can be found in a variety of materials. For example, the Family Questionnaire (described earlier) features a scale for "Response to other's feedback" rated in terms of "Shows negative or no response to feedback" contrasted with "Attends to and responds to feedback". It is likely, however, that clinicians would need to search diligently to combine enough items to assess listening skills comprehensively, though Hartley's (1995) checklist is a good starting point.

SUMMARY

This chapter has explored the notion that the comprehensive assessment of communication skills after TBI requires that the process should go beyond testing of specific skills and observation in various settings to include information elicited from as many other sources as possible. The potential sources include the person with TBI, their carers and friends, and other (non-speech and language) professionals involved in their care. The benefits of using multiple sources of information are discussed in terms of ensuring that a variety of settings, contexts, and roles is sampled, diluting examiner bias and raising informants' awareness of the nature of communication and TBI. It is suggested that when considering available tools for eliciting others' perceptions, speech and language therapists working in this field need not restrict themselves to materials specifically designed for communication in TBI but can look wider to general assessments of behaviour and to other areas of speech pathology. The issues that arise from this selection process are discussed in terms of their applicability to TBI, the type of respondent, the method of administration, the format of the items, the focus on pre- or post-injury skills, the terminology employed, and the balance between listening and speaking skills.

NOTE

1. Interest has also been shown in the comparative usefulness of different forms of assessment, including questionnaires. For example, Crockford and Lesser (1994) investigated the use of the Communicative Effectiveness Index (CETI) (Lomas, Pickard, Bester, Elbard, Finlayson, & Zoghaib, 1989) in comparison with analysis of speech elicited through role-play and a conversational analysis. They found the CETI to be of limited clinical use either for diagnosis or test-retest, but noted "the incidental utility of drawing aspects of communication to the carers' attention which they may not previously have considered".

REFERENCES

Armstrong, E. (1987). Cohesive harmony in aphasic discourse and its significance to listener perception of coherence. In R.H. Brookshire (Ed.), *Clinical aphasiology conference proceedings, 17.* Minneapolis, MN: BRK Publishers.

Bayles, K.A., & Tomoeda, C.K. (1991). Caregiver report of prevalence and appearance order of linguistic symptoms in Alzheimer's patients. *The Gerontologist*, *2*, 210–216.

Benton, A.L., & Hamsher, K. de S. (1989). *Multilingual Aphasia Examination*. Iowa City, IA: AJA Associates.

Body, R., Herbert, C., Campbell, M., Parker, M., & Usher, A. (1996). An integrated approach to team assessment in head injury. *Brain Injury*, *10*, 311–318.

Body, R., & Perkins, M.R. (1998). Ecological validity in assessment of discourse in traumatic brain injury: Rating by clinicians and non-clinicians. *Brain Injury, 12*, 963–976.

Cohen, G. (1989). *Memory in the real world*. Hove, UK: Lawrence Erlbaum Associates Ltd.

Crockford, C., & Lesser, R. (1994). Assessing functional communication in aphasia: Clinical utility and time demands of three methods. *European Journal of Disorders of Communication*, *29*, 165–182.

Damico, J.S. (1985). Clinical discourse analysis: A functional approach to language assessment. In C.S. Simon (Ed.), *Communication skills and classroom success* (pp.165–203). London: Taylor & Francis.

Dewart, H., & Summers, S. (1988). *The Pragmatics Profile of Early Communication Skills*. London: NFER.

Douglas, J., O'Flaherty, C., & Snow, P. (in press). Measuring perception of communicative ability: The development and evaluation of the La Trobe Communication Questionnaire. *Aphasiology*.

Ellmo, W.J., Graser, J.M., Krchnavek, E.A., Calabrese, D.B., & Hauck, K. (1995). *Measure of cognitive-linguistic abilities*. Florida: The Speech Bin.

Elsass, L., & Kinsella, G. (1987). Social interaction following severe closed head injury. *Psychological Medicine*, *17*, 67–78.

Finset, A., Krogstad, J.M., Hansen, H., Berstad, J., Haarberg, D., Kristansen, G., Sæther, K., & Wand, M.D. (1995). Team development and memory training in traumatic brain injury rehabilitation: Two birds with one stone. *Brain Injury*, *9*, 495–507.

Gil, M., Cohen, M., Korn, C., & Groswasser, Z. (1996). Vocational outcome of aphasic patients following severe traumatic brain injury. *Brain Injury*, *10*, 39–45.

Giles, G.M., & Clark-Wilson, J. (1993). *Brain injury rehabilitation: A neurofunctional approach*. London: Chapman & Hall.

Godfrey, H.P.D., Knight, R.G., Marsh, N.V., Moroney, B.M., & Bishara, S.N. (1989). Social interaction and speed of information processing following very severe closed head injury. *Psychological Medicine*, *19*, 175–182.

Hagan, C. (1981). Language disorders secondary to closed head injury: Diagnosis and treatment. *Topics in Language Disorders, September*, 73–87.

Hartley, L.L. (1990). Assessment of functional communication. In D.E. Tupper & K.D. Cicerone (Eds.), *The neuropsychology of everyday life, Volume 1: Assessment and basic competencies* (pp.125–167). Boston, MA: Kluwer Academic Publishers.

Hartley, L.L. (1995). *Cognitive-communicative abilities following brain injury: A functional approach*. San Diego, CA: Singular Publishing.

Hartley, L.L., & Levin, H. (1990). Linguistic deficits after closed head injury: A current appraisal. *Aphasiology*, *4*, 353–370.

Heilman, K.M., Safran, A., & Geschwind, N. (1971). Closed head trauma and aphasia. *Journal of Neurology, Neurosurgery and Psychiatry*, *34*, 265–269.

Knights, R.M., Ivan, L.P., Ventureyra, E.C.G., Bentivoglio, C., Stoddart, C., Winogron, W., & Bawden, H.N. (1991). The effects of head injury in children on neuropsychological and behavioural functioning. *Brain Injury*, *5*, 339–351.

Lees-Haley, P.R., Williams, C.W., Zasler, N.D., Marguilies, S., English, L.T., & Stevens, K.B. (1997). Response bias in plaintiffs' histories. *Brain Injury, 11*, 791–799.

Leinonen, E., & Smith, B.R. (1993). Characterisation of disordered functioning in children with pragmatic difficulties. In M.M. Leahy & J.L. Kallen (Eds.), *Inter-disciplinary perspectives in speech and language pathology* (pp.252–256). Dublin: Trinity College.

Linscott, R.J., Knight, R.G., & Godfrey, H.P.D. (1996). The Profile of Functional Impairment in Communication (PFIC): A measure of communication impairment for clinical use. *Brain Injury*, *10*, 397–412.

Lomas, J., Pickard, L., Bester, S., Elbard, H., Finlayson, A., & Zoghaib, C. (1989). The Communicative Effectiveness Index: Development and psychometric evaluation of a functional communication measure for adult aphasia. *Journal of Speech and Hearing Disorders*, *54*, 113–124.

Macdonald, S., & Johnson, C.J. (1996). Utility of a verbal reasoning test in indicating vocational readiness following traumatic brain injury. *Brain Injury*, *10*, 531–542.

Manochiopinig, S., Sheard, C., & Reed, V.A. (1992). Pragmatic assessment in adult aphasia: A clinical review. *Aphasiology*, *6*, 519–533.

Manochiopinig, S., Sheard, C., Reed, V.I., & Choo, P. (1996). Communication disruption as perceived by significant others of Thai aphasic speakers. *Aphasiology*, *10*, 657–670.

McDonald, S. (1993). Pragmatic language skills after closed head injury: Ability to meet the informational needs of the listener. *Brain and Language*, *44*, 28–46.

McGann, W., & Werven, G. (1995). Social competence and head injury: A new emphasis. *Brain Injury*, *9*, 93–102.

McKinlay, W.W., & Brooks, D.N. (1984). Methodological problems in assessing psychological recovery following severe head injury. *Journal of Clinical Neuropsychology*, *6*, 87–89.

Miller, T.K., Halper, A.S., & Cherney, L.R. (1991). Evaluation of communication problems in the traumatic brain-injured adult. In A.S. Halper, L.R. Cherney, & T.K. Miller (Eds.), *Clinical management of communication problems in adults with traumatic brain injury* (pp.27–56). Gaithersburg: Aspen Publishers.

Oxenham, D., Sheard, C., & Adams, R. (1995). Comparison of clinician and spouse perceptions of the handicap of aphasia: Everybody understands "understanding". *Aphasiology*, *9*, 477–493.

Penn, C. (1985). The profile of communicative appropriateness. *The South African Journal of Communication Disorders*, *32*, 18–23.

Perkins, M., Body, R., & Parker, M. (1995). Closed head injury: Assessment and remediation of topic bias and repetitiveness. In M. Perkins & S. Howard (Eds.), *Case studies in clinical linguistics* (pp.293–320). London: Whurr Publishing.

Powell, J.A., Hale, M.A., & Bayer, A.J. (1995). Symptoms of communication breakdown in dementia: Carers' perceptions. *European Journal of Disorders of Communication*, *30*, 65–75.

Powell, T., Partridge, T., Nicholls, T., Wright, L., Mould, H., Cook, C., Anderson, A., Blakey, L., Boyer, M., Davis, L., Grimshaw, J., Johnsen, E., Lambert, L., Page, J., Pearce, D., Smith, A., Sturman, S., Searle, Y., & Tatter, S. (1994). An inter-disciplinary approach to the rehabilitation of people with brain injury. *British Journal of Therapy and Rehabilitation*, *1*, 8–13.

Prigatano, G.P., Altman, I.M., & O'Brien, K.P. (1991). Behavioural limitations traumatic brain-injured patients tend to underestimate. *BNI Quarterly*, *7*, 27–33.

Prigatano, G.P., Roueche, J.R., & Fordyce, D.J. (1985). Non-aphasic language disturbances after closed head injury. *Language Sciences*, *7*, 217–229.

Prutting, C.A., & Kirchner, D.M. (1987). A clinical appraisal of the pragmatic aspects of language. *Journal of Speech and Hearing Disorders*, *52*, 105–119.

Robertson, I.H., Ward, T., Ridgeway, V., & Nimmo-Smith, I. (1994). *The Test of Everyday Attention*. Bury St Edmunds, UK: Thames Valley Test Company.

Santos, M.E., Castro-Caldas, A., & De Sousa, L. (1998). Spontaneous complaints of long-term traumatic brain injured subjects and their close relatives. *Brain Injury*, *12*, 759–767.

Sarno, M.T. (1969). *The Functional Communication Profile: Manual of directions*. New York: Institute of Rehabilitation Medicine, New York University Medical Center.

Sinnott, J.D. (1989). *Everyday problem solving: Theory and applications*. New York: Praeger.

Snow, P., Douglas, J., & Ponsford, J. (1995). Discourse assessment following traumatic brain injury: A pilot study examining some demographic and methodological issues. *Aphasiology*, *9*, 365–380.

Snow, P., & Ponsford, J. (1995). Assessing and managing changes in communication and interpersonal skills following TBI. In J. Ponsford with S. Sloan & P. Snow, *Traumatic brain injury: Rehabilitation for everyday adaptive living* (pp.137–164). Hove, UK: Lawrence Erlbaum Associates Ltd.

Spitzberg, B.H., & Hurt, H.T. (1987). The measurement of interpersonal skills in instructional contexts. *Communication Education*, *36*, 28–45.

Swindell, C.S., Pashek, G.V., & Holland, A.L. (1982). A questionnaire for surveying personal and communicative style. In R.H. Brookshire (Ed.), *Clinical aphasiology conference proceedings*. Minneapolis, MN: BRK Publishers.

Ulatowska, H., Allard, L., Donnell, A., Bristow, J., Haynes, S.M., Flower, A., & North, A.J. (1988). Discourse performance in subjects of the Alzheimer type. In H.A. Whitaker (Ed.), *Neuropsychological studies of non-focal brain damage*. New York: Springer-Verlag.

Varney, N.R. (1991). Iowa Collateral Head Injury Interview 1989. *Neuropschology*, *5*, 223–225.

Varney, N.R., & Menefee, L. (1993). Psychosocial and executive deficits following closed head injury: Implications for orbital frontal cortex. *Journal of Head Trauma Rehabilitation*, *8*, 32–44.

Wilson, B., Alderman, N., Burgess, P.W., Emslie, H., & Evans, J.J. (1996). *Behavioural Assessment of the Dysexecutive Syndrome*. Bury St Edmunds, UK: Thames Valley Test Company.

Wilson, B., Cockburn, J., & Baddeley, A. (1985). *The Rivermead Behavioural Memory Test*. Reading, UK: Thames Valley Test Company.

World Health Organisation (1980). *International classification of impairments, disabilities and handicaps: A manual of classification relating to the consequences of disease*. Geneva: WHO.

World Health Organisation (1997). *ICIDH-2: International classification of impairments, activities and participation*. Geneva: WHO.

Ylvisaker, M., & Szekeres, S.F. (1986). Communication disorders associated with closed head injury. In R. Chapey (Ed.), *Language intervention strategies in adult aphasia* (3rd ed.) (pp.474–490). Baltimore, MD: Williams & Wilkins.

CHAPTER SEVEN

Social skill deficits following traumatic brain injury: Assessment and treatment

Nigel V. Marsh
Department of Psychology, University of Waikato, Hamilton, New Zealand

Chronic social isolation appears to be the defining characteristic of the long-term psychosocial consequences of traumatic brain injury (TBI) (Boake, 1991; Marsh, Knight, & Godfrey, 1990; Morton & Wehman, 1995). The often reported inability of the individual who has suffered a TBI to maintain, or initiate new, social relationships results in their decreased social contact. Those behaviours that occur during social interaction and that are necessary for the formation and maintenance of social relationships are collectively known as "social skills".

At the core of socially skilled behaviour is the ability to communicate effectively. The vast majority of human communication occurs through the use of language. At a general level the study of language can be broken down into the four major branches of phonology, syntax, semantics, and pragmatics (Medin & Ross, 1992). TBI can affect all aspects of language. However, recent research suggests that it is loss of the knowledge of the social rules of language—the pragmatics—or the failure to apply that knowledge during social interaction that has the greatest impact on the long-term psychosocial functioning of TBI patients. The application of different theories concerning the pragmatics of language to the description of communication following TBI was described in detail in Chapter 4. This chapter takes a broader focus, considering language as part of a constellation of behaviours that comprise social skill.

Before considering the findings from recent research in any detail, it is useful to gain an understanding of the theoretical and clinical context from which these findings have emerged. An appreciation of the conceptual issues associated with the assessment and treatment of social skills, and how they relate to working with adult TBI patients is a necessary first step. This is followed by a discussion of the methods available to assess social skill, and the findings that have been obtained when these methods have been used with TBI patients. I then turn to consider the treatment of social skill problems in adult TBI populations, including the treatment approaches available, and the use of these procedures in dealing with both the behavioural excesses and deficits that can contribute to a lack of social skill. Finally, I outline some factors that need to be considered when planning an assessment of social skills with TBI patients, and a number of key issues that need to be resolved before further advances are made in the training of social skills in TBI patients.

CONCEPTUAL ISSUES

Definitions

A precise and universally accepted definition of social skill is notably absent from the vast amount of literature that is available on the subject. This is understandable given the complexity and comprehensiveness of the topic; no one definition is adequate or sufficiently comprehensive to describe all social interactions. In reviewing the various definitions available at that time, Bellack (1979, p.77) noted that there were four elements common to most definitions:

1. Performance in interpersonal situations depends on a set of discrete verbal and non-verbal response components. This allows for the identification of the specific parameters that determine the adequacy of social behaviour.
2. The particular parameters that comprise adequate behaviour, and their configuration, vary according to the situation. Therefore, social skills are situationally specific.
3. The various component elements that comprise adequate social behaviour are learned response capabilities. Consequently individuals may vary in their overall level of social skill, as well as their skilfulness in different specific situations.
4. When specific social skill deficits can be identified, they can be targeted and remediated by training. In order for a valid assessment of social skill to be undertaken, these elements need to be reflected in the methods and procedures used.

Despite the absence of a precise definition for social skill, inadequate social skill has been viewed as a causal factor in many different behavioural disorders (Trower, Bryant, & Argyle, 1978). The variety of social situations in which a skill deficit may manifest itself has led to the development of a variety of social skills training programmes. A review of the literature indicates that there are primarily three different varieties of social skill training programmes: assertion training (for situations where assertiveness is appropriate); heterosocial training (for developing dating skills); and basic interpersonal skills training (to assist those who have general problems in relating to others and making friends). The assertiveness and heterosocial programmes have been developed primarily in the United States of America, while the research on basic interpersonal training has been developed primarily in England.

In the same way that assertion can be viewed as a subset of social skill, so too can social skill be viewed as a component of social competence. That is, the individual who displays skilled behaviour in a social situation will be viewed as socially competent by others. Therefore, while the assessment and treatment of social skill problems in TBI patients focuses on specific behaviours, the goal is to improve the extent to which the TBI patient is viewed as socially competent by others in their environment.

Models of social skill

Information-processing models

Conceptual models of social skills are almost as prolific as the different definitions of social skill (Trower, 1995). One of the more comprehensive information-processing models is that proposed by McFall (1982). Although not without its critics (e.g. Bellack, 1983; Curran, Farrell, & Grunberger, 1984), McFall's model is similar to other more recent models (e.g. Hargie, Saunders, & Dickson, 1994) which include cognitive and perceptual factors in their consideration of the process leading to socially skilled behaviour. McFall proposed that there were three relatively distinct systems involved in producing the specific abilities that enable a person to perform competently at particular social tasks. These systems were designated physiological, cognitive, and overt motor.

Physiological skills included all sensory processes and all aspects of autonomic regulation and control. Very little research has been conducted on the role that sensory deficits resulting from TBI may play in the social skill problems exhibited by this population. Cognitive skills included the decoding of the incoming sensory information, the decision-making process involved in selecting an appropriate response, and encoding the selected response into the necessary behavioural acts. Given the deficits in information-processing ability that are commonly reported following TBI, impairment in the necessary cognitive skills may be a primary reason for the social skill deficits evident in TBI patients. Finally, the overt motor skills system included the verbal and non-verbal expressive behaviours that play a significant role in social interaction. Such behaviours have been the prime focus of social skill research with non-TBI populations, and deficits in this system readily lend themselves to being transformed into specific goals for treatment programmes.

As well as understanding the ways in which social skill problems may result from TBI, it is also necessary to consider the ways in which these problems may affect the social behaviour of the TBI patient. The person with a social skill problem may be perceived as being socially incompetent for three different reasons. First, they may have a skill deficit, which results from their never having learnt the requisite cognitive and social skills. Secondly, they may have a performance deficit, which results when the skill has been acquired but there is a failure to perform it. Thirdly, they may have impaired self-control, which results in their disruptive behaviour interfering with the acquisition and performance of appropriate social skills. The first two of these would present as behavioural deficits (absence of pro-social behaviour), while the third would present as a behavioural excess (presence of anti-social behaviour).

Communication models

Human beings are inherently social animals. The successful establishment and maintenance of interpersonal relationships can be considered to be fundamental to the survival of a person (Trower, 1995). As already noted in this chapter, the ability to communicate effectively is the basis of socially skilled behaviour and in humans language is the primary method of communication. It is this functional, rather than the structural, aspect of language that has been the focus of developments within cognitive psychology (e.g. Schiffrin, 1994). Similarly, developments within linguistics have emphasised the social context of communication and the role of language in social interaction (Slobin, Gerhardt, Kyratzis, & Guo, 1996).

These developments have had an impact on recent theories of social skill following TBI. One of the models that has incorporated the dimension of communication into a consideration of social skill following TBI is that proposed by Ylvisaker, Urbanczyk, and Feeney (1992). These authors proposed a five-factor model of social skills. The first factor is concerned with the TBI individual's knowledge of self. This allows for consideration of the fact that many people following TBI are unaware of their strengths and weaknesses, and may become angry and depressed as a result of their inability to achieve their goals. The second factor is the extent to which TBI patients attend to their personal appearance, including dressing and hygiene. These are aspects of behaviour that can be neglected following TBI. The third factor is cognition. Here, Ylvisaker et al. emphasise the consequences of impairment in social cognition. It is training in these aspects of social perception, social knowledge, and social decision making that is frequently needed when teaching social skills to TBI patients. The fourth factor is communication. Ylvisaker et al. take issue with the usual distinction that is made between verbal and non-verbal communication. They state that this distinction has led to an artificial treatment dichotomy, wherein speech-language therapists deal with verbal aspects of communication and behavioural psychologists deal with non-verbal aspects of communication. Ylvisaker et al. claim that both speech-language therapists and behavioural psychologists have an equal role to play in treating deficits in the pragmatics of language, which form the communication core of social skills. The fifth and final factor is the social environment. This factor emphasises that when undertaking a comprehensive social skills training programme, significant people in the TBI patient's natural environment should also be trained as part of the communication skills programme.

The models that incorporate communication as an aspect of social skill hold considerable promise for the development of more comprehensive approaches to the assessment and treatment of social skill deficits following TBI. In particular, their emphasis on the metacognitive, or social cognition, aspects of social skill highlights the need to include training in the processing of social information and social decision making in social skill training programmes. Therefore, in addition to the traditional behavioural focus on the development of specific repertoires of positive behaviours, social skill programmes for TBI patients should include training in cognitive skills. Unfortunately, to date, the application of communication models of social skill has been restricted to paediatric TBI populations (e.g. Ylvisaker, Feeney, & Szekeres, 1998). The majority of the work with adult TBI populations has had its origins in behavioural psychology, and it is this approach that will form the basis for the remainder of this chapter. I will return to the role of communication in social skill following TBI when discussing future directions at the end of the chapter.

Behavioural changes following TBI

Impairment in social skill following TBI can be evident as either a behavioural deficit or a behavioural excess. These behavioural changes have been described in various ways by different authors. One of the earlier attempts to develop a typology of the behavioural changes that follow TBI was that of Stern, Melamed, Silberg, Rahmani, and Groswasser (1985). They described two distinct clusters of behavioural change that they labelled "extroversion" and "introversion". Within the extroversion cluster they included aggressiveness, acting out, egocentricity, over demanding, lack of attention, and increased distractibility. Within the introversion cluster they included passivity, slowed mental processes, lowered self-esteem, dependency on others, withdrawal, and the minimising of interpersonal relationships. Stern et al. concluded that the more severe the TBI the more likely the person was to exhibit the behaviours associated with the introversion syndrome, whereas mild TBI resulted in the development of behaviours associated with the extroversion syndrome. These results indicate that there are different types, or forms, of the behavioural expression of social skill problems following TBI. Although the idea that the severity of injury determines the type of social skill problem remains controversial, there is considerable support for the notion that social skill difficulties can take more than one form following TBI.

A more recent attempt to describe the types of behavioural changes that follow TBI has been provided by Garcia (1994). This model classifies the behavioural changes in terms of three categories of expected potential outcome, and presents a classification system that differs from those traditionally derived from medical models. The three categories of outcome are transient, modifiable, and chronic. Transient behaviours are those that are presumed to be a consequence of temporary neuropathological factors that affect brain function, such as metabolic disturbance, hydrocephalus, intracranial bleeding, and seizures. They usually disappear spontaneously within the first few months following TBI. Transient behaviours include screaming, verbal abuse, agitation, poor arousal, wandering, hallucinations, delusions, enuresis, and confabulation. Modifiable behaviours are those that are acquired and maintained following TBI through processes such as operant and classical conditioning, and modelling. They require assessment by means of a functional analysis of behaviour, and are changed by systematic behavioural intervention. Such behaviours include aggression, social skill deficits, excessive anxiety, verbal outbursts, eating problems, non-adherence to treatment, manipulative behaviours, dependent behaviours, sexual acting-out, and sexual inhibition. Impaired cognitive functioning may contribute to the development and maintenance of such patterns of behaviour, although these behaviours are primarily learnt and are therefore modifiable. Finally, chronic behaviours result from permanent neuropathological damage to the brain involving the limbic system, reticular activating system, and the frontal lobes. The presentation of these behavioural changes may also be affected by premorbid factors. Chronic behaviours, as the term implies, tend to be permanent sequelae of TBI and require special consideration when planning for community re-entry. These behaviours include episodic dyscontrol, lack of initiation, irritability, decreased ability to learn, disinhibition, impulsiveness, depression, and isolation.

As is evident from both of these models, problems in social interaction following TBI can result from either an increase or decrease in various types of behaviour, or both. For example, the TBI patient who speaks too much is as likely to become as socially isolated as the TBI patient who speaks too little. Similarly, an aggressive TBI patient will have as much difficulty as a socially anxious TBI patient in developing social networks. Garcia's (1994) model also highlights two important issues in the assessment and treatment of social skill following TBI. The first of these is the timing of such procedures. Although Garcia avoids imposing a temporal sequence on the development of behaviours within his three categories, it is obvious that, if the problematic behaviours are of a "transient" nature then there is little to be gained from attempting to implement a behaviour modification programme. This is particularly so when such programmes require considerable staff time and resources. Also, individuals experiencing the neuropathological conditions associated with such behaviours are unlikely to respond to any but the most stringent behavioural procedures and, given the temporary nature of these behaviours, such an approach appears unwarranted.

The second issue involves the nature of the requirements placed on the TBI patient who is undergoing a social skill training programme. The assessment and training procedures need to take into account, and be modified in response to, those behaviours that Garcia (1994) has labelled "chronic". Of particular importance are the deficits in attention, memory, and executive control, which can be a permanent consequence of TBI. Even the chronic susceptibility to fatigue that is experienced by many TBI patients can necessitate changes to the pace and complexity of a social skill training programme. The extent to which cognitive deficits can compromise the TBI patient's progress in social skill training is an important issue that is discussed in more detail later in this chapter. At this point it is sufficient to state that such deficits should not preclude TBI patients from benefiting from an appropriate social skills training programme. As Wood (1987) and many others have demonstrated, TBI patients can learn. It's just that sometimes it takes them a little bit longer! However, the first step in designing and implementing an effective social skills training programme for TBI patients is the completion of a broad-based and comprehensive assessment of the social behaviours of the TBI patient.

ASSESSMENT OF SOCIAL SKILLS

Methods of assessment

The use of various forms of questionnaires and checklists to assess communication skills following TBI has been described in Chapter 6. What follows here is a broader coverage of the different ways in which the more global construct of social skill can be assessed following TBI. Similar to the perspective presented in Chapter 6, the procedures described here encourage the use of multiple informants when assessing social skill following TBI. At a minimum, information should be obtained from the person with TBI, their family, and through clinical examination.

Interview

Despite the lack of convincing evidence for its reliability or validity, the interview is still the most frequently used method of assessment. Although the clinical assessment interview of TBI patients may include semi-structured formats relevant to their mental or neurological status (Hersen & Turner, 1994), such procedures will provide little information of direct relevance to the assessment of social skill deficits. However, the standard problem-orientated behavioural interview (Peterson, 1968) provides a useful structure for the initial assessment of socially skilled behaviour in TBI patients.

Wilson, Spence, and Kavanagh (1989) have provided a useful summary of topics that should be included when conducting assessment interviews focused on social skill. These include the frequency of social interaction and the person's level of satisfaction with this frequency, the quality of social interaction and a description of occasions that the person considers were either satisfactory or unsatisfactory in terms of their outcome, the extent to which a person considers their behaviour contributed to both satisfactory and unsatisfactory social interactions, and a description of which of their own specific behaviours the person considers were instrumental in determining the outcome of both satisfactory and unsatisfactory social interactions. Other topics that can be covered include the extent to which the person feels uncomfortable in social situations, and the degree to which they seek to avoid social interaction. The interview can also provide some indication of the historical aspects of the person's social development. It does not necessarily follow that the TBI patient who is now socially isolated was, prior to their TBI, socially skilled and successfully integrated into a social community.

Once the interviewer has obtained an understanding of the antecedents, behaviour, and consequences of the social behaviour of the TBI patient, they can then focus on getting clarification of specific instances of social interaction. Such questioning should elicit a detailed description of a problem situation and its parameters, including the physiological, cognitive, and overt behaviours experienced by the TBI patient. Obviously many of the topics and techniques used in interviewing the TBI patient can also be used when interviewing their family members. This allows for corroborating information on the TBI patient's social behaviour, and may also provide information about aspects of the TBI patient's behaviour of which they are unaware. Despite the large amount of information that can be obtained from interviewing the TBI patient and their family, the use of further assessment procedures is necessary before planning a treatment programme.

Self-report methods

A vast number of self-report questionnaires are available for the assessment of social skill deficits. Recent comprehensive listings of these are available in Spitzberg and Cupach (1989) and Fischer and Corcoran (1994). The available questionnaires differ in terms of their emphasis; some assess social anxiety, others assertiveness, and others interpersonal behaviour. Listed below is a brief description and psychometric evaluation of some of the more frequently used self-report questionnaires from each of these three areas.

Social anxiety. Watson and Friend (1969) developed a Fear of Negative Evaluation Scale and a Social Avoidance and Distress Scale. Both of these concepts may be useful in determining the causal factors associated with an absence of socially skilled behaviours in a person who has suffered a TBI. While it is doubtful that the original normative data obtained on these scales would be of much current use, they could have a role as pre-post measures. The Fear of Negative Evaluation Scale contains 30 items, which are answered true/false, and assesses an individual's concern, apprehension, and worry about how they are evaluated by others. The reliability data for the Fear of Negative Evaluation Scale are acceptable, with high internal consistency and reasonable one-month test-retest coefficients being reported. Similarly, there is evidence for its convergent and discriminant validity.

The Social Avoidance and Distress Scale assesses an individual's self-reported tendency to avoid social interactions, and to feel anxious while in them. The 24 items were originally presented in a true/false format, but many researchers have used five-point scales. Similar to the Fear of Negative Evaluation Scale, the Social Avoidance and Distress Scale has high internal consistency, acceptable test-retest reliability, and evidence for both convergent and discriminant validity. Factor analytic studies have suggested that the questionnaire assesses social avoidance more than social anxiety. The Social Avoidance and Distress Scale remains one of the most widely used questionnaires in the area of social skill. Use of either or both of these scales may be helpful in determining the extent to which issues related to social anxiety and the consequent avoidance of social situations need to be emphasised in a social skills training programme with TBI patients.

Assertiveness. Gambrill and Richey's (1975) Assertion Inventory is one of the most widely known instruments of its type. Each of the 40 items is answered 3 times, allowing for the calculation of 3 different scores for discomfort with assertion, probability of responding in an assertive manner, and the identification of specific situations where assertion is lacking. The pattern of answers also allows for respondents to be characterised as either assertive, unassertive, an anxious performer, or as unconcerned. The use of such a typology provides obvious direction in determining the nature of the intervention programme that could be used with TBI patients. Additional scales, relating to the specific types of situation that result in discomfort, can also be calculated. Although there are no data on the internal consistency of the Assertion Inventory, its high test-retest correlations provide evidence for its stability. Evidence for its validity is quite impressive; the Assertion Inventory has been successfully used to discriminate between clinical and non-clinical groups, and has demonstrated sensitivity to the effects of treatment.

The Simple Rathus Assertiveness Schedule (McCormick, 1985) is a useful revision of the well-established Rathus Assertiveness Schedule. The nature of the revision involved rewriting the 30 items using more simple language. Therefore, this version can be used with a wide range of people, including those with poor reading ability. Each item is rated on a six-point scale from "very much like me" to "very unlike me". The total score is the sum of all items, with higher scores reflecting more assertion. Evidence for reliability, as provided by a measure of internal consistency, was very good. Although there is little specific information on the validity of the Simple Rathus Assertiveness Schedule, its high correlation with the original Rathus Assertiveness Schedule suggests that the two may be thought of as parallel forms. Therefore, the concurrent and construct validity demonstrated for the original instrument can reasonably be assumed to also apply to the Simple Rathus Assertiveness Schedule. Given that language difficulties (including reading problems) are such a common consequence of TBI, the simplified language format of the Simple Rathus Assertiveness Schedule suggests that it may be a particularly useful measure to be used with TBI patients.

Interpersonal behaviour. Levenson and Gottman's (1978) Dating and Assertion Questionnaire has 18 items that cover the 2 areas of dating and assertion. Respondents are required to indicate not only the frequency with which they engage in relevant behaviours, but also the degree of comfort they would experience in a number of given situations. Such a distinction may be particularly useful when working with TBI patients. Although it has been well established that TBI patients display a low frequency of heterosocial behaviours, the reasons for this remain unclear. Therefore, the assessment of heterosocial behaviour in TBI patients needs to have a broad focus. The Dating and Assertion Questionnaire has good reliability, as demonstrated by both internal consistency and test-retest procedures. Similarly, acceptable validity data has been established by the Dating and

Assertion Questionnaire's ability to distinguish between different groups, and its sensitivity to the effects of treatment.

The Test of Negative Social Exchange (Ruehlman & Karoly, 1991) represents a unique approach to the assessment of social interaction. Here the emphasis is not on how the respondent has behaved or how comfortable they have felt in social situations, but on how many negative social interactions they have experienced in the past month. Obviously this aspect of social interaction—the person's perception of the unpleasantness of their social experiences—may have a role in providing an explanation for the social isolation experienced by TBI patients. Similarly, administration of this questionnaire to significant people in the TBI patient's environment may assist in determining if there are any aspects of the TBI patient's behaviour that discourage others from regular social contact with them. The Test of Negative Social Exchange has 16 items that provide 4 subscale scores of hostility/impatience, interference, insensitivity, and ridicule. It has acceptable reliability and there is good evidence for its construct validity.

Behavioural observation

Behavioural observation is the *sine qua non* of psychological assessment. The sophistication of observational procedures ranges from the most fundamental of approaches—the Mental Status Examination—through to the use of very elaborate and comprehensive coding procedures. A wide variety of rating scales is available, including those designed for use with only one gender (e.g. Kolko & Milan, 1985) and those that concentrate on frequently neglected aspects of social interaction such as "tenderness" (Warren & Gilner, 1978). Reviews of the various coding systems are available in Grotevant and Carlson (1987) and Spitzberg and Cupach (1989). The advent of commercially available video has simplified the collection of observational data and allowed such assessment procedures to be used in clinical as well as research settings (Summerfield, 1983).

The assessment settings used in the behavioural observation of social skill have included *in vivo*, naturalistic, and role-play. Real-life, or *in vivo*, situations have rarely been used and present difficulties for obvious practical and ethical reasons. In naturalistic, or simulated, interactions an attempt is made to parallel real-life situations, and the subject and confederate are given minimal instructions. Role-play situations are more structured and can be of a single-response format or multiple-response format (Meier & Hope, 1998).

Observational coding systems differ in terms of their level of measurement. The vast majority of coding systems are designed to assess behaviour at either a molar or molecular level. Molar analysis typically involves trained judges or peers rating individual subjects on global, qualitative dimensions (e.g. ratings of overall anxiety, assertiveness, skill, interpersonal effectiveness). Molecular measurements target specific response characteristics (e.g. eye contact, speech duration, speech latency, smiles) and involve more direct recording (e.g. frequency, duration). Several complex microanalytic coding systems based on "type" or "class" of behaviour (e.g. agreement, problem solving, expressing feelings) have also been devised. An outstanding example of the microanalytic approach is the Couples Interaction Scoring System (Gottman, 1979). Unfortunately, the cost and complexity of these microanalytic coding systems means that they are mainly used for research purposes, and clinical assessment procedures tend to use molar or molecular approaches to assessment.

There are a number of difficulties, however, associated with the sole use of either molar or molecular levels of measurement in the assessment of social skill (Bellack, 1983). Molecular measurements have not been useful in validating assessment measures, and typically fail to correlate meaningfully across situations or methodologies. On the other hand, molar ratings are too ambiguous to help specify which potential behaviours contribute to a rating of skilled or unskilled and, consequently, which behaviours should be targeted for change. In response to these difficulties, many researchers use both molar and molecular ratings when assessing social skill. However, a recent development in this area has been the introduction of coding systems that offer a compromise between the molar and molecular levels; these are usually known as intermediate level coding systems. Before examining the research findings from those studies that have used behavioural observation to assess social skill in TBI patients, it is useful to briefly review some examples of different coding systems that are applicable to the assessment of social skill in TBI populations (see Table 7.1).

Heterosocial Skills Behaviour Checklist. The Heterosocial Skills Behaviour Checklist (Barlow, Able, Blanchard, Bristow, & Young, 1977) has 11 verbal (e.g. loudness, pitch) and non-verbal (e.g. initiation, flow) items, which are assumed to be skills involved in conducting a heterosocial conversation. The items are grouped into the three categories of voice, form of conversation, and affect. Raters are initially required to rate each item as appropriate or inappropriate. They then indicate on a five-point scale the degree to which the rating applies. Scoring consists of summing across items within each category to derive subscale scores, and summing across the categories to provide a total heterosocial conversation competence score. Although the items of the Heterosocial Skills Behaviour Checklist are supposedly all molecular, some (e.g. interest) are arguably molar in nature. Despite the fact that it was originally designed for use in assessing males in heterosocial conversation, the Heterosocial Skills Behaviour Checklist can be used to rate performance during any instance of dyadic interaction.

TABLE 7.1
Content of social skill observational rating scales

Scale	*Type*	*Subscales*	*Components*
Heterosocial Skills Behavioural Checklist (Barlow et al., 1977)	Molecular	Voice	Loudness, pitch, inflection, use of dramatic effects
		Form	Initiation, follow-up, flow, interest
		Affect	Facial, eye contact, laughter
Social Interaction Test (Trower et al., 1978)	Molecular	Voice	Volume, tone, pitch, clarity, pace, speech disturbances
		Non-verbal	Proximity, orientation, appearance, face, gaze, posture tonus, posture position, gesture, autistic gesture
		Conversation	Length, generality, formality, variety, humour, non-verbal "grammar", feedback, meshing, turn-taking, questions, supportive routines, assertive routines, behaviour in public, situation-specific routines
	Molar		Warm/like–cold/dislike, superior/dominant–inferior/submissive, socially anxious–relaxed, happy–sad, rewarding–unrewarding, controlling–uncontrolling, feminine–masculine, attractive–unattractive, poised–awkward, passive–active, difficult–easy, emotional–unemotional, socially skilled–socially unskilled
Simulated Social Interaction Test (Curran, 1982)	Molar	Anxiety and skill	Disapproval or criticism, social assertiveness or visibility confrontation and anger expression, heterosexual contact, interpersonal warmth, conflict with or rejection by parent or relative, interpersonal loss, receiving compliments
Communication Skills Test (Floyd & Markman, 1984)	Molar	Very positive	Summarising other or both, checking out, opinion/feeling probe, specific plan, specific feedback, back on beam, metacognition, validation
		Positive	Feeling statement, agree or disagree with rationale provided, plan suggestion that is non-specific, compliment, clarification request, accept responsibility, empathy—mind reading with positive affect, summarising self concisely or to clarify a point, humour, positive non-verbal

(continued)

Table 7.1 continued

Scale	*Type*	*Subscales*	*Components*
		Neutral	Problem talk—offering an opinion, asking a question, agreement statement without providing a rationale, information statement
		Negative	Problem talk that is confusing or unclear, opinions without rationale provided, disagreement without rationale, disruptive extraneous comments, negative non-verbal behaviours
		Very negative	Off-beam, kitchen sinking, mind reading with negative affect, putdown, summarising self when not requested or no clarification is needed, blaming, character assassination, deny responsibility, very negative non-verbal
Behaviourally Referenced Rating System of Intermediate Social Skills (BRISS) (Farrell et al., 1985)	Intermediate	Head	Movement, position
		Facial	Smiles, animation, tension
		Eyes	Contact, movement, characteristics
		Arms/hands	Movement, position
		Body and legs	Movement, position
		Language	Words, grammar, syntax
		Delivery	Fluency, rate, quality, mannerism
		Structure	Fluency, topic change
		Content	Topic interest, topic substance
		Style	Self-disclosure, humour, manners
		Partner	Use of reinforcers, self-centred, partner involvement

Social Interaction Test. The rating scale of the Social Interaction Test (Trower et al., 1978) has two sections. The first section consists of 29 molecular behaviours that cover the three categories of voice quality, non-verbal, and conversation. The second section provides bipolar ratings on thirteen seven-point molar scales (Table 7.1). Scoring of the molecular scales can be either on the basis of individual items for diagnostic purposes, or across items for various broad categories of behaviour. Scoring of the molar scales is achieved by reverse scoring the negatively worded items, and then summing across items.

Originally designed for use with psychiatric populations, the Social Interaction Test has also been used with student populations. Although primarily used to assess behaviour recorded in simulated or naturalistic interactions; the Social Interaction Test rating scale is obviously applicable to the analysis of social skill in any type of social interaction. The Social

Interaction Test rating scale is one of the few measures that allows for both too much and too little of a behaviour to be rated as less competent, and this useful feature may contribute to its enduring role in social skill assessment.

Simulated Social Interaction Test. The Simulated Social Interaction Test (Curran, 1982) provides the stimulus situations as well as the rating scales for the assessment of social skill. It is therefore an example of social skill assessment using a naturalistic or simulated interaction. The stimulus situations consist of eight descriptions of hypothetical problematic interpersonal situations (e.g. disapproval or criticism, receiving compliments). The inclusion of such a broad range of social situations makes the Simulated Social Interaction Test a useful instrument for assessing the various ways in which social skill deficits may present in a clinical situation.

A narrator describes the context of the situation, and a confederate makes a stimulus comment. The subject's response to the confederate is then rated. The original rating scales used in the Simulated Social Interaction Test consisted of two eleven-point molar scales (social anxiety and social skill). Subjects therefore receive a social anxiety and a social skill score for each of the eight situations. Although the use of only two global scales is unlikely to provide sufficient information for designing a social skills treatment programme for TBI patients, it does allow for an initial assessment of the type of social situations in which the person has difficulty. Information specific to the development of treatment programmes could be provided through the use of further assessment procedures. Alternatively, more detailed analysis of the stimulus situations contained in the Simulated Social Interaction Test could provide useful information for such programmes. To date, the Simulated Social Interaction Test has been used in assessing social behaviour with a wide range of population groups including psychiatric patients, students, and non-clinical samples of adults.

Communication Skills Test. The authors (Floyd & Markman, 1984) state that the Communication Skills Test was developed to achieve the three goals of (a) assessing both verbal and non-verbal communication skills displayed by couples during brief problem-solving interactions, (b) to provide a numerical summary index of the dyad's overall level of communication proficiency while maintaining at least some of the descriptive richness of other observational measures and fidelity to the interaction sequence, and that (c) with a minimum of training it would allow experienced observers to make reliable evaluations with only a single viewing of the interaction sequence (p.98). The Communication Skills Test uses as its coding unit the entire statement made by a person during an interaction. Each statement receives a rating on a five-point scale from "very positive" to "very negative". The rating reflects the degree of communication proficiency exhibited by the speaker, and the authors provide various behavioural referents for determining how to award ratings. There are eight referents for a "very positive" rating, ten referents for a "positive" rating, four referents for a "neutral" rating, five referents for a "negative" rating, and nine referents for a "very negative" rating (Table 7.1).

Scoring is completed by averaging the ratings across all statements for each person in the interaction. Ratings would also be averaged across raters in those instances when more than one rater was used. Although the Communication Skills Test was originally developed on a sample of dating couples planning their first marriage, it would be suitable for use in assessing the problem-solving interaction of any type of dyad. Not only does the Communication Skills Test provide a global rating of skill, but the behavioural referents used in determining the overall level of skill also allow for a detailed description of an individual's communication behaviours. Such a description could be used in developing an individualised treatment plan for a social skills training programme. Research conducted during the development of the Communication Skills Test demonstrated that it had an acceptable level of inter-rater agreement, was sensitive to change, and had concurrent validity with another measure of dyadic communication. Overall, the Communication Skills Test shows promise as a functionally useful procedure for the assessment and training of social skills with TBI populations.

Behaviourally Referenced Rating System of Intermediate Social Skills (BRISS). The BRISS (Wallander, Conger, & Conger, 1985; Farrell, Rabinowitz, Wallander, & Curran, 1985) represents a significant development in the assessment of social skill. It is an intermediate level coding system and, as such, use of the BRISS avoids the difficulties associated with the sole use of either a molar or molecular analysis of observational data. The BRISS provides qualitative ratings for 11 specific behavioural components of heterosocial skill. There are five non-verbal components and six verbal components. Raters assign a value on a seven-point scale from "very inappropriate" to "very appropriate". Each scale has a number of behavioural referents that provide guidance to the rater in arriving at a rating value.

The five non-verbal scales consist of use of head, use of facial expressions, use of eyes, use of arms and hands, and use of overall body and legs. The six verbal scales consist of language (the technical quality of the subject's expressions, largely independent of the content of these expressions), speech delivery (the sound of the subject's speech or utterances, largely independent of the content of the speech), conversational structure (the progression of the conversation at a general level), conversational content (the subject matter talked about in the conversation), personal conversational style (the general communication pattern of the subject), and partner-directed behaviour (behaviour that facilitates the involvement of the partner in the conversation and that is not subsumed under other categories).

Whereas the Communication Skills Test is designed solely for analysing social skill during problem-solving dyadic interactions, the BRISS can be used to assess social skill in a wide variety of situations. It has been used in assessing social skill with many different populations including students, clinic psychiatric patients, non-clinic psychiatric patients, community adults, and TBI patients. When using multiple raters, scoring is achieved by averaging across each component. The BRISS was designed from a sound theoretical basis and has displayed high inter-rater reliability, concurrent validity with other measures of social skill, and a reasonable ability to discriminate between groups differing in their level of social skill. A difficulty with the original BRISS (Wallander et al., 1985) was the limited range reported on each scale. However, a revision of the referent positioning on the scales by Farrell et al. (1985) has overcome this limitation. Despite the complexity of the BRISS and the associated need for significant training of raters, it appears to be one of the most useful procedures for the assessment of social skill currently available. As well as providing for an overall assessment of a person's level of social skill, analysis of the person's performance on each of the BRISS components provides sufficient information for the development of individualised social skills training programmes.

Research findings in the assessment of social skill following TBI

Many studies have assessed the social behaviour of TBI patients using unstructured, semi-structured, or structured interviews of the TBI patient and members of their family. The use of self-report questionnaires completed by the TBI patient and/or their family members have also been a frequent method of assessment. Those studies that have used interviews and questionnaires to assess social behaviour following TBI report a relatively consistent pattern of results. In general, TBI patients and their family members report substantial changes in the social behaviour of the TBI patient (this is often referred to as "personality changes"). These changes result in difficulties in social interaction, a lower frequency of social relationships, and a tendency to rely on family for social contact (Marsh et al., 1990; Whalley Hammell, 1994). These changes also play a role in determining the experience of caregiver burden by family members (Godfrey, Knight, & Bishara, 1991; Marsh, Kersel, Havill, & Sleigh, 1998; Stratton & Gregory, 1994).

In a review of the literature where interview and questionnaire methods have been used to assess the social behaviour of TBI patients, Godfrey, Marsh, and Partridge (1987) stressed the need for future studies to employ behavioural observation as their primary method of assessment. Further

TABLE 7.2
Studies that have used behavioural observation in the assessment of social skill following severe TBI in adults

Authors	*Subjects*	*Level of measurement*	*Result*
Newton & Johnson (1985)	11 TBI, 20 out-patients, 32 non-clinical	3 molar scales, 12 molecular scales summed to give molar rating	TBI patients rated as poorer on measures of social performance, than both comparison groups
Godfrey et al. (1993)	24 TBI 6 months, 19 TBI 1 year, and 23 TBI 2–3 years post-injury, plus 27 orthopaedic controls	1 molar scale	All 3 TBI groups rated as less socially skilled than control group
Spence et al. (1993)	14 TBI, 19 orthopaedic controls	1 molar scale	TBI rated as less socially skilled during the initial stages of the interaction
Godfrey et al. (1989)	18 TBI, 18 controls	5 molar scales, 10 molecular scales	TBI rated as less interesting, likeable, and skilled. TBI spoke less, slower, more monotonously, and less spontaneously than controls
Bond & Godfrey (1997)	62 TBI, 25 orthopaedic controls	4 molar scales, 2 molecular scales	TBI rated less appropriate, interesting, rewarding, and more effortful. TBI required more prompting and prompted less
Marsh & Knight (1991a)	18 TBI, 18 controls.	6 intermediate scales	TBI rated less appropriate on language, speech delivery, and partner-directed behaviour

progress in determining the exact nature of the social skill deficits that result from TBI cannot be made through the sole use of interviews and questionnaires. Also, the development of therapy programmes for the treatment of social skill deficits following TBI requires a precise description of the specific behaviours that need to be targeted by the treatment programme, and information on whether these behaviours need to be decreased or increased. Fortunately, several research groups have utilised behavioural observation as the primary method of assessment when investigating social skill following TBI. A summary of these studies is presented in Table 7.2.

Behavioural assessment of social skill following TBI

Molar/global analysis of social skill following TBI. One of the first studies to use behavioural observation in the assessment of social skill following TBI was that of Newton and Johnson (1985). The performance of 11 adult, severe TBI patients was compared with that of both an out-patient group referred for social interaction difficulties and a non-clinical group. The TBI patients were assessed at least two years post-injury. The patient's performance during a semi-structured social interaction with a stranger was evaluated on three five-point global scales of performance, anxiety, and assertiveness. In addition, a total performance score was calculated on the basis of ratings from twelve three-point molecular scales assessing various aspects of verbal and non-verbal social behaviour. The TBI patients' performance was rated as poorer than that of the comparison groups on both the performance scale and total performance scale. Despite this, there was no significant difference between the groups on either the anxiety or assertiveness rating scales. Newton and Johnson concluded by suggesting that the social interaction difficulties of TBI patients may lead to their poor social adjustment and social isolation.

A seven-point Likert scale of global social skill was used by the three raters employed in Godfrey, Partridge, Knight, and Bishara's (1993) study of three adult groups of severe TBI patients at different stages post-injury. The first group was six months, the second group one year, and the third group two to three years post-injury. The level of social skill displayed by the three groups during an unstructured conversation with a stranger was compared with that of an orthopaedic control group. All three groups of TBI patients were rated as less socially skilled than the control group of orthopaedic patients. This suggests that the social skill deficits evident in TBI patients' social behaviour do not change significantly as a function of time since injury. The results obtained by Godfrey et al. demonstrated that social skill deficits in TBI patients are evident as early as six months post-injury and are still present up to three years post-injury.

Using similar procedures, Spence, Godfrey, Knight, and Bishara (1993) investigated the social skills of 14 adult, severe TBI patients during a semi-structured social interaction at 4 months post-injury. Three raters evaluated the level of social skill displayed by the TBI patients in response to seven specific prompts (e.g. "What do you do to keep yourself busy?") delivered by the female experimenter. Ratings were made on a 7-point Likert scale of global social skill. When the results of the TBI patients were compared with those of an orthopaedic control group, the TBI patients were rated as less socially skilled on the basis of their performance during the whole interaction. However, further analysis of the TBI patients' behaviour in response to the specific prompts showed that the difference between the two groups was only evident in the early part of the interaction. Spence et al. concluded by suggesting that TBI patients may be primarily disadvantaged in the initial stages of a social interaction, and that it is their failure to interact effectively during the early stages of a conversation that leads to them being excluded from further social interaction and contact.

Molecular analysis of social skill following TBI. Godfrey, Knight, Marsh, Moroney, and Bishara (1989) reported results from the first of two studies of 18 male, adult, very severe TBI patients. The patients were assessed at least 18 months post-injury. The TBI patients' performance during two social interactions—an unstructured heterosocial conversation with a stranger and a role-play job interview—were videotaped and later assessed by 2 independent raters on 15 7-point Likert scales. The raters evaluated the TBI patients' performance on 5 global rating scales (interesting, pleasant, likeable, skilful, apathetic) and 10 specific verbal (voice speed, speech length, spontaneity, emotion, question frequency, speech pitch) and non-verbal (looking duration, gesture frequency, smiling frequency, laughing frequency) molecular rating scales. When compared with a matched control group, the TBI patients' performance was rated as less interesting, likeable, and skilled. However there was no difference between the two groups in terms of the ratings of pleasantness and animation. The TBI group was also rated as less skilled on the five molecular rating scales of speech speed, spontaneity, speech length, speech pitch, and looking duration. There were no significant between group differences on the other five molecular rating scales of specific social skills. It is noteworthy that it was the specific impairments in the TBI patients' verbal, not non-verbal, behaviour that resulted in global ratings documenting their lack of social skill.

Bond and Godfrey (1997) used four 9-point global rating scales and two molecular scales to further analyse the social skills of 62 TBI patients and 25 orthopaedic control patients from Godfrey et al. (1993). The results from this further analysis of the videotapes made during the earlier study showed that the TBI patients were rated more poorly on the four global scales of appropriateness, effortful, interesting, and rewarding. Using two molecular scales of prompt frequency and turn duration they found that interactors prompted more frequently and spoke for a shorter time during interactions with TBI patients than with control patients. TBI patients prompted less and spoke for longer than control patients. In attempting to explain the specific behaviours that resulted in the poorer overall evaluation of the TBI patients' social skill, Bond and Godfrey found that the TBI patients' failure to use prompts during the conversation was strongly related to the global measures of social skill.

Intermediate level analysis of social skill following TBI. In one of only two studies to utilise an intermediate level assessment of social skill following TBI, Marsh and Knight (1991a) reported the results from a further assessment of the 18 TBI patients assessed by Godfrey et al. (1989). The patients' performance during an unstructured heterosocial conversation with a stranger and two problem-solving tasks with a significant other were analysed using the six verbal scales of the revised BRISS (Farrell et al., 1985). The performance of the TBI group was rated as significantly less appropriate than the performance of the matched control group on the two BRISS scales of language and speech delivery. In addition, the TBI group was rated as less appropriate on the partner-directed scale during the heterosocial conversation, and this difference became stronger as the interaction progressed.

Use of the BRISS scales allowed Marsh and Knight (1991a) to provide what is currently the most detailed analysis available of the social skills of TBI patients. These results indicated that the communication of the TBI patients was characterised by a difficulty finding appropriate words, an inability to express ideas clearly, and the use of inappropriate expressions. These difficulties were reflected in speech that lacked fluency, clarity, and continuity. Perhaps most important were the communication problems evident only during the heterosocial conversation with a stranger. During this interaction the verbal behaviour of the TBI patients suggested that they were more passive and failed to attend to, or show interest in, the other person. It is these deficits in their pragmatic language behaviours that appear to be the defining aspect of their social skill deficits.

TREATMENT OF SOCIAL SKILL DEFICITS

Treatment approaches

The procedures involved in conducting a social skills training programme have been standardised and established for over 20 years (Lange & Jakubowski, 1976). The components of such programmes usually include behavioural rehearsal, feedback, prompting, model presentation, programming of change, and homework assignments (Trower, 1995). Results from the assessment procedures should provide sufficient detailed information to allow the components of the programme to be tailored to suit an individual's specific behavioural excesses and deficits, and the particular situations in which they have difficulty. A relatively recent innovation in social skills training has been the development of board games that provide the players with the opportunity to practise and receive feedback on their responses to various social situations requiring different types of social skill (Foxx & McMorrow, 1983).

Social skills training can be undertaken as either an individual or a group treatment. Preliminary assessment of individuals prior to their inclusion in a social skills training group would allow for the formation of homogeneous groups with respect to the nature of the social skill deficits and/or excesses. However, a heterogeneous grouping of individuals may still be able to benefit from a comprehensive, broad-based programme.

Obviously the group format provides a useful setting to practise many of the skills that are taught within social skills training programmes. Despite this there are methods that would allow for similar procedures to be used on an individual basis, and encourage the generalisation of the skills learnt across a variety of settings (Shelton & Levy, 1981). More detailed descriptions of the components of social skills training programmes are available in Kanfer and Goldstein (1991) and Masters, Burish, Hollon, and Rimm (1987).

The elimination of anti-social behaviours

The history of the use of behaviour modification procedures with different patient groups seems remarkably similar. In the first stage, practitioners of both pharmacological and psychotherapeutic approaches resist the application of such methods to the patient groups they work with. Following this, behaviour therapists are provided with limited access for the purpose of developing treatment programmes for severe behavioural disorders (e.g. aggression, self-mutilation, etc.) that have failed to respond to other treatment methods. Finally, once the efficacy of behaviour therapy has been demonstrated in controlling or eliminating such behavioural excesses, the technology of behaviour modification is accepted for use in teaching new skills and overcoming difficulties that result from behavioural deficits.

The history of the use of behavioural procedures with TBI patients follows this general trend. Much of the early work in this area was undertaken by Wood and Eames (Wood & Eames, 1981; Eames & Wood 1985a, b). These early studies demonstrated the success that could be achieved by behavioural procedures in treating the severe behavioural disturbances that can follow TBI. Similarly, Horton and Howe (1981) provided one of the early demonstrations of the use of behaviour therapy with TBI patients. They reported a case study in which a report card system and a response cost procedure were used to eliminate swearing and biting in a 40-year-old male with a history of head trauma. Lewis, Nelson, Nelson, and Reusink (1988) also used a case study approach to demonstrate how behaviour therapy could be employed to modify disruptive social behaviours following brain injury. They evaluated the effects of three feedback contingencies (attention and interest, systematic ignoring, and correction) on the occurrence of socially inappropriate talk in a 21-year-old male who had suffered anoxic brain injury. Data were collected during naturalistic dyadic conversations with three different therapists. These two-minute conversations occurred five times per day and were audiotaped for later analysis. The use of correction resulted in the greatest decrease in socially inappropriate remarks. As expected, attention and interest increased the rate of socially inappropriate talk, demonstrating that such talk was likely maintained by social reinforcement. Similar procedures were reported to be effective by Giles, Fussey, and Burgess (1988) in improving the conversational behaviours of a 27-year-old male with severe TBI.

The use of behavioural procedures to reduce or eliminate behaviours that disrupt the social interaction of TBI patients is now a well-established practice (Hopewell, Burke, Weslowski, & Zawlocki, 1990). Indeed, Godfrey and Knight (1988) have demonstrated how such approaches can be more effective than cognitive rehabilitation in contributing to the successful community placement of TBI patients. Peters, Gluck, and McCormick (1992) have described how behavioural principles can be successfully used to develop comprehensive rehabilitation programmes for the most difficult of TBI patients; those that remain confused and agitated. Such patients usually display physical and vocal aggression, destroy property, abscond from care, engage in self-injurious behaviour, and are generally noncompliant with the process of rehabilitation. Obviously, such behaviours need to be reduced or eliminated before treatments aimed at remediating behavioural deficits and teaching new social behaviours can be introduced. However, the most recent advances in the area of social skills training following severe TBI have been made with those who, by medical standards, have made a good recovery following their injury. Such TBI patients do not usually exhibit disruptive behaviours; they frequently reside in the community, and may even have returned to some form of employment. Despite the possibility of ongoing physical and cognitive consequences from their TBI, for these patients it is their difficulties in social interaction that present the greatest obstacle to their complete reintegration into the community. These are the TBI patients for whom social isolation appears to be the most enduring and disabling consequence of TBI.

The training of pro-social behaviours

Despite the somewhat ambiguous diagnostic status of their patient, Turner, Hersen, and Bellack's (1978) study is frequently cited as one of the early examples of social skills training with TBI patients. They evaluated the effects of a social skills training programme (consisting of behavioural rehearsal, modelling, instruction, feedback, and verbal reinforcement) on the pro-social behaviours of an "organically" impaired patient. They used a multiple baseline design to assess change across six molecular behaviours (eye contact, response latency, loudness of speech, number of words spoken, smiles, and physical gestures), and also made a global rating of overall assertiveness. They reported an improvement in all the targeted pro-social behaviours following initial training and that, six months after treatment, booster sessions rapidly reinstituted any lost treatment gains. A summary of more recent studies that have implemented social skill training programmes with TBI patients is presented in Table 7.3.

Utilising two of the core components of social skills training (feedback and self-monitoring), Gajar, Schloss, Schloss, and Thompson (1984) taught appropriate group conversational behaviours to 2 23-year-old male TBI patients. Both patients had received their TBI in separate road traffic crashes 18 months prior to social skills training. Feedback consisted of providing a light signal to the patients indicating whether they were behaving positively or negatively during the group social interaction. The self-monitoring procedure required the patients to indicate whether their conversational

TABLE 7.3
Studies that have used social skills training to improve the social interaction skills of adult TBI patients

Author	*Subjects*	*Type of programme*	*Results*
Gajar et al. (1984)	2 TBI	Individual	Feedback and self-monitoring increased appropriate conversational behaviours
Schloss et al. (1985)	2 TBI	Individual	Self-monitoring increased frequency of questions, compliments, and self-disclosures
Braunling-McMorrow et al. (1986)	3 TBI	Board game	Use of game increased all 6 social skill components during game and in natural setting
Brotherton et al. (1988)	4 TBI	Individual	Training resulted in improvement for three patients
Johnson & Newton (1987)	10 TBI	Group	Group performance did not improve significantly. Evidence for improvement in some individuals
Flanagan et al. (1995)	5 TBI	Group	Improvement found for some individuals

behaviours were positive or negative. By utilising an alternating treatments design these researchers were also able to assess the relative efficacy of each treatment. Both treatments were effective in improving the appropriate conversational behaviours of the patients to levels similar to that displayed by a group of non-TBI peers. The treatment effects also showed generalisation to settings outside of the training setting.

In a further development of these procedures, Schloss, Thompson, Gajar, and Schloss (1985) examined the effect of self-monitoring on three heterosexual conversation behaviours for two severe TBI patients. One patient was a 20-year-old male who had received his injury 2 years prior to training. The other patient was a 21-year-old male who had received his injury 1 year prior to training. Schloss et al. assessed treatment effectiveness by using a multiple baseline design across the three behaviours of complimenting others, asking others questions about themselves, and telling others about themselves. This was combined with an alternating treatment design, wherein on some occasions the patients were instructed to self-monitor and on other occasions they were not instructed to self-monitor. The results showed that the "instructions to self-monitor" condition produced an increase in compliments and questions, and a decrease in self-disclosure. These increases in socially appropriate behaviours generalised across settings, and were maintained at follow-up.

The use of a social skill training game to teach social skills to three severe TBI patients was reported by Braunling-McMorrow, Lloyd, and Fralish (1986). The 3 patients, 2 females and 1 male, were aged between 18 and 27 years and they had received their injuries at least 2 years prior to training. These researchers used a revision of the general social skills curriculum from the training programme, "Stacking the Deck" (Foxx & McMorrow, 1983). The six components of social skill targeted by this game are compliments, social interaction, politeness, criticism, social confrontation, and questions/answers. As the game proceeded, the TBI patients received cards that required them to either initiate an interaction (the "actor" condition) or respond to an interaction initiated by someone else (the "reactor" condition). There were 48 cards, 8 for each of the 6 component areas of social skill, with 4 of the cards for each area depicting "actor" situations and the remaining 4 cards relating to "reactor" situations. The patients' ability to progress in the game was contingent upon them providing a correct response to the situation depicted on the game card. The game appeared to be an effective procedure for the teaching of social skills. The TBI patients not only increased their social skills during training, but these skills generalised to a natural setting (meal times in a residential setting). The improvements in social skill were evident across all six social skill components, as well as in both "actor" and "reactor" situations. Braunling-McMorrow et al. concluded by highlighting a number of advantages from using a "game" procedure for the training of social skills, but also highlighted the need for future studies to investigate the long-term maintenance of social skills learnt through playing board games.

Brotherton, Thomas, Wisotzek, and Milan (1988) used a multiple baseline across behaviours design to evaluate the impact of their social skills training programme with four severe TBI patients. The patients, 1 female and 3 males, were aged between 20 and 27 years and they had received their injuries at least 3 years prior to training. All patients were individually videotaped during both structured and unstructured social interactions with two confederates. Two raters then evaluated the patients' performance across six target behaviours (self-manipulation, posture, speech dysfluencies, personal attention, reinforcing feedback, and positive statements) to determine the training goals for each patient. After treatment, three patients showed improvement across some of the targeted behaviours, and these improvements generalised to other settings and were still evident at a one-year follow-up. Brotherton et al. noted that the patients' performance improved despite their cognitive impairments, although this improvement occurred for simple, motoric behaviours (e.g. self-manipulation, posture) rather than more complex verbal behaviours.

In a larger group study, Johnson and Newton (1987) reported the results from a 12-month social skill training programme. They used the same assessment procedures and patients as reported in Newton and Johnson (1985). The 10 TBI patients who completed the programme were initially assessed during a 5-minute conversation with a stranger, and 2 raters then evaluated the patients' performance on 3 global scales (performance, anxiety, and assertiveness) and 12 molecular scales measuring various aspects of verbal and non-verbal behaviour. The ratings from the molecular scales were combined to give a total performance score. The TBI patients were reassessed on the same measures following the completion of their group social skills training programme. No significant differences emerged between the pre- and post-treatment scores for the group as a whole. However, the authors pointed out that the group results masked the improvements made by some individual patients and, when the performance of the TBI patients was considered individually, over half the group had made some improvement in social performance.

In what is arguably the most methodologically sophisticated study to date, Flanagan, McDonald, and Togher (1995) evaluated the effectiveness of a social skills training programme with five males in the chronic stage following severe TBI. Pre-intervention assessment was undertaken using the six verbal scales of the revised BRISS (Farrell et al., 1985). The patients' performance during three naturalistic interactions with an opposite-sex stranger was rated on the BRISS scales by two postgraduate psychologists. Ratings from the initial interaction were used to develop individualised intervention plans for each of the five TBI patients. Following the three assessment interactions and the development of the intervention plans, the TBI patients took part in a three-month, group-based social skills training programme that allowed for each individual's specific deficits to be addressed. Therefore, although the programme was conducted in a group format, the goals for each individual were devised from the results of individualised assessments.

The social skills training programme consisted of weekly two-hour group sessions held over the three-month period (S. Flanagan, personal communication, February 1997). Components of the programme included instruction, modelling, role-play, feedback, and "homework" assignments. To allow for the patients' cognitive impairments sessions were heavily structured and involved simple, concrete language, repetition, frequent rest breaks, and a variety of activities. A system of non-verbal signals was taught and used throughout the training sessions to indicate to the patients when their behaviour was socially inappropriate. Role-plays were frequently videotaped and immediately replayed to facilitate the provision of feedback. In addition to practising specific social skills, patients were encouraged to attend to social cues provided by the social interaction partner and during modelling sessions the behaviour therapist would occasionally articulate their interpretation of the social cues being provided by the social interaction partner.

Finally, a post-intervention assessment was completed using the same procedure as for the three pre-intervention assessments. Despite the relatively large within-patient variability evident on some of the scales pre-intervention, one patient showed significant changes on three of the BRISS scales and this improvement in his social skills was confirmed by reports from independent sources. One other patient showed improvement on one of the BRISS scales. The authors commented that the use of global scales would compliment the effectiveness of the BRISS in detecting probable areas of behavioural change.

Overall, the Flanagan et al. (1995) study shows a number of significant improvements over the procedures used in Johnson and Newton's (1987) study. While both studies used behavioural observation as their primary assessment procedure, the intermediate level BRISS rating scale employed by Flanagan et al. allowed for the development of individualised social skills training programmes, and demonstrated that such individualised treatment programmes can still be delivered in the preferred group format. Use of the BRISS scales also allowed for the analysis of improvement in specific skill areas. Finally, the BRISS scales can be used to demonstrate change through either statistical analysis based on group data or through the examination of changes in an individual case. Which one of these two methodologies is best suited to evaluating the effects of social skills training programmes remains one of the issues that need to be addressed by researchers working in this area.

FUTURE DIRECTIONS

During the past decade, considerable advances have been made in the assessment of social skill following TBI. Current clinicians and researchers working in this area have an established and sound methodology with regard to the use of questionnaires, behavioural observation, and procedures to be followed when completing such assessments. However, the application of social skills training programmes to TBI populations is comparatively less advanced. Although the methodology for treating the behavioural disturbances that lead to anti-social behaviour is well established, the development and evaluation of effective programmes for the training of pro-social behaviour requires further research. Such research needs to address issues related to the appropriateness of the methodology used, the role of cognitive deficits, and the actual willingness of TBI patients to engage in social interaction.

Issues in assessment

Use of self-report methods

The use of questionnaires in assessment assumes that the respondents answer in a reliable manner. Early researchers cast doubt on the reliability of self-report methods when used with TBI patients, and advocated the more reliable nature of reports from the patients' caregivers (McKinlay & Brooks, 1984). There is also considerable evidence that some TBI patients may be unaware of their deficits (McGlynn, 1990) and that there can be significant variation in the level of agreement between patients and their caregivers on the problems and changes that follow TBI (Cavallo, Kay, & Ezrachi, 1992; Tepper, Beatty, & Dejong, 1996).

However, recent research has also demonstrated that TBI patients can reliably and validly report on their own social behaviour (Dodwell, 1988; Elsass & Kinsella, 1987; Marsh et al., 1990). Therefore, there continues to be a role for the reliable and valid use of self-report methods when assessing the social behaviour of TBI patients.

Use of observational methods by clinicians

There appears to be little doubt in the literature that the preferred means for assessing social skill is behavioural observation. The use of interview and questionnaire procedures undoubtedly adds to the comprehensiveness of any social skill assessment. However, such procedures do not provide sufficient information for an accurate assessment if they are used to the exclusion of behavioural observation. Despite the ready availability of video equipment, many practitioners working in clinical settings still seem to be of the opinion that behavioural observation is an assessment procedure that is costly, time consuming, and impractical. The idea seems to persist that such procedures are a luxury, only available in large, well-funded research institutions.

While acknowledging the practical difficulties associated with the use of behavioural observation in clinical settings, Foster, Bell-Dolan, and Burge (1988) have suggested six ways in which behavioural observation data can be made both easier to collect and more useful for the clinician. These comprise arranging the job setting to make observation easier, systematically observing in-session behaviour, integrating direct observation with other assessment methods, designing the observational system to suit its purpose, borrowing from pre-existing observational systems when relevant, and using participant observers. The adoption of such practices should increase the use of behavioural observation as an assessment method used by practising clinicians who wish to accurately and usefully assess the social skills of their TBI patients.

Procedural factors

One of the decisions that needs to be made when planning for the behavioural assessment of social skill is the type of setting in which the assessment will occur. The use of simulated, or naturalistic, settings appears to be most prominent in the recent literature. While *in vivo*, or real-life, settings may be preferred for demonstrating the generalisation of learnt skills, naturalistic observation appears adequate for the purposes of assessment and provides sufficient information to allow for the development of treatment programmes. Although role-play assessments may have a place in social skills assessment with TBI patients, recent evaluations of their validity and utility (e.g. Kern, 1994) have not been encouraging.

The assessment situations utilised by recent researchers in this area have included problem-solving interactions with a significant other, simulated job interviews, and heterosocial interactions with an opposite-sex stranger. Obviously, the nature of the research question that is being asked may determine to some extent the type of assessment situation that is appropriate. For an overall evaluation of social performance, however, the opposite-sex stranger interaction seems most useful. There is certainly a wealth of theoretical information available on heterosocial behaviour (e.g. Conger & Conger, 1982) to assist in the development of appropriate rating scales for such situations.

The type of rating scale used in the behavioural assessment of social skill is the final procedural issue that needs to be addressed by future researchers. The intermediate level scales have the advantage of providing sufficient information on the molecular components of behaviour to allow for the development of individualised training programmes, while at the same time providing the validity of measurement usually only found with the use of global scales. Despite some difficulties with the use of these scales (e.g. Flanagan et al., 1995), further development of such scales using either the behaviour analytic method (Goldfried & D'Zurilla, 1969) or the utility X generalisability decision approach (Curran & Mariotto, 1980) offers considerable promise for progress in this area. The behaviour analytic method assumes that the target of assessment is well defined and that it can be conceptualised in terms of problem solving. This method uses a five-step procedure of situation analysis, response enumeration, response evaluation, construction of instrument format, and instrument evaluation to develop a procedure for assessing an individual's ability to respond to problematic situations. The utility X generalisability decision approach to instrument development is concerned with the reliability of a measure across various aspects of the assessment situation such as raters and settings. The more aspects of the assessment situation that need to be taken into account, the greater the required utility of the instrument. Such utility is provided by establishing the reliability, or generalisability, of the instrument across a broad number of aspects of the assessment situation. This approach has been reflected in the development of new instruments in this area that, at least, report rater reliability in terms of generalisability coefficients (e.g. Linscott, Knight, & Godfrey, 1996).

Treatment issues

A methodology for demonstrating change

There are two different methodologies available for demonstrating the effectiveness of social skills training programmes with TBI patients. The issue is whether the group comparison approach and its associated use of inferential statistics, or the case study approach and the use of single case experimental designs is the most appropriate methodology to be used. The authors of the two studies that used the group comparison approach (Flanagan et al., 1995; Johnson & Newton, 1987) commented, however, that the evaluation of average group performance failed to demonstrate the significant change that occurred for some individuals.

It appears, therefore, that single case experimental designs may be the most useful methodology for assessing the results of social skill training programmes with TBI patients (Sunderland, 1990). The use of such procedures does not preclude the normative evaluation of outcome (e.g. Flanagan et al., 1995), and may be more readily adopted in a clinical setting than the complex statistical procedures (e.g. Gardner, 1993) that are available for research purposes.

The role of cognitive deficits

As described in McFall's (1982) model, one of the systems involved in socially skilful performance is the cognitive process of decoding incoming information, deciding the appropriate response, and encoding the correct behavioural expression of that response. Other models of social skill also emphasise the role of metacognitive, or information-processing, factors in socially skilled behaviour (Ylvisaker et al., 1992). Despite the high prevalence of a variety of cognitive deficits following TBI, only a small number of researchers have attempted to determine the relationship between deficits in cognitive functioning and the presence of deficits in social functioning. One possible reason for this may be that the identification of the cognitive deficits that result in impaired social performance does not necessarily result in improvements in the treatment procedures available for social skills training. Indeed the early promise offered by cognitive rehabilitation procedures has failed to be realised in practice (Benedict, 1989; Robertson, 1990), and the most useful approach to neuropsychological rehabilitation is proving to be the adoption of behavioural procedures (Peters & McLean, 1995).

However, the nature of the TBI patient's cognitive deficits can have substantial implications for their progress in behavioural social skills training programmes. Research has indicated that TBI patient's deficits in social skills are unrelated to either their general intellectual abilities (Marsh & Knight, 1991a; Newton & Johnson, 1985) or their deficits in speed of information processing and memory functioning (Marsh & Knight, 1991a). There is evidence, however, of a relationship between impairment in another class of cognitive functions—namely executive functions—and the level of social skill displayed by TBI patients.

Impaired executive functions are associated with damage to the frontal, particularly the prefrontal regions, of the brain. Alexander, Benson, and Stuss (1989) outlined 10 relatively distinct adult frontal lobe communication syndromes. Marsh and Knight (1991b) have shown that one form of these—decreased verbal fluency—is related to the level of social skill displayed by adult, severe TBI patients. The relationship between pragmatic language and executive dysfunction was explored in detail in Chapter 4. Further research examining the interaction between TBI patients' cognitive deficits and their level of social skill, more broadly defined, is clearly needed to further our understanding of the complex relationship between these two aspects of behaviour. Ylvisaker et al. (1992) have also highlighted the importance of establishing the relationship between cognitive impairment and decreased ability to correctly perceive and interpret social cues in TBI patients.

Other aspects of behaviour that are related to executive, or frontal lobe function, have also been found to be impaired in TBI patients (Hartman, Pickering, & Wilson 1992). This has important treatment implications given recent findings that TBI patients accurately report that they experience social isolation, but do not report being distressed or concerned by their lack of social contact (Elsass & Kinsella, 1987; Marsh et al., 1990). The TBI patients' failure to view their social isolation as problematic has obvious consequences for their willingness and motivation to complete social skills training programmes or behave in a skilful manner during social interaction. It is possible that the TBI patients' failure to be distressed by their social isolation is a further manifestation of a central executive deficit. Further research on the role of executive deficits in the social behaviour of TBI patients seems warranted.

Finally, the central role of verbal communication in establishing and maintaining social relationships (e.g. Ralph & Lee, 1994) and the consistent finding of pragmatic language deficits following TBI (e.g. McDonald, 1992; Sohlberg & Mateer, 1990) means that social skills training programmes, focusing on verbal skills, will continue to play a major role in the rehabilitation of the TBI patient. Further progress in this area is most likely to result from inter-disciplinary endeavours (e.g. Ylvisaker & Feeney, 1994). In this way, the devastating impact of that most enduring psychosocial consequence of TBI—social isolation—will be lessened.

REFERENCES

Alexander, M.P., Benson, D.F., & Stuss, D.T. (1989). Frontal lobes and language. *Brain and Language, 37,* 656–691.

Barlow, D.H., Abel, G.G., Blanchard, E.B., Bristow, A.R., & Young, L.D. (1977). A heterosocial skills behavior checklist for males. *Behavior Therapy, 8,* 229–239.

Bellack, A.S. (1979). Behavioural assessment of social skills. In A.S. Bellack & M. Hersen (Eds.), *Research and practice in social skills training* (pp.75–104). New York: Plenum.

Bellack, A.S. (1983). Recurrent problems in the behavioural assessment of social skill. *Behavior Research and Therapy, 21,* 29–41.

Benedict, R.H.B. (1989). The effectiveness of cognitive remediation strategies for victims of traumatic head-injury: A review of the literature. *Clinical Psychology Review, 9,* 605–626.

Boake, C. (1991). Social skills training following head injury. In J.S. Kreutzer & P.H. Wehman (Eds.), *Cognitive rehabilitation for persons with traumatic brain injury: A functional approach* (pp.181–189). Baltimore, MD: Paul H. Brookes.

Bond, F., & Godfrey, H.P.D. (1997). Conversation with traumatically brain-injured individuals: A controlled study of behavioural changes and their impact. *Brain Injury, 11,* 319–329.

Braunling-McMorrow, D., Lloyd, K., & Fralish, K. (1986). Teaching social skills to head-injured adults. *Journal of Rehabilitation, 52(1),* 39–44.

Brotherton, F.A., Thomas, L.L., Wisotzek, I.E., & Milan, M.A. (1988). Social skills training in the rehabilitation of patients with traumatic closed head injury. *Archives of Physical Medicine and Rehabilitation, 69,* 827–832.

Cavallo, M.M., Kay, T., & Ezrachi, O. (1992). Problems and changes after traumatic brain injury: Differing perceptions within and between families. *Brain Injury, 6,* 327–335.

Conger, J.C., & Conger, A.J. (1982). Components of heterosocial competence. In J.P. Curran & P.M. Monti (Eds.), *Social skills training: A practical handbook for assessment and treatment* (pp.313–347). New York: Guilford.

Curran, J.P. (1982). A procedure for the assessment of social skills: The Simulated Social Interaction Test. In J.P. Curran & P.M. Monti (Eds.), *Social skills training: A practical handbook for assessment and treatment* (pp.348–373). New York: Guilford.

Curran, J.P., Farrell, A.D., & Grunberger, A.J. (1984). Social skills: A critique and a rapprochement. In P. Trower (Ed.), *Radical approaches to social skills training* (pp.16–46). London: Croom Helm.

Curran, J.P., & Mariotto, M.J. (1980). A conceptual structure for the assessment of social skills. In M. Hersen, R.M. Eisler, & P.M. Miller (Eds.), *Progress in behavior modification* (Vol. 10, pp.1–37). New York: Academic Press.

Dodwell, D. (1988). The heterogeneity of social outcome following head injury. *Journal of Neurology, Neurosurgery, and Psychiatry, 51,* 833–838.

Eames, P., & Wood, R. (1985a). Rehabilitation after severe brain injury: A follow-up study of a behaviour modification approach. *Journal of Neurology, Neurosurgery, and Psychiatry, 48,* 613–619.

Eames, P., & Wood, R. (1985b). Rehabilitation after severe brain injury: A special-unit approach to behaviour disorders. *International Rehabilitation Medicine, 7,* 130–133.

Elsass, L., & Kinsella, G. (1987). Social interaction following severe closed head injury. *Psychological Medicine, 17,* 67–78.

Farrell, A.D., Rabinowitz, J.A., Wallander, J.L., & Curran, J.P. (1985). An evaluation of two formats for the intermediate-level assessment of social skill. *Behavioural Assessment, 7,* 155–171.

Fischer, J., & Corcoran, K. (1994). *Measures for clinical practice: A source book* (2nd ed.). New York: Free Press.

Flanagan, S., McDonald, S., & Togher, L. (1995). Evaluating social skills following traumatic brain injury: The BRISS as a clinical tool. *Brain Injury, 9,* 321–338.

Floyd, F.J., & Markman, H.J. (1984). An economical observational measure of couples' communication skill. *Journal of Consulting and Clinical Psychology, 52,* 97–103.

Foster, S.L., Bell-Dolan, D.J., & Burge, D.A. (1988). Behavioural observation. In A.S. Bellack & M. Hersen (Eds.), *Behavioural assessment: A practical handbook* (3rd ed., pp.119–160). New York: Pergamon.

Foxx, R.M., & McMorrow, M.J. (1983). *"Stacking the Deck": A social skills game for retarded adults.* Champaign, IL.: Research Press.

Gajar, A., Schloss, P.J., Schloss, C.N., & Thompson, C.K. (1984). Effects of feedback and self-monitoring on head trauma youth's conversation skills. *Journal of Applied Behavior Analysis, 17,* 353–358.

Gambrill, E.D., & Richey, C.A. (1975). An assertion inventory for use in assessment and research. *Behavior Therapy, 6,* 550–561.

Garcia, J. (1994). Behavior after a traumatic brain injury: Toward a classification based on three outcome categories. *Rehabilitation Education, 8,* 259–274.

Gardner, W. (1993). Hierarchical continuous-time sequential analysis: A strategy for clinical research. *Journal of Consulting and Clinical Psychology, 61,* 975–983.

Giles, G.M., Fussey, I., & Burgess, P. (1988). The behavioural treatment of verbal interaction skills following severe head injury: A single case study. *Brain Injury, 2,* 75–79.

Godfrey, H.P.D., & Knight, R.G. (1988). Memory training and behavioural rehabilitation of a severely head-injured adult. *Archives of Physical Medicine and Rehabilitation, 69,* 458–460.

Godfrey, H.P.D., Knight, R.G., & Bishara, S.N. (1991). The relationship between social skill and family problem-solving following very severe closed head injury. *Brain Injury, 5,* 207–211.

Godfrey, H.P.D., Knight, R.G., Marsh, N.V., Moroney, B., & Bishara, S.N. (1989). Social interaction and speed of information processing following very severe head injury. *Psychological Medicine, 19,* 175–182.

Godfrey, H.P.D., Marsh, N.V., & Partridge, F.M. (1987). Severe traumatic head injury and social behaviour: A review. *New Zealand Journal of Psychology, 16,* 49–57.

Godfrey, H.P.D., Partridge, F.M., Knight, R.G., & Bishara, S. (1993). Course of insight disorder and emotional dysfunction following closed head injury: A controlled cross-sectional follow-up study. *Journal of Clinical and Experimental Neuropsychology, 15,* 503–515.

Goldfried, M.R., & D'Zurilla, T.J. (1969). A behavior-analytic model for assessing competence. In C.D. Spielberger (Ed.), *Current topics in clinical and community psychology* (Vol. 1, pp.151–196). New York: Academic Press.

Gottman, J.M. (1979). *Marital interaction: Experimental investigations.* New York: Academic Press.

Grotevant, H.D., & Carlson, C.I. (1987). Family interaction coding systems: A descriptive review. *Family Process, 26,* 49–74.

Hargie, O., Saunders, C., & Dickson, D. (1994). *Social skills in interpersonal communication* (3rd ed.). London: Routledge.

Hartman, A., Pickering, R.M., & Wilson, B.A. (1992). Is there a central executive deficit after severe head injury? *Clinical Rehabilitation, 6,* 133–140.

Hersen, M., & Turner, S.M. (1994). *Diagnostic interviewing* (2nd ed.). New York: Plenum.

Hopewell, C.A., Burke, W.H., Weslowski, M., & Zawlocki, R. (1990). Behavioral learning therapies for the traumatically brain-injured patient. In R.L. Wood & I. Fussey (Eds.), *Cognitive rehabilitation in perspective* (pp.229–245). London: Taylor & Francis.

Horton, A.M., Jr., & Howe, N.R. (1981). Behavioural treatment of the traumatically brain-injured: A case study. *Perceptual and Motor Skills, 53,* 349–350.

Johnson, D.A., & Newton, A. (1987). Social adjustment and interaction after severe head injury: II. Rationale and bases for intervention. *British Journal of Clinical Psychology, 26,* 289–298.

Kanfer, F.H., & Goldstein, A.P. (1991). *Helping people change: A textbook of methods* (4th ed.). New York: Pergamon.

Kern, J.M. (1994). The use of role-plays in behavioural assessment. In M. Hersen, R.M. Eisler, & P.M. Miller (Eds.), *Progress in behavior modification* (Vol. 29, pp.73–97). Pacific Grove, CA: Brooks/Cole.

Kolko, D.J., & Milan, M.A. (1985). A woman's heterosocial skill observational rating system. *Behavior Modification, 9,* 165–192.

Lange, A.J., & Jakubowski, P. (1976). *Responsible assertive behavior: Cognitive/behavioural procedures for trainers.* Champaign, IL.: Research Press.

Levenson, R.W., & Gottman, J.M. (1978). Toward the assessment of social competence. *Journal of Consulting and Clinical Psychology, 46,* 453–462.

Lewis, F.D., Nelson, J., Nelson, C., & Reusink, P. (1988). Effects of three feedback contingencies on the socially inappropriate talk of a brain-injured adult. *Behavior Therapy, 19,* 203–211.

Linscott, R.J., Knight, R.G., & Godfrey, H.P.D. (1996). The Profile of Functional Impairment in Communication (PFIC): A measure of communication impairment for clinical use. *Brain Injury, 10,* 397–412.

Marsh, N.V., Kersel, D.A., Havill, J.H., & Sleigh, J.W. (1998). Caregiver burden at 6 months following severe traumatic brain injury. *Brain Injury, 12,* 225–238.

Marsh, N.V., & Knight, R.G. (1991a). Behavioural assessment of social competence following severe head injury. *Journal of Clinical and Experimental Neuropsychology, 13,* 729–740.

Marsh, N.V., & Knight, R.G. (1991b). Relationship between cognitive deficits and social skill after head injury. *Neuropsychology, 5,* 107–117.

Marsh, N.V., Knight, R.G., & Godfrey, H.P.D. (1990). Long-term psychosocial adjustment following very severe closed head injury. *Neuropsychology, 4,* 13–27.

Masters, J.C., Burish, T.G., Hollon, S.D., & Rimm, D.C. (1987). *Behavior therapy: Techniques and empirical findings* (3rd ed.). New York: Harcourt Brace Jovanovich.

McCormick, I.A. (1985). A simple version of the Rathus Assertiveness Schedule. *Behavioural Assessment, 7,* 95–99.

McDonald, S. (1992). Communication disorders following closed head injury: New approaches to assessment and treatment. *Brain Injury, 6,* 283–292.

McFall, R.M. (1982). A review and reformulation of the concept of social skills. *Behavioural Assessment, 4,* 1–33.

McGlynn, S.M. (1990). Behavioural approaches to neuropsychological rehabilitation. *Psychological Bulletin, 108,* 420–441.

McKinlay, W.W., & Brooks, D.N. (1984). Methodological problems in assessing psychosocial recovery following severe head injury. *Journal of Clinical Neuropsychology, 6,* 87–99.

Medin, D.L., & Ross, B.H. (1992). *Cognitive psychology.* New York: Harcourt Brace Jovanovich.

Meier, V.J., & Hope, D.A. (1998). Assessment of social skills. In A.S. Bellack & M. Hersen (Eds.), *Behavioural assessment: A practical handbook* (4th ed., pp.232–255). Needham Heights, MA: Allyn & Bacon.

Morton, M.V., & Wehman, P. (1995). Psychosocial and emotional sequelae of individuals with traumatic brain injury: A literature review and recommendations. *Brain Injury, 9,* 81–92.

Newton, A., & Johnson, D.A. (1985). Social adjustment and interaction after severe head injury. *British Journal of Clinical Psychology, 24,* 225–234.

Peters, M.D., Gluck, M., & McCormick, M. (1992). Behaviour rehabilitation of the challenging client in less restrictive settings. *Brain Injury, 6,* 299–314.

Peters, M.D., & McLean, A.Jr. (1995). The evolution of the clinician-scientist model of neurological rehabilitation. *Brain Injury, 9,* 543–552.

Peterson, D.R. (1968). *The clinical study of social behavior.* Englewood Cliffs, NJ: Prentice-Hall.

Ralph, A., & Lee, E. (1994). The effects of interpersonal verbal behaviour of varying participant role in initial dyadic conversations. *Scandinavian Journal of Behaviour Therapy, 23,* 155–175.

Robertson, I. (1990). Does computerized cognitive rehabilitation work? A review. *Aphasiology, 4,* 381–405.

Ruehlman, L.S., & Karoly, P. (1991). With a little flack from my friends: Development and preliminary validation of the Test of Negative Social Exchange (TENSE). *Psychological Assessment, 3,* 97–104.

Schiffrin, D. (1994). *Approaches to discourse.* Cambridge: Blackwell.

Schloss, P.J., Thompson, C.K., Gajar, A.H., & Schloss, C.N. (1985). Influence of self-monitoring on heterosexual conversational behaviors of head trauma youth. *Applied Research in Mental Retardation, 6,* 269–282.

Shelton, J.L., & Levy, R.L. (1981). *Behavioural assignments and treatment compliance: A handbook of clinical strategies.* Champaign, IL.: Research Press.

Slobin, D.I., Gerhardt, J., Kyratzis, A., & Guo, J. (1996). *Social interaction, social context, and language: Essays in honor of Susan Ervin-Tripp.* Mahwah, NJ.: Lawrence Erlbaum Associates.

Sohlberg, M.M., & Mateer, C.A. (1990). Evaluation and treatment of communicative skills. In J. S. Kreutzer & P. Wehman (Eds.), *Community integration following traumatic brain injury* (pp.67–83). Baltimore, MD: Paul H. Brookes.

Spence, S.E., Godfrey, H.P.D., Knight, R.G., & Bishara, S.N. (1993). First impressions count: A controlled investigation of social skill following closed head injury. *British Journal of Clinical Psychology, 32,* 309–318.

Spitzberg, B.H., & Cupach, W.R. (1989). *Handbook of interpersonal competence research.* New York: Springer-Verlag.

Stern, J.M., Melamed, S., Silberg, S., Rahmani, L., & Grosswasser, Z. (1985). Behavioral disturbances as an expression of severity of cerebral damage. *Scandinavian Journal of Rehabilitation Medicine, 17,* (Suppl 12), 36–41.

Stratton, M.C., & Gregory, R.J. (1994). After traumatic brain injury: A discussion of consequences. *Brain Injury, 8,* 631–645.

Summerfield, A.B. (1983). Recording social interaction. In P.W. Dowrick & S.J. Biggs (Eds.), *Using video* (pp.3–11). New York: Wiley.

Sunderland, A. (1990). Single-case experiments in neurological rehabilitation. *Clinical Rehabilitation, 4,* 181–192.

Tepper, S., Beatty, P., & Dejong, G. (1996). Outcomes in traumatic brain injury - self-report versus report of significant others. *Brain Injury, 10,* 575–581.

Trower, P. (1995). Adult social skills: State of the art and future directions. In W. O'Donohue & L. Krasner (Eds.), *Handbook of psychological skills training: Clinical techniques and applications* (pp.54–80). Boston, MA: Allyn & Bacon.

Trower, P., Bryant, B., & Argyle, M. (1978). *Social skills and mental health.* London: Methuen.

Turner, S.M., Hersen, M., & Bellack, A.S. (1978). Social skills training to teach pro-social behaviors in an organically impaired and retarded patient. *Journal of Behaviour Therapy and Experimental Psychiatry, 9,* 253–258.

Wallander, J.L., Conger, A.J., & Conger, J.C. (1985). Development and evaluation of a behaviorally referenced rating system for heterosocial skills. *Behavioural Assessment, 7,* 137–153.

Warren, N.J., & Gilner, F.H. (1978). Measurement of positive assertive behaviors: The behavioural test of tenderness expression. *Behavior Therapy, 9,* 178–184.

Watson, D., & Friend, R. (1969). Measurement of social-evaluative anxiety. *Journal of Consulting and Clinical Psychology, 33,* 448–457.

Whalley Hammell, K.R. (1994). Psychosocial outcome following severe closed head injury. *International Journal of Rehabilitation Research, 17,* 319–332.

Wilson, P.H., Spence, S.H., & Kavanagh, D.J. (1989). *Cognitive behavioural interviewing for adult disorders: A practical handbook.* London, UK: Routledge.

Wood, R.L. (1987). *Brain injury rehabilitation: A neurobehavioural approach.* London: Croom Helm.

Wood, R.L., & Eames, P. (1981). Application of behaviour modification in the rehabilitation of traumatically brain-injured patients. In G. Davey (Ed.), *Applications of conditioning theory* (pp.81–101). London: Methuen.

Ylvisaker, M., & Feeney, T.J. (1994). Communication and behavior: Collaboration between speech-language pathologists and behavioral psychologists. *Topics in Language Disorders, 15,* 37–54.

Ylvisaker, M., Feeney, T.J., & Szekeres, S.F. (1998). Social-environmental approach to communication and behavior. In M. Ylvisaker (Ed.), *Traumatic brain injury rehabilitation: Children and adolescents* (2nd ed., pp.271–302). Boston, MA: Butterworth-Heinemann.

Ylvisaker, M., Urbanczyk, B., & Feeney, T.J. (1992). Social skills following traumatic brain injury. *Seminars in Speech and Language, 13,* 308–322.

CHAPTER EIGHT

Dysarthria following traumatic brain injury

Bruce E. Murdoch and Deborah G. Theodoros
Motor Speech Research Unit, Department of Speech Pathology and Audiology, University of Queensland, Brisbane, Australia

Dysarthria constitutes one of the most persistent sequelae of severe traumatic brain injury (TBI), often remaining beyond the resolution of any concomitant language disorder (Najenson, Sazbon, Fiselzon, Becker, & Schechter, 1978; Sarno & Levin, 1985). Despite this recognition, the literature relating to the prevalence and natural course of post-TBI dysarthria is unclear. Depending on factors such as the measures used, the stage post-injury when the measures were taken, the population studied, etc., estimates of the prevalence of dysarthria following TBI vary from 8–100% (Dresser, Meirowsky, Weiss, McNeel, Simon, & Caveness, 1973; Groher, 1977; Rusk, Block, & Lowmann, 1969; Sarno, Buonaguro, & Levita, 1986). Rusk et al. (1969) reported that approximately one-third of 96 survivors of severe TBI exhibited dysarthria during the acute phase of their recovery. Sarno et al. (1986) observed dysarthria in 34% of their 124 subjects with severe TBI. This was recently corroborated by Olver, Ponsford, and Curran (1996) who also reported that motor speech problems were evident in 34% of their 103 severe TBI subjects 5 years post-injury. Two separate long-term follow-up studies of children who had suffered severe TBI indicated that 10% of children and 8% of adolescents were unintelligible (Ylvisaker, 1986). In a study of 14 TBI patients, Groher (1977) noted that all demonstrated dysarthria shortly after regaining consciousness.

One frequently observed feature of the dysarthria following TBI is the persistent nature of the disorder. In a follow-up study of 40 severe TBI cases, Thomsen (1984) reported that all 15 subjects who exhibited dysarthria in the acute stage (approximately 4 months post-injury) continued to demonstrate dysarthria 10–15 years later. Rusk et al. (1969) noted that, of their original 30 TBI subjects diagnosed as dysarthric, half of those subjects remained unimproved 5–15 years later. The remaining 50%, however, had made significant improvements in speech production. Such findings suggest that the prognosis for complete resolution of the dysarthric speech disturbance in individuals with severe TBI is poor (Hartley & Levin, 1990). Despite the often persistent and resilient nature of dysarthria post-TBI, however, the findings of several studies suggest that restoration of functional verbal communication is possible in TBI cases many years post-injury, and certainly long after the accepted period of "neurological recovery" has passed (Beukelman & Garrett, 1988; Enderby & Crow, 1990; Workinger & Netsell, 1992).

The presence of a persistent dysarthria has important implications for the long-term quality of life of survivors of severe TBI. As pointed out by Beukelman and Yorkston (1991), the presence of such a disorder reduces the individual's ability to function in communication situations that require understandable, efficient, and natural sounding speech (e.g. public speaking, vocational positions that require independent interaction with the public, etc.). In its most severe form, the dysarthria may necessitate the use of alternative and/or augmentative communication systems to bypass the impaired speech production apparatus. Put simply, the presence of a dysarthria may impede the successful return of the affected TBI patient to study, work or general social activities, leading to loss of vocational standing and social isolation.

Despite the persistent nature of dysarthria in TBI and its potentially devastating social and economic impact on the lives of many survivors of TBI, very little research into its nature and severity has been reported. In particular, until recently there has been a conspicuous lack of research into the physiological bases of the motor breakdown in the various major components of the speech production mechanisms of TBI subjects. Most reports in the literature have included only clinical descriptions of the speech disturbances, single case studies, or physiological investigations of small groups of TBI cases. Kent, Netsell, and Bauer (1975) in a cinefluorographic study and Lehiste (1965) in an acoustic analysis provided case studies of dysarthria following TBI that detailed deficits in lingual movement, slow rate and incoordination in articulatory activity. Detailed physiological investigations of the functioning of the speech mechanism in survivors of TBI with dysarthria have yet to be reported. Because physiological assessment of the individual motor subsystems of the speech mechanism (i.e. respiratory, laryngeal, velopharyngeal, and articulatory subsystems) is crucial in defining the underlying speech motor pathophysiology necessary for the development of optimal treatment programmes (Abbs & De Paul, 1989; Netsell, 1986), further research of this type is necessary. In one of the few systematic attempts to address this area, a series of perceptual and physiological studies by Theodoros and colleagues (Murdoch, Theodoros, Stokes, & Chenery, 1993; Theodoros & Murdoch, 1994: Theodoros, Murdoch, & Chenery, 1994; Theodoros, Murdoch, & Stokes, 1995; Theodoros, Murdoch, Stokes & Chenery, 1993) provide some insights and will be detailed in the following sections.

SEVERITY AND TYPE OF DYSARTHRIA FOLLOWING TBI

Examination of the literature reveals wide variability in the severity and type of dysarthria reported to occur in association with TBI, with the severity covering the entire spectrum of dysfunction from mild articulatory imprecision through to total unintelligibility (Sarno et al., 1986). Consistent with the multi-focal nature of the brain damage associated with TBI and, depending on the specific site of the lesion, a number of different types of dysarthria have been reported to occur following TBI (Theodoros et al., 1994). As would be expected based on the pathophysiology of TBI, the majority of dysarthric TBI patients exhibit a mixed form of dysarthria reflecting involvement of multiple motor systems, with a preponderance of spastic and ataxic features (Theodoros et al., 1994). In an investigation of the perceptual speech characteristics of 27 TBI subjects with dysarthria, Theodoros et al. (1994) identified the presence of 4 specific types of dysarthria (spastic, hypokinetic, ataxic, and flaccid) and 4 mixed dysarthrias (spastic-ataxic, spastic-hypokinetic, spastic-flaccid, and flaccid-ataxic). Marquardt, Stoll, and Sussman (1990) suggested that the most frequently occurring form of dysarthria post-TBI is spastic dysarthria, characterised by imprecise articulation, harsh voice quality, reduced stress, monopitch, and monoloudness. Spastic dysarthria was also observed by Theodoros et al. (1994) to be one of the most frequently occurring components of the mixed dysarthrias exhibited by their TBI patients but only occurring in 3 (11%) cases in isolation. Spastic dysarthria is generally regarded as resulting from bilateral upper motor neurone lesions (Murdoch, 1990). According to Marquardt et al. (1990), spastic dysarthria following TBI usually occurs in conjunction with spastic quadriplegia.

Damage to the bulbar cranial nerve nuclei within the brain stem or to the bulbar cranial nerves in their peripheral course (due to either direct insult and/or the shearing effects of acceleration/deceleration in TBI) leads to flaccid dysarthria. Depending on which particular cranial nerves/nuclei are damaged, the characteristics of the flaccid dysarthria will vary, however, nasal emission, hypernasality, breathiness and consonant imprecision are features of flaccid dysarthria frequently reported in TBI cases. Theodoros et al. (1994) identified flaccid dysarthria in 4 (15%) of their TBI cases in isolation and as part of a mixed dysarthria in 3 other TBI cases.

Some authors have reported the dysarthria evidenced in their TBI cases to be predominantly of the ataxic type (Simmons, 1983), a condition usually associated with generalised damage to the cerebellum or its connections in the brain stem. In support of these findings, Theodoros et al. (1994) identified the features of ataxic dysarthria in the speech of approximately 41% of their TBI group. The most frequently occurring form of dysarthria reported by Theodoros et al. (1994) was mixed spastic-ataxic, occurring in 30% of their subjects. Excess and equal stress, irregular articulatory breakdown, distorted vowels, and a harsh voice quality are commonly reported features of ataxic dysarthria (Darley, Aronson, & Brown, 1975).

Although less common, hypokinetic and hyperkinetic dysarthria may also occur in TBI patients, reflecting damage to the extrapyramidal pathways in the region of the basal ganglia and upper brain stem nuclei (Murdoch, 1990). Theodoros et al. (1994) reported that 4 of their 27 dysarthric TBI subjects exhibited hypokinetic dysarthria, with a further 3 subjects demonstrating mixed spastic-hypokinetic dysarthria.

Perceptual features of dysarthria following TBI

The perceptual features of dysarthria following TBI encompass a broad range of abnormal speech features involving all aspects of the speech production process. Abnormal speech features reported to be exhibited by TBI patients include imprecise articulation, phonatory weakness, reduced pitch and loudness variation, hypernasality, a slow or rapid rate of speech, and excessively increased or decreased loudness (Ylvisaker, 1992).

The most frequently occurring deviant speech dimensions identified by Theodoros et al. (1994) in 27 severe TBI cases included disturbances of prosody, resonance, articulation, and respiration, with those deviant speech dimensions pertaining to phonation being less apparent in the speech output of their cases. Abnormal prosodic features noted to be present by Theodoros et al. (1994) included impaired rate (70% of TBI subjects exhibited a reduction in rate, while 30% of subjects demonstrated an increased rate of speech), rate fluctuations, short rushes of speech, reduced variation of pitch and loudness, impaired maintenance of loudness, unsteadiness of pitch, excess and equal stress, reduced phrase length, and prolonged inter-word and/or inter-syllable intervals. The deviant prosodic features reported by Theodoros et al. (1994) are consistent with those observed in the speech of TBI subjects by other researchers (Bellaire, Yorkston, & Beukelman, 1986; Vogel & von Cramon, 1983; Yorkston, Beukelman, Minifie, & Sapir, 1984; Ziegler, Hoole, Hartmann & von Cramon, 1988).

Disorders of resonance, in particular hypernasality, have frequently been observed clinically in the speech of individuals following TBI, and the prevalence of this disorder was confirmed by Theodoros et al. (1994) who reported that their TBI dysarthric subjects exhibited greater levels of nasality and mixed nasality than non-speech impaired controls with 26/27 or 96% of their subjects exhibiting hypernasality. Resonatory disturbances have also been reported in several case studies of TBI individuals (McHenry, Wilson, & Minton, 1994; Workinger & Netsell, 1992).

Articulatory imprecision is another major component of dysarthria following TBI. Theodoros et al. (1994) found consonant imprecision to be present in 26 (i.e. 96%) of their 27 TBI cases with dysarthria and was the most discriminating deviant speech feature for differentiating TBI subjects from normal controls. An increase in the length of phonemes and distortion of vowels was also present in the speech output of 75% of these TBI subjects.

Certain perceptual characteristics of the speech output of TBI patients with dysarthria also indicate that the majority of these cases have inadequate respiratory support for speech production. Theodoros et al. (1994) reported that 24/27 (88%) of their TBI cases were perceived to exhibit insufficient supply and/or control of expiratory air flow to enable them to phrase correctly and maintain adequate pitch and volume control during speech.

Individual case studies of TBI subjects have indicated the presence of weak, breathy phonation in some subjects (McHenry et al., 1994; Netsell & Daniel, 1979), whereas other patients have presented with strained-strangled vocal quality (Workinger & Netsell, 1992). The perceptual analysis of phonation in TBI patients reported by Theodoros et al. (1994) indicated that the deviant phonatory features of hoarseness, harshness, and intermittent breathiness were more evident in 81%, 48%, and 46% of the TBI subjects respectively, compared with normal speaking controls.

Overall, the intelligibility of TBI subjects with dysarthria has been reported to be significantly reduced compared with matched controls in relation to single word and sentence intelligibility, rate of intelligible speech, and communication efficiency (Theodoros et al., 1994). The reduction in intelligibility appears to be the result of the combined effects of deficits in all five aspects of speech, namely prosody, articulation, resonance, respiration, and phonation.

Acoustic features of dysarthria following TBI

To date, the acoustic characteristics of dysarthria associated with TBI have been poorly defined. By far the majority of studies have only involved single cases, or at best only small groups of TBI patients. Further, in many reported studies, the acoustic features of the speech of TBI patients have been reported in conjunction with acoustic features of other neurologically disordered groups (e.g. cerebrovascular accident cases) making it impossible to identify the specific acoustic anomalies attributable to TBI. Those acoustic studies that have been reported have identified disorders in the areas of articulation, prosody, and phonation post-TBI.

Acoustic features indicative of articulatory disorders identified by Ziegler and von Cramon (1983a, b, 1986) included centralisation of vowel formants (leading to vowel reduction and distortion), articulatory undershoot on lip rounding and protrusion, lingual undershoot, increased word and syllable durations, inadequate voicing, spirantisation (i.e. frication of stop gaps due to incomplete constriction), evidence of tongue retraction, and the presence of slow, large amplitude cycles in formant trajectories, indicating slow, exaggerated protrusions and retractions of the tongue. Prosodic disturbances identified by way of acoustic analysis in a single TBI case with ataxic dysarthria by Simmons (1983) included changes in fundamental frequency contour as well as alterations in the temporal aspects of speech and articulatory gestures. Specifically, Simmons (1983) identified the presence of a flat fundamental frequency contour and the lack of high frequency energy in the vowel formants, consistent with the perceptual qualities of monotonous and unnatural speech. Alterations in the temporal aspects of speech identified by Simmons (1983) using temporal acoustic measures included equal syllable duration with no variation in pause time, consistent with a speech pattern of excess and equal stress. Simmons (1983) also observed syllable durations in this TBI case to be longer than normal.

In an evaluation of the phonatory function of 24 subjects with central dysphonia (18 subjects with TBI), Hartmann and von Cramon (1984) identified specific acoustic features associated with "breathy", "rough", and "tense" vocal qualities. Increased time lag of pre-exhalation and spectral energy above 5kHz typified "breathy" vocal quality, while increased fundamental frequency perturbation (jitter), especially in males, was characteristic of "rough" voice quality. An increase in spectral energy in the 1–5kHz range as well as increased variance of spectral energy above 5kHz was associated with "tense" vocal quality.

Physiological features of dysarthria following TBI

Little research has been directed at defining the pathophysiological bases of dysarthric speech disturbance in TBI subjects. With the exception of the series of studies reported by Theodoros and colleagues noted earlier, most reports in the literature have been confined to case studies (McHenry et al., 1994; Netsell & Daniel, 1979; Netsell, Lotz, & Barlow, 1989; Workinger & Netsell, 1992).

Physiological assessment of the respiratory function of persons following TBI has identified impaired lung volumes and abnormal chest wall movements during speech breathing. McHenry et al. (1994), using respiratory inductance plethysmography, identified reduced inspiratory volume (11% of vital capacity) in a traumatically brain-injured woman with flaccid dysarthria. Spirometric and kinematic assessment of the respiratory function of 20 severe TBI subjects conducted by Murdoch et al. (1993) using strain-gauge pneumographs revealed the presence of (1) significantly reduced lung capacities (i.e. vital capacity (VC) and forced expiratory volume in one second (FEV[SUB]1) compared with those of matched controls and (2) abnormalities in the two-part coordination of the chest wall, involving the rib cage and abdomen, during expiration.

Physiological assessments have demonstrated contrasting patterns of laryngeal function in TBI patients with the findings of some studies suggestive of hypofunction and others, hyperfunctional patterns. Netsell and Daniel (1979), in a single case study of a severe TBI person, recorded high glottal air flows consistent with hypoadduction of the vocal folds, compared with normative data (Iwata, von Leden, & Williams, 1972). Using a pneumotachometer and differential transducer attached to a face mask, Netsell et al. (1989) recorded considerably higher laryngeal air flow during vowel production for a TBI subject with dysarthric speech compared with a normal individual. Netsell et al. (1989) inferred from these results that the dysarthric speaker demonstrated problems with rapid abduction and adduction of the vocal folds, in addition to inefficient vocal fold adduction in the midline. Similarly, McHenry et al. (1994) recorded laryngeal aerodynamic data consistent with a hypofunctioning larynx in an 18-year-old female following a severe TBI. Specifically, the subject recorded low subglottal pressures and laryngeal resistance values in conjunction with high air flows.

In contrast, Theodoros and Murdoch (1994) identified hyperfunctional laryngeal activity as the predominate form of laryngeal dysfunction in a group of TBI subjects, with five different patterns of laryngeal hyperfunction being identified. Hyperfunctional vocal fold vibratory patterns and aerodynamic characteristics, such as increased fundamental frequency, decreased duty cycle and closing time, increased glottal resistance and subglottal pressure, and reduced phonatory air flow and ad/abduction rate of the vocal folds, were evident in the instrumental findings, but never altogether in the one subject (Theodoros & Murdoch, 1994). Statistical analysis identified five subgroups of TBI subjects with varying degrees and combinations of hyperfunctional laryngeal features. It was suggested by Theodoros and Murdoch (1994) that the hyperfunctional laryngeal activity identified in their subjects could be accounted for by both diffuse cortical and subcortical neuronal damage that is commonly sustained in TBI and that would account for bilateral lesions of the upper motor neurones and corticobulbar fibre tracts resulting in spasticity of the laryngeal musculature. Furthermore, Theodoros and Murdoch (1994) proposed that the different manifestations of hyperfunctional laryngeal activity reflected a combination of the various glottal and respiratory force adjustments deployed by the individual subjects in response to spasticity in the vocal folds and strategies to compensate for impairment in other subsystems of the speech production mechanism.

Velopharyngeal incompetence is a prominent physiological characteristic of the dysarthric speech disturbance associated with TBI. Several individual case studies have identified velopharyngeal dysfunction in traumatically brain-injured persons with dysarthric speech (McHenry et al., 1994; Netsell & Daniel, 1979; Netsell et al., 1989; Workinger & Netsell, 1992). Essentially, these studies identified high nasal air flows and nasalance values, in addition to reduced velopharyngeal resistance and intraoral pressures (McHenry et al., 1994; Netsell et al., 1989). McHenry et al. (1994) reported the findings of an increased nasalance score (50%), reduced velopharyngeal resistance, increased nasal air flow and a reduced intraoral pressure in their severely brain-injured case. Similarly, Netsell et al. (1989) identified the presence of a very high nasal air flow with a concomitant reduction in intraoral pressure in a TBI person during the production of the word "pamper", indicating that the subject failed to close the velopharynx for the /p/ segment following the nasal /m/.

Confirmation of the frequent occurrence of velopharyngeal dysfunction in the TBI population has been provided by a group study in which an indirect instrumental assessment of velopharyngeal competency was performed on 20 dysarthric TBI subjects and their matched controls (Theodoros et al., 1993). The results of this study revealed significantly increased nasality, based on a nasality index across non-nasalised utterances, in the speech output of TBI subjects compared with the controls. The findings were suggestive of impaired functioning of the velopharyngeal valve.

Physiological deficits in the articulatory components of the speech mechanism, such as the lips, tongue, and jaw, have also been reported in brain-injured individuals. Kent et al. (1975), in an early case study of a person with dysarthria following head trauma, identified a reduction in the ranges of lingual mobility, restrictions in the direction of tongue movements, and a slow rate of articulation, using cineradiographic techniques. Several aspects of lip force control such as peak force overshoot, force stability during the hold phase of muscle contraction, and the rate of force recruitment have also been found to be significantly impaired in TBI subjects (Barlow & Burton, 1988, 1990; Barlow & Netsell, 1989). In addition, greater force impairment of the lower lip compared with the upper lip, and a relationship between deficits in lip force control and the magnitude of the target force have been identified in this population (Barlow & Netsell, 1989). Barlow and Burton (1990), in applying a ramp-and-hold force paradigm in a preliminary investigation to assess the upper and lower lips of four TBI adults with dysarthric speech, identified a degree of force control impairment affecting one or both lips in each subject with considerable individual variation in the manifestation of this impairment. Using a similar ramp-and-hold task, McHenry et al. (1994) identified an impaired ability to rapidly recruit lingual force when attempting to reach a target level in a severely brain-injured subject. Furthermore, the subject demonstrated reduced maximum voluntary forces for the upper and lower lips and the tongue. In another single case study of a TBI subject with mild spastic-flaccid dysarthria, Robin, Somodi, and Luschei (1991) assessed the tongue strength of the subject on a maximum tongue pressure task and found that the TBI subject produced a weaker maximum tongue pressure compared with a matched control subject. Theodoros, Murdoch, and Stokes (1995) also identified significant impairment of lip and tongue function in a group of 18 TBI subjects with dysarthric speech, based on strength, endurance, and rate measures. Overall, the study indicated the presence of a slightly greater degree of impairment in tongue function compared with lip function.

The differing degrees of impairment of lip and tongue function are consistent with previous reports of differential subsystem impairment in dysarthric speakers (Abbs, Hunker, & Barlow, 1983; Hunker, Abbs, & Barlow, 1982). The findings highlight the importance of assessing each functional component of the speech mechanism independently in TBI patients, to accurately define the nature of the underlying pathophysiological deficits of the perceived articulatory disorder.

SUMMARY OF DYSARTHRIA FOLLOWING TBI

Consistent with the diffuse nature of the pathology following TBI, a wide array of deviant perceptual, acoustic, and physiological characteristics have been identified by the limited number of investigations of dysarthria post-TBI reported to date. Although the few physiological investigations that have been reported do provide a rudimentary profile of the functioning of the speech mechanism in TBI patients, the high inter-subject variability reported makes interpretation of their findings difficult. Further physiological studies using larger subject numbers are needed to more clearly define the nature and severity of the physiological breakdown in the various components of the speech production apparatus of survivors of TBI. Only then will it be possible to determine appropriate strategies for the treatment of dysarthria following TBI using objective, physiological techniques as suggested by Murdoch (1996).

Finally, the heterogeneity of the speech impairments manifest in persons following TBI necessitates the need for clinicians to develop individualised treatment programmes for each case. These programmes should be based as far as possible on the findings of comprehensive physiological analyses of the functioning of the various subcomponents of the speech production apparatus in combination with appropriate perceptual and acoustic measures of the client's speech output.

TREATMENT OF DYSARTHRIA ASSOCIATED WITH TBI

Clinically, recovery from a dysarthric speech disturbance following TBI has been found to be a variable and unpredictable process. Indeed, some TBI individuals have been reported to maintain severe dysarthric speech impairments over a long periods of time post-injury, whereas others have exhibited varying degrees and rates of improvement in speech production abilities following the initial brain damage (Netsell & Lefkowitz, 1992). Although dysarthria following TBI is noted for its resilience, the majority of TBI cases retain at least some degree of potential with respect to rehabilitation of speech function. Indeed, several case studies reported in the literature have demonstrated that intervention can be very effective in restoring functional speech, long after the acute and short-term rehabilitation periods have ceased (Beukelman & Garrett, 1988; Light, Beesley, & Collier, 1988; McHenry et al, 1994; Workinger & Netsell, 1992). Such findings suggest that, where possible, clinicians should provide ongoing, albeit, intermittent treatment in the long term, to establish functional communication for dysarthric speakers following TBI (Enderby & Crow, 1990).

The aim of intervention for TBI individuals with dysarthria is to develop early and effective communication skills by enhancing physiological support for speech and teaching compensatory speech behaviours (Beukelman & Yorkston, 1991; Caligiuri & Murry, 1983; Rosenbek & LaPointe, 1991). Several different therapy approaches, including behavioural, instrumental, prosthetic, surgical, and augmentative and alternative communication (AAC) techniques have been utilised in the treatment of the dysarthric speech disturbance in the head-injured population (Kearns & Simmons, 1990). The following sections provide a summary of a number of treatment techniques, relating to each subsystem of the speech production mechanism, that have been used successfully with TBI patients with dysarthria or, alternatively, have the potential to be beneficial to this clinical population. Due to the differential, multi-subsystem impairment evident in TBI individuals, the importance of developing flexible, hierarchial treatment plans that allow for the simultaneous and/or sequential treatment of particular subsystems is emphasised in this population. In general, the treatment of these patients requires a combination of strategies and techniques that are selected on an individual basis.

Treatment of respiratory dysfunction

Based on previous findings (McHenry et al., 1994; Murdoch et al., 1993), it would appear that the remediation of respiratory deficits in TBI individuals should involve techniques to improve reduced lung volumes and abnormal control of respiratory muscles during speech breathing. As suggested by Beukelman and Yorkston (1991), however, techniques designed to increase primary physiological support may be restricted to the severely dysarthric patient rather than the moderately severe speaker who would seem to benefit more from treating speech as an integrated activity rather than focusing on exercises to improve a specific component of respiratory function.

Undoubtedly, one of the simplest and most effective behavioural techniques used in the treatment of respiratory impairment is modification of posture to avoid a slumped shoulder position that restricts rib cage and abdominal movement. In addition, simplified information and instruction regarding the normal process of respiration, and improving the patient's self-monitoring of their own respiratory patterns have been found clinically to be important prerequisites to further treatment. Netsell and Hixon (1992) found that a behavioural technique known as "inspiratory checking" was effective in increasing breath support and control for speech in head-injured patients. Essentially, the technique requires the patient to inhale deeply and then "let the air out slowly", which capitalises on the passive recoil pressures of the lungs and forces the patient to use the inspiratory muscle forces in order to maintain a relatively constant subglottal air pressure. The Accent Method (Kotby, 1995), a behavioural technique that involves rhythmic breathing exercises designed to assist voicing control, has also been found to be effective with patients with dysarthria (Shimizu, Watanabe, & Hirose, 1992). Although the primary aim of therapy is to maximise respiratory support and control for speech in most cases, the majority of TBI patients will derive additional speech benefits from using compensatory techniques such as altering breath phrase length and varying breath patterning. In addition to behavioural techniques, some TBI patients may require prosthetic devices such as an abdominal binder, overhead slings, and an expiratory "board" attached to a wheelchair (Rosenbek and LaPointe, 1991) to support expiratory muscles during speech. A number of instrumental techniques have been developed to provide the dysarthric patient with feedback of physiological parameters of respiratory function such as subglottal pressure and chest wall movements. Netsell and Daniel (1979) reported the successful use of a U-tube manometer (as described by Rosenbek & LaPointe, 1991), to train a severely head-injured patient with flaccid dysarthria to generate and sustain air pressures within the range for normal speech (5 cm H[SUB]2O for 5 seconds). Following 8 20-minute sessions, the patient was able to generate 10 cm H[SUB]2O for 10 seconds. Respiratory kinematic instrumentation has also been used to provide feedback to TBI patients concerning the movements and coordination of the chest wall and lung volumes during speech and non-speech breathing tasks. Murdoch, Sterling, Theodoros, and Stokes (1995), while examining the efficacy of both behavioural and kinematic biofeedback-based therapy techniques for two TBI mixed dysarthria speakers, found that the biofeedback techniques were more effective in achieving greater and more consistent changes in respiratory parameters than the behavioural techniques. Similarly, Yorkston, Beukelman, and Bell (1988) found that displaying feedback of the patient's respiratory-phonatory timing via a Respitrace (Ambulatory Monitoring, Inc.) signal together with a raw acoustic waveform was an effective means of creating an improvement in this respiratory feature.

Treatment of laryngeal dysfunction

As TBI patients have been found to exhibit either hyperfunctional (Theodoros & Murdoch, 1994) or hypofunctional laryngeal behaviour (McHenry et al., 1994; Netsell & Daniel, 1979), and possible phonatory instability and incoordination, specific treatment techniques for the management of these abnormal laryngeal manifestations need to be carefully selected and implemented. The major treatment approaches for the management of laryngeal dysfunction in TBI patients include behavioural and instrumental techniques with the possible use of prosthetic compensatory devices such as voice amplifiers (Yorkston et al., 1988). Surgical intervention, involving the reduction or enhancement of vocal fold adduction, to create a more suitable laryngeal valving mechanism may be advocated in specific cases (Blitzer, Brin, Fahn, & Lovelace, 1988; Dedo & Izdebski, 1983; Facs & Beery, 1986; Ford, Martin, & Warner, 1984).

A range of behavioural techniques are used with TBI patients to reduce hyperadduction of the vocal folds. These methods include tension reduction techniques such as the chewing method, the yawn-sigh approach, and gentle voice onsets (Boone, 1977; Froeschels, 1952). Smitheran and Hixon (1981) suggested phonating at a high lung volume which results in passive abduction of the vocal folds and reduced hyperadductory vocal fold activity. In contrast, therapy techniques for hypoadduction of the vocal folds are designed to maximise vocal fold adduction through increased physiological effort. These techniques include isometric exercises (pushing and pulling), the production of hard glottal attack, postural adjustment of the head (e.g. turn head to affected side to decrease distance between vocal folds), and use of higher pitch (Aronson, 1985; Boone, 1977; Colton & Casper, 1996). A recent technique, the Lee Silverman Voice Treatment (LSVT) programme, originally designed to address the hypoadduction of the vocal folds associated with Parkinson's disease, has the potential to be effective in the treatment of TBI patients with hypofunctional laryngeal behaviour, with its focus on an intensive, high effort, voice treatment (Ramig, Bonitati, Lemke, & Horii, 1994). McHenry et al. (1994) utilised a similar approach to the LSVT in their management of the laryngeal function of a young head-injured person. Phonatory stability in TBI patients may be improved through the use of techniques such as initiating phonation at the beginning of exhalation (Yorkston et al., 1988), maximum duration vowel phonation (Ramig, Mead, & DeSanto, 1988), frequent inhalations, and the production of fewer syllables on exhalation (Linebaugh, 1983; Ramig & Scherer, 1989). Phonatory incoordination may be effectively addressed using the Accent Method (Kotby, 1995) because this technique is designed to create an appropriate balance between expiration and vocal fold muscle power.

Instrumental or biofeedback techniques for the treatment of laryngeal dysfunction in TBI cases involve the use of instruments that display vocal parameters such as pitch, vocal intensity, and duration. Such instruments include the VisiPitch (Yorkston et al., 1988), the VisiSpeech (Johnson & Pring, 1990), the Speech Viewer (Bougle, Ryall, & Le Dorze, 1995), the storage oscilloscope (Berry & Goshorn, 1983; Caligiuri & Murry, 1983), and transducers that monitor phonatory air flow and air pressure. Using visual feedback of air flow, Netsell and Daniel (1979) reported a marked reduction in air flow in a TBI patient with flaccid dysarthria, resulting in a 25% increase in vocal loudness. For those TBI patients with hyperadduction of the vocal folds, electromyographic (EMG) feedback of laryngeal muscle tension may prove to be of assistance in these cases (Prosek, Montgomery, Walden, & Schwartz, 1978).

Treatment of velopharyngeal dysfunction

TBI patients with velopharyngeal dysfunction may benefit from four types of approaches to the management of velopharyngeal dysfunction, namely behavioural, prosthetic, instrumental, and surgical. The behavioural and instrumental approaches are mainly applied to patients with mild to moderate velopharyngeal dysfunction while the more severe forms of impairment require prosthetic and/or surgical intervention. For the TBI patients who are able to achieve adequate velopharyngeal closure inconsistently, and present with mild to moderate hypernasality, behavioural therapy is generally directed towards increasing articulatory precision (Rosenbek & LaPointe, 1991), maintaining adequate oral resonance (Moncur & Brackett, 1974), and controlling rate of speech to ensure greater articulatory precision and velopharyngeal closure (Yorkston & Beukelman, 1981).

Although a number of instrumental techniques have been developed to provide visual feedback of velar movements, only a few remain clinically useful for the treatment of velopharyngeal dysfunction in patients with TBI. The Nasometer (Kay Elemetrics), a commonly used clinical tool, may be used as a biofeedback instrument providing visual feedback of levels of "nasalance" produced during speech. Similarly, nasal accelerometry in which miniature accelerometers positioned on the side of the nose and throat detect vibrations of sound, can provide the TBI patient with visual feedback of increased or decreased nasal vibrations during speech (Stevens, Kalikow, & Willemain, 1975). Electromyographic (EMG) biofeedback techniques have also been used in the treatment of velopharyngeal impairment in individuals following TBI. Draizar (1984) reported on the effectiveness of this technique in improving velar function in a TBI patient, after two to three therapy sessions per week for a month.

In addition to the use of biofeedback instrumentation for the treatment of velopharyngeal dysfunction, another instrumental technique, continuous positive airway pressure (CPAP) therapy, has been developed recently to exercise and strengthen the soft palate (Kuehn, 1991; Kuehn & Wachtel, 1994; Liss, Kuehn, & Hinkle, 1994). An air pressure flow device, which delivers positive air pressure to the nasal cavities via a hose and mask assembly, creates resistance against which the soft palate muscles must act to achieve velopharyngeal closure (Kuehn, 1991). While using the CPAP device, the patient practises speech drills of utterances consisting of VNCV (V = vowel, N = nasal consonant, C = pressure consonant) sequences, with stress placed on the second syllable. Although the efficacy of this technique has not been established, the results of preliminary clinical trials with patients with TBI indicate that the technique at least has potential for the management of velopharyngeal dysfunction in these patients.

The most common prosthetic device used in the treatment of velopharyngeal impairment in TBI patients is the palatal lift prothesis, a device designed to partially elevate the soft palate and provide a contact surface for the lateral pharyngeal walls. A number of different types of palatal lifts have been designed (Aten, McDonald, Simpson, & Gutierrez, 1984; Schweiger, Netsell, & Sommerfield, 1970; Spratley, Chenery, & Murdoch, 1988) and used with patients with TBI (Grand, Matsko, & Avart, 1988; McHenry et al., 1994; Netsell & Daniel, 1979). Several guidelines for the selection of patients for a palatal lift have been documented in the literature and include consideration of severity of dysfunction, impairment of other speech components, co-operation, palatal spasticity, swallowing difficulties, dentition, and hypersensitivity (Beukelman & Yorkston, 1991; Gonzales & Aronson, 1970; Netsell & Rosenbek, 1985; Rosenbek & LaPointe, 1991). One of the major issues involved in the use of palatal lifts in patients with TBI relates to the timing of the fitting of the prosthesis due to the potential for ongoing neurological and velopharyngeal improvement in this clinical population. Beukelman and Yorkston (1991) advocated the fitting of a palatal lift prothesis early in the course of recovery from TBI to prevent the patient from becoming dependent upon augmentative communication, overdriving the respiratory system, and failing to use residual speech capabilities. As an alternative to a palatal lift prosthesis, Stewart and Rieger (1994) reported the successful use of a temporary nasal obturator to eliminate nasal emission and regulate air flow in a severely TBI male. After approximately two years of intermittent use, the patient no longer used the nasal obturator, having eliminated nasal emission and attained a speech intelligibility rating of 95% to 100% for conversational speech.

In carefully selected cases, velopharyngeal impairment may be modified through surgical intervention, although Yorkston et al., (1988) have suggested that this approach is not as effective in the neurologically impaired individual as it is with patients with structural deficits of the velopharyngeal mechanism. The benefits of surgical procedures for patients with velopharyngeal dysfunction following TBI have not yet been established.

Treatment of articulatory dysfunction

A range of behavioural, instrumental, and prosthetic treatment techniques are available for the management of the articulatory disorders evident in persons following TBI. The most common behavioural methods of remediation include strategies to normalise the function of the oral articulators and reduce impairment, and techniques that assist the patient to compensate for the motor speech impairment. Treatment strategies to normalise the function of the articulators include alteration of muscle tone, muscle strengthening techniques, and speech drills to normalise speech movements (Rosenbek & LaPointe, 1991; Yorkston et al., 1988). Rosenbek and LaPointe (1991) advocated the use of an integral stimulation approach involving auditory, visual, and imitative learning, selection of appropriate speech targets, phonetic placement, and speech drills to consolidate the targeted speech sounds. Compensatory strategies to improve speech intelligibility include the use of contrastive and intelligibility speech drills in which the speaker concentrates on achieving the highest level of intelligibility based on feedback from the clinician (Rosenbek & LaPointe, 1991; Yorkston et al., 1988).

Electromyographic biofeedback therapy to alter muscle tone and strength by decreasing or increasing muscle activity has been found to result in improvement of articulatory function in several TBI patients. Specifically, EMG biofeedback therapy has been used to reduce hypertonia in facial and jaw muscles of dysarthric speakers following TBI (Draizar, 1984; Nemec & Cohen, 1984) while in other cases EMG has been shown to be effective in increasing muscle activity of the oral articulators (Draizar, 1984; Netsell & Daniel, 1979). In addition to EMG techniques, a number of the instruments used in the assessment of articulatory function have application for use as biofeedback tools for the treatment of articulatory impairments in TBI patients. For example, the strain-gauge transduction systems and pressure transducers developed for assessment of lip and tongue function can be adapted for biofeedback training of lip and tongue strength, endurance, and fine motor control (Abbs, Hunker, & Barlow, 1983; Robin, Somodi, & Luschei, 1991; Thompson, Murdoch, Theodoros, & Stokes, 1996). A further assessment tool that has application for biofeedback training in the TBI population is the electropalatograph which provides visual details of the location and timing of tongue contact during speech via electrodes embedded in an artificial palate (Gibbon, Dent, & Hardcastle, 1993; Hardcastle, Morgan Barry, & Clark, 1985).

Prosthetic devices available for the treatment of articulatory disorders in TBI patients are limited, and to date would appear to be restricted to the use of a bite block to stabilise the jaw, allowing optimum functioning of the remaining articulators (Barlow & Abbs, 1983), a jaw sling to maintain jaw closure, and a palatal prothesis designed to lower the palatal contact surface to within the range of movement of the tongue (Kearns & Simmons, 1988).

Treatment of prosodic dysfunction

Prosodic dysfunction is a common feature of the dysarthric speech disturbance exhibited by patients following TBI (Theodoros et al., 1994). Several behavioural, instrumental, and prosthetic treatment strategies are available to address the recognised disorders in stress patterning, intonation, and rate in this population. Disorders of stress patterning may involve a reduced ability to differentiate the prominence of syllables within a word (word stress) and/or words within a group (group stress) (Rosenbek & LaPointe, 1991). The most common behavioural treatment strategy for improving either word or group stress involves the use of contrastive stress drills in which the core component of the drill consists of two or more features that can be differentiated in meaning by varied stress patterns (Rosenbek & LaPointe, 1991).

According to the breath group theory of intonation, the breath group is considered the unit of prosody, and intonation is the result of variations in the fundamental frequency of speech within a breath group (Liebermann, 1967). The remediation of impaired intonation involves improving, or in some cases, establishing a patient's breath group capacity and pattern of use (Yorkston et al., 1988). Improvement in breath group capacity may be achieved by remediation of respiratory-phonatory control to enable the patient to produce longer breath groups, while improved breath patterning may be accomplished through reading tasks in which prepared passages are marked according to the breath group length appropriate for the individual (Yorkston et al., 1988). Intonational contours may then be improved through the use of contrastive intonational drills (Rosenbek & LaPointe, 1991). Impaired intonation, however, may also be the result of excessive uniformity across breath groups as identified in a head-injured patient by Bellaire et al. (1986). To overcome this problem, the patient was trained to vary the length of breath groups, and increase the frequency of pauses without inhalation (Bellaire et al., 1986).

A number of techniques are available to increase the slow rate of speech observed in the majority of TBI patients (Theodoros et al., 1994). These strategies involve both rigid rate control techniques (e.g. controlled reading tasks, hand tapping with speech at a specific rate), those that attempt to preserve speech naturalness (e.g. rhythmic cueing), and strategies that indirectly affect rate control (e.g. appropriate stress and breath patterning) (Yorkston et al., 1988). Instrumental techniques devised for rate control mainly involve feedback of various parameters associated with stress, intonation, and rate (intensity, fundamental frequency, intraoral pressure, etc.) (Berry & Goshorn, 1983; Bougle et al., 1995; Caligiuri & Murry, 1983), computer-controlled stimulus presentation (PACER) (Beukelman, Yorkston, & Tice, 1988), and altered auditory feedback (Yorkston et al., 1988). Prosthetic devices designed to assist rate control include a pacing board (Helm, 1979) and alphabet supplementation (Beukelman & Yorkston, 1978; Crow & Enderby, 1989).

Augmentative and alternative communication for TBI dysarthric speakers

For those TBI individuals who exhibit severe dysarthric speech disturbances and non-functional communication skills, the augmentative and alternative communication (AAC) approach to the management of the communication deficit may be the treatment of choice. As suggested by Light et al. (1988), the delivery of AAC strategies to head-injured patients differs from other severely disabled populations in that there is a need to introduce the AAC systems early in the recovery period to relieve frustration, promote interaction, and support the patient's complete participation in the rehabilitation process. With documented evidence of recovery of natural speech function several years post-trauma in some patients where AAC techniques were utilised (Beukelman, Yorkston, & Dowden, 1985; Beukelman, Yorkston, Mitsuda, & Kenyon, 1981; Light, et al., 1988), it has been recommended that AAC should be integrated into regular therapy programmes to maximise recovery of functional speech (DeRuyter & Kennedy, 1991; Light et al., 1988). Furthermore, to ensure that the most appropriate AAC system is selected and progressively modified with recovery, it is essential that the patient's cognition, language use, behaviour, positioning, motor access site, and visual abilities are continually monitored (DeRuyter & Kennedy, 1991).

Cohen and DeRuyter (1982) categorised the various types of AAC systems available to TBI patients into three groups: simple systems (picture, symbol, alphabet and communication boards, gestures, yes/no questions, and writing), dedicated devices (e.g. Canon communicator) that serve a specific function, and multi-purpose systems (e.g. Scanwriter) which serve a variety of purposes within different settings. The AAC systems are generally referred to as temporary or permanent with the temporary systems consisting of simple and dedicated devices, while the permanent systems include a combination of the different systems (DeRuyter & Kennedy, 1991). By far the majority of non-speaking TBI patients (over 76%) use simple AAC systems consisting mainly of communication boards (DeRuyter & Kennedy, 1991). As indicated by DeRuyter and Kennedy (1991), the application of AAC systems to the head-injured population is a complex process requiring considerable expertise on the part of the clinician, as well as dedicated involvement from the patients, their families, and caregivers. For the more severely communicatively impaired patients with TBI, however, the AAC approach provides the patient with a means of communication that enhances the ability of the individual to exist as a functional member of society.

In conclusion, the treatment of the dysarthric speech disturbance associated with TBI encompasses a wide range of treatment techniques that are available to address the diverse motor speech impairments evident in this population. Of particular importance to the clinician is an awareness of the impact of the cognitive deficits demonstrated by these patients on motor speech function, and the need to develop long-term individualised treatment programmes to account for the variability that exists within the head-injured group and the potential for ongoing recovery of speech function in this population (Yorkston & Beukelman, 1991).

REFERENCES

Abbs, J.H., & De Paul, R. (1989). Assessment of dysarthria: The critical prerequisite to treatment. In M.M. Leahy (Ed.), *Disorders of communication: The science of intervention* (pp.206–277). London: Taylor & Francis.

Abbs, J.H., Hunker, C.J., & Barlow, S.M. (1983). Differential speech motor subsystem impairments with suprabulbar lesions: Neurological framework and supporting data. In W.R. Berry (Ed.), *Clinical dysarthria* (pp.21–56). San Diego, CA: College-Hill Press.

Aronson, A.E. (1985). *Clinical voice disorders* (2nd ed.). New York: Thieme.

Aten, J., McDonald, A., Simpson, M., & Gutierrez, R. (1984). Efficacy of modified palatal lifts for improved resonance. In M. McNeil, J. Rosenbek, & A. Aronson, (Eds.), *The dysarthrias: Physiology, acoustics, perception, management*. San Diego, CA: College-Hill Press.

Barlow, S.M., & Abbs, J.H. (1983). Force transducers for the evaluation of labial, lingual, and mandibular function in dysarthria. *Journal of Speech and Hearing Research, 26*, 616–621.

Barlow, S.M., & Burton, M.K. (1988). Orofacial force control impairments in brain injured adults. *Association for Research in Otolaryngology Abstracts, 218.*

Barlow, S.M., & Burton, M.K. (1990). Ramp-and-hold force control in the upper and lower lips: Developing new neuromotor assessment applications in traumatically brain-injured adults. *Journal of Speech and Hearing Research*, *33*, 660–675.

Barlow, S.M., & Netsell, R. (1989). Clinical neurophysiology for individuals with dysarthria. In K.M. Yorkston, & D.R. Beukelman (Eds.), *Recent advances in clinical dysarthria* (pp.53–82). Boston, MA: College-Hill Press.

Bellaire, K., Yorkston, K.M., & Beukelman, D.R. (1986). Modification of breath patterning to increase naturalness of a mildly dysarthric speaker. *Journal of Communication Disorders, 19*, 271–280.

Berry, W.R., & Goshorn, E.L. (1983). Immediate visual feedback in the treatment of ataxic dysarthria: A case study. In W.R. Berry (Ed.), *Clinical dysarthria* (pp.253–265). San Diego, CA: College-Hill Press.

Beukelman, D.R., & Garrett, K. (1988). Augmentative and alternative communication for adults with acquired severe communication disorders. *Augmentative and Alternative Communication*, *4*, 104–121.

Beukelman, D.R., & Yorkston, K.M. (1978). Communication options for patients with brain stem lesions. *Archives of Physical Medicine and Rehabilitation, 59*, 337–340.

Beukelman, D.R., & Yorkston, K.M. (1991). Traumatic brain injury changes the way we live. In D.R. Beukelman & K.M. Yorkston (Eds.), *Communication disorders following traumatic brain injury* (pp.1–13). Austin, TX: Pro-Ed.

Beukelman, D.R., Yorkston, K.M., & Dowden, P.A. (1985). *Communication augmentation: A casebook of clinical management*. Boston, MA: College-Hill Press.

Beukelman, D.R., Yorkston, K.M., Mitsuda, P., & Kenyon, T. (1981). Canon communicator use: A retrospective study. *Journal of Speech and Hearing Disorders*, *46,* 374–388.

Beukelman, D.R., Yorkston, K.M., & Tice, B. (1988). *Pacer/Tally*. Tuscon, AZ: Communication Skill Builders.

Blitzer, A., Brin, M., Fahn, S., & Lovelace, R. (1988). Localized injections of botulinum toxin for the treatment of focal laryngeal dystonia (spastic dysphonia). *Laryngoscope*, *98*, 193–197.

Boone, D.R. (1977). *The voice and voice therapy* (2nd ed.). Englewood Cliffs, NJ: Prentice-Hall.

Bougle, F., Ryall, J., & Le Dorze, G. (1995). Improving fundamental frequency modulation in head trauma patients: A preliminary comparison of speech-language therapy conducted with and without IBM's SpeechViewer. *Folia Phoniatrica Logopedics*, *47*, 24–32.

Caligiuri, M.P., & Murry, T. (1983). The use of visual feedback to enhance prosodic control in dysarthria. In W.R. Berry (Ed.), *Clinical dysarthria* (pp.267–282). San Diego, CA: College-Hill Press.

Cohen, C.G., & DeRuyter, F. (1982). Technology for the communicatively impaired: A perspective for future clinicians. *Journal of the National Student Speech-Language-Hearing Association, 10*, 67–76.

Colton, R., & Casper, J.K. (1996). *Understanding voice problems: A physiological perspective for diagnosis and treatment*. Baltimore, MD: Williams & Wilkins.

Crow, E., & Enderby, P. (1989). The effects of an alphabet chart on the speaking rate and intelligibility of speakers with dysarthria. In K.M. Yorkston & D.R. Beukelman (Eds.), *Recent advances in clinical dysarthria* (pp.99–107). Boston, MA: College-Hill Press.

Darley, F.L., Aronson, A.E., & Brown, J.R. (1975). *Motor speech disorders*. Philadelphia: Saunders.

Dedo, H.H., & Izdebski, K. (1983). Intermediate results of 306 recurrent laryngeal nerve sections for spastic dysphonia. *Laryngoscope, 93*, 9–16.

DeRuyter, F., & Kennedy, M.T. (1991). Augmentative communication following traumatic brain injury. In D.R. Beukeleman & Yorkston, K.M. (Eds.), *Communication disorders following traumatic brain injury: Management of cognitive, language, and motor impairments* (pp.317–366). Austin, TX: Pro-Ed.

Draizar, A. (1984). Clinical EMG feedback in motor speech disorders. *Archives of Physical Medicine and Rehabilitation, 65*, 481–484.

Dresser, A.C., Meirowsky, A.M., Weiss, G.H., McNeel, M.L., Simon, G.A., & Caveness, W.F. (1973). Gainful employment following head injury: Prognostic factors. *Archives of Neurology, 29*, 111–116.

Enderby, P., & Crow, E. (1990). Long-term recovery patterns of severe dysarthria following head injury. *British Journal of Disorders of Communication, 25*, 341–354.

Facs, M.M., & Beery, Q. (1986). Muscle-nerve pedicle laryngeal reinnervation. *Laryngoscope, 96*, 1196–1200.

Ford, C.N., Martin, D.W., & Warner, T.F. (1984). Injectable collagen in laryngeal rehabilitation. *Laryngoscope, 94*, 513–518.

Froeschels, E. (1952). Chewing method as therapy. *Archives of Otolaryngology, 56*, 427–434.

Gibbon, F., Dent, H., & Hardcastle, W. (1993). Diagnosis and therapy of abnormal alveolar stops in a speech-disordered child using electropalatography. *Clinical Linguistics and Phonetics, 7*, 247–267.

Gonzalez, J.B., & Aronson, A.E. (1970). Palatal lift prosthesis for treatment of anatomic and neurologic palatopharyngeal insufficiency. *Cleft Palate Journal, 7*, 91–104.

Grand, H., Matsko, T., & Avart, H. (1988). Speech prosthesis retention problems in dysarthria: Case report. *Archives of Physical Medicine and Rehabilitation, 69*, 213–214.

Groher, M. (1977). Language and memory disorders following closed head trauma. *Journal of Speech and Hearing Research, 20*, 212–223.

Hardcastle, W.J., Morgan Barry, R.A., & Clark, C.J. (1985). Articulatory and voicing characteristics of adult dysarthric and verbal dyspraxic speakers: An instrumental study. *British Journal of Disorders of Communication, 20*, 249–269.

Hartley, L.L., & Levin, H.S. (1990). Linguistic deficits after closed head injury: A current appraisal. *Aphasiology, 4*, 353–370.

Hartmann, E., & von Cramon, D. (1984). Acoustic measurement of voice quality in central dysphonia. *Journal of Communication Disorders, 17*, 425–440.

Helm, N.A. (1979). Management of palilalia with a pacing board. *Journal of Speech and Hearing Disorders, 44*, 350–353.

Hunker, C., Abbs, J.H., & Barlow, S.M. (1982). The relationship between parkinsonian rigidity and hypokinesia of the orofacial system: A quantitative analysis. *Neurology, 32*, 755–761.

Iwata, S., von Leden, H., & Williams, D. (1972). Air flow measurement during phonation. *Journal of Communication Disorders, 5*, 67–69.

Johnson, J.A., & Pring, T.R. (1990). Speech therapy and Parkinson's disease: A review and further data. *British Journal of Disorders of Communication, 25*, 183–194.

Kearns, K.P., & Simmons, N.N. (1988). Motor speech disorders: The dysarthrias and apraxia of speech. In N.J. Lass, I.V. McReynolds, J.L. Northern, & D.E. Yoder (Eds.), *Handbook of speech-language pathology and audiology* (pp.592–621). Toronto: B.C. Decker.

Kearns, K.P., & Simmons, N.N. (1990). The efficacy of speech-language pathology intervention: Motor speech disorders. *Seminars in Speech and Language, 11*, 273–295.

Kent, R., Netsell, R., & Bauer, L. (1975). Cineradiographic assessment of articulatory mobility in the dysarthrias. *Journal of Speech and Hearing Disorders, 40*, 467–480.

Kotby, M.N. (1995). *The Accent Method of voice therapy*. San Diego, CA: Singular Publishing.

Kuehn, D.P. (1991). New therapy for treating hypernasal speech using continuous positive airway pressure (CPAP). *Plastic and Reconstructive Surgery, 88*, 959–966.

Kuehn, D.P., & Wachtel, J.M. (1994). CPAP therapy for treating hypernasality following closed head injury. In J.A. Till, K.M.Yorkston, & D.R. Beukelman (Eds.), *Motor speech disorders: Advances in assessment and treatment* (pp.207–212). Baltimore, MD: Paul H. Brookes.

Lehiste, I. (1965). Some acoustic characteristics of dysarthric speech. *Biblotheca Phonetica*, *2*, 1–124.

Liebermann, P. (1967). *Intonation, perception, and language*. Cambridge: MIT Press.

Light, J., Beesley, M., & Collier, B. (1988). Transition through multiple augmentative and alternative communication systems: A three-year case study of a head-injured adolescent. *Augmentative and Alternative Communication*, *4*, 2–14.

Linebaugh, C.W. (1983). Treatment of flaccid dysarthria. In W.H. Perkins (Ed.), *Current therapy of communication disorders: Dysarthria and apraxia* (pp.59–67). New York: Thieme Medical Publishers.

Liss, J.M., Kuehn, D.P., & Hinkle, K.P. (1994). Direct training of velopharyngeal musculature. *Journal of Medical Speech-Language Pathology*, *2*, 243–249.

Marquardt, T.P., Stoll, J., & Sussman, H. (1990). Disorders of communication in traumatic brain injury. In E.D. Bigler (Ed.), *Traumatic brain injury: Mechanisms of damage, assessment, intervention and outcome* (pp.181–205). Austin, TX: Pro-Ed.

McHenry, M., Wilson, R.L., & Minton, J.T. (1994). Management of multiple physiologic system deficits following traumatic brain injury. *Journal of Medical Speech-Language Pathology, 2*, 59–74.

Moncur, J.P., & Brackett, I.P. (1974). *Modifying vocal behaviour*. New York: Harper & Row.

Murdoch, B.E. (1990). *Acquired speech and language disorders: A neuroanatomical and functional neurological approach*. London: Chapman & Hall.

Murdoch, B.E. (1996). Physiological rehabilitation of disordered speech following closed head injury. In B.P. Uzzell & H.H. Stonnington (Eds.), *Recovery after traumatic brain injury* (pp.163–184). Hillsdale, NJ: Lawrence Erlbaum Associates Inc.

Murdoch, B.E., Sterling, D., Theodoros, D.G., & Stokes, P.D. (1995). Physiological rehabilitation of disordered speech breathing in dysarthric speakers following severe closed head injury. In J. Fourez & N. Page (Eds.), *Treatment issues and long-term outcomes* (pp.137–146). Brisbane: Academic Press.

Murdoch, B.E., Theodoros, D.G., Stokes, P.D., & Chenery, H.J. (1993). Abnormal patterns of speech breathing in dysarthria following severe closed head injury. *Brain Injury, 7*, 295–308.

Najenson, T., Sazbon, L., Fiselzon, J., Becker, E., & Schechter, I. (1978). Recovery of communicative functions after prolonged traumatic coma. *Scandinavian Journal of Rehabilitation Medicine, 10*, 15–21.

Nemec, R.E., & Cohen, K. (1984). EMG biofeedback in the modification of hypertonia in spastic dysarthria: Case report. *Archives of Physical Medicine and Rehabilitation*, *65*, 103–104.

Netsell, R. (1986). *A neurological view of speech production and the dysarthrias*. San Diego, CA: College-Hill Press.

Netsell, R., & Daniel, B. (1979). Dysarthria in adults: Physiologic approach in rehabilitation. *Archives of Physical Medicine and Rehabilitation*, *60*, 502–508.

Netsell, R., & Hixon, T.J. (1992). Inspiratory checking in therapy for individuals with speech breathing dysfunction. *American Speech and Hearing Association*, *34*, 152.

Netsell, R., & Lefkowitz, D. (1992). Speech production following traumatic brain injury: Clinical and research implications. *Neurophysiology and Neurogenic Speech and Language Disorders*, *2*, 1–8.

Netsell, R., Lotz, W.K., & Barlow, S.M. (1989). A speech physiology examination for individuals with dysarthria. In K.M. Yorkston & D.R. Beukelman (Eds.), *Recent advances in clinical dysarthria* (pp.4–37). Boston, MA: College-Hill Press.

Netsell, R., & Rosenbek, J. (1985). Treating the dysarthrias. In J. Darby (Ed.), *Speech and language evaluation in neurology: Adult disorders* (pp.363–392). Orlando, FL: Grune & Stratton.

Olver, J.H., Ponsford, J.L., & Curran, C.A. (1996). Outcome following traumatic brain injury: A comparison between 2 and 5 years after injury. *Brain Injury*, *10(11)*, 841–848.

Prosek, R.A., Montgomery, A.A. Walden, B.E., & Schwartz, D.M. (1978). EMG biofeedback in the treatment of hyperfunctional voice disorders. *Journal of Speech and Hearing Disorders*, *43*, 282–294.

Ramig, L.O., Bonitati, C.M., Lemke, J.H., & Horii, Y. (1994). Voice treatment for patients with Parkinson's disease: Development of an approach and preliminary efficacy data. *Journal of Medical Speech-Language Pathology*, *2*, 191–209.

Ramig, L.O., Mead, C.L., & DeSanto, L. (1988). Voice therapy and Parkinson's disease. *Journal of American Speech and Hearing Association*, *30*, 128.

Ramig, L.O., & Scherer, R.C. (1989). Speech therapy for neurologic disorders of the larynx. In A. Blitzer, C. Sasaki, S. Fahn, M. Brin, & K. Harris (Eds.), *Neurological disorders of the larynx* (pp.163–181). New York: Thieme Medical Publishers.

Robin, D.A., Somodi, L.B., & Luschei, E.S. (1991). Measurement of strength and endurance in normal and articulation disordered subjects. In C.A. Moore, K.M. Yorkston, & D.R. Beukelman (Eds.), *Dysarthria and apraxia of speech: Perspectives on management* (pp.173–184). Baltimore, MD: Paul Brookes Publishing Company.

Rosenbek, J.C., & LaPointe, L.L. (1991). The dysarthrias: Description, diagnosis, and treatment. In D.F. Johns (Ed.), *Clinical management of neurogenic communication disorders* (pp.97–152). Boston, MA: Little Brown.

Rusk, H., Block, J., & Lowmann, E. (1969). Rehabilitation of the brain-injured patient: A report of 157 cases with long-term follow-up of 118. In E. Walker, W. Caveness, & M. Critchley (Eds.), *The late effects of head injury* (pp.327–332). Springfield, MA: Charles C. Thomas.

Sarno, M.T., Buonaguro, A., & Levita, E. (1986). Characteristics of verbal impairment in closed head-injured patients. *Archives of Physical Medicine and Rehabilitation*, *67*, 400–405.

Sarno, M.T., & Levin, H.S. (1985). Speech and language disorders after closed head injury. In J.K. Darby (Ed.), *Speech and language evaluation in neurology: Adult disorders* (pp.323–339). New York: Grune & Stratton.

Schweiger, J., Netsell, R., & Sommerfield, R. (1970). Prosthetic management and speech improvements in individuals with dysarthria of the palate. *Journal of the American Dental Association*, *80*, 1340.

Shimizu, M., Watanabe, Y., & Hirose, H. (1992). *Use of the Accent Method in training for patients with motor speech disorders*. Paper presented at the XXII World Congress of the International Association of Logopedics and Phoniatrics, Hannover, Germany.

Simmons, N. (1983). Acoustic analysis of ataxic dysarthria: An approach to monitoring treatment. In W. Berry (Ed.), *Clinical dysarthria* (pp.283–294). San Diego, CA: College-Hill Press.

Smitheran, J.R., & Hixon, T.J. (1981). A clinical method for estimating laryngeal airway resistance during vowel production. *Journal of Speech and Hearing Disorders*, *46*, 138–146.

Spratley, M.H., Chenery, H.J., & Murdoch, B.E. (1988). A different design of palatal lift appliance: Review and case reports. *Australian Dental Journal*, *33*, 491–495.

Stevens, K.N., Kalikow, D.N., & Willemain, T.R. (1975). A miniature accelerometer for detecting glottal waveforms and nasalisation. *Journal of Speech and Hearing Research*, *18*, 594–599.

Stewart, D.S., & Rieger, W.J. (1994). A device for the management of velopharyngeal incompetence. *Journal of Medical Speech-Language Pathology*, *2*, 149–155.

Theodoros, D.G., & Murdoch, B.E. (1994). Laryngeal dysfunction in dysarthric speakers following severe closed head injury. *Brain Injury*, *8*, 667–684.

Theodoros, D.G., Murdoch, B.E., & Chenery, H.J. (1994). Perceptual speech characteristics of dysarthric speakers following severe closed head injury. *Brain Injury*, *8*, 101–124.

Theodoros, D.G., Murdoch, B.E., & Stokes, P.D. (1995). A physiological analysis of articulatory dysfunction in dysarthric speakers following severe closed head injury. *Brain Injury*, *9*, 237–254.

Theodoros, D.G., Murdoch, B.E., Stokes, P.D., & Chenery, H.J. (1993). Hypernasality in dysarthric speakers following severe closed head injury: A perceptual and instrumental analysis. *Brain Injury, 7,* 59–69.

Thompson, E.C., Murdoch, B.E., Theodoros, D.G., & Stokes, P.D. (1996). *Physiological assessment of interlabial contact pressures in normal and neurologically impaired adults.* Paper presented at the Fifth Conference of the International Association for the Study of Traumatic Brain Injury, Melbourne, Australia.

Thomsen, I.V. (1984). Late outcome of severe blunt head injury: A ten to fifteen year second follow-up. *Journal of Neurology, Neurosurgery and Psychiatry*, 47, 260–268.

Vogel, M., & von Cramon, D. (1983). Articulatory recovery after traumatic midbrain damage: A follow-up study. *Folia Phoniatrica*, *35*, 294–309.

Workinger, M., & Netsell, R. (1992). Restoration of intelligible speech 13 years post-head injury. *Brain Injury*, *6*, 183–187.

Ylvisaker, M. (1986). Language and communication disorders following pediatric head injury. *Journal of Head Trauma Rehabilitation*, *1*, 48–56.

Ylvisaker, M. (1992). Communication outcome following traumatic brain injury. *Seminars in Speech and Language, 13*, 239–250.

Yorkston, K.M., & Beukelman, D.R. (1981). Ataxic dysarthria: Treatment sequences based on intelligibility and prosodic considerations. *Journal of Speech and Hearing Disorders*, *46*, 398–404.

Yorkston, K.M., & Beukelman, D.R. (1991). Motor speech disorders. In D.R. Beukelman & Yorkston, K.M. (Eds.), *Communication disorders following traumatic brain injury: Management of cognitive, language, and motor impairments* (pp.251–316). Austin, TX: Pro-Ed.

Yorkston, K.M., Beukelman, D.R., & Bell, K.R. (1988). *Clinical management of dysarthric speakers*. Boston, MA: Little Brown.

Yorkston, K.M., Beukelman, D.R., Minifie, F.D., & Sapir, S. (1984). Assessment of stress patterning in dysarthric speakers. In M. McNeil, A. Aronson, & J. Rosenbek (Eds.), *The dysarthrias: Physiology, acoustics, perception, management* (pp.131–162). San Diego, CA: College-Hill Press.

Ziegler, W., Hoole, P., Hartmann, E., & von Cramon, D. (1988). Accelerated speech in dysarthria after acquired brain injury: Acoustic correlates. *British Journal of Disorders of Communication*, *23*, 215–228.

Ziegler, W., & von Cramon, D. (1983a). Vowel distortion in traumatic dysarthria: A formant study. *Phonetica, 40*, 63–78.

Ziegler, W., & von Cramon, D. (1983b). Vowel distortion in traumatic dysarthria: Lip rounding versus tongue advancement. *Phonetica*, *40,* 312–322.

Ziegler, W., & von Cramon, D. (1986). Spastic dysarthria after acquired brain injury: An acoustic study. *British Journal of Disorders of Communication*, *21*, 173–187.

CHAPTER NINE

Communication problems resulting from brain injury in children: Special issues of assessment and management

Sandra Bond Chapman
Brain Research and Treatment Center, University of Texas at Dallas, Texas, USA

Harvey S. Levin
Baylor College of Medicine, Houston, Texas, USA

Stacy L. Lawyer
Callier Center for Communication Disorders, University of Texas at Dallas, Texas, USA

INTRODUCTION

In developed countries, brain injury is the leading cause of death in children. In America, the death rate associated with paediatric brain injury is five times greater than the second major cause which is leukaemia (Zitnay, 1995). Fortunately, recent advances in emergency medical treatment have reduced the risk of death. Improving the prognosis for survival, however, has not reduced the long-term disability associated with paediatric brain injury that remains a major public health problem. Since the majority of brain injuries occur sometime between early childhood and young adulthood, many individuals with brain injury live out most of their life coping with varying degrees and types of disability. In order to mitigate the long-lasting effects of brain injury in children, it is essential to recognise the scope of the problem.

This chapter reviews the literature on the associated linguistic and cognitive factors that contribute to communication breakdown in paediatric brain injury. Whereas early reports signalled a good prognosis for recovery of communication skills even after severe paediatric brain injury in children (Klonoff, Low, & Clark, 1977), more recent evidence dampens this optimistic view. A majority of children who sustain a severe brain injury reportedly show some form of communication disability, although the nature of communication outcome is not readily measurable and is highly variable across individuals (Blosser & DePompeii, 1994). The extent of the problems is realised predominately through consideration of the numerous factors that influence the outcome profile in paediatric brain-injured populations and utilisation of appropriate measures that are sensitive to the neurobehavioural outcome and effects of treatment.

Definition

Confusion in terminology used to refer to different types of brain injury arises from the misuse and overlap in the meaning of labels. Some labels pertain to the time of injury and others the nature of injury (Blosser & DePompei, 1994). Regarding time of brain injury, the brain injury may be specified as either congenital (occurring prior to or during birth) or acquired (occurring after birth). Acquired brain injuries are further subclassified according to the nature of the injury including traumatic (i.e. open head injury and closed head injuries) or non-traumatic (e.g. anoxia, infection, tumour, or stroke) causes.

In this chapter, the discussion focuses on traumatic brain injury (TBI) with closed head injury (CHI) comprising the largest segment of the population studied. To date, CHI represents the largest aetiological category of acquired brain injury in children. For comparative purposes other types of pediatric brain injury are mentioned when relevant. A CHI is defined as a non-penetrating injury to the brain usually associated with motor vehicle, motor-bicycle, motor-pedestrian, sports-related injuries, falls, or child abuse (Savage & Wolcott, 1994). As detailed in Chapter 2, the impact of a CHI typically involves widespread areas of the brain resulting in diffuse as well as focal injuries (Levin, Culhane, Mendelsohn, et al., 1993). There is often extensive stretching and tearing of the nerve fibres in the white matter of the cerebral hemispheres.

Nature of the problem

Communication disability in children with TBI is poorly understood and consequently often overlooked. Whereas some researchers describe the residual communication deficits in head injury as subtle or subclinical (Jaffe, Brink, Hays, & Choraze, 1990; Sarno, 1980), others claim that such designation of the deficits may lead to mismanagement. Recent evidence has shown that the deficits may be quite severe. The distinction is that the impairment is more apparent at higher-level aspects of language representation, specifically at discourse levels (Chapman, 1995; Dennis & Barnes, 1990), than at lower levels (e.g. vocabulary).

The misconception that residual communication deficits in TBI are rare may be based on a narrow view in which language and communication are treated as synonymous behaviours (Chapman, 1997). Language in this context refers to the formal components of the language system including phonology, lexical semantics, morphology, and syntax. In contrast, communication entails the ability to use the formal language components to convey information—i.e. the pragmatic dimension. The neglect of communication disability in TBI could result largely from the reliance on criteria used to identify linguistic impairment (LI) in children with developmental language problems (i.e. children with LI) (Chapman, Watkins, Gustafson, Moore, Levin, & Kufera, 1997). The criteria are based on extensive evidence that children with LI readily show deficits on measures of morphology and syntax. In contrast, the majority of children with TBI have minimal difficulty in the formal components of the language system. This is to say that despite an initial impairment after brain injury, children with TBI typically recover the formal domains of language (Klonoff et al., 1977; Ylvisaker, 1993). The ability to utilise the lexical and grammatical aspects of language, however, does not necessarily correspond with the ability to manipulate the language system to convey information at a discourse level for communication (Chapman et al., 1997). Clearly the residual communication ability is dependent on linguistic, cognitive, behavioural, and psychosocial functioning.

This chapter discusses five major issues related to pediatric brain injury. First, the prevalence and nature of formal language problems identified in children with TBI are discussed. This information provides empirical evidence to guide clinical practice in adopting the most sensitive measures to assess the linguistic sequelae of TBI. Secondly, the evidence from discourse studies in TBI are summarised. A case is made that discourse measures should be used to complement traditional measures to ensure a more complete assessment of the cognitive-communicative disability in TBI. The clinical need to go beyond the superficial aspect of language structure to discourse level measures is vividly illustrated through studies of children with brain injury. The following quote from Damico (1985, p.165) epitomises the elusiveness of the language disability in children with acquired brain injury:

> If you just listen to him, he seems to have a problem. He's hard to follow and the other kids don't really like to interact with him. His teachers say that he isn't a very good student . . . but I can't seem to find any specific problems according to my diagnostic battery.

Thirdly, the factors that contribute to communicative disability, such as severity of injury and neuropathophysiologic aspects of the injury, are delineated. Fourthly, the relationship between discourse function and related cognitive abilities are considered and, finally, the implications for treatment are examined.

FORMAL LANGUAGE PROBLEMS IN CHILDREN WITH TBI

Classically, much of paediatric clinical practice and available language tests have been based on the language disturbances characteristic of children with isolated problems in the language domain—a disorder commonly referred to as specific language impairment (Chapman, 1997). The label of specific language impairment (SLI) refers to a child whose language fails to develop normally in the absence of mental handicap, hearing loss, emotional disorder, or environmental deprivation (Bishop, 1992). In order to understand the language problems of children with acquired brain damage, it is important to recognise how their language disturbances parallel and diverge from those seen in children with developmental language impairments such as SLI.

For children with developmental language problems, the most consistently documented deficits involve protracted acquisition of phonology, grammar, and lexicon (Bishop, 1992; Leonard, 1989). In contrast, the majority of children with TBI not only acquire the phonological, lexical, and grammatical aspects of language normally, but typically they regain the ability to comprehend language and to manipulate these components for the purposes of verbal expression to their premorbid level (Chapman, Levin, Matejka, Harward, & Kufera, 1995b; Klonoff et al., 1977; Ylvisaker, 1993). Chapman et al. (1995b) and Chapman, Levin, Wanek, Weyrauch, and Kufera (1998) reported that the amount and complexity of language in narrative productions were minimally affected in the majority of children with TBI ranging from mild to severe as early as three months post-injury. Even the lexical specificity in referential noun phrases for children with TBI was similar to typically developing peers and superior to that of children with LI (Chapman & Gustafson, 1994). Thus, there appears to be a striking disparity between children with TBI and children with LI in the lexical and grammatical domains of language functioning.

Recent evidence asserts that residual communication disturbances in paediatric TBI are more likely to be identified outside the formal linguistic domains. Nevertheless, some children with TBI do show language-specific problems. That is, the optimistic prognosis for recovery of the formal components of the linguistic system does not necessarily generalise to all children with TBI (Chapman et al., 1997; Dennis, 1992; Jordan, Murdoch, Hudson-Tennent, & Boon, 1996; Levin, 1996). For example, Chapman et al. (1997) found that approximately one-third of their paediatric head-injured population (n = 24) with moderate to severe TBI exhibited language problems on structured language measures.

Although the form and the range of language disturbances are poorly understood, the aspects of tasks that appear to be more sensitive to the effects of head injury are those that require efficiency of responding (e.g. response time), productivity (e.g. fluency of words or ideas, and alternative solutions), and inferencing (e.g. interpreting ambiguous sentences and non-literal language). Table 9.1 summarises recent findings of the prevalence of language disturbances in TBI on standardised language measures. The most frequently occurring deficits have been identified on tasks of word fluency (Dennis & Barnes, 1990; Ewing-Cobbs, Miner, Fletcher, & Levin, 1989; Jordan & Murdoch, 1994; Jordan et al., 1996; Levin, 1996), confrontation naming, and latency of naming (Chadwick, Rutter, Shaffer, & Shrout, 1981; Ewing-Cobbs, Levin, Eisenberg, & Fletcher, 1987; Jordan et al., 1996; Jordan & Murdoch, 1993). Other studies have used a cluster of tasks to identify language impairment such as measures of receptive vocabulary, defining vocabulary items, semantic word fluency for categories, and ability to ask generalised questions to more efficiently solve a problem (e.g. "Is it a vehicle?" as contrasted with lower-level questions, "Is it a car?") (Chapman et al., 1997). Whereas a proportion of children with moderate to severe TBI demonstrated disturbances on structured language measures, the disturbances occurred in a more restricted set of tasks than is typical of children with developmental language problems (SLI, LI).

Another way that children with TBI differ from children with LI is in syntactic complexity. The majority of children with LI exhibited notable deficiencies in morphology and syntax as compared with normal control children. In contrast, children with TBI do not typically differ from normal control children on measures of amount and complexity of sentences comprising a narrative discourse sample (Chapman et al., 1997). This finding persists even in the subgroup of TBI children who exhibit significant problems on standardised language measures. It appears that most children with TBI regain the ability to utilise linguistic knowledge to formulate sentences. Additionally, Chapman and Gustafson (1994) found children with TBI produced more complex referential noun phrases than children with LI, allowing them to distinguish linguistically two ambiguous participants in their narrative productions more clearly. The most important implication from the above findings is that linguistic measures such as amount and complexity of sentences are insensitive to the long-term outcome of brain injury. The evidence of a relative preservation in amount and complexity of verbal output may help explain why many of the communication deficits in TBI go unnoticed and therefore untreated. Strong evidence of untreated communication problems in TBI was shown when only one child out of 24 moderate to severely injured children was found to be enrolled in speech-language services at three months post-injury even though one-third exhibited linguistic disturbances on structured measures and three-quarters

TABLE 9.1
Summaries of studies of language deficits in childen with TBI

Task	*Test*	*Age range/time post-injury*	*Severity levels in deficits observed*	*Reference*
Naming	Boston Naming Test[1]	18 months post-injury	Severe, significantly worse than controls	Jordan & Murdoch (1993); Jordan et al. (1988)
Verbal fluency	FAS: Spreen Aphasia Battery[2];	Ages 17–50 years at time of assessment, ages 5–16 years at time of injury	Severe deficits seen into adulthood	Jordan & Murdoch (1994); Dennis & Barnes (1990)
	NCCEA[2]	Ages 5–15 years tested within 6 months post-injury	30% severe/mod pts 8% mild (<60%tile)	Ewing-Cobbs et al. (1987)
Visual naming/tactile naming	NCCEA[2]	Ages 5–15 years tested within 6 months post-injury	15% severe/mod pts 8% mild pts (<60%tile)	Ewing-Cobbs et al. (1987)
Description of use			25% severe/mod pts 12% mild	
Sentence repetition			34% severe/mod pts 12% mild	
Writing to dictation			35% severe/mod pts 12% mild	
Writing to copy			22% severe/mod pts 15% mild pts (<60%tile)	
Expressive language	SICD[3]	Children under 6 years	Most affected in children less than 31 months of age at time of injury	Ewing-Cobbs et al. (1989)
Overall language	TOLD-P[4]; TOLD-I[5]; TOAL-2[6]	7–17 years	Severe did worse than controls	Jordan et al. (1995)
Ambiguous sentences; figurative language; inferences	Test of Language Competence - Expanded Edition[7]	Ages 5–16 years at time of injury	67% were impaired on composite score; at least 80% were impaired on at least one discourse task	Dennis & Barnes (1990)

continued

Table 9.1 continued

Task	*Test*	*Age range/time post-injury*	*Severity levels in deficits observed*	*Reference*
Discourse	Clinical Discourse Analysis[8]	Ages 8–16 years	Conversational discourse was analysed and no differences between CHI and control groups due to wide variety	Jordan & Murdoch (1990)

[1]Kaplan et al. (1983).
[2]Neurosensory Center Comprehensive Examination for Aphasia (Spreen & Benton, 1969).
[3]Sequenced Inventory of Communication Disorders (Hedrick, Pather, & Tobin, 1974).
[4]Test of Language Development – Primary (Hammill & Newcomer, 1982).
[5]Test of Language Development – Intermediate (Hammill & Newcomer, 1982).
[6]Test of Adolescent Language (Hammill et al., 1987).
[7]Wiig and Secrod (1989).
[8]Damico (1985).

showed discourse disturbances (Chapman et al., 1997). Because children with TBI may talk a lot, they may be under-referred for language services.

DISCOURSE AS AN OUTCOME MEASURE

An increasing number of empirical studies show that discourse measures are more sensitive to the sequelae of paediatric TBI than classic language measures or even amount and complexity measures of verbal output. Children with TBI produce stories that are fragmented and difficult to follow, even though they tend to use as much language as normal children (Biddle, McCabe, & Bliss, 1996; Chapman et al., 1992; Chapman et al., 1997). Paradoxically, children with moderate to severe TBI without measurable language deficits reportedly perform as poorly as the children with developmental language problems on the organisation measure of narrative discourse (Chapman et al., 1998). Furthermore, some investigations have failed to find a relationship between isolated vocabulary measures and measures of discourse function (Chapman et al., 1992; Chapman et al., 1997), while other studies have indicated that difficulties on verbal fluency or word definition tasks co-occur with difficulties in processing discourse information (Dennis, 1992; Dennis & Barnes, 1990). Nonetheless, the relationship between the formal aspects of the language system and discourse is not straightforward.

Clearly, diagnostic protocols must retain traditional measures that evaluate primarily linguistic functions because a number of children with acquired brain injury exhibit language disturbances. Nonetheless, the state-of-the-art assessment procedures for cognitive-communication disability in the paediatric brain-injured population have moved beyond solely determining whether specific language problems exist. Presently, research and clinical efforts are directed at identifying how the cognitive and linguistic disturbances contribute to the disruption in ability to use language for social and academic purposes using discourse analysis.

Definition and significance

For our purposes, discourse is defined as a sequence of ideas typically expressed in sentences that serve the communicative function of conveying a message (Ulatowska, Allard, & Chapman, 1990). Discourse is a generic term that refers to a variety of discourse types such as descriptive, conversational, narrative, procedural, or expository discourse. Discourse functioning in adult TBI is discussed in detail in Chapter 3. As highlighted there, discourse processing entails a complex interplay of linguistic abilities, cognitive abilities, and information-processing abilities. Each genre has different cognitive and linguistic requirements as well as unique properties that define its well-formedness in terms of organisation and content.

Although a few studies of conversational discourse in paediatric brain-injured populations exist (Jordan & Murdoch, 1990), the majority of studies have utilised narrative discourse (Campbell & Dollaghan, 1990; Chapman, 1995; Chapman et al., 1992; Chapman et al., 1995b; Chapman et al., 1998; Dennis, 1980; Dennis, Jacennik, & Barnes, 1994; Jordan, Murdoch, & Buttsworth, 1991). Narrative discourse is a logical sequence of events that unfold through the actions of the characters. The major components of narrative discourse include a setting (i.e. identification of characters, time, and/or place), action sequence (i.e. sequence of events and turning point), and resolution (i.e. final outcome of the characters' actions) (Labov, 1972).

Narrative discourse measures may be particularly relevant for paediatric populations due to the developmental aspects, educational implications, and functional salience of narratives (Chapman et al., 1997). In order to determine the long-term outcome in pediatric brain-injured populations, assessment methods must be effective in evaluating the degree of recovery as well as the rate of continued development. The rudiments of narrative discourse develop relatively early in life, at around the age of two-and-a-half years, with more complex forms of linguistic and information structure unfolding with later cognitive stages (Applebee, 1978; Stein & Glenn, 1979; Westby, 1984). The identified stages of development provide useful guidelines for measuring recovery and continued development after brain injury (Chapman et al., 1997).

Educationally, narrative ability is associated with academic performance and may even be a precursor to literacy (Bishop & Edmundson, 1987;

Feagans & Applebaum, 1986; Westby, 1989). The majority of children who suffer moderate to severe brain injuries require some form of special education services for at least two years or longer after the injury (Klonoff, Clark, & Klonoff, 1993). The academic failure has been attributed to a wide range of underlying cognitive and linguistic deficits identified as common sequelae to brain injury (Ewing-Cobbs et al., 1989; Levin & Eisenberg, 1979). Chapman, Levin, and Harward (1996) have proposed that disability in processing discourse information may be directly related to poor classroom performance in paediatric populations with TBI.

Recent evidence suggests that discourse provides a functional basis for intervention because it represents language in context and is relevant to the social use of language (Chapman et al., 1995b; Gillam, McFadden, & van Kleek, 1995). Problems in social interaction is perhaps one of the most common and persistent deficits in children who suffer moderate to severe brain injuries (Brown, Chadwick, Shaffer, Rutter, & Traub, 1981; Fletcher, Ewing-Cobbs, Miner, Levin, & Eisenberg, 1990). Inability to manipulate discourse may be related to lack of success in developing and maintaining adequate peer interactions (Roth & Spekman, 1989; Westby, 1989).

In summary, discourse disturbances in acquired brain injury are more prevalent and longer-lasting than specific language problems (Chapman et al., 1992; Dennis & Barnes, 1990; Ylvisaker, 1993). An estimated 75% of children who sustain a severe brain injury show persistent deficits in narrative discourse as late as three years post-injury or longer (Chapman, 1997; Dennis & Barnes, 1990). Additionally, discourse disturbances may become more prominent at later stages post-injury as the child fails to develop more complex narrative structures (Chapman et al., 1995b; Chapman, Levin, & Harward, 1996). For children with mild to moderate brain injury, the prognosis for recovery of normal discourse function is generally more favourable than in children with severe injuries (Chapman et al., 1992; Chapman, 1995).

Nature of impairments

The majority of children with severe TBI experience difficulties conveying their ideas, despite normal or near normal performance on traditional language measures by three months post-injury (Chapman, Levin, & Culhane, 1995a). Although discourse ability associated with brain injury is extremely heterogeneous, several common patterns have been identified. First, the discourse impairment in TBI is more commonly revealed by information measures than by language measures (Chapman et al., 1995b; Chapman et al., 1997). The disruption of information measures for narration takes the form of (a) a reduction in the amount of information provided, (b) an impairment in story structure/organisation (i.e. setting, action, and resolution), (c) a failure to paraphrase the most central information when retelling or generating stories, and (d) an inability to synthesise and abstract the global meaning of the story (Chapman et al., 1992; Chapman et al., 1995b; Chapman et al., 1997). Secondly, narrative discourse skills are more likely to be impaired than are conversational discourse abilities in pediatric TBI populations (Chapman et al., 1997; Jordan & Murdoch, 1990). The greater impairment in narrative discourse abilities is likely to be due to the requirements to manipulate longer units of discourse text during narrative production. In contrast, conversational discourse can be achieved with a minimal response such as a single word.

Although few empirical studies of written language exist, the limited data indicate that this modality may be even more vulnerable to the effects of severe brain injury than verbal expression (Ewing-Cobbs et al., 1987; Yorkston, Jaffe, Polissar, Liao, & Fay, 1997). Ewing-Cobbs and colleagues identified a positive relationship between severity of TBI and writing ability (Table 9.1). The primary error categories included omissions, misspellings, and capitalisation disturbances. The errors were attributed to attentional and organisational difficulties as opposed to specific breakdown in semantics or syntax. Moreover, memory did not appear to be a factor because the sentences were presented as often as required.

With regard to written discourse level language, children with severe TBI (ages 8 to 10 at injury) were found to be significantly impaired compared to children with mild TBI (Chapman & Lawyer, 1997). The impairment was evident at both a 3- and 12-month interval post-injury. The children with severe brain injuries produced significantly less core information, less complete episodic structure, and exhibited a trend towards producing less of the gist information in the written narrative productions than children with mild TBI. Although the children with severe TBI produced fewer sentences in generating a written story than did the children with mild TBI, the complexity of the written sentences did not differ according to severity of the brain injury. Evaluation of the mechanical errors in writing revealed that the children with moderate to severe brain injury exhibited more errors in spelling, punctuation, and capitalisation than manifested by the children with mild brain injuries. This difference remained significant even after controlling for the amount of written output (i.e. total number of words) because more errors are possible the more output produced.

Comparisons of oral versus written narrative discourse using the same story revealed greater reductions in the amount of language and in the amount of total information produced with a trend towards increased disruptions in episodic structure for children with severe TBI for the written modality. The differences in quantity of output is likely to be due to the inherent features of the respective modality. We all tend to say more than we write because of efficiency of expression. Nonetheless, the tendency towards greater disturbances in episodic structure (suggestive of greater impairment in discourse organisation) supports the possibility that written expression may be more vulnerable to the effects of TBI than the verbal modality. No differences were found in the complexity of language or the amount of gist information between the two modalities across either mild, moderate, or severe TBI. It is interesting to note that the differences between modalities occurred even though the written stories were always produced after the oral version providing some practice. The effects of a severe TBI on the written modality are likely to be stronger when a written sample is obtained without a prior oral formulation. This prediction is based on the complex cognitive demands required when simultaneously creating a story and transposing it in written form. The greater vulnerability of the written modality is instructive for assessment and treatment for paediatric TBI populations given the central role of writing in education, one of the primary contexts to which the brain-injured child must be reintegrated.

FACTORS CONTRIBUTING TO OUTCOME

Although discourse appears to be a sensitive outcome measure of the long-term communication sequelae associated with severe brain injury in children, the relationship is not absolute. Considerable heterogeneity and variability in formal aspects of language and in discourse abilities are identified across paediatric populations with brain injury. The most relevant factors that contribute to the residual profile of disabilities and abilities include initial injury severity, the nature of the brain injury (including mechanism of injury, site and size of focal lesion), the age at the time of injury, the stage at the time of follow-up evaluation, and the premorbid characteristics of the child. Each variable must be considered in order to accurately predict long-term prognosis for recovery in an individual child and to establish protocols for evaluating the effects of treatment and prevention efforts (Fletcher, Ewing-Cobbs, Francis, & Levin, 1995).

Injury severity

Severity of the initial injury is one of the most consistently reliable variables related to discourse outcome in children with TBI (Chapman, 1995). In a series of discourse studies, Chapman and co-workers (1992, 1995, 1998) found discourse measures to be significantly lower in children who suffered a severe TBI with inconsistent findings for children with moderate degree of severity. In general, children with mild TBI performed comparably to normal controls and were even used as the control group in some studies. The findings of discourse impairment after severe TBI were consistent across a variety of ages evaluated in individual studies; i.e. 9–18 years

(Chapman et al., 1992), 6–8 years (Chapman et al., 1998), and 7–14 years (Chapman et al., 1995b), and across different narrative tasks, some auditory retell, and others generating a story from sequence pictures. Moreover, the findings were manifested at all stages of recovery, ranging from three months to five years post-injury. Injury severity was assessed using the lowest post-resuscitation Glasgow Coma Scale (GCS) score (Teasdale & Jennett, 1974), length of coma, and brain imaging findings. A mild severity judgement was made if the GCS score was greater than 12 and CT and/or MRI findings were normal. A classification of moderate impairment was made for GCS scores of 9–12 or if the child had a positive finding on the brain scan. A severe rating was associated with a GCS score of 8 or less, a level indicative of coma regardless of structural brain imaging results.

Although research consistently supports the notion that severity of initial injury is an important variable influencing degree of language/discourse recovery, severity alone does not account for degree of recovery in all cases (Levin, Ewing-Cobbs, & Eisenberg, 1995). When recovery patterns are examined for individual children, a different pattern may emerge because group results often obscure individual patterns of recovery. For example, a proportion of patients with mild to moderate injuries may show poor recovery, while some children with severe injuries may exhibit relatively good recovery (Chapman et al., 1992; Chapman et al., 1995b; Chapman et al., 1997, 1998).

In sum, the more severe the initial injury, the poorer the long-term prognosis. However, the relationship between severity and discourse outcome is not so straightforward, because severity alone does not always correspond to the degree of recovery (Chapman. et al., 1997; Levin, Ewing-Cobbs, & Eisenberg, 1995). The inconsistency in the relationship may arise from the influence of additional variables such as the mechanism of injury, the method used to measure severity, and from the pathophysiological effects of injury on the brain (Fletcher et al., 1995).

Site and size of lesion

Focal brain lesions have been associated with persistent linguistic disturbances in children by a number of investigations (Aram, Ekelman, & Whitaker, 1987; Chapman et al., 1992; Dennis, 1980; Dennis & Lovett, 1990; Lovett, Dennis, & Newman, 1986). Children who sustain early left hemisphere vascular lesions show compromised syntactic ability to a greater degree than children with early right hemisphere lesions (Aram, Ekelman, Rose, & Whitaker, 1985; Aram, Ekelman, & Whitaker, 1986, 1987). Children with left hemisphere lesions subsequent to TBI are also more likely to show specific language disturbances on traditional language measures than children with intact left hemispheres (Chapman, 1997).

A frontal lobe injury may correspond to severity of discourse disability as well as affect the nature of the impairment in children with TBI (Chapman, 1995; Chapman et al., 1992; Chapman et al., 1998). For example, children with relatively large frontal lobe injuries after TBI reportedly exhibited greater discourse deficits than those observed in a group with a comparable severity of brain injury not involving the frontal lobes. The discourse disruptions were manifested on measures of information organisation and content. Differences in the nature of the impairment have been identified based on the lateralisation of frontal lesions. For example, children with left frontal lesions produced simplified narratives at both sentential and discourse levels (Chapman et al., 1992; Dennis, 1980; Dennis & Lovett, 1990; Lovett, Dennis, & Newman, 1986). In contrast, a right frontal lobe lesion was associated with a reduction in information content on narrative retell tasks; however, the amount and complexity of the sentences comprising the story were preserved.

The size or volume of resultant lesion is also related to outcome measures after TBI (Levin, Ewing-Cobbs, & Eisenberg, 1995) and interacts with the location of the lesion. For example, the volume of left or right frontal lesions increased the predictive value of performance on verbal fluency for generating as many words as possible beginning with a specific letter (i.e. *f, a, s*) and on a response modulation task (i.e. respond to one stimulus and withhold response to another stimulus), whereas volume of extra frontal lesion failed to significantly enhance prediction on any cognitive or linguistic measure (Levin et al., 1995). The relationship between volume of frontal lobe lesion and behavioural sequelae of TBI remained even after accounting for severity of injury. Specifically, the larger lesions were associated with greater impairment.

Age at injury

The evidence regarding the relationship between age at the time of brain injury and language outcome is equivocal. Nonetheless, recent findings indicate that a younger age at injury may have a more deleterious impact on long-term recovery (Chapman, 1995; Chapman et al., 1998; Chapman et al., 1997; Ewing-Cobbs, Levin, Eisenberg, & Fletcher, 1987). Hebb (1942) was perhaps the first to suggest that brain injury may have the greatest effect on the acquisition of new skills rather than the recovery of previous abilities.

More severe discourse impairment has been identified in children who were injured at younger ages. In particular, children who sustained a severe brain injury prior to five years of age showed consistently lower performance on discourse measures than children who suffered brain injuries at five years or older (Chapman et al., 1998). Both groups, comparable in age at the time of testing (between the ages of six to eight years), severity, gender, and socioeconomic status, were all evaluated at least one year post-injury. These findings were particularly striking because the children injured at a younger age had a longer recovery period. A brain injury incurred before five years of age may disrupt the critical period in which basic narrative structure is evolving (Applebee, 1978; Westby, 1984).

Ewing-Cobbs and colleagues (1989) identified age-at-injury effects on expressive language measures but not on receptive skills. The younger age-at-injury group (<31 months) performed lower than the older age-at-injury (>31 months) group. In another study, Ewing-Cobbs et al. (1987) found that written language was significantly more affected in children than in adolescents. These researchers postulated that emerging written language skills are more prone to disruption when the injury occurs prior to the stage when these skills are well established. A similar relationship was found between age-at-time of brain injury and reading ability (Shaffer, Bijur, Chadwick, & Rutter, 1980). That is, children who sustained early, severe brain injuries (i.e. prior to age eight) had significant reading disorders whereas children injured later were less impaired.

Age has also been postulated as a possible explanation for the relatively good recovery of the lexical and grammatical aspects of language. The argument offered is that many children with acquired brain injuries benefit from the premorbid stages of normal acquisition. That is, most children and adolescents may be fortunate enough to regain the lexical and grammatical language components because these abilities may have been well established prior to the brain injury.

Alternative evidence suggests that the lexical and grammatical systems may be likely to recover regardless of age at injury. Studies of children who suffer pre- or perinatal brain injuries reported recovery of language skills to normal levels by five years of age, despite earlier evidence of delay in language acquisition (Stiles, 1996). Moreover, the delay in acquisition of language and subsequent recovery occurred regardless of the site of brain lesion. It is important to note that measurement of language recovery did not include assessment of discourse. Nonetheless, the degree of cognitive-linguistic recovery in children is influenced to some extent by the stage of cognitive and brain development at the time of injury (Jellinger, 1983).

Recovery stage at follow-up evaluation

Recovery of language function in children who sustain a severe brain injury is clearly not a one-time phenomenon (Bates, Reilly, & Marchman, 1992). For some time now it has been speculated that some children with severe brain injury may show deficits at later developmental stages despite an apparent recovery at one year post-injury. Evidence from retrospective studies indicate that the scope of the problem may not be fully realised until the brain-injured child reaches maturity or even adulthood (Eslinger, Grattan, Damasio, & Damasio, 1992).

Although interesting patterns have emerged from retrospective studies, the only way to examine the evolution of the problems is through prospective evaluations where the same child is evaluated at subsequent developmental stages. A case is summarised to illustrate how changes may evolve. Chapman and colleagues reported a single case study of a child whose behavioural deficits became more conspicuous as she reached later developmental stages (Chapman, Levin, & Harward, 1996). She sustained a severe TBI at approximately six years of age. She showed relatively good recovery at both a three-month and a twelve-month follow-up evaluation, whereas by three years post-injury, there was a marked gap between her performance and that of her peer group. In contrast to the expected recovery pattern of continued improvement over time, this patient's performance became increasingly more divergent from normal with increased time post-injury. With regard to discourse performance, this child generated stories at a level appropriate for her age at the 3- and 12-month post-injury evaluations. Unfortunately, no improvement in narrative ability was observed at two years post-injury. By the time she was 10;11, at her 3-year post-injury assessment, her ability to formulate more complete and complex stories fell significantly below that of her age group. She tended to express isolated pieces of information without any clear connection from one idea to the next. Whereas this behaviour is normal for very young children, it is abnormal for older children who have typically mastered the ability to produce well organised and coherent stories by the second or third grade. Moreover, she exhibited a marked deficiency in synthesising the central meaning of the story in the form of a generalised statement. Normal children are able to produce a generalised statement by at least eight years of age (Chapman et al., 1997). Similar to other children with severe TBI, this child produced as much and as complex language in telling a story as normal children. Classroom performance also supported a decrement in development over time. This child returned to the normal classroom within three months after the injury when she was in the first grade. She performed at or above an average level as compared with other children in the classroom until the middle of the third grade. By the end of the third grade, she began experiencing considerable trouble keeping up with her peer group particularly in reading and English composition. Additional evidence of individual children who showed latent manifestations of disturbances at three years post-injury has been reported (Chapman & Levin, 1994).

At present it is unclear what mechanisms contribute to the latent presentation of behavioural disturbances. The two most commonly proposed explanations are that (a) children with severe brain injury may fail to acquire higher cognitive levels necessary to support later developmental processes, and (b) the later emerging symptoms may result from an injury to an immature brain region causing a delay of symptoms until the region subserving the specific ability has reached functional maturity (Chapman et al., 1996; Goldman-Rakic, 1987; Levin et al., 1993). The underlying cause of the delayed behavioural symptoms may result from an interaction of these two mechanisms.

Premorbid characteristics

Another important variable to consider when determining the nature and extent of the disability associated with the brain injury is the patient's pretraumatic behavioural and psychological status. The victims of brain injury do not form a random sample of their age group (Jennett, 1990). It is commonly postulated that children with attention deficit disorders or those who are risk-takers premorbidly are more likely to sustain a brain injury (Jennett, 1990). Shaffer (1995) found that the presence of pre-injury behavioural problems was a strong predictor of later problems in children with mild to severe brain injuries. Moreover, it is unclear how the endogenous changes associated with development in adolescence interact with the behavioural changes resulting from the TBI.

Children with TBI are likely to have pre-existing conditions, such as attention deficit-hyperactivity disorder or developmental language problems that confound the outcome profile. For example, a number of common discourse disturbances have been identified in children with attention deficit-hyperactivity disorder and in children with TBI, such as a failure to retain the most essential or gist information (Chapman, 1994; Tannock, 1994). Given the possibility of premorbid attention deficits in children who suffer TBI, a lower discourse performance may be due largely to pre-injury status rather than the sole consequences of the neurological injury.

Additionally, children with TBI may have had pre-existing language impairments that went undetected for a variety of reasons, such as an early age at injury. In a recent study, some degree of language impairment was found in two brothers (Chapman, Weyrauch, & Harrison, 1993). One brother had suffered a severe brain injury at five years of age and the younger was believed to have had normal language development. In fact, neither child had a suspected language problem prior to the brain injury. The brother who suffered a TBI exhibited a marked language impairment when evaluated at four years post-injury at nine years of age. This child had positive and compatible findings on both MRI and SPECT (single photon emission computed tomography measuring cerebral brain blood flow) scans showing involvement in the left temporal lobe, a region that supports language function. For comparative purposes, his brother was tested when he reached nine years of age and a mild language impairment was identified. This finding suggested a possible familial language problem, although the sibling with a TBI clearly had a more severe language disturbance. Thus, the measured language impairment in the child with TBI may represent the combined effects of a pre-existing language disturbance that was exacerbated by a subsequent brain injury with the focus of injury in the language cortex.

Language comparisons across brain aetiologies

The literature suggests that brain damage in general, regardless of the mechanism of injury, may produce a global reduction in language performance levels. In support of this view, Jordan et al., (1995) found a significant depression on a composite language score in three diverse pathologies; i.e. children with closed head injury, children treated for acute lymphoblastic leukaemia, and children treated for posterior fossa tumour. No single language measure alone was found to be consistently depressed for any group. Similarly, Dennis (1992) reported a general lowering of word-finding abilities in separate studies of paediatric clinical populations with various etiologies. The aetiologies included: (a) unilateral congenital brain malformations and subsequent hemidecortication (Lovett, Dennis, & Newman 1986); (b) early hydrocephalus (Dennis, Hendrick, Hoffman, & Humphreys, 1987; Dennis, Jacennik, & Barnes, 1994); (c) left hemisphere stroke (Dennis, 1980); and (d) traumatic head injury (Dennis & Barnes, 1990). All four types of brain pathology reportedly had an adverse effect on word-finding ability. For the most part, the word-finding deficits were more readily apparent on timed tasks or on word-finding tasks tested in the context of discourse.

Some evidence points to a differential effect of brain aetiology on language functions, with some suggesting qualitative differences and others revealing primarily quantitative discrepancies. Differences in the nature of disturbances were asserted by Jordan et al. (1996) who found that children with TBI were impaired on both confrontation naming and verbal fluency (e.g. categories of foods and animals) measures, whereas children treated for leukaemia and posterior fossa tumours were impaired only on verbal fluency measures (Jordan et al., 1996). Qualitative differences were implicated between the aetiologies of closed head injuries (CHI) and open head injuries (OHI). Chapman, Wanek, and Sharpe (1994) compared the discourse profile of children with focal injuries following open head injuries (e.g. gunshot wound) to children with focal plus diffuse injuries associated with CHI and found different degrees of discourse impairment when matching the children on severity of injury and site of focal lesions. The findings of this latter study revealed that the individual children with CHI exhibited more severe disturbances in narrative discourse than the children with other types of TBI (see original story and sample stories in the Appendix to this chapter). Similarly, children with frontal lesions associated with a CHI were found to manifest greater disturbances in discourse ability than a child who sustained bilateral frontal lobe lesions subsequent to a traumatic aneurysm (Chapman et al., 1992). It is important to note that when the lesion focus was comparable across aetiological categories, there was more overlap in the discourse profiles.

At present, the degree to which the mechanism of injury produces divergent behavioural profiles is unclear. The divergent causes of trauma vary in the amount of force affecting the brain (Fletcher et al., 1995), consequently injuring the brain to different degrees. For example, minor injuries are more likely to occur in accidents that do not involve motor vehicles. Although ratings of the initial injury severity can be higher in OHI, the degree of disability associated with OHI is often comparable to that seen in severe CHI (Ewing-Cobbs, Thompson, Miner, & Fletcher, 1994; Ewing-Cobbs et al., 1989). Moreover, the differences in degree of recovery associated with various mechanisms of injury interact with the localisation and size of the resultant lesion.

COGNITIVE CORRELATES OF DISCOURSE DISABILITY

In order to understand the cognitive-linguistic deficits associated with discourse impairment or communication breakdown in general, it is important to go beyond determining whether specific language or even discourse-level problems exist. A more integrated clinical approach is to determine how cognitive and linguistic disturbances interact to disrupt communicative competence. As stated previously, discourse processing entails a complex interaction of linguistic knowledge and the supporting cognitive abilities including working memory, planning, problem solving, and attention, to mention a few. It is necessary to examine the relationship between discourse and cognitive abilities to effectively manage the long-term communicative disabilities manifested in severe brain injury.

In the next section we focus on the relationships between discourse processing and cognitive abilities of executive functioning. The relatively high prevalence of discourse disturbances in paediatric TBI has already been discussed. Disturbances in executive function also represent persistent sequelae of head trauma incurred during childhood, particularly for those children with injuries involving the prefrontal network (Hendryx & Verduyn, 1995; Levin, Goldstein, Williams, & Eisenberg, 1991; Sohlberg & Mateer, 1989). Chapman and colleagues (1996) claim that the pervasive deficits documented in higher-level discourse processing for children with severe brain injury may be associated with deficits in cognitive abilities of executive control and metacognition.

Cognitive abilities of executive control and neural representation

Cognitive abilities of executive control, commonly referred to as executive functions, include the cognitive processes involved in attainment of a future goal, such as the strategic planning and problem solving that goes into completing a project (Luria, 1966; Pennington, 1991). Executive functions include organisation of memory (i.e. the guidance of cognitive processing by a symbolic or mental representation—semantic organisation), planning and problem solving (i.e. the ability to visualise subgoals and to monitor the performance of carrying out the subgoals to achieve a goal), elaboration or creativity (i.e. the application of information to previous knowledge or novel contexts—e.g. fluency of ideas or tokens), and self-regulation of responses (as achieved through the processes of initiating, monitoring, inhibiting, set-shifting, and revising responses as needed to accomplish a task). Strongly associated with executive function is metacognition, which refers to the ability to reflect on what and how one processes information and to proactively apply strategies to improve performance or learning (Borkowski & Kurtz, 1987). The development and intactness of metacognitive ability is associated with the ability to orchestrate cognitive processes to enhance learning and to monitor the consequences of one's behaviour (Borkowski & Cavanaugh, 1979; Flavell, 1978).

The prefrontal region of the brain and its interconnections appear to play a central and pervasive role in controlling executive functions (Case, 1992; Goldman-Rakic, 1987; Stuss, 1992). The unique and complex interconnectivity of the prefrontal to other brain regions including the posterior neocortex, basal ganglia, thalamus, hippocampus, and brain stem nuclei supports the special role of the prefrontal cortex in coordinating diverse cognitive functions (Goldman-Rakic, 1988). It is important to recognise that the specialisation of frontal lobe functions emerges in a "multi-stage process" (Passler, Isaac, & Hynd, 1985). That is, cognitive abilities of executive functioning are present early in development and continue to evolve in a protracted course of development (Welsh & Pennington, 1988).

Relationship between discourse and cognitive variables

Few empirical studies have directly examined the relationship between discourse and cognitive variables of executive function. However, the limited evidence suggests that a relationship may exist providing a theoretical basis for intervention. Studies linking executive function to communication in TBI adults are discussed in Chapter 4 and specific links between discourse and executive dysfunction in TBI adults are explored in detail in Chapter 3. In a recent study, a relationship was found between the ability to utilise organisational schemas during discourse production and performance on cognitive measures of semantic organisation in children with TBI and control children (Culhane, Chapman, & Levin, 1993). Specifically, performance on a group of cognitive measures of executive function was found to be significantly related to the ability to plan and formulate well-organised discourse. The positive relationship could not be attributed to a general cognitive factor because the relationship was over and above what could be accounted for by non-verbal cognitive measures.

In a longitudinal case study, impairments were documented in both cognitive measures of executive control and discourse abilities in a child with bilateral frontal lobe involvement identified on functional brain imaging (Chapman et al., 1996). This child was able to retain isolated pieces of discourse information but was unable to make inferences and adequately interpret the information at a higher level of semantic representation. With regard to cognitive function, this child failed to consistently use a semantic clustering strategy to guide recall of a list of words as typically expressed by normally developing children.

Regarding interdependencies across discourse and cognitive abilities of executive control, Chapman and Levin (1994) proposed a set of possible relationships (Table 9.2). One proposed relationship is between the executive function of utilising a symbolic representation to guide future cognitive processing and the ability to process the global semantic meaning of a discourse text. For example, an individual with the aforementioned executive dysfunction may have difficulty interpreting the gist or theme of a narrative. Moreover, if an individual is unable to either establish or to hold a generalised semantic representation of discourse meaning in working memory, they may be unable to process subsequent content in the context of previous information. This pattern may explain why children with severe TBI are unable to integrate information across sentences although they retain isolated pieces of information. In addition, an impairment in the capacity for planning may be manifested in discourse as an incoherent unfolding of information content. Moreover, cognitive organisational structures such as episodic structure or scripts of regularly occurring everyday events are used to guide narrative discourse comprehension, storage, and subsequent recall, and may potentially be disrupted as a consequence of executive impairment.

TABLE 9.2
Impact of cognitive disturbances of executive functions on discourse abilities

Impaired executive functions	*Resulting discourse behaviours*
Impaired global semantic representation	Unable to grasp the central meaning of discourse; or hold it in memory to use later for social or learning purposes.
Unable to utilise organised memory systems	Impairment in episodic structure resulting in disorganisation of information related to everyday happenings.
Poor capacity for planning	Difficulty unfolding discourse coherently.
Limited flexibility in problem solving	Difficulty conceiving of alternative interpretations, narrow or rigid interpretations of text, fluency of ideas reduced.
Poor inhibitory control	Stream of consciousness in discourse producing intrusions of tangentially related information, unable to inhibit ideas that come to mind during talk or learning.

Discourse ability and working memory

Recall studies of discourse indicate that normal individuals process and store information at higher levels of semantic representation than is represented in the original text (Frederiksen, Bracewell, Breuleux, & Renuas, 1990; van Dijk, 1995). Evidence for higher-level processing during encoding of discourse information is supported by the fact that individuals typically recall little of the original story verbatim even on immediate recall. In fact, only 10% to 25% of the original content is retold on immediate reproduction (Kintsch & van Dijk, 1978). Rather, a condensed version of the text is recalled that represents the global meaning of the text represented in a higher-level, abstract paraphrase of the original information (Kay & Black, 1986). Limited memory of the precise words and sentences remain, although knowledge of the general meaning is retained. In fact, individuals are typically able to elaborate on the relationship in meaning expressed across sentences when probed.

The fact that individuals do not retain the exact wording of discourse is commonly attributed to working memory limitations. Working memory is a transient, prospective form of memory, while semantic memory deals with a more permanent storage of knowledge (Baddeley & Della Sala, 1996; Pennington, 1991). Working memory is conceptualised as a computational workspace in which one is able to make response choices while inhibiting competing, less appropriate responses. Models of discourse processing predict that information must be stored at higher levels of meaningful representation in order to effectively use the information for learning purposes (Kintsch & van Dijk, 1978; Winograd, 1984). In view of capacity limitations, an information-processing system cannot operate effectively if it is limited to lower levels of information (Pennington, 1991). Therefore it may be possible to hold in working memory the central meaning of a whole text while processing the incoming information by encoding the information at a condensed, higher level of semantic representation. The relationship between TBI and impaired working memory is reviewed in Chapter 2 and specific empirical studies linking poor working memory with discourse processing in adult TBI are detailed in Chapter 4. Similarly, working memory deficits have implications for discourse function in the paediatric TBI population.

A majority of children with a severe TBI display significant difficulty in paraphrasing the story information and retaining the central meaning (Chapman et al., 1992; Chapman, 1995; Chapman et al., 1996; Chapman et al., 1997). Even though many children with severe TBI are able to understand and remember isolated pieces of information, they have difficulty making inferences between ideas. It has been suggested that these children have marked difficulty integrating information at higher levels of semantic representation due, in part, to limitations in working memory. Moreover, they experience significant problems in condensing information in the form of a generalised statement (Chapman et al., 1997). This later ability is a prerequisite to successful academic performance (Hill, 1991; Kay & Black, 1986).

Management implications

Based on the research findings discussed above, a number of guidelines can be formulated to provide quality assessment and treatment of the cognitive-communicative sequelae of TBI.

Assessment framework

The framework for assessment should include structured language measures making sure to include tasks that rely on strategic-cognitive operations such as (a) verbal fluency for categories or fluency of solutions to everyday problems (e.g. "What are some different things you could do if you forgot your keys and found yourself locked out of the house?"), (b) resolving ambiguous sentences, (c) concept formation such as word definitions, and (d) formulation of semantically constrained responses—e.g. use of

20 questions to guess an item with as few yes-no questions as possible or determination of how two concepts are alike.

It is equally important to incorporate discourse measures for both oral and written modalities in the diagnostic protocol. While the structured language measures will identify problems in a proportion of the population, the discourse measures will prove to be a more sensitive measure of the cognitive-communicative sequelae in a majority of children with TBI at chronic stages of recovery.

In addition, assessment procedures should include collection of comprehensive case information. The case history should document the mechanism of brain injury, the initial injury severity, the site and extent of brain damage identified on brain scans, age at injury, and as complete a profile as possible of premorbid characteristics and learning capacity. Determining the child's previous level of function requires identifying any potential at-risk factors such as any concerns regarding a learning disability, attention deficit hyperactivity disorder, developmental language problem, or affective disorder. It is also important to inquire about any familial problems. Evaluation of each variable is essential in establishing the degree to which the child's disabilities will be amenable to treatment.

Perhaps the greatest void in management of cognitive-linguistic sequelae of paediatric TBI today is the failure to provide stage-by-stage evaluation and treatment, when indicated. That is, the resultant disability associated with severe brain injury is rarely fully realised in the early stage post-injury (from 3 to 12 months following injury) and may become more apparent at later stages post-injury (from 3 to 5 years following injury). Growing evidence points to a more profound effect of early brain injury on later developing skills or even skills in the process of development at the time of injury (Chapman et al., 1996; Fletcher, Miner, & Ewing-Cobbs, 1987). The impact at later developmental stages is often more pronounced than the loss or disruption of skills acquired prior to the trauma. In contrast, skills acquired prior to the injury during a period of normal development can show relatively good recovery following brain trauma. Finally, measures of cognitive abilities of executive function will provide a more comprehensive profile of the impairments and preservations.

Treatment framework

Any general statements made regarding prescribed treatment for children with TBI must be interpreted cautiously. Because each child presents a unique profile of strengths and weaknesses, the treatment programme must be individually designed. Despite this caveat, some general suggestions can be offered to direct management of the residual and perhaps later-appearing cognitive-linguistic deficits associated with paediatric TBI. First, it is important to recognise that few children with TBI are likely to need traditional remediation of specific language abilities as required for children with congenital or developmental language impairments. Secondly, many children who sustain a severe TBI will exhibit significant impairments in discourse skills that should be remediated. No single discourse programme will be appropriate for all children with TBI because the nature and degree of the discourse disruption will vary across individual children. A treatment programme that is directed at improving the ability to manipulate, paraphrase, and condense text level information may facilitate discourse function for brain-injured children who show these specific problems. This recommended focus is based on evidence that the most common discourse sequelae in brain-injured children (Chapman et al., 1992; Chapman et al., 1995b; Chapman et al., 1997; Dennis & Barnes, 1990; Szekeres & Meserve, 1994; Ylvisaker & Feeney, 1994) include difficulties in:

(1) retaining the most important information from the text
(2) producing organised discourse
(3) making inferences and realising meaning relations between adjacent ideas
(4) paraphrasing information contained in texts, and
(5) condensing and transforming the textual information into synthesised, generalised statements.

Generally, treatment goals should be directed toward facilitating discourse processing at global levels of information processing, including intermediate levels (e.g. combining information in adjacent sentences) and at higher levels (e.g. abstracting main ideas or themes across entire texts) of processing. Training should include strategies to condense and transform discourse information in the form of main ideas, summary statements, and interpretive responses, that generalise the information to other contexts (Borkowski & Kurtz, 1987; Kay & Black, 1986; Winograd, 1984). The discourse content for the therapeutic sessions should be derived from the child's functional context—e.g. personal interest reading (like sports or mysteries), hobbies, activities, academic information from classroom texts, and personal letters. Discourse treatment should be integrated within the context of teaching specific cognitive strategies to process and organise new information. For example, helping the child to plan, monitor, and revise oral and written assignments can be implemented in various stages (Borkowski & Kurtz, 1987). The planning component might entail the child identifying the subgoals required to complete a written project. Monitoring would help the child to review his or her own performance in completing the necessary steps to complete a project. Revising would give the child practice in recognising the need to improve the quality of this output at different stages of treatment based on their level of competence.

CONCLUSIONS

On the basis of the current review, the most important conclusion to be drawn is that the communication disability associated with paediatric brain injury is distinct from the classic profile of children with developmental language problems. Unlike children with specific developmental language problems, children and adolescents with acquired brain injuries do not commonly exhibit specific language impairments in the formal domains of language (i.e. phonology, morphology, and syntax). If deficits are present, they will be most prominent on structured language measures that place high demands on cognitive processing—e.g. rapid access of information as required on verbal fluency tasks. However, the majority of children with severe brain injuries will exhibit significant impairments in discourse function.

It is essential to recognise the distinction between developmental and acquired communication problems given that traditional clinical practice for paediatric populations has been derived primarily from the profile of developmental language disturbances. The differences have important implications for assessment and treatment. In assessment, there is consensus that traditional language measures, when used alone, are insufficient to tap the full scope of the communicative disability in brain-injured populations. Children with brain injury tend to perform relatively well on formal language tests because the cognitive demands are low and the tasks are well structured (Ylvisaker, 1993). Consequently, the more complex disturbances in manipulating larger chunks of language (i.e. discourse level) common to severe brain injury often go undetected if higher-level measures are not employed. The evidence overwhelmingly indicates that discourse measures must be incorporated in diagnostic protocols for brain-injured children to effectively characterise the pervasive cognitive-communicative disability. Moreover, assessment should include evaluations of both oral and written modalities involving retellings and paraphrasing of prescribed discourse information as well as self-created discourse texts.

A second conclusion related to assessment is that accurate prognostication about long-term recovery from acquired brain injury is possible only by registering the influence of injury severity, site and extent of lesion, age at injury, and stage of development at follow-up assessments. Assessment of cognitive-linguistic abilities at any time post-injury should be integrated within the context of these injury variables to make more accurate predictions about recovery and continued development.

Another important principle relevant to assessment and treatment is that both should be ongoing processes throughout the academic years following a severe brain injury because latent disturbances in communication ability may evolve. Unlike adults who manifest a loss soon after the brain insult, children with acquired brain injuries may not exhibit the greatest impact until they reach a developmental stage far removed from the time of injury (Dennis & Lovett, 1990). Finally, discourse abilities in paediatric brain injury should not be treated in isolation. Rather, discourse should be managed within the context of related cognitive abilities of executive control—e.g. planning, problem solving, and organised memory. Moreover, the ability to exchange information in a social interaction should be targeted. Clearly the treatment framework should focus on discourse, cognitive, and social abilities simultaneously to provide a functional, integrated approach.

In sum, assessment of discourse will provide a more complete characterisation of the nature of the broad-based cognitive-communicative deficits associated with paediatric brain injury that go beyond isolated language disturbances. Moreover, the assessment of discourse will contribute to establishing functional goals that target everyday communicative activities in social and academic contexts. The characterisation of discourse abilities at subsequent stages of development following a moderate to severe brain injury will lead to better understanding of the long-term recovery potential from a developmental perspective. We believe application of discourse tasks during assessment and intervention will insure the highest level of care in children and adolescents with cognitive-communicative disorder subsequent to acquired brain injury.

ACKNOWLEDGEMENTS

Research reported in this chapter was supported by grant NS-21889. The authors gratefully acknowledge the children and families whose commitment made this project possible.

REFERENCES

Applebee, A.N. (1978). *The child's concept of story*. Chicago, IL: University of Chicago Press.

Aram, D.M., Ekelman, B.L., Rose, D.F., & Whitaker, H.A. (1985). Verbal and cognitive sequelae following unilateral lesions acquired early in childhood. *Journal of Clinical and Experimental Neuropsychology, 7(10)*, 55–78.

Aram, D.M., Ekelman, B.L., & Whitaker, H.A. (1986). Spoken syntax in children with acquired unilateral hemisphere lesions. *Brain and Language*, *31*, 61–87.

Aram, D.M., Ekelman, B.L., & Whitaker, H.A. (1987). Lexical retrieval in left and right brain lesioned children. *Brain and Language, 27(1)*, 75–100.

Baddeley, A., & Della Sala, S. (1996). Working memory and executive control. *Philosophical Transactions of the Royal Society of London*, *351*, 1397.

Bates, E., Reilly, J., & Marchman, E. (1992, October). *Discourse and grammar after early focal brain injury*. Abstract from Academy of Aphasia Meeting, Toronto, Canada.

Biddle, K.R., McCabe, A., & Bliss, L.S. (1996). Narrative skills following traumatic brain injury in children and adults. *Journal of Communication Disorders*, *29(6)*, 447–470.

Bishop, D.V. (1992). The underlying nature of specific language impairment. *Journal of Child Psychiatry and Allied Disciplines, 33,* 3–66.

Bishop, D.V., & Edmudson, A. (1987). Language-impaired four-year-olds: Distinguishing transient from persistent impairment. *Journal of Speech and Hearing Disorders, 52,* 156–173.

Blosser, J.L., & DePompeii, R. (1994). *Pediatric traumatic brain injury proactive intervention.* San Diego, CA: Singular Publishing Group, Inc.

Borkowski, J.G., & Cavanaugh, J.C. (1979). Maintenance and generalization of skills and strategies by the retarded. In N.R. Ellis (Ed.), *Handbook of mental deficiency: Psychological theory and research* (pp.569–618). Hillsdale, NJ: Lawrence Erlbaum Associates Inc.

Borkowski, J.G., & Kurtz, B.E. (1987). Metacognition and executive control. In J.G. Borkwoski & J.D. Day (Eds.), *Cognition in special children* (pp.123–152). Norwood, NJ: Ablex Publishing.

Brown, G., Chadwick, O., Shaffer, D., Rutter, M., & Traub, M. (1981). A prospective study of children with head injuries: III. Psychiatric sequelae. *Psychological Medicine, 11,* 63–78.

Campbell, T.F., & Dollaghan, C.A. (1990). Expressive language recovery in severely brain-injured children and adolescents. *Journal of Speech and Hearing Disorders, 55(3),* 567–581.

Case, R. (1992). The role of frontal lobes in the regulation of cognitive development. *Brain and Cognition, 20,* 51–73.

Chadwick, O., Rutter, M., Shaffer, D., & Shrout, P.E. (1981). A prospective study of children with head injuries: Specific cognitive deficits. *Journal of Clinical Neuropsychology, 3(2),* 101–120.

Chapman, S.B. (1994, January). *Discourse and pediatric head injury: Consideration of cognitive/linguistic, psychosocial, and neuropathological factors.* Paper presented at the meeting of the International Society for Research in Child and Adolescent Psychopathology, Santa Monica, CA.

Chapman, S.B. (1995). Discourse as an outcome measure in pediatric head-injured populations. In S.H. Broman & M.E. Michel (Eds.), *Traumatic brain injury in children* (pp.95–116). New York: Oxford University Press.

Chapman, S.B. (1997). Cognitive-communication abilities in children with closed head injury. *American Journal of Speech-Language Pathology, 6(2),* 50–58.

Chapman, S.B., Culhane, K.A., Levin, H.S., Harward, H., Mendelsohn, D., Ewing-Cobbs, L., Fletcher, J.M., & Bruce, D. (1992). Narrative discourse after closed head injury in children and adolescents. *Brain and Language, 43,* 42–65.

Chapman, S.B., & Gustafson, C. (1994, April). *Narrative discourse in language impaired and head injured children.* Paper presented at the meeting of the Texas Speech-Language-Hearing Association, San Antonio, TX.

Chapman, S.B., & Lawyer, S.L. (1997, April). *Recovery of written discourse abilities in children following closed head injury at three and twelve months post-injury.* Paper presented at the meeting of the Texas Speech-Language-Hearing Association, Austin, TX.

Chapman, S.B., & Levin, H.S. (1994, November) *Discourse abilities and executive function in head-injured children.* Paper presented at the American Speech-Language and Hearing Association Convention, New Orleans, LA.

Chapman, S.B., Levin, H.S., & Culhane, K. (1995a). Language impairment in closed head injury. In H. Kirschner (Ed.), *Handbook of neurological speech and language disorders* (pp.387–414). New York: Marcel Dekker, Inc.

Chapman, S.B., Levin, H.S., & Harward, H.N. (1996). Long-term recovery of discourse, cognitive, and psychological abilities in pediatric head injury: A case illustration. In A. Balejko (Ed.), *Diagnoza i terapia osób z różnymi zaburzeniami językowymi.* Bialystok, Poland: Wydaniel.

Chapman, S.B., Levin, H.S., Matejka, J., Harward, H.N., & Kufera, J. (1995b). Discourse ability in head-injured children: Considerations of linguistic, psychosocial, and cognitive factors. *Journal of Head Trauma Rehabilitation, 10,* 36–54.

Chapman, S.B., Levin, H.S., Wanek, A., Weyrauch, J., & Kufera, J. (1998). Discourse after closed head injury in young children: Relation of age to outcome. *Brain and Language, 61,* 420–449.

Chapman, S.B., Wanek, A., & Sharpe, S. (1994, September). *Narrative discourse in pediatric head injury: What a story!* Paper presented at the Meeting of the Colorado Speech and Hearing Association, Denver, CO.

Chapman, S.B., Watkins, R., Gustafson, C., Moore, S., Levin, H.S., & Kufera, J.A. (1997). Narrative discourse in children with closed head injury, children with language impairment, and typically developing children. *American Journal of Speech-Language Pathology, 6,* 66–75.

Chapman, S.B., Weyrauch, J., & Harrison, S. (1993, April). *Neurobehavioral sequelae and discourse abilities: Is there improvement beyond one year post-injury in CHI children and adolescents.* Paper presented at the meeting of the Texas Speech-Language-Hearing Association, Corpus Christi, *TX.*

Culhane, K.A., Chapman, S.B., & Levin, H.S. (1993, February). *The relationship of discourse and cognitive task performance following closed head injury.* Paper presented at the International Neuropsychological Society Meeting, San Antonio, TX.

Damico, J.S. (1985). Clinical discourse analysis: A functional approach to language assessment. In C.S. Simon (Ed.), *Communication skills and classroom success* (pp.165–206). San Diego, CA: College-Hill Press.

Dennis, M. (1980). Capacity and strategy for syntactic comprehension after left or right hemidecortication. *Brain and Language, 10(2),* 287–317.

Dennis, M. (1992). Word finding in children and adolescents with a history of brain injury. *Topics in Language Disorders, 13(1),* 66–82.

Dennis, M., & Barnes, M.A. (1990). Knowing the meaning, getting the point, bridging the gap, and carrying the message: Aspects of discourse following closed head injury in childhood and adolescence. *Brain and Language, 39(3),* 428–446.

Dennis, M., Hendrick, E.B., Hoffman, H.J., & Humphreys, R.P. (1987). Language of hydrocephalic children and adolescents. *Journal of Clinical and Experimental Neuropsychology, 9(5),* 593–621.

Dennis, M., Jacennik, B., & Barnes, M.A. (1994). The content of narrative discourse in children and adolescents after early-onset hydrocephalus and in normally developing age peers. *Brain and Language, 46(1),* 129–165.

Dennis, M., & Lovett, M.W. (1990). Discourse ability in children after brain damage. In Y. Joanette & H.H. Brownell (Eds.), *Discourse ability and brain damage: Theoretical and empirical perspectives* (pp.199–223). New York: Springer-Verlag.

Eslinger, P., Grattan, L.M., Damasio, H., & Damasio, A.R. (1992). Developmental consequences of childhood frontal lobe damage. *Archives of Neurology, 49,* 764–769.

Ewing-Cobbs, L., Levin, H.S., Eisenberg, H.M., & Fletcher, J.M. (1987). Language functions following closed head injury in children and adolescents. *Journal of Clinical and Experimental Neuropsychology, 9(5)* 575–592.

Ewing-Cobbs, L., Miner, M.E., Fletcher, J.M., & Levin, H.S. (1989). Intellectual motor, and language sequelae following closed head injury in children and adolescents. *Journal of Pediatric Psychology, 9(5),* 575–592.

Ewing-Cobbs, L., Thompson, N.M., Miner, M.E., & Fletcher, J.M. (1994). Gunshot wounds to the brain in children and adolescents: Age and neurobehavioral development. *Neurosurgery, 35,* 225–233.

Feagans, L., & Applebaum, M. (1986). Validation of language subtypes in learning of disabled children. *Journal of Educational Psychology, 78,* 358–364.

Flavell, J.H. (1978). Metacognitive development. In J.M. Scandura & C.J. Brainerd (Eds.), *Structural/process theories of complex human behavior* (pp.213–245). Aphen ad. Rign, The Netherlands: Sijhoff & Noordhuff.

Fletcher, J.M., Ewing-Cobbs, L., Francis, D.J., & Levin, H.S. (1995). Variability in outcomes after traumatic brain injury in children: A developmental perspective. In S.H. Broman & M.E. Michel (Eds.), *Traumatic brain injury in children* (pp.95–116). New York: Oxford University Press.

Fletcher, J.M., Ewing-Cobbs, L., Miner, M.E., Levin, H.S., & Eisenberg, H.M. (1990). Behavioral changes after closed head injury. *Journal of Consulting Clinical Psychology, 58,* 93–98.

Fletcher, J.M., Miner, M., & Ewing-Cobbs, L. (1987). Age and recovery from head injury in children: Developmental issues. In H.S. Levin, H. Eisenberg, & J. Grafman (Eds.), *Neurobehavioral recovery from head injury* (pp.279–291). New York: Oxford University Press.

Frederiksen, C.H., Bracewell, F.J., Breuleux, A., & Renuas, A. (1990). The cognitive representation and processing of discourse: Function and dysfunction. In Y. Joanette & H.H. Brownell (Eds.), *Discourse ability and brain damage: Theoretical and empirical perspectives* (pp.69–112). New York: Springer-Verlag.

Gillam, R., McFadden, T.U., & van Kleek, A. (1995). Improving the narrative abilities of children with language disorders: Whole language and language skills approaches. In M. Fey, J. Windsor, & J. Reichie (Eds.), *Communication intervention for school-age children* (pp.145–182). Baltimore, MD: Paul Brookes.

Goldman-Rakic, P.S. (1987). Circuitry of primate prefrontal cortex and regulation of behavior by representational knowledge. In F. Plum (Ed.), *Handbook of physiology: Section 1. The nervous system: Vol 5. Higher functions of the brain* (pp.373–417). New York: Oxford University Press.

Goldman-Rakic, P.S. (1988). Topography of cognition: Parallel distributed networks in primate association cortex. *Annual Review of Neuroscience, 11,* 137–156.

Hammill, D.D., Brown, V.L., & Larsen, S.C. (1987). *Test of adolescent language – 2.* Austin, TX: Pro-Ed.

Hammill, D.D., & Newcomer, P.L. (1982). *Test of language development – Primary.* Austin, TX: Pro-Ed.

Hammill, D.D., & Newcomer, P.L. (1982). *Test of language development – Intermediate.* Austin, TX: Pro-Ed.

Hebb, D.O. (1942). The effect of early and late brain injury upon test scores and the nature of abnormal adult intelligence. *Proceedings of the American Philosophical Society, 1,* 265–292.

Hedrick, D.L., Prather, E.M., & Tobin, A.R. (1974). *Sequenced inventory of communication development: Examiner's manual.* Seattle, WA: University of Washington Press.

Hendryx P.M. & Verduyn, M. (1995). Diagnosis and treatment strategies for the latent sequelae of head trauma in children. *Journal of Cognitive Rehabilitation, 13,* 8–12.

Hill, M. (1991). Writing summaries promotes thinking and learning across the curriculum: But why are they so difficult to write? *Journal of Reading, 34(7)*, 536–539.

Jaffe, K.M. Brink, J.D., Hays, R.M., & Choraze, A.J.L. (1990). Specific problems associated with pediatric head injury. In M. Rosenthal, E.R. Griffith, M.R. Bond, M.D. Miller (Eds.), *Rehabilitation of the adult and child with traumatic brain injury* (pp.539–557). Philadelphia, PA: F.A. Davis Company.

Jennett, B. (1990). Scale and scope of the problem. In M. Rosenthal, E.R. Griffith, M.R. Bond, M.D. Miller (Eds.), *Rehabilitation of the adult and child with traumatic brain injury* (pp.3–7). Philadelphia, PA: F.A. Davis Company.

Jellinger, K. (1983). The neuropathology of pediatric head injury. In K. Shapiro (Ed.), *Pediatric head trauma* (pp.87–115). Mount Kisco, NY: Futura.

Jordan, F.M., & Murdoch, B.E. (1990). A comparison of the conversational skills of closed head injured children and normal children. *Australian Journal of Human Communication Disorders, 18(1)*, 69–82.

Jordan, F.M., & Murdoch, B.E. (1993). A prospective study of the linguistic skills of children with closed head injuries. *Aphasiology, 7(5)*, 503–512.

Jordan, F.M., & Murdoch, B.E. (1994). Severe closed head injury in childhood: Linguistic outcomes into adulthood. *Brain Injury, 8(6)*, 501–508.

Jordan, F.M., Murdoch, B.E., & Buttsworth, D.L. (1991). Closed head injured children's performance on narrative tasks. *Journal of Speech and Hearing Research, 34(3)*, 572–582.

Jordan, F.M., Murdoch, B.E., Buttsworth, D.L., & Hudson-Tennent, L.J. (1995). Speech and language performance of brain-injured children. *Aphasiology, 9(1)*, 23–32.

Jordan, F.M., Murdoch, B.C., Hudson-Tennent, L.J., & Boon, D.L. (1996). Naming performance of brain-injured children. *Aphasiology, 19(8)*, 755–766.

Jordan, F.M., Ozanne, A.E., & Murdoch, B.E. (1988). Long-term speech and language disorders subsequent to closed head injury in children. *Brain Injury, 2(3)*, 179–185.

Kaplan, E., Goodglass, H., & Weintraub, S. (1983). *Boston Naming Test*. Philadelphia, PA: Lea & Febiger.

Kay, D.S., & Black, J.S. (1986). Explanation-driven processing in summarization: The interaction of content and process. In J.A. Galambos, R.P. Abelson, & J.B. Black (Eds.), *Knowledge structure* (pp.211–236). Hillsdale, NJ: Lawrence Erlbaum Associates Inc.

Kintsch, W., & van Dijk, T. (1978). Toward a model of text comprehension and production. *Psychological Review, 85*, 363–394.

Klonoff, H., Clark, C., & Klonoff, P.S. (1993). Long-term outcome of head injuries: A 23-year follow-up of children with head injuries. *Journal of Neurology, Neurosurgery and Psychiatry, 56*, 410–415.

Klonoff, H., Low, M.D., & Clark, C. (1977). Head injuries in children: A prospective five-year follow-up. *Journal of Neurology, Neurosurgery and Psychiatry, 40,* 1211–1219.

Labov, W. (1972). *Language in the inner city: Studies in the black vernacular*. Philadelphia, PA: University of Pennsylvania Press.

Leonard, L.B. (1989). Language learning ability and specific language impairment in children. *Applied Psycholinguistics, 10,* 179–202.

Levin, H.S. (1996, December). *Recovery and reorganization after diffuse brain injury*. Paper presented at The NIH Workshop on Neuroplasticity and Reorganization of Function after Brain Injury, Baltimore, MD.

Levin, H.S., Culhane, K.A., Mendelsohn, D. Lilly, M.A., Bruce, D., Fletcher, J., Chapman, S., Harward, H., & Eisenberg, H.M. (1993). Cognition in relation to magnetic resonance imaging in head-injured children and adolescents. *Archives of Neurology, 50,* 897–905.

Levin, H.S., Ewing-Cobbs, L., & Eisenberg, H.M. (1995). Neurobehavioral outcome of pediatric closed head injury. In S.H. Broman & M.E. Michel (Eds.), *Traumatic head injury in children* (pp.70–94). New York: Oxford University Press.

Levin, H.S., & Eisenberg, H.M. (1979). Neuropsychological outcome of closed head injury in children and adolescents. *Child's Brain, 5,* 1–10.

Levin, H.S., Goldstein, F.C., Williams, D.H., & Eisenberg, H.M. (1991). The contribution of frontal lobe lesions to the neurobehavioral outcome of closed head injury. In H.S. Levin, H.M. Eisenberg, & A.L. Benton (Eds.), *Frontal lobe function and dysfunction* (pp.318–338). New York: Oxford University Press.

Lovett, M.W., Dennis, M.W., & Newman, J.E. (1986). Making reference: The cohesive use of pronouns in the narrative discourse of hemidecorticate adolescents. *Brain and Language, 29(2)*, 224–251.

Luria, A.R. (1966). *Higher cortical functions in man,* New York: Basic Books.

Passler, M.A., Isaac, W., & Hynd, G.W. (1985). Neuropsychological development of behavior attributed to frontal lobe functioning in children. *Developmental Neuropsychology, l,* 349–370.

Pennington, B.E. (1991). Genetics of learning disabilities. *Seminars in Neurology, 11* (1), 28–34.

Roth, F.P., & Spekman, N.J. (1989). Higher-order language processes and reading disabilities. In A.G. Kamhi & H.W. Catts (Eds.), *Reading disabilities: A developmental language perspective* (pp.159–197). Boston/Toronto: Little Brown.

Sarno, M.T. (1980). The nature of verbal impairment after closed head injury. *Journal of Nervous and Mental Disorders, 168(11),* 685–692.

Savage, R.C., & Wolcott, G.C. (1994). Overview of acquired brain injury. In R.C. Savage & G.D. Wolcott (Eds.), *Educational dimensions of acquired brain injury* (pp.3–12). Austin, TX: Pro-Ed.

Shaffer, D. (1995). Behavioral sequelae of serious head injury in children and adolescents: The British Studies. In S.H. Broman & M.E. Michel (Eds.), *Traumatic head injury in children* (pp.55–69), New York: Oxford University Press.

Shaffer, D., Bijur, P., Chadwick, O.F., & Rutter, M.L. (1980). Head injury and later reading disability. *Journal of the American Academy of Child Psychiatry, 19(4)*, 592–610.

Sohlberg, M., & Mateer, C. (1989). *Introduction to cognitive rehabilitation: Theory and practice.* New York: Guilford Press.

Spreen, O., & Benton, A.L. (1969). *Neurosensory center comprehensive examination for aphasia: Manual of directions.* Victoria, BC: Neuropsychology Laboratory, University of Victoria.

Stein, N.L., & Glenn, C.G. (1979). An analysis of story comprehension in elementary school children. In R.O. Freedle (Ed.), *New directions in discourse processing* (pp.53–120). Norwood, NJ: Ablex.

Stiles, J. (1996, December). *The effects of early focal brain injury on the development of spatial analytic processing.* Paper presented at the NIH Workshop on Neuroplasticity and Reorganization of Function after Brain Injury, Baltimore, MD.

Stuss, D.T. (1992). Biological and psychological development of executive function. *Brain and Cognition, 20,* 8–23.

Szekeres, S.F. (1989). Clinical illustration: Cognitive-communicative problem. *Journal of Children in a Contemporary Society, 21(1–2)*, 167–172.

Szekeres, S.F., & Meserve, N.F. (1994). Collaborative intervention in schools after traumatic brain injury. *Topics in Language Disorders, 15(1)*, 21-36.

Tannock, R. (1994, January). *Discourse deficits in ADHD: Executive dysfunction as an underlying mechanism.* Paper presented at the meeting of the International Society for Research in Child and Adolescent Psychopathology, Santa Monica, CA.

Teasdale, G., & Jennett, B. (1974). Assessment of coma and impaired consciousness: A practical scale. *Lancet, 2(872)*, 81–84.

Ulatowska, H.K., Allard, L., & Chapman, S.B. (1990). Narrative and procedural discourse in aphasia. In Y. Joanette & H. Brownell (Eds.), *Discourse ability and brain damage.* (pp.180–198). New York: Springer-Verlag.

van Dijk, T.A. (1995). On macrostructure, mental models, and other inventions: A brief personal history of the Kintsch–van Dijk Theory. In C.A. Weaver, S. Mannes, & C.R. Fletcher (Eds.), *Discourse comprehension* (pp.383–410). Hillsdale, NJ: Lawrence Erlbaum Associates Inc.

Welsh, M.C., & Pennington, B.F. (1988). Assessing frontal lobe functioning in children: Views from developmental psychology. *Developmental Neuropsychology, 4, 199–230.*

Westby, C. (1984). Development of narrative abilities. In G. Wallach & K.G. Butler (Eds.), *Language learning disabilities in school-age children* (pp.103–127). Baltimore, MD: Williams & Wilkins.

Westby, C. (1989). Assessing and remediating text comprehension problems. In S. Kamhi & H. Catts (Eds.), *Reading disabilities: A developmental language perspective* (pp.199–259). Boston, MA: Little Brown.
Wiig, E.H., & Secord, W. (1989). *Test of language competence: Expanded edition.* San Antonio, TX: Psychological Corporation.
Winograd, P.N. (1984). Strategic difficulties in summarizing texts. *Reading Research Quarterly, 19(940)*, 404–425.
Ylvisaker, M. (1993). Communication outcome in children and adolescents with traumatic brain injury. *Neuropsychological Rehabilitation, 3,* 367–387.
Ylvisaker, M., & Feeney, T.J. (1994). Communication and behavior: Collaboration between speech-language pathologists and behavioral psychologists. *Topics in Language Disorders, 15(1)*, 37–54.
Yorkston, K.M., Jaffe, K.M., Polissar, N.L., Liao, S., & Fay, G.C. (1997). Written language production and neuropsychological function in children with traumatic brain injury. *Archives of Physical Medicine and Rehabilitation, 78(10),* 1096–1102.
Zitnay, G.A. (1995). Foreword. In D.G. Stein, S. Brailowsky, & B. Will (Eds.), *Brain Repair* (pp.v–vi). New York: Oxford University Press.

APPENDIX

Narrative Stimulus with Delineation of Core Propositions, Gist Propositions, and Episodic Structure (from Chapman, Wanek, & Sharpe, 1994)

Original story: "Two Roosters"

Once upon a time, there were two roosters. They were always fighting over who would be ruler of all the hens. One day, they decided to really fight it out. Finally, one rooster was beaten. The poor defeated rooster hid himself in the corner. The other rooster, who won the fight, flew to the very top of the henhouse, and began crowing and flapping his wings to brag about his victory over the other rooster. Suddenly, an eagle swooped down, grabbed the boasting rooster and carried him far away. Now, this was good luck for the defeated rooster because now he could rule over the chicken yard and have all the hens that he wanted.

A priori propositions

Note that semantically equivalent statements are acceptable.

Episode 1

Setting	1. There were two roosters.
	2. They were in the chicken yard.
Action	3. The roosters were fighting.
Resolution	4. One rooster was defeated.

Episode 2

Setting	5. He hid himself in the corner.
	6. The other rooster flew to the top of the roost.
Action	7. He began crowing.
	8. He began flapping his wings.
	9. He boasted of his victory.
	10. An eagle/hawk/crow swooped down/came by.
	11. The eagle grabbed the rooster.
	12. The eagle carried him away.
Resolution	13. This was good for the defeated rooster.
	14. He could rule over the hens.
	15. He could have all the hens.

Gist propositions

That is, the central information depicting the role reversal in which the defeated rooster won in the end.

1. The two roosters are fighting/there is a fight.
2. Someone won/lost the fight.
3. The winner bragged.
4. The eagle carried the winner away.
5. The defeated rooster/the one that remained won/ruled over the chickens.

Examples of narratives

Sample A: Age-equivalent control, age 10;10

There were two roosters. And they were going they were fighting over who would rule over all the hens. And then so they really fought it out. And the one rooster won. And the other one, he went into the barn and hid. And then the other one who went up to the top of the barn and started flapping his wings and bragging about it. And a eagle came and got him and took him away as far as he could. So that was good luck for the rooster who lost. So he could, he rule, he could rule over all the other hens.

Observations: The child uses relatively long sentences with increased clausal embedding particularly at the turning point. Vocabulary usage is consistent with the level contained in the story. With regard to information, the child produces the majority of core and gist propositions as well as intact episodic structure. The child is able to clearly distinguish the two rooster characters and does so with expanded noun phrases when necessary.

Sample B: Child with severe TBI secondary to a motor vehicle accident. Age 10;4 at time of test, 36 months post-injury. MRI findings: increased signal intensity noted in the deep white matter of the left frontal lobe

One day there was two little chickens. And they were fighting over who was go be the chicken thing. And (one one) one chicken bit the one chicken and flew to the top of the chicken house. And (he he) he was yellin'. (Cau) because he bit the chicken, he can be that thing. (And and) and the crow came along and took him up and flew him. And that chicken could be the chicken farm.

Observations: Notice the relative preservation in the amount and complexity of language. Problems in naming are quite obvious ("chicken thing", "yellin'" for bragging).

With regard to information, there is a reduction in the amount of core and gist propositions. The flow of information is disjointed and incoherent.

Sample C: Child with developmental language impairment, age 9;2

Once there were these two roosters who always fighted. As they one day they um fought to the end. And well one rooster was beated to the wall. And the other rooster flew up on something. And he bragged about it, clocking and waving his um feathers. And an eagle swat just got him. And the other eagle I mean rooster was proud of him I mean proud because now he can.

Observations: This child exhibits marked language problems evident in the lexicalisation of the information (e.g. coinage of novel expressions, "clocking and waving his feathers" for bragging), a regularisation of "fight", and simple and sometimes incomplete sentences.

The child seems to have experienced some comprehension problems as he is unclear who is "proud". The information is disrupted at all levels (i.e. amount and structure). Conceptualisation of the gist (i.e. the losing rooster won at the end) is not evident in this retell.

Sample D: Child with gunshot wound. Age 12;3. Bullet penetrated the skull at the level of the ventricles resulting in underlying skull fractures of the left frontal and parietal bones and subsequent focal damage to the left frontal and parietal regions of the cortex

There was two rooster. (Uh) They were fighting over who would be (uh) the leader. (Uh) But one day they fought it out. And (the uh) the rooster won. The rooster that (uh) didn't win he hid hisself in the corner. And (he) the rooster that did won (uh) he flyed all the way to (uh) the henhouse. And a big (uh a) eagle spotted him. And he grabbed him. And he took him far far far far away. But the other rooster that defeated him, (uh he) he was leader.

Observations: This case of a focal TBI (gunshot) is presented as a comparison with a CHI plus a focal injury (Sample B). Both children had relatively large left frontal lesions. In contrast to Child B, this child's deficits are more evident in the language domain. Notice the marked syntactic simplification, especially for a 12-year-old. While this child does not connect ideas cohesively, the ideas are concatenated in a logical order such that the events are easy to follow. The child conveys most of the core information and expresses the role reversal for the two roosters.

CHAPTER TEN

Discourse rehabilitation following traumatic brain injury

Pamela Snow and Jacinta Douglas
School of Human Communication Sciences, Faculty of Health Sciences, Latrobe University, Bundoora, Victoria, Australia

Traumatic brain injury (TBI) is a catastrophic event that alters the course of the injured individual's life, and usually has serious and complex ramifications for spouses and close family members. In previous chapters the nature of the communication impairment associated with TBI has been discussed in some detail, and a number of assessment approaches have been suggested and described. The purpose of this chapter is to address the complex questions associated with understanding and managing the impact of cognitive-communicative changes associated with TBI on discourse abilities, so that readers may more confidently design and implement efficacious treatment programmes. It should be noted that there are special considerations in the evaluation of brain-injured patients during the period of initial confusion and disorientation known as post-traumatic amnesia (PTA). These are beyond the scope of this chapter, but have been described in Chapter 2 and also by Snow and Ponsford (1995a).

We have seen that TBI typically occurs in young males in the 17 to 30 year age group. Such individuals may not have completed their educational/vocational training, and are typically enjoying a period of relatively new-found personal and social independence. Because road trauma is the single most common cause of TBI (Kraus et al., 1984), such injuries are often associated with multiple-trauma (e.g. orthopaedic and/or internal injuries). TBI is associated with a pattern of diffuse axonal injury throughout the cerebral white matter, and may be accompanied by focal injuries to the frontal and/or temporal regions (Pang, 1985; Richardson, 1990). This pattern of injury is associated with certain characteristic neurobehavioural changes in the individual. In particular, difficulties with planning/initiating, organisation, attention/concentration, insight, self-monitoring, and flexibility of thought have been found to characterise the profile of deficits associated with TBI (see Chapter 2 for a review).

So, the individual who presents (sometimes reluctantly, and often with some bewilderment) for speech pathology assessment brings with him or her a unique set of pre-injury characteristics (age, sex, educational/vocational background, socioeconomic status, family/social supports, culture, religion, values and expectations about disability), which interact with factors such as injury severity, the presence of associated trauma, and personal response to disability. Factors relating to the circumstances of the accident itself may also be relevant. For example the death/serious injury of friends or family members, and issues of blame and criminal prosecution all impact on the injured person as soon as he or she is able to understand and retain such information. This complex mix of premorbid and injury-related factors results in one of the defining characteristics of TBI rehabilitation—heterogeneity. This poses important challenges for the clinician, who firstly needs to understand what defines "typical" in terms of demography and pathophysiology, but secondly needs to be sensitive to the unique factors associated with each individual's circumstances. Such an understanding forms the basis of a working relationship with the patient, and should ensure that rehabilitation goals and activities are always considered in terms of their relevance to the individual concerned.

Most people who sustain TBI receive speech-language pathology and neuropsychology services as in-patients or out-patients in a "fast stream" rehabilitation setting, followed by an ever-diminishing period of ongoing service provision. Funding arrangements vary widely from country to country, and even between different states or provinces within countries. Funding bodies everywhere, however, are imposing significant constraints on the duration and frequency of therapy. Rehabilitation services in general tend to be disproportionately skewed in favour of the acute and subacute end of the continuum, with few, if any services available to support the injured individual at later, often more complex stages in the community re-entry process. This poses a significant challenge to clinicians concerned with minimising the impact of cognitive-communicative problems in real-world contexts in the longer term. It is vital that rehabilitation services shift their emphasis to community re-entry, and maintenance of everyday skills in the individual's real world. All clinicians have a responsibility to educate funding bodies and administrators, so that sparse services are more equitably distributed across the time continuum after injury. Enormous financial and practical resources are mobilised to save the lives of people who sustain severe TBI, and to address their early (largely physical) rehabilitation needs.

There is a glaring need, however, to balance this with community-based services that can build on the gains made in acute and subacute rehabilitation, and maximise injured peoples' ability to regain their status as productive members of society. The psychosocial problems associated with TBI are not acute, and do not, in themselves, require hospital-based services. They are, however, chronic, and demand skilled intervention from a range of professionals with expertise in rehabilitation and counselling.

In this chapter we describe the broad context in which communication needs to be investigated for rehabilitation and community re-entry. We provide a conceptual framework for identifying and changing problematic communicative behaviours following TBI. Central to this framework is the development of communication awareness as a basis for behavioural change. After the general principles of this approach have been presented, a detailed case study is used to illustrate its clinical application. This framework for intervention can be readily applied by clinicians new to the area of TBI rehabilitation.

ISSUES IN ASSESSING COMMUNICATION AS A BASIS FOR REHABILITATION

The assessment of an individual's communication abilities needs to be seen as a dynamic, continuous process, rather than a "snapshot" at arbitrary points during rehabilitation. Although the administration of formal measures has its place as an index of change (and to a limited extent as a measure of treatment efficacy), clinicians cannot rely on this alone as a basis for intervention. Rather, it is important that subtle changes in parameters such as self-awareness, concentration, and ability to utilise feedback effectively are noted as they occur, so that appropriate adjustments can be made to treatment programmes on a continuous basis.

It should be remembered that some cognitive-communicative deficits may, on formal assessment, appear to be subtle, while exerting damaging and wide-ranging effects in everyday activities that lack the structure and predictability of a clinical examination (Naugle & Chelune, 1990; Prigatano, 1987; Ylvisaker & Holland, 1985). Great caution needs to be exercised, then, in interpreting data derived from structured, formal assessments. These are normally conducted in quiet, distraction-free settings, employing clear stimulus–response paradigms. As will be emphasised throughout this chapter, formal measures should be complemented by a range of other assessment tools, such as direct observation, and self/close-other report data.

With the ever-increasing emphasis on treatment that is "functional", clinicians need to consider the theoretical and practical implications of concepts defined within models of the consequences of disablement. In 1997, the

World Health Organisation introduced its revision of the International Classification of Impairment Disability and Handicap, ICIDH-2. While the definition of impairment remained essentially the same (i.e. loss or abnormality of structure or function), the terms "disability" and "handicap" were revised and replaced by "activity limitation" and "participation restriction", respectively. Activities are defined as the nature and extent of functioning at the level of the person. Thus, activity limitation is associated with the tasks and actions of everyday life and relates to the actual rather than potential performance or execution of a task or activity. Many of the assessment tools (and consequently many treatment tasks) traditionally employed by speech-language pathologists are concerned predominantly with the measurement of impairment, and to a lesser extent, disability or activity limitation. This approach probably grew out of aphasia (stroke) rehabilitation, where the relationship between focal injury and the physical, cognitive, and/or communicative changes observed in the individual formed the basis for the organisation of the multi-disciplinary team. As McGrath and Davis (1992) have observed, the language of disability sits readily alongside traditional role definitions of the various professions involved, and lends itself to the "partitioning" of a patient into a collection of disabilities. These can then be allocated to different professionals, assessed, and treated, in the hope that the individual somehow emerges better equipped to resume valued life roles. Unfortunately, this approach offers little to the understanding of the brain-injured patient, whose complex psychosocial difficulties cross all disciplinary boundaries, and pervade attempts at community re-entry.

This leads then to consideration of the concept of participation or participation restriction (formerly "handicap" in ICIDH, 1980). Participation is described by the WHO (1997) as the lived experience of people with a health condition, impairment or activity limitation. Participation restriction refers to the extent to which a person's involvement is restricted in life situations in relation to impairments, activities, health conditions, and contextual factors. Participation is classified according to "domains" of life experience, which enables the identification of facilitators and barriers to participation. McGrath and Davis (1992) noted that each individual will value a unique set of social roles, which may be many and varied, ranging from spouse, family member, student, colleague, sexual partner, and citizen. Conceptual models of disablement also inform the debate on outcome measurement and the efficacy and cost effectiveness of rehabilitation for persons with TBI. The subjective as well as the objective experience of disability along with life satisfaction and subjective well-being are also important concepts to include within the models we use to guide functional assessment and outcome evaluation (Johnston, Hall, & Banja, 1994; Johnston, Hall, Carnevale, & Boake, 1996).

All members of the treating team need to develop an understanding of the relevance of participation and life satisfaction as being driving factors that motivate the brain-injured person to progress beyond the rehabilitation phase. "I just want to get back to my job again" and "If I could just go home and look after my family" are some of the common pleas from people undergoing rehabilitation, particularly if the tasks presented to them have little face validity in relation to what they perceive as relevant activities for their everyday lives. It is easy to dismiss such requests as reflecting a lack of insight, but they should also be seen as a message to staff about the injured person's priorities.

A question that frequently confronts speech-language pathologists assessing people who have sustained TBI is the extent to which premorbid factors are at least contributing to, if not accounting for, the verbal behaviour displayed by the injured person. This question of normal sociolinguistic influences on verbal behaviour requires close consideration with the TBI population. Snow, Douglas, and Ponsford (1995, 1997a) have pointed out that because there is a premorbid demographic profile of the "at-risk" individual, it is reasonable to expect that certain sociolinguistic characteristics might be associated with this. There is a large body of sociolinguistic literature attesting to the link between verbal skills and demographic factors such as race, geographical location, and education (e.g. Edwards, 1989; Hudson, 1980; Poole, 1976; Stubbs, 1983; Trudgill, 1983). Such demographic variables can exert powerful influences on what sociolinguists refer to as "linguistic items"—e.g. lexical choice (vocabulary)—and the phonological and grammatical rules a speaker employs during connected discourse. It must be stressed, however, that the presence of differences between speaker groups with respect to linguistic items does not imply superiority of one group over another. Trudgill (1983), for example, observed that "All varieties of a language are structured, complex, rule-governed systems which are wholly adequate for the needs of their speakers" (p.20). The relevance of sociolinguistics to TBI lies in its representation of premorbid verbal behaviour, which may, in some cases be erroneously judged as inferior on societal, rather than linguistic grounds.

Assessment measures, then, need to be sensitive to behaviours uniquely associated with brain injury, not to normal variants present in the wider community. McGann and Werven (1995) have observed that a clinician's definition of what is "normal" is generally based on a concept of central tendency, with behaviours that are unfamiliar to the observer being those that attract attention. These workers noted that there are variations in the allowances made for individual differences, depending on who the individual is, and the level of his or her perceived social status. Hudson (1980) also cautioned about the difficulties of making judgements about an individual's communication behaviour noting that "... personal experience is a very limited base from which to generalise about language in society, since it does not take account of all the other societies, where things are arranged very differently" (p.2).

It is most important, therefore, to gain a clear understanding of the injured individual's personal, cultural, social, educational, vocational, and recreational background, as a basis for understanding the significance of this injury, for this individual, at this point in his or her life. A number of workers (e.g. Crisp, 1993; Hartley, 1996; McGann & Werven, 1995; Rees & Gerber, 1992; Spencer, 1993) have recently advocated the use of qualitative data collection techniques in the clinical assessment of people who have sustained TBI. These techniques are drawn from the field of anthropology, and include ethnography, phenomenology, storytelling (narratives), and grounded theory. *Ethnography* refers to the direct observation of the activity of members of a particular social group, and the subsequent description and evaluation of such activity (Minichiello, Aroni, Timewell, & Alexander, 1995). Phenomenology, however, refers to the study of how events and experiences are interpreted by the individual (Minichiello et al., 1995). Storytelling (as distinct from story grammar, which has been discussed in Chapter 3), is a means of directing an interview in order to elicit a story (e.g. of a past experience) from the informant's perspective. As Spencer (1993) has observed, personal narratives and metaphors are fundamental and universal ways of interpreting and understanding one's own life experiences. "Grounded theory" refers to the "teasing out" of theories and ideas about an individual from the data he or she supplies, rather than from the clinician's set of preconceived ideas or values about behaviour after TBI. As McGann and Werven (1995) have observed, the challenge facing us as clinicians is to observe behaviour without invoking our personal collection of stereotypes and stigmas—i.e. to consider people and their behaviour as separate from the diagnosis that has brought them to our attention. This view was also expressed by Spencer (1993), who noted that traditionally, rehabilitation professionals have made judgements about a person's readiness for one or another standard treatment programmes, based on their own beliefs about that person's needs, rather than on an understanding of the context of this injury within the individual's life story.

Ethnographic techniques should be employed in the collection of background demographic information, and also in the establishment of treatment goals and priorities. As well as providing a rich body of information about the individual and his or her interpretation of the significance of the injury, these techniques allow the clinician and patient to establish rapport, and instil confidence in patients that they are not "just a number" in the rehabilitation setting. These methods allow for continuous modification and checking of perceptions and goals, so that small adjustments can be made to the emphasis of treatment as they are needed. Hartley (1996) suggested that the collection of data in this manner helps to expose information that may be perceived by the clinician as unexpected and, in so doing, ensures that intervention will be more specifically tailored to the needs of the individual. This, in turn, should help to alleviate some of the well-known difficulties with generalisation of new skills from the rehabilitation setting to the individual's real world, as ethnographic techniques lead away from so-called "cook book" approaches to a more systematic and personalised approach to treatment planning.

Other ethnographic methods that are useful to employ are participant observation and triangulation. Participant observation requires the clinician to place him- or herself in the real-world contexts (e.g. home, school, work) that are relevant to the individual, and observe "on-line" both the strengths and difficulties the person experiences. Triangulation is a means by which data gathered using qualitative methods can be checked and verified. This might be done, for example, by comparing data from direct observation with those from self-perceptions and close-other perceptions, so that areas of overlap, and areas of discrepancy can be identified, and investigated further. Kazdin (1995) has cautioned that multiple measures should be taken of behavioural constructs, because of the limited extent to which generalisations can be made from both data derived from direct sampling and that which is based on self/close other report. A lack of correspondence between so-called "objective" data, such as language test scores, and "subjective" data, such as self-perceptions should not, however, automatically call into question the validity of the latter. As Wolf (1978) has observed, the use of qualitative methods does not necessarily seek to define cause–effect relationships, but rather reflects efforts to understand the dimensions of complex reinforcers of behaviour. As such, these methods should have greater face validity for the survivor of TBI, and hence form a basis for a therapeutic partnership between patient and clinician.

CRITICAL ISSUES IN THE REHABILITATION OF DISCOURSE IN TBI SPEAKERS

Explain the speech-language pathologist's role to the injured person and his or her family members

Many TBI speakers (and sometimes their families) are initially puzzled at the involvement of a speech-language pathologist in their rehabilitation, as "there's nothing wrong with my speech". Therefore, in establishing rapport with the injured person and family members, speech-language pathologists need to spend time explaining the breadth of their role, and in particular the fact that this extends well beyond a simple concern with "speaking". Clinicians should take time to explain that they are concerned with all aspects of communication, stressing that this encompasses listening, understanding, concentrating, idea generation (or, put more simply, "thinking of things to say"), word finding ("coming up with the right words"), turn-taking, knowing how to interpret non-verbal cues from the listener, and understanding the subtle conventions surrounding context and "appropriateness".

It also needs to be explained to patients and family members that language can be seen as a "tool" of thought, and thus changes in cognitive abilities will impact on the person's ability to use this tool effectively in everyday life. As Hartley (1995) has pointed out, the common cognitive impairments associated with TBI manifest themselves in the person's communication in typical ways. Poor concentration, for example, manifests as difficulty following group conversations, and/or a tendency to ask questions about material that has previously been covered. Poor self-monitoring may result in verbosity, inappropriate volume, and/or difficulty relinquishing a conversational turn. Rigid thinking will manifest as difficulty appreciating another person's perspective, which may in turn be interpreted as stubbornness. Egocentricity will tend to limit the range of subjects about which the injured person will converse, and may also result in turn-taking difficulties. Examples that are relevant to the individual concerned should be used to illustrate the intrinsic nature of the link between cognition ("thinking") and communication. Great care needs to be taken, however, to use simple, everyday terms, and to avoid the use of professional jargon, because the latter will be interpreted both as uninformative and unfriendly to those for whom it is an unfamiliar language.

Giving and receiving feedback, and dealing with limited insight

During the early stages of rehabilitation, the injured person may have limited awareness about his or her communication difficulties. Feedback, therefore, needs to be provided with this in mind. It should be remembered that few of us welcome negative feedback under any circumstances, and feedback about deficiencies in how they relate to others can be potentially damaging to injured people's self-esteem, and hence motivation in therapy. When negative feedback is to be given, it can be "sandwiched" between two pieces of positive feedback, so that the integrity of the individual's self-esteem is maintained at all times. Further, therapists need to provide concrete suggestions as to how the injured person might approach the same task next time (Crosson, 1987). Opportunities also need to be created for injured people to experience changes in themselves at first hand—e.g. through day/week-end leave with family members, participation in group treatment (see below)—so that self-perceptions can form a meaningful and dynamic part of the evaluation process.

In addition to giving the injured person feedback about "test" results and the overall profile of needs that has emerged from the evaluation process, clinicians need to elicit feedback from TBI speakers about their perceptions of the relevance of assessment, and any questions they may have about the treatment in which they will be participating. A number of workers over the past decade have questioned the long-held belief that survivors of TBI are not capable of "accurate" perceptions about their performance or their rehabilitation needs (e.g. Elsass & Kinsella, 1987). Traditionally, rehabilitation workers have adopted a rather paternalistic stance on the relevance and validity of the injured person's view. If this did not concur with difficulties apparent on formal, clinic-based assessment measures, he or she was labelled as lacking in insight. If, however, the injured person reported difficulties that were not detected by formal assessment, doubts were expressed about the genuineness of his or her motivation to improve.

The relationship between self- and close other-ratings is not simply summarised by the generalisation that TBI patients rate themselves more optimistically than do their close others or their therapists. Important factors that need to be considered include the nature of the task/function in question, and the time post-injury at which self-awareness is considered. Further, as Allen and Ruff (1990) observed, the willingness to disclose negative self-perceptions may not be present in all individuals, regardless of the presence of brain damage. Goldstein and McCue (1995) have also observed that some functional losses may be associated with greater amounts of stigma than others, and this may influence reporting of perceived negative change post-injury.

Prigatano (1991) noted that brain-injured individuals typically rate themselves more positively than relatives rate them on measures of cognitive function, memory, and social skill. On measures concerning self-care ability, however, patients and close others are more likely to concur. Goldstein and McCue (1995) have noted that the self-ratings of TBI patients are sometimes more negative than the ratings of a close other, or neuropsychological test scores. These workers also noted that the face validity of measures of self-awareness needs to be considered carefully, because this may influence respondents' reporting. Self-report measures may be compromised by impaired insight, although it is important to remember that self-awareness tends to change over time as a function of factors such as severity of injury, amount of recovery, life experience, the development of depression, and the availability of feedback (Godfrey, Partridge, Knight, & Bishara, 1993; Prigatano, 1987; Sbordone, 1991).

In a comparison between neuropsychological test scores and self-ratings, Allen and Ruff (1990) found that severely injured TBI patients tended to overestimate their performance on sensori-motor and attentional tasks, although self-ratings and test scores were more congruent on measures of arithmetic and language skill. Mildly injured subjects, however, were pessimistic about their performance on sensori-motor, language, and reasoning tasks. Allen and Ruff also found that TBI respondents become more pessimistic about their performance over time. This latter finding was endorsed by findings reported by Godfrey et al. (1993). These workers found that in comparison with objective indices, TBI respondents under-reported behavioural and cognitive problems at six months post-injury. On reassessment at one year, and two to three years post-injury, however, TBI survivors reported higher levels of behaviour problems, emotional distress, and depression, together with lower self-esteem, than did a group of orthopaedically injured controls. Godfrey et al. found that such reports did not correlate significantly with injury severity indices, nor with the presence of CT scan abnormalities. Their findings led them to speculate that the relatively rapid improvement in *physical* functioning that occurs soon after injury may promote unrealistic optimism about eventual *psychosocial* recovery. Godfrey et al.'s findings suggest that by one to three years post-injury, however, this optimism is giving way to a more pessimistic self-perception.

Great care needs to be taken, then, with attempts to engage people who are reluctant to participate in therapy. Clinicians need to recognise that what they perceive as a glaring need for therapy, may be perceived by the patient as a manifestation of premorbid characteristics ("I've always been this way"), or as irrelevant to roles he or she urgently wishes to resume. In disputing the validity of either or both of these claims, it should be remembered that with the passage of time, most people begin to experience the effects of their difficulties "on-line" in the real world. Many then seek, or are at least receptive to, professional assistance. A great deal of damage can be done, however, to this later adjustment if the patient feels alienated by a clinician's earlier forceful attempts to engage him or her in therapy. It is common for young TBI patients to be largely preoccupied with physical rehabilitation, in particular learning to walk again. It is important, therefore, that clinicians consider the context of communication for each individual, and allow for the possibility that difficulties may be easier to address (a) when insight/awareness have improved and (b) when real-world settings can be utilised as the context for rehabilitation. Naturally this requires a re-education of funding bodies, which may operate on inflexible and outdated concepts relating to the timing (acute to subacute) and location (rehabilitation setting) of therapy.

Sometimes, problems of reduced insight persist, even in the face of what seems to be overwhelming evidence about the person's difficulties. In such cases, direct confrontation should still be avoided, because this merely acts to fortify the injured person's belief that the treating team is "against" him or her. It may be necessary to systematically address the person's beliefs about why failure has occurred (e.g. in the case of an unsuccessful return to work), and to give clear and honest feedback about this. Reviewing an unsuccessful experience also allows the patient and therapist to "brainstorm" suggestions as to how to proceed in the future. This can help to minimise defensiveness and restore enthusiasm to try again at some later stage. A number of workers (e.g. Ben-Yishay & Prigatano, 1990; Gillis, 1996; Sloan & Ponsford, 1995b; Snow & Ponsford, 1995b) have advocated the use of audio/videotape feedback, to help brain-injured people to make judgements about their own performance. Behaviour checklists should be provided to the injured person to help structure judgements, and to draw attention to particular facets of performance. Ethical issues pertaining to the use of videotaping have been considered by Gillis (1996).

An individual's resistance to therapy should also signal to the clinician that the tasks being offered may need to be reviewed in terms of their face validity for the person concerned. Although a therapist may see a link between structured activities aimed at, for example, improving the individual's auditory processing skills and return to work, this link may not be at all obvious to the individual concerned. Two possibilities need to be considered in this situation: (1) inadequate time has been spent in discussing assessment findings, treatment planning, and goal setting with the injured person, and/or (2) greater flexibility is required on the part of the clinician with respect to designing an intervention programme that is both relevant and engaging to the person concerned. Specifically, more emphasis may need to be given to activities/treatment tasks that facilitate awareness of maladaptive communication behaviour and its consequences for interpersonal interactions.

The rationale behind rehabilitation: Restitution or compensation?

Although the heterogeneity associated with TBI will always demand that highly individualised intervention programmes are developed for each person, it is important that clinicians work within a theoretical framework with respect to notions of recovery following brain injury. The diffuse nature of the pathology associated with TBI, together with the vulnerability of the frontal and temporal lobes to focal damage frequently results in a pattern of pervasive, multi-modality neurobehavioural disturbance. A number of mechanisms by which "recovery" (perhaps more correctly termed "improvement") occurs after brain injury have been described (Finger & Stein, 1982; Gillis, 1996; Miller, 1984; Richardson, 1990; Sloan & Ponsford, 1995b; Whyte, 1990). Family members are often anxious to understand (a) the mechanism by which "recovery" will occur in their loved one's brain, and (b) what they can do to maximise this. The term "recovery" has unfortunate lay connotations of restoration to wellness after a period of ill-health, and is thus a term about which staff and family need to come to some mutual understanding. While it is generally agreed that physiologic changes are responsible for much of the early improvement that occurs after severe TBI (Richardson, 1990; Schoenfeld & Hamilton, 1977), there is less certainty about the mechanism(s) by which change occurs in response to specific therapeutic efforts. The term "improvement" is probably a more accurate descriptor of the positive changes that are sought after severe TBI, and does not carry with it an assumption of 100% restoration to pre-injury levels of functioning. As such, it is a concept that can enable the injured person and family members to focus on strengths, while not unrealistically awaiting a full "recovery".

A number of approaches to rehabilitation of cognitive deficits have been described. Some (e.g. restoration/remediation) are specifically aimed at improving core cognitive abilities (such as attention, planning, self-monitoring) while others (e.g. compensation, environmental manipulation, and behavioural adaptation) are more wide-ranging and multi-factorial in their efforts to increase the opportunities available to the TBI survivor. Although there is some overlap between the last three techniques, restoration/remediation approaches have as their focus specific and isolated neuropsychological impairments that are targeted through repeated practice on highly structured clinic-based activities (e.g. Ben-Yishay, Piasetsky, & Rattok, 1987; Sohlberg & Mateer, 1987, 1989). The rationale for this type of treatment is that amelioration of the underlying deficit should result in improvement of all functions associated with it. Unfortunately, however, such models have two major flaws. First, people who have sustained TBI typically have great difficulty generalising from structured clinic-based tasks to activities they must perform in more cognitively demanding environments in the real world (Ben-Yishay & Prigatano, 1990; Gillis, 1996; Lennox & Brune, 1993; Prigatano, 1987; Sloan & Ponsford, 1995b; Webb, 1991; Ylvisaker & Szekeres, 1994). For this reason, improvements that can be demonstrated as a consequence of repeated practice on specific tasks do not automatically manifest as improved performance on related tasks of personal salience in everyday life (e.g. conversing with friends, or attending to the information contained within a lecture). Secondly, as Ben-Yishay and Prigatano (1990) have noted, our current understanding of the neuropathology underlying many of the impairments observed after TBI is not yet sufficiently sophisticated to form a basis for therapy aimed at restoration of function.

Because of the inherent limitations in restoration models of recovery, most workers (e.g. Ben-Yishay & Prigatano, 1990; Gillis, 1996; Hartley, 1995; Sloan & Ponsford, 1995b) advocate the use of intervention methods aimed at maximising both recovery and functional adaptation. *In other words, the goal of intervention is to reduce activity limitation and to increase participation.* Such approaches require the clinician and patient to work together to identify salient real-life goals, and then to analyse features of the activity that the person can perform, and those that he or she cannot.

This approach therefore incorporates feedback about strengths, as well as weaknesses, and emphasises residual abilities that can be utilised to overcome persisting disabilities. This should be the focus of communication therapy from the outset, rather than being an unhappy compromise after attempts at direct restitution have failed. Communication in everyday contexts is an inherently complex, multi-factorial skill. The individual must learn how to self-monitor in a range of settings, how to "read" cues from the other speaker, how to utilise different discourse genres within conversation, how to take turns in conversation, and how to repair breakdowns in information transfer. Not all aspects of the communication process will be equally affected, and wide variations will exist from one individual to the next. It is unrealistic, therefore, to expect treatment aimed at isolated subcomponents of this complex process to "flow on" automatically in an integrated manner to the end-product of effective communication skills in a range of everyday settings.

It is important, therefore, that clinicians explain to family members that:

- Much of the early and quite rapid improvement that occurs reflects physiological changes such as the resolution of swelling (oedema) around the brain.
- Improvement will be most rapid in the first six months post-injury, but will potentially continue for many months, or even years after this. Factors that may influence the amount of ongoing improvement include severity of injury, age at injury, the presence of other injuries, awareness and motivation, the availability of personal supports, and the rehabilitation options that are available to the injured person. For this reason, precise prognostic statements cannot be made in the early stages of rehabilitation.
- Although the rate and consistency of improvement tends to slow over time, this does not mean that further functional gains cannot be made. It may mean, however, that systematic efforts need to be made to promote learning for the individual concerned. This requires careful attention to task analysis, as well as consideration of the individual's strengths and weaknesses. Achieving and sustaining improvements after the period of more rapid initial change also requires that careful consideration is given to ways of maximising carry-over or generalisation of new skills to different contexts.

Goal setting in rehabilitation

Goal setting might be seen as a systematic process of attempting to influence the future, in the light of the restrictions acting on the present. Many factors will impact on the number, complexity, time-frame, and life domains targeted by goals (Gillis, 1996; Hartley, 1995; Hopewell, Burke, Weslowski, & Zawlocki, 1990; Sloan & Ponsford, 1995b; Ylvisaker & Holland, 1985), and goals should address domain-specific acquisition of functional skills, rather than "global mental improvement" (Hopewell et al., 1990). In the early stages of rehabilitation, the patient's goals may be perceived by staff as unrealistic, because they are concerned with role normalisation (e.g. return to work/driving/school). Clinicians need to teach the skill of differentiating between long-term and short-term goals, recognising that the development of awareness on the part of the injured person will facilitate this process. At the outset of rehabilitation, the patient and clinician need to agree on a small number of goals that will be the focus of treatment for a foreseeable period of time. Important concepts to consider with respect to goal setting are:

1. Whose goal is it? If treatment goals are formulated by the clinician in isolation, they will be the clinician's goals. In this case, the patient's participation will be passive at best. If, however, the clinician takes time to listen to the patient's aspirations and concerns, and to involve the injured person in the process of goal setting, joint ownership is more likely. This in turn helps to enhance motivation, and also creates an atmosphere in which goals can be modified by either party, and where successes can be celebrated along the way (Prigatano, 1987).
2. It is important to recognise the need to modify goals in relation to progress/lack of it, changing needs concerning community re-entry, and changes in level of insight and awareness. Goals must serve the therapeutic alliance, not vice versa.
3. Goals need to be clearly distinguished from the procedures that serve them. Administering assessment tasks, giving the patient feedback, and counselling family members are all procedures, not goals. Corresponding goals might be to determine the person's comprehension of conversational discourse, to ensure that the person understands the nature and implications of his or her difficulties, and to ensure that family members understand the nature of their relative's injuries and the implications for communication. The goal should answer the question "what do we want to achieve at this point in time?" It should be accompanied by a rationale, and then the procedure(s) likely to achieve the goal.
4. In articulating the rationale behind a goal, the clinician needs to ask two questions: (i) How does this goal relate to the neurobehavioural disturbances associated with this person's TBI? and (ii) What contribution to a particular everyday skill would achieving this goal make? The answer to the first question is relevant to the issue of ensuring that behaviours resulting from the TBI, rather than premorbid difficulties,

are being addressed. The answer to the second question relates directly to treatment efficacy, and should offer face validity to the injured person.

5. The language used to express goals should be as simple as possible, taking into account the injured person's premorbid and current English language proficiency, vocabulary level, and level of cognitive functioning. Wherever possible, goals should be expressed using the language of activities or disability (i.e. relating to specific everyday tasks or actions the person is having difficulty performing) and the language of participation or handicap (i.e. relating to the specific life domains in which the injured person wishes to participate). It is not appropriate, however, to express goals in terms of the language of impairment (underlying deficits that might be measured by specific test items). Restated, then, the goal of therapy is not to see a percentage improvement on a particular test. Such improvement may or may not occur in parallel with increased performance of everyday tasks or increased participation. A number of workers have cautioned that structured assessments of executive functioning have clear limitations in the evaluation of the abilities of TBI individuals (e.g. Naugle & Chelune, 1990; Sloan & Ponsford, 1995a; Tupper & Cicerone, 1990; Ylvisaker & Holland, 1985), so that TBI survivors may actually function far above or below the levels suggested by their neuropsychological profile.
6. Careful consideration needs to be given to the method by which progress will be recorded. Where possible, charts or graphs should be employed, and the injured person him- or herself should be encouraged to record the results of each treatment session. This maximises ownership of the goal (together with responsibility for improvement) and can therefore be a motivating aspect of therapy. Ideally, goals should be stated at the outset of each treatment session, so that they can be reviewed at the conclusion of the session.
7. At the time they are set, a date needs to be determined for the formal review of treatment goals. This will depend on the degree of difficulty inherent in the skills being targeted. If set too soon, the injured person may be disappointed in what he or she sees as a lack of progress. If set too far ahead, however, both patient and therapist may become bored with therapy that is no longer challenging or relevant. Care needs to be taken, therefore, with selecting a review date, and both parties need to be flexible, in the light of the patient's rate of progress, in making appropriate adjustments to this.

In summary, goals need to focus on the actual performance of tasks and activities in everyday life and to promote participation in the life domains relevant to and valued by the individual. They need to be achievable in a reasonable period of time, shared by both patient and therapist, and reviewed at regular intervals.

The role of cooperative teamwork in rehabilitation

As described earlier in this chapter, the "segmentation" of patients into categories of impairments and disabilities lends itself to the maintenance of rigid role boundaries within the treating team. Traditionally, the management of neurologically impaired patients has been carried out in such a way as to demarcate and maintain professional role definitions: the physiotherapist rehabilitating walking, the speech-language pathologist focusing on communication skills, and the occupational therapist on activities of daily living. Taken literally, the term "multi-disciplinary" simply means "lots of disciplines". It does not, however prescribe nor imply that strategic efforts will be made by team members to interact and work cooperatively towards common goals. Rather, multi-disciplinary models tend to create service gaps between role boundaries, and many of the individual's personal difficulties in resuming valued life roles fall between these gaps (McGrath & Davis, 1992). It is thus particularly inappropriate for TBI rehabilitation, where all team members must grapple with the same pervasive neurobehavioural impairments. Disorders such as impaired concentration, impulsivity, and poor self-monitoring are great levellers within the team as they manifest in a range of treatment settings and, if not addressed systematically and cooperatively, cause frustration for staff, patients and families, together with a slowing of overall progress.

Inter-disciplinary teams, then, are concerned with cultivating role overlap, so that all team members have a clear understanding of the factors that will work against the injured person in his or her efforts to re-enter the community. This means that staff from all disciplines need to be educated about psychosocial dysfunction after TBI, and need to understand the complex neurobehavioural factors that will reduce the effectiveness of learning and generalisation from therapy. All staff also need to understand that patients and families will find many aspects of the rehabilitation process frustrating, confusing, and sometimes intimidating. The focus of the inter-disciplinary team is the injured person and his or her family, and their complex, ever-changing needs. In order to achieve this focus, staff need to relinquish their hold on professional boundaries in the interests of educating other team members about their area of special expertise, and, in turn, learning from colleagues about the unique contribution they bring to the challenge of community re-entry for TBI survivors. A number of workers have noted that ongoing staff training and support are crucial for the development and maintenance of effective inter-disciplinary TBI rehabilitation teams (e.g. Carpino & Newman, 1991; Crosson, 1987; Melvin, 1989). Teamwork skills need to be learnt, refined, modified in response to changing economic and service provision constraints, and shared with less experienced colleagues.

Inter-disciplinary teamwork has a number of special implications for the management of cognitive-communicative disorders after TBI. First, how should the injured person be assessed, and by whom? There is a certain amount of overlap between the assessment tools employed by speech-language pathologists and those employed by neuropsychologists, and to a lesser extent, occupational therapists. There may also be a passionate belief on the part of clinicians within the team that they, and they alone, are qualified and equipped to assess certain functions. This is an issue that needs to be considered in a patient-centred way. Team members need to ask themselves, and each other, the following questions: (i) "What are the skills which need to be assessed?", (ii) "What measures are available to assess these?", and finally (iii) "Who in the team is best qualified to administer, score, and interpret these measures?"

Being able to ask these questions and discuss the answers in a constructive manner demands a high level of maturity and trust on the part of team members. It is not good use of anyone's time (staff, patient, funding body) for a patient to be subjected to two or three administrations of similar (and sometimes frankly identical) tests. A clear distinction needs to be made between role overlap, which should be encouraged, and role duplication, which simply represents a waste of resources. Instead, time should be made available for staff to cooperate in assessment—e.g. by designing joint assessment protocols and then spending time discussing and interpreting assessment findings—as a basis for team goal setting. Such a process creates opportunities for professionals to learn from and teach each other, and allows more experienced team members to act as mentors for newer staff. This in turn enhances trust within the team and creates a sense of shared responsibility for addressing the more complex neurobehavioural sequelae associated with TBI.

In addition to its special implications for assessment, inter-disciplinary teamwork also requires close cooperation and liaison between staff where the management of cognitive-communicative disorders is concerned. For this to happen, speech-language pathologists must move away from models of intervention that comprise almost exclusively individual, didactic therapy. Instead, clinicians need to create opportunities to work with brain-injured people "*in vivo*"—i.e. in contexts in which they experience difficulty (Hartley, 1995; Snow & Ponsford, 1995b; Ylvisaker & Holland, 1985). This should supplement, not replace, individual therapy, and requires systematic consideration of the community re-entry goals being addressed by other team members. If the occupational therapist, for example, is working on banking, the speech-language pathologist can accompany the injured person to the bank and set specific communication tasks, such as requesting information at the enquiries counter. Similarly, if the physiotherapist would like the injured person to attend a gymnasium in the community, the speech-language pathologist can create opportunities for the patient to plan and make telephone enquiries to a number of gyms (see Chapter 5). These can be audio-taped, to allow immediate review by patient and therapist. It is important to remember that the speech-language pathologist's office can provide a venue for practice on specific tasks; however, it is not a microcosm of the everyday environments in which the injured person will be communicating. By liaising closely with other team members, the speech-language pathologist will encounter a large number of contexts that give the patient "real-world" opportunities to practise specific communication skills. Cooperative teamwork creates scope for mutual support, and creative problem solving, particularly as applied to the frustrations of working with people whose slow and fragmented learning ensures that gains are difficult to achieve, and even harder to maintain over time.

A number of workers have emphasised the importance of all team members being familiar with, and consistently employing behaviour management principles in their dealings with people who have sustained TBI (e.g. Crosson, 1987; Hartley, 1995; Prigatano, 1987; Sloan & Ponsford, 1995; Wood, 1984). Although the consistent application of behavioural principles is widely agreed to underpin successful intervention, it must be emphasised that a supportive treatment milieu is also critical in addressing the injured individual's personal responses (e.g. a sense of loss of identity) to injury (Crosson, 1987; Prigatano, 1987). Behavioural principles are summarised in Table 10.1.

Individual and group therapy: Their roles and limitations

As has been indicated already in this Chapter, speech-language pathologists cannot expect to tackle the rebuilding of effective communication skills simply by working with the injured person within the confines of a quiet clinic office. Ylvisaker and Holland (1985) cited a number of features of one-to-one clinical settings that threaten the ecological validity of the assessments that take place in them. These factors are equally relevant to treatment. Ylvisaker and Holland noted that attention and concentration difficulties may be masked by the orderly and isolated nature of the environment, and the natural tendency of clinicians to simplify and repeat instructions may create a "halo effect" where judgements about the person's real levels of ability are concerned. Further, problems in domains such as

TABLE 10.1
Employing behaviour management principles in rehabilitation

- Base treatment around an unconditional positive regard for the injured person.
- Always look for opportunities to reward (positively reinforce) behaviour.
- Employ the principle of successive approximation: be prepared to reinforce progress towards the attainment of goals.
- Always collect baseline information before commencing intervention.
- Ensure that feedback is immediate, clear, specific, and not emotive.
- Encourage consistency across all staff and family members.
- Look at the person's environment to determine antecedent events and random reinforcers of behaviour.
- Label the behaviour and not the person—e.g. "That response was quite impulsive", rather than "You were impulsive when you answered my question".
- Use "I" statements not "you" statements when giving feedback—e.g. "Sometimes I have trouble following what you are saying", rather than "You go on and on and get off the track".
- Remember that negative attention may be seen by the injured person as being better than no attention at all.
- Consider the role of the overall environment in both creating and sustaining maladaptive behaviours—e.g. is the person bored/easily influenced by others/highly distractable?

initiation and information processing may be masked by the fact that one-to-one therapy is generally structured in a stimulus–response pattern, so that there is at least a covert expectation that the session will be lead by the clinician and the injured person will "follow". The injured person's real level of ability can be further obscured by the fact that one-to-one therapy is usually carried out in a supportive atmosphere, where failure is expected, and the real-life consequences of this (e.g. loss of face, embarrassment, listener confusion) are minimised. Finally, containing therapy to one-to-one contact will restrict the risk-taking necessary for the injured person to regain the confidence to attempt activities in the real world, and eliminates a vast range of opportunities to utilise personal experience as a catalyst for change.

In spite of these limitations, one-to-one therapy does play an important role in the evaluation and management of cognitive-communicative difficulties after TBI. This type of therapy allows the TBI speaker and the therapist to establish rapport, and enables detailed setting and discussion of personally salient goals. Given that not all communication occurs in group contexts, individual therapy is an obvious medium for teaching listening, turn-taking, and topic management skills during one-to-one conversation. It also allows the clinician to provide informational counselling about the ways in which communication can be affected by TBI, together with feedback about the specific nature of the injured person's strengths and weaknesses. Further, individual therapy is a venue in which the injured person can disclose concerns and anxieties about his or her skills, without fear of ridicule or misunderstanding (as can occur in group settings).

With respect to intervention, individual therapy provides the injured person with opportunities to practise emergent skills he or she may be wishing to employ in the community. This should be done in as realistic a manner as possible (e.g. using role-plays), and every opportunity should be provided for the injured person to self-evaluate. Ideally this should be done using audio- or videotaped feedback, which patient and therapist can review together.

Group treatment for TBI speakers has been advocated as a powerful medium in which people who have sustained TBI can practise and consolidate new skills in the relative security of the company of peers (Ben-Yishay & Prigatano, 1990; Cockburn & Wood, 1995; Crosson, 1987; Deaton, 1991; Ehrlich & Sipes, 1985; Flanagan, McDonald, & Togher, 1995; Gillis, 1996; Hartley, 1995; Prigatano et al., 1984; Snow & Ponsford, 1995b; Sohlberg & Mateer, 1989). Groups offer opportunities to practise the more complex processing required when more than one person is speaking at a time, and also provide TBI speakers with experience engaging in one-to-one conversation with a range of speakers.

Careful consideration needs to be given to the constellation of a group in terms of patient numbers, therapist–patient ratios, and the relative cognitive-communicative strengths and weaknesses of the participants. Ideally, conversational skills groups should meet at a regular time, more than once a week, and preferably in the same venue. Participants can share responsibilities such as booking the room, setting up the seating arrangements, and organising refreshments. Every effort needs to be made to promote a sense of shared ownership for the planning, organisation, and ultimate success of a group.

Conducting groups requires experience and assertiveness on the part of the facilitator, and professional supervision/mentoring is important in this respect. There should be a clear rationale for bringing a particular group of individuals together as a group, and specific goals need to be developed for each individual, in consultation with the treating speech-language pathologist. In group sessions, each individual works on specific goals identified through individual therapy, and participates as part of a supportive milieu for fellow group members. This requires that each person is taught how to give and receive feedback (positive and negative) in a fair and constructive manner. In selecting group activities, clinicians should aim for a balance between instruction, experience, and enjoyment. No person should be allowed to feel humiliated as a result of an experience in a group, although participants should feel comfortable to take risks and experience "controlled failure".

At the outset, staff need to explain why the group is meeting, so that sessions are seen as purposeful and goal-oriented. The factors that promote successful communication (such as eye-contact, appropriate body language, showing interest, attentive listening) need to be described and discussed, together with behaviours that can be damaging to communication. Staff can model both appropriate and inappropriate communication behaviours, and these can be observed, identified, and discussed by group participants. Groups should provide opportunities for repeated practice of key skills so that behavioural principles such as shaping, fading of cues, and successive approximation can be employed to maximal advantage. The use of groups in retraining social skills has been described by Nigel Marsh in Chapter 7.

The overriding aim of both individual and group therapy is to teach TBI speakers communication skills and behaviours they can successfully employ in the real world. Because it is difficult for people who have sustained TBI to generalise new skills acquired in the rehabilitation setting to more cognitively demanding settings in the real world (Ylvisaker & Szekeres, 1994), the question of generalisation, or "carry-over" needs to be addressed from the outset. Table 10.2 summarises some ways in which rehabilitation professionals can do this.

Some people remain in rehabilitation for many months after TBI, and it is natural that their enthusiasm and motivation will fluctuate during this time. Because motivation is central to learning, it is essential that clinicians consider ways in which this valuable resource can be harnessed and maximised throughout the person's rehabilitation. Table 10.3 outlines some ways in which motivation can be addressed.

Issues in the evaluation of treatment efficacy

During the past decade, the question of treatment efficacy and the evaluation of outcomes has become a major issue confronting all rehabilitation professionals. A quarter of a century ago, Jennett (1972) touched on the subtle and

TABLE 10.2
Promoting generalisation from therapy to the "real world"

- Recognise that generalisation will not occur spontaneously from therapy.
- Where possible, make activity and participation limitations the focus of rehabilitation, identifying and working on tasks that are relevant to the person in question.
- As far as possible, work on tasks in the environments in which they will be performed. This will mean that the injured person must accommodate to real-life visual and auditory distractions, and learn ways of dealing with them "*in vivo*". This helps to increase awareness and motivation on the part of the injured person. These, in themselves, are essential to generalisation.
- Help the injured person to understand the similarities and differences between different communication tasks, so that he or she can gain a more systematic understanding of why some tasks cause repeated difficulties, while others are more manageable.
- Use group treatment as a "stepping stone" between the rehabilitation setting and the "real world".

TABLE 10.3
Suggested ways of maintaining motivation over time

- Encourage the setting of small, achievable, and measurable goals.
- Make as much use of videotaping as possible. This allows the injured person to view and judge his or her own performance, and provides objective evidence of change over time.
- Make sure that all successes, even small ones, are acknowledged and "celebrated".
- Set dates for reviewing progress.
- Encourage short breaks from rehabilitation, or from specific therapies if boredom and/or frustration seems to be interfering with progress.
- Avoid patronising behaviour.
- Take every opportunity to remind the person of how far they have progressed, while acknowledging that they may still fall far short of their own long-term goals.
- Explain that progress cannot be expected to be observable every day, but what they do every day can make a contribution to continued improvement.
- If the person seems totally unrealistic, try to harness the positive aspects of this (e.g. motivation to return to work, school) while gently reminding them of the benefits of allowing themselves sufficient time to improve specific skills.

elusive nature of outcome measurement when he observed that "A different view of recovery may be taken by the patient himself, who knows only how well he was before the injury, by the doctor, who knows only how bad he was after the injury, and by the family, who know something of both" (p.18). A quarter of a century later, rehabilitation professionals are still largely at odds with issues such as (a) linking outcomes to therapeutic inputs and (b) demonstrating participation at the community re-entry stage (Johnston & Wilkerson, 1992). A number of challenges in outcome measurement remain, as this aspect of TBI rehabilitation is still largely in its infancy. Kearns (1993) observed that so-called "functional assessments" are often more concerned with programme evaluation than they are with the evaluation of a particular individual's unique strengths and weaknesses. While this stems from an understandable need for programme-level efficacy data, clinicians need to recognise that many tools are grossly insensitive as measures of change for a given individual. This issue, together with the relative strengths and weaknesses of a number of so-called "functional" measures of communication, has been discussed in some depth elsewhere (e.g. Body & Campbell, 1995; Frattali, 1992; Manochiopinig, Sheard, & Reed, 1992).

Although much has been made of the methodological issues that need to be addressed by researchers conducting group studies in the field of outcome measurement (e.g. High, Boake, & Lehmkuhl, 1995; Prigatano, Parsons, & Bortz, 1995), a responsibility also lies with individual clinicians to conduct therapy in such a way that its effects may be distinguished from other variables—in particular, spontaneous recovery. The use of single-case methodology, with clear definitions of dependent and independent variables, is an obvious approach for clinicians working in rehabilitation settings (e.g.

McReynolds & Kearns, 1983). Clinicians should give close consideration to factors such as stable baselines, and the threats to validity and reliability of single-case methodology of not employing a rater who is blind to the details of clinical intervention (Robertson, 1994). A range of measures should be selected, targeting the actual performance of specific activities and the resultant restrictions on participation in life domains.

The perceptions of the injured person and/or a close other should also be elicited, because both false positives and false negatives can emerge if only clinic-based measures are employed. Tools such as the La Trobe Communication Questionnaire (Douglas, O'Flaherty, & Snow, in press) allow systematic data collection about perceptions of communication parameters other than those commonly assessed by speech-language pathologists in clinical, rather than "real-world" settings. Further, tools such as the Craig Hospital Assessment and Reporting Technique (CHART; Whiteneck, Charliefue, Gerhart, Overholser, & Richardson, 1992a, b) provide a measure of what the World Health Organisation defined as "handicap" in its 1980 model of disablement. The CHART was originally developed for use with spinal-cord injury patients, but has recently been revised to include items relevant to outcome after severe TBI (Whiteneck, 1996). The revised CHART employs an interview-questionnaire format to elicit information about everyday independence in multiple outcome domains, as follows: physical independence, cognitive independence, mobility, occupation, social integration, and economic self-sufficiency. Boake and High (1996) compared CHART scores on a group of 67 moderately-to-severely injured TBI survivors with their scores on two uni-dimensional indices of outcome—the Disability Rating Scale (DRS) (Rappaport, Hall, Hopkins, Belleza, & Cope, 1982), and the Glasgow Outcome Scale (GOS) (Jennett & Bond, 1975)—and concluded that outcome after severe TBI is not adequately accounted for by single summary scores. Further, they noted that DRS and GOS scores may be overly sensitive to physical outcomes at the expense of outcome in vocational and social domains. The Outcome Measures Subcommittee of the (US) National Institutes of Health/National Institute of Neurologic Disorders and Stroke has recently recommended the inclusion of the CHART as an outcome measure for use with TBI survivors (Hannay, Ezrachi, Contant, & Levin, 1996).

At what time post-injury should "outcome" be evaluated? This is an important question, and one which rehabilitation providers and funding bodies need to consider closely. The most optimistic view of "outcome" may be derived from evaluation at the point of discharge from rehabilitation. At this time, maximal supports are in place, and the injured person and family members are often enthusiastic and confident about the future (sometimes unreasonably so). Discharge, however, is not synonymous with outcome, which needs to be constantly re-evaluated with respect to the personally valued roles the individual is striving to fulfil (Johnston & Wilkerson, 1992). Outcome needs to be considered in terms of the individual's ability to maintain gains made in therapy, and consolidate these gains in different contexts within the community.

SPECIFIC APPROACHES TO NARRATIVE, PROCEDURAL, AND CONVERSATIONAL DISCOURSE

Hartley and Griffith (1989) defined discourse as "... connected speech, a group of utterances related in some manner and treated as a unified whole" (p.51). These workers noted that the four most commonly studied forms of discourse in adult neurological populations are conversation, narrative, procedural, and expository discourse. These have been described in detail in Chapters 1 and 3. Smith and Leinonen (1992) observed that discourse analysis embraces many fields of enquiry such as sociolinguistics, psycholinguistics, ethnomethodology, and cognitive psychology. Discourse is, however, regarded as something of a latecomer in the field of linguistic analysis, thus there are many gaps in the current understanding of what constitutes "normal" performance, and how "abnormal" discourse should be approached. It has been suggested that this reflects the complex ways in which discourse differs from syntax, semantics, and phonetics. Specifically, Patry and Nespoulous (1990) noted that the analysis of discourse is closely related to the study of meaning, it is "multi-levelled", it relies on contextual factors, and is subject to individual variation. It must be stressed, then, that discourse skills can break down at a number of levels (e.g. information transfer, turn-taking, communicative efficiency). Consequently each speaker needs to be carefully evaluated in order to maintain a prescriptive link between assessment and intervention.

Over recent years, there has been a strong groundswell of opinion that clinicians should utilise connected discourse, rather than isolated linguistic parameters as the focus of assessment (and to a lesser extent intervention) with TBI patients (Coelho, 1995; Hartley, 1995; Mentis & Prutting, 1987). This shift to what should be a more "functional" focus is, however, plagued by methodological problems of its own (Snow et al., 1995, 1997a). Merely sampling connected discourse does not ensure that a representative sample of an individual's verbal skills has been obtained, and there are unfortunately a number of ways in which clinicians can reduce the ecological validity of discourse assessment. Consideration needs to be given to the context and relevance of sampling techniques (particularly for conversational discourse), and the types of measures that will be applied to a sample once it has been elicited. Other factors to consider include the role of premorbid sociolinguistic characteristics, and the individual's motivation to perform.

In the absence of normative data that systematically controls for basic factors such as age, gender, and educational background, clinicians must recognise that subjective assessment plays a significant role in the clinical decision-making process. While this involves an element of social validation, it also leaves scope for both false positives and false negatives in the evaluation process.

There is evidence to indicate that different discourse genres (conversation, narrative, procedural), may place different cognitive and/or linguistic demands on both TBI and normal speakers (Coelho, Liles, & Duffy, 1991; Hartley & Jensen, 1991; Shadden, Burnette, Eikenberry, & DiBrezzo, 1991; Togher, Hand, & Code, 1997; Ulatowska, Allard, & Chapman, 1990). Regardless of the discourse genre in question, however, it would seem clear that the major challenge facing TBI speakers is making judgements about information transfer. Problems in parameters such as "insufficient information", "informational redundancy", and "poor topic maintenance" have been reported on Damico's (1985) "Clinical Discourse Analysis" across all of the discourse genres discussed in this chapter (Snow, 1995; Snow et al., 1997a, b). Difficulties making judgements about how much information to convey to a listener, together with related difficulties with topic maintenance, and difficulty structuring discourse, appear to underpin TBI performance in both interactive and monologue (e.g. McDonald, 1993; McDonald & Pearce, 1995) discourse genres. Such difficulties need to be addressed as they apply to each genre, on tasks that are relevant to the person concerned.

Researchers, and to a lesser extent clinicians, make distinctions between different discourse genres, although these will not be immediately obvious to the injured person. Therapy should begin, therefore, with some background explanations and descriptions that will need to be modified in relation to each individual's conceptual abilities. First, it should be explained that there are two broad categories of discourse ("talking") tasks. The first is conversation, a process by which two or more people convey social greetings and/or information. The clinician should discuss with the patient the fact that conversation is a rule-governed activity. Patient and therapist can then compile a list of some of the rules pertaining to conversational behaviour (e.g. turn-taking, topic maintenance, eye-contact, physical proximity mores), and discuss the implications of violations of these rules. It should then be explained that other types of talking are sometimes used within (or completely separately from) conversation. These are narratives (stories) and procedures.

Improving narrative discourse skills

Hedberg and Stoel-Gammon (1986) have observed that individuals who lack knowledge of story grammar will have difficulty reconstructing their own experiences in order to share these with others. The clinician should explain that a narrative has a logical, sequential structure, which enables the speaker to organise information in such a way as to maximise the listener's understanding and enjoyment. Listing and discussing the seven story grammar elements (setting, initiating event, internal responses, plan, attempt, direct consequences, and reactions) proposed by Stein and Glenn (1979) may help to illustrate this concept, particularly if this can be assigned meaning relevant to the patient's recent experience. The name of each story grammar element can be written in red, and information inserted in another colour under the relevant heading. For example: This morning on the ward {setting}, the doctor came to see me {initiating event}. I was worried that he would say I couldn't weight-bear on my broken leg {internal response}, and I was going to ask for another opinion if he said I couldn't {plan}. He had a good look at my leg and the x-rays {attempt}, and then said I could start weight-bearing this week {direct consequences}. I was rapt {reaction}.

It must be stressed that this is an exercise in illustrating to the patient the logical and sequential relationships between the parts of a story. The story grammar elements are provided merely as "sign-posts", not as a list to be rote-learned. It should also be noted that not all stories contain all elements. Sometimes some elements are omitted altogether, or may be implied rather than overtly stated (in particular the plan). It should be explained that when a speaker using narrative forms fails to establish clear temporal and/or cause–effect relationships between the elements in a story, a greater burden is shifted to the listener, who must make inferences and reconstruct events from the incomplete information that has been conveyed. This can result in frustration, confusion, and diminished communicative satisfaction for both parties. Illustrative examples in which the clinician systematically omits different story grammar elements should be employed, so that the patient can identify the effect that this has on the effectiveness of information transfer to the listener.

Liles (1993) has emphasised the cognitive nature of story grammar knowledge, pointing out that "... episodes display logical relationships, usually either temporal or causal, that are thought to transcend the meaning of specific words" (p.870). There is some evidence to suggest that the ability to use story grammar schema may be disturbed by TBI (Coelho et al., 1991, 1995; Liles, Coelho, Duffy, & Zalagens, 1989), although this is equivocal at present. Snow (1995), for example, found that although a group of severely recently injured TBI speakers did not differ significantly from controls with respect to the number of story grammar elements present, they did differ with respect to qualitative aspects of the information contained within these elements. This phenomenon is well illustrated by the following narrative transcript, which was a narrative description of the "Flowerpot Incident" cartoon (Fig. 10.1) produced by a 27-year-old woman, two years after a severe TBI (Snow, Douglas, & Ponsford, in press):

Well he's approaching maybe his house or someone's house with something on his head, a pot plant and then, then he, he get there and he dropped the pot plant so he's probably calling for help, and any rate they open the door, and the pot plant ends up staying there. And oh he's probably gone up and down the stairs, and he's knocking on the, at the door, to see if the person's there. And that person finally comes out and pats the dog, and greets the person, the guy. And now the person's going away. He's um kissing her hand. I suppose he's not going to see her um too often. He kisses her hand and then he's making his way out. And the dog's running around. He's excited. Got a bone. (Reproduced by permission of Taylor & Francis from Snow, Douglas & Ponsford, © in press, *Aphasiology*.)

FIG. 10.1 Picture stimulus "The Flowerpot Incident" (Adapted from "so ein Dackel! 22 Bildergeschichten für den Sprachunterricht" by H. Kossatz (1972). Berlin: Tomus-Verlag. Reproduced with permission.)

This speaker was able to produce information pertaining to the setting *(Well he's approaching maybe his house or someone else's house with something on his head)*, an **initiating event** *(and he dropped the pot plant)*, an **internal response** *(so he's probably calling for help)*, an **attempt** *(and he's knocking on the, at the door, to see if the person's there)*, **direct consequences** *(and that person finally comes out and pats the dog, and greets the person, the guy)*, and a **reaction** *(He's um kissing her hand. I suppose he's maybe not going to see her um too often. He's kissing her hand and then he's making his way out. And the dog's running around. He's excited. Got a bone)*. This speaker failed, however, to establish clear and logical sequential links between the events in the story, resulting in a narrative that was disjointed and inconclusive. Had a listener been naïve about the content of the picture stimuli, it is doubtful that adequate information transfer would have taken place. Interestingly, a similar phenomenon has recently been reported with respect to the discourse of right hemisphere stroke patients (Davis, O'Neil-Pirozzi, & Coon, 1997). These workers also employed the "Flowerpot Incident" cartoon, and found that accuracy of storytelling may be independent of logical cohesion. As Coelho et al. (1991) have observed, then, normal performance on one discourse dimension does not justify an assumption of normality on others.

Thus it is important that each individual's ability to utilise story grammar is evaluated from both a *structural* and a *content* perspective, so that intervention addresses the appropriate level(s) of breakdown. If information transfer is deemed to be deficient because of structural deficiencies, then intervention should commence at this level. If, however, the individual can demonstrate the ability to incorporate and link story grammar elements in narratives, attention needs to be focused on the adequacy, clarity, and relevance of the information contained within the elements. Table 10.4 summarises some useful cues and prompts for the review of narrative practice attempts.

Improving procedural discourse skills

According to Ulatowska et al. (1990) the principal difference between narrative and procedural discourse is that while the primary function of a narrative is to entertain, the main purpose of procedural discourse is to inform or instruct. Like narrative discourse, procedural discourse is a monologue genre that relies on the speaker's ability to plan and organise verbal output in a particular sequence, so that it can be readily understood by the

TABLE 10.4
Questions the speaker needs to consider when producing narrative and procedural genres

- How much does this listener already know?
- How much time is available?
- If I have used a pronoun (e.g. "he/we/they"), have I first told the speaker who I mean?
- Did I start at the beginning, and move from one idea to the next in a logical way?
- Am I staying on the topic, or am I going off the track?
- Am I repeating some information unnecessarily?
- Did I include all of the steps/elements I intended to?
- What sort of non-verbal cues is the listener giving about his or her level of interest in the topic? (Consider eye-contact, restlessness, attempts to interject.)
- Does the listener seem to be following what I am saying? (Note head-nodding for signs of understanding, confused looks for signs that the listener is "getting lost".)
- Did I ask the listener if he or she had any questions, or would like to clarify anything?

listener. Ulatowska, Weiss Doyel, Freedman Stern, and Macaluso Haynes (1983) have proposed that the information contained within procedural discourse is organised into steps, which may be designated as "essential" (containing information which is central to the procedure) or "optional" (providing clarification and/or extra detail about information contained in the "essential" steps). The theoretical structure of procedural discourse is, however, less well understood than that of the narrative genre, and as Snow et al. (1997b) point out, a number of factors need to be taken into account when making clinical judgements about the adequacy or otherwise of a given individual's procedural discourse abilities. These include the fact that the distinction between so-called "essential" and "optional" information is quite an arbitrary one, and could vary with respect to assumptions made by the speaker about shared world knowledge with the listener.

Further, many of the procedures that have traditionally been employed in clinical assessment protocols have required quite simple, well learned activities (e.g. making a sandwich, writing a letter) to be described. Under these circumstances, it is doubtful that the individual's cognitive-communicative skills are taxed in the same way they would be if he or she was required to explain a novel procedure to a naïve listener (as in the studies described by McDonald, 1993 and McDonald & Pearce, 1995). It may simply be that when providing procedural descriptions of common daily activities, the speaker is doing little more than reciting from procedural memory or "script" knowledge. A script was defined by Schank and Abelson (1977) as a predetermined stereotyped sequence of actions that defines a well-known situation. Scripts are said to represent an individual's knowledge about everyday goal-oriented events that are so familiar that their performance is stereotyped in terms of temporal ordering of events, main characters, and setting (Abbott, Black, & Smith, 1985; Nelson, 1981; Ross & Berg, 1990). Ross and Berg (1990) have observed that although scripts are derived from common experience, speakers may include idiosyncratic information from their unique experience. Further, speakers may differ with respect to their interpretations of events, and these, in turn, will influence their personal scripts. These workers cautioned, therefore, that valid individual differences are likely to exist with respect to the nature and amount of information contained within speakers' scripts for given events. Such differences are likely to manifest as varying levels of detail when producing procedural discourse.

Thus, asking an individual to outline the steps in a familiar daily procedure, such as writing a letter, may be so contrived that, in spite of its face validity, it tells us little about the person's ability to utilise this discourse genre in everyday contexts where shared world knowledge cannot be assumed. Because there are currently no clinical tools that are based on normative data about how non-TBI speakers approach the selection and organisation of information to be contained within procedures, clinicians need to take great care in using this genre as an assessment task. The available evidence suggests that there is a considerable degree of normal variability in even such basic parameters as the amount speakers say when producing procedural discourse (Snow et al., 1997b).

Procedural discourse may have special relevance to the individual who is attempting to return to work, particularly if his or her job requires the teaching or supervision of other staff. It is interesting to note the findings of a study reported by Brooks et al. (1987), who examined return to work after brain injury. These workers reported that the presence of what they termed "conversational" difficulties was highly predictive of failure to sustain employment after TBI. Unfortunately, they did not provide a detailed description of the behaviours they encountered; however, their findings suggest that TBI speakers had difficulty conveying specific information to work peers in a clear and concise manner. Individuals who are being prepared for return to work require a careful "needs assessment" (described in detail by Hartley, 1995) in order to determine whether proficiency with procedural discourse will be required in the workplace. If this proves to be so, then individual therapy can provide direct teaching about how to present information clearly, and sequentially, using examples from the injured person's work setting. The clinician should spend time with the injured person during a work trial, so that performance can be monitored directly and problems identified. The self-checking questions outlined in Table 10.4 can form a basis for review of audio/videotaped practice attempts, and later for attempts that occur "on-line" in the workplace.

Improving conversational skills

Modifying an individual's conversational behaviour can be a key to improving the individual's chances of resuming and sustaining pre-existing personal relationships, and forming meaningful new relationships as part of the return to the community. Nofsinger (1991) has observed that conversation is the medium through which we build and maintain contacts with people in order to carry out the business of everyday life. On the surface, everyday conversation may appear ordinary and effortless; its complexity and intricacy are not to be underestimated, however, because these are the very facets of interpersonal behaviour that remain confusing and elusive to the TBI speaker. Therapy aimed at improving conversational skills is inextricably linked to the individual's so-called "social skills", and hence his or her opportunity to achieve a successful outcome with respect to psychosocial functioning in the longer term. In a recent follow-up investigation into the discourse abilities of a group of severely injured TBI speakers, Snow, Douglas, and Ponsford (1998) found conversational abilities did not improve over time (i.e. at nearly 3 years post-injury, compared with a mean of 18 weeks post-injury). Further, conversational abilities were significantly associated with speakers' level of psychosocial handicap, as measured by the CHART social integration subscale (Whiteneck, 1996; Whiteneck et al., 1992a, b). These findings lend support to the notion that conversational difficulties are intimately related to psychosocial functioning, and may well be associated with a contracted and diminishing social circle in the longer term. Therapy aimed at ameliorating conversational difficulty requires a special level of rapport and trust between the injured person and the clinician, and no intervention should be attempted without a thorough assessment that incorporates information from as many sources as possible.

Although the conversational assessment tools available to clinicians all have limitations with respect to validity, reliability, and practical application, they form an important part of the problem-solving process for determining treatment priorities. Every effort should be made, however, to incorporate self and significant other reports (as in, for example, the La Trobe Communication Questionnaire, Douglas et al., in press; see also Chapter 6), in order to increase the ecological validity of both assessment and intervention.

As described earlier in this chapter, both individual and group therapy should be available to TBI speakers who are experiencing conversational difficulties. Individual therapy provides opportunities for clear, sensitive feedback and role-play practice on specific activities (e.g. conveying information in a concise manner, taking turns in conversation, employing appropriate non-verbal behaviours), whereas groups offer more realistic and more challenging arenas in which to practise these skills. Groups also allow TBI speakers to give and receive feedback about their skills in a relatively "safe" context. This not only allows failure to be experienced in a more realistic manner than can be achieved in individual therapy, it provides opportunities for confidence to be regained in ways that individual therapy cannot provide—e.g. through the approval/social validation of peers.

Like group therapy, individual treatment sessions should begin with discussion between therapist and patient about behaviours that promote conversational success, and those that inhibit it. Parameters to consider include the physical proximity of the speakers, the degree of familiarity between speakers, the extent to which speakers "cooperate" through observance of turn-taking rituals, speakers' ability to stay on topic/make smooth shifts between topics, and the clarity of expression of ideas. There should also be discussion of the non-verbal behaviours interactants display during conversation, and what these might signal—e.g. poor eye-contact indicating a desire not to engage in conversation, moving away from the other speaker indicating a desire to terminate an interaction, and excessive head-nodding, indicating that the listener has "got the message" and no further detail is required. Clinicians need to discuss ways in which conversational rules alter in response to changes in context—for example, the relationship between the speakers (e.g. boss and employee, as opposed to two friends), the purpose of the interaction (e.g. discussing a sales contract, as opposed to making plans for a barbecue at the week-end), and the physical surroundings in which a conversation is taking place (e.g. a quiet living-room as opposed to a noisy city street). The therapist can model a variety of communication behaviours, and ask the patient to identify (a) what the speaker did, and (b) why this had a positive or a negative effect on the interaction.

In both individual and group therapy, specific conversational behaviours identified through assessment need to be targeted. TBI speakers need to be given opportunities to observe themselves on video, and rate specific parameters of their own performance. It is also helpful to give the patient opportunities to observe and rate other TBI speakers on video, as this will be less personally threatening at the outset of therapy. Naturally consent should be sought from other speakers before videotaped samples are used in this way. Agreement and discrepancies between therapist and patient ratings provide rich sources of information about personal values and self-perception where particular communication behaviours are concerned and can therefore assist with the setting of treatment priorities.

There is clear evidence that significant gains in communication abilities can be achieved if the individual's unique and specific needs are targeted using behaviour management principles, preferably utilising single-case methodology, as described in the case study later in this chapter (e.g. Blair & Lanyon, 1987; Braunling-McMorrow, Lloyd, & Fralish, 1986; Brotherton, Thomas, Wisotzek, & Milan, 1988). The need to address maintenance and generalisation within the context of treatment, not as an after-thought, cannot, however, be overemphasised. Central to the question of promoting generalisation is the issue of teaching the injured person to self-monitor. This is often a slow process and requires that TBI speakers have repeated opportunities to view themselves on video before developing strategies to use "on-line" during everyday conversations. Such strategies might entail the use of self-talk phrases such as "keep it brief", or may focus on responding to the reactions of the other speaker. Therapy aimed at the management of cognitive-communication disorders will necessarily overlap with what has traditionally been known as "social skills training" (see Chapter 7), and may, therefore call on the expertise of other team members, such as the occupational therapist and psychologist. More recently, formal input regarding decision-making skills has also been provided to TBI individuals within the context of this type of therapy (e.g. Hartley, 1995; Rolan, Williams, & Crawford, 1996).

Many of the communication problems identified through the formal and informal assessment procedures outlined in this and earlier chapters will impact directly on the individual's ability to return to work and/or study following rehabilitation. Discourse, then, needs to be viewed broadly as a tool by which the individual negotiates a wide range of interactions—at home, at work, and/or in educational settings. Consequently, speech-language pathologists need to view these settings as appropriate contexts in which to conduct therapy. Models of supported employment have been described by a number of workers over recent years (e.g. Abrams, Barker, Haffey, & Nelson, 1993; Wehman et al., 1990; Wehman & Kreutzer, 1994), although the role of impaired discourse skills has received little attention with respect to difficulties experienced by TBI survivors who attempt to re-enter the workforce. This neglect of communication has occurred in spite of Brooks et al.'s (1987) finding that difficulty engaging in conversation was a significant predictor of failure to resume working after TBI. This area is ripe for further research and is a context to which speech-language pathologists need to devote time and resources during rehabilitation. Similarly, successful return to educational settings, be they primary, secondary, or tertiary, depends heavily on the individual's ability to use and understand a variety of discourse genres (including written text). Speech-language pathologists have a role in assessing readiness for return to study, selection of course/curriculum content, liaising with teaching staff, and monitoring progress over time (Stewart-Scott & Douglas, 1996, 1998). Cognitive-communicative changes may manifest in subtle and perplexing ways for individuals who face the challenge of return to employment and/or study. It is the role of the speech-language pathologist to anticipate and ameliorate such difficulties and to educate significant others (e.g. supervisors, teachers, year coordinators) about ways in which compromised communication skills may impact on performance in these cognitively challenging settings.

COMMUNICATION AWARENESS TRAINING: A CASE STUDY

Communication Awareness Training (CAT) (Douglas, 1990, 1992) represents a systematic behavioural approach to the identification and amelioration of discourse changes associated with TBI. CAT should ideally be employed within an inter-disciplinary team framework and should involve family members wherever possible. CAT applies to both individual and group intervention. The overriding focus of CAT is giving assistance to TBI speakers in their efforts to return to as many of their valued life roles as possible, while recognising that the process of adjustment to permanent disability can be long and difficult.

CAT has several features in common with other intervention programmes described in the TBI literature (e.g. Ehrlich & Sipes, 1985; Gillis, 1996;

Hartley, 1995; Ponsford, Sloan, & Snow, 1995; Sohlberg & Mateer, 1989) and builds on the principles outlined in previous sections of this chapter.

There are three principal stages or components of CAT. The first component requires investigation and facilitation of speakers' awareness—that is, their ability to perceive and identify problem behaviours. The second requires development and implementation of an agreed-upon strategy for change in defined rehabilitation settings. The third requires systematic introduction of the treatment strategy to novel situations and post-treatment evaluation of maintenance of gains in other situations. Three steps are specified for each stage of intervention and these are outlined in Table 10.5. The CAT framework allows for ready application of multiple baseline procedures across communicative behaviours, communication situations and settings, and across individual patients. Patients working within the CAT framework are required to participate in all stages—awareness, treatment across differing situations, and review. Treatment within all phases is flexible and the number of situations and settings in which the treatment is introduced may vary across patients.

The following case study describes the use of the three stages and associated steps of CAT and illustrates the intervention principles that we have described in this chapter. BR was a 22-year-old male who had sustained an extremely severe TBI (post-traumatic amnesia of 112 days duration) as a result of a motor vehicle accident. At the time of commencing CAT, he was 27 months post-injury. He had been discharged from a primary care rehabilitation facility and

TABLE 10.5
Communication awareness training: Stages and associated steps

STAGE 1:	**To change a problem behaviour one must experience/perceive that a problem exists**
• Step i.	Develop a simple method for demonstrating a particular maladaptive communicative behaviour.
• Step ii.	Define the target behaviour objectively and establish goal levels.
• Step iii.	Make baseline recordings in treatment-designated situations.
STAGE 2:	**To change a problem behaviour a simple strategy must be used**
• Step i.	Agree upon a strategy or a control mechanism with the client.
• Step ii.	Implement treatment within a designated situation.
• Step iii.	Record behaviour response in designated treatment and non-treatment situations/settings.
STAGE 3:	**To be successful a treatment response must be stable and generalise to novel situations**
• Step i.	Implement treatment in non-treatment situations.
• Step ii.	Record behaviour response.
• Step iii.	Check response level in non-treatment situations and review performance following treatment termination.

had been living at home with his parents and two brothers in a small country town for 14 months. BR was assessed and began attending a private rehabilitation programme following several failed attempts to develop vocational skills. By report, failure in vocational programmes had not been due to lack of cognitive skills but rather inappropriate interpersonal behaviour. The most outstanding features of BR's neuropsychological assessment were significantly impaired performance on the Halstead Category Test (DeFilippis, McCampbell, & Rogers, 1979), the Wisconsin Card Sorting Test (Heaton, Chelune, Talley, Kay, & Curtiss, 1993), and the Stroop Test (Trenerry, Crosson, DeBoe, & Leber, 1989) implicating severe frontal lobe dysfunction. Wechsler intelligence and memory scale scores were commensurate with a full scale intelligence quotient of 102 and a memory quotient of 84, indicating significant verbal memory problems. In addition to his neuropsychological deficits, BR presented with a marked overlay of anger concerning his injury, its circumstances, and its consequences. He was extremely angry with the world and everybody in it. With BR, it was particularly important to present rehabilitation as an education/training programme entered into as an agreement between himself and the centre.

BR and his mother rated his communication behaviour using the Communication Performance Scale (CPS) (Ehrlich & Sipes, 1985) during a structured interview session. Two clinicians also rated BR's communication using the CPS. The CPS comprises 13 items measuring intelligibility, prosody/rate, body posture, facial expression, lexical selection, syntax, cohesiveness, variety of language uses, topic, initiation of conversation, repair, interruption, and listening. BR himself did not report any difficulties/problems in any of these areas in the structured interview session. He did, however, make a comment on one item—Listening: "Nobody f—ing listens to anything I say, so why should I listen to them?" Problems related to 9 of the 13 areas were identified by his mother as indicated by the following comments:

- Intelligibility: "Sometimes difficult to understand, I often have to ask him to repeat what he says; (this) makes him mad sometimes."
- Rate: "Speaks a little slow, not really a problem, it helps us to understand him really."
- Syntax: "He does tend to talk in short sentences but it's not really a problem."
- Cohesiveness: "Things are often mixed up ... hard to follow."
- Topic: "Definitely gets stuck on things."
- Initiation: "Doesn't really have anybody else to talk to much."
- Repair: "Mostly gets angry ... yells or won't talk at all."
- Interruption: "Yes all the time, it's awful!"
- Listening: "Seems to depend on whether he wants to or not."

When asked to rank problem behaviours from most to least disruptive/difficult to deal with, BR's mother nominated excessive interruptions as being the most difficult communication problem. This problem was rated at one on the five-point scale of the CPS where one represents frequent interruption and five represents good conversation flow with appropriate interruption. Both clinicians identified some degree of difficulty on all 13 areas of the CPS. However, both strongly agreed with BR's mother that BR's interruptions severely hampered his communication interactions. He simply did not stop interrupting. Frequently, it was not possible to complete a simple instruction or make a brief comment to BR without interruption. His pattern of interruption reflected severely reduced ability to inhibit verbal comment on a thought as it popped into his mind. In addition, his interruptions were frequently characterised by aggressive and provocative content. Consequently, interruptions were selected as the first behaviour to modify in BR's communication interactions. Unfortunately, although this behaviour was seen as problematic by BR's family and the clinicians working with him, it was not seen as problematic from BR's perspective. Thus, Stage 1 in CAT was particularly important for BR.

Stage 1: To change a problem behaviour one must perceive that it exists

Stage 1, Step (i)

The challenge for clinicians was to develop a simple method that allowed BR to experience his interruptive behaviour as maladaptive behaviour. The method chosen for increasing BR's awareness was directed specifically at experiencing a negative consequence for his own interruptive behaviours. BR was passionately interested in working with and learning about computers and computer programs. This interest had played a major role as incentive for BR to attend the centre. Fifty minutes per day had been scheduled for computer work in BR's programme. This interest was selected as the reinforcement activity for CAT. Loss of time for computer work was set up as the negative consequence of interruptive behaviours. To promote BR's awareness of his interruptions in Stage 1 of CAT, the clinician instructed BR that each time he interrupted the message delivery at the beginning of the session she would restart the message. This would continue until the message was completed. It took nine minutes to complete the following instruction: "Today we're going to begin the session with a quick review of the work you completed on Friday and then move to some work on identifying different sorts of interruptive behaviours in group conversations. We'll try and work out when something is an interruption and when it's not." The time taken to complete the message was deducted from the duration of his computer session. This interaction was videotaped and viewed by BR with his clinician. The goal of the activity was for BR to see how his interruptions prevented the delivery of the message and needlessly reduced the time available for a desirable activity.

Stage 1, Step (ii)

In order to define the target behaviour, three ten-minute video recordings of group communication interactions were then viewed by the therapist and BR and were used as training trials. These recordings were of conversation groups conducted in the rehabilitation centre. BR was not involved in the interactions that were viewed. The goal of this task was to identify occurrences within an interaction whereby transfer of a message was delayed or prevented by an interruption. During observation of the videos and discussion of identified interruptions, BR and the therapist together developed a definition of the target behaviour: an interruption occurs whenever an individual verbally disrupts the flow of conversation and/or prevents a speaker from finishing a statement when there is no verbal or non-verbal cue given by the speaker to indicate that this response is appropriate. Requests for clarifications were not included as interruptive behaviours. Viewing videos of other interactants also assisted BR in identifying interruptions as a negative communicative behaviour. When he was not evaluating or defending his own behaviours, he was able to describe the negative consequences of interruptive/disruptive behaviour. He could see people being "put off" and made "upset" or "angry" by this behaviour. He could also see how it frequently made both the speaker and the interrupter "forget" or "lose track of" what they had been talking about. After perceiving these phenomena as unpleasant or difficult in other speakers, he was able to choose the goal of decreased interruptions for himself. Having agreed upon the definition and the personal acceptability of the goal, BR and his clinician agreed that no more than two interruptions per therapy session would be an appropriate level to aim for.

Stage 1, Step (iii)

BR was involved in three different situations within his rehabilitation programme: (a) individual treatment sessions (five per week); (b) group treatment sessions (four per week); and (c) socialisation sessions (one per week). Individual sessions were highly structured and involved one-to-one contact with a clinician. Communicative interaction in these sessions included initial conversation, review of progress, preview of current session goals, task instruction, and review of performance during the session. Group treatment sessions were less structured than individual sessions and were conducted by two clinicians with six clients. Several skill areas were addressed through the different groups run in the centre. These included groups for behaviour management, conversational skills, leisure activities, problem solving, organisation, and planning. Communicative interactions in these sessions included activities such as group introductions, group discussion of problems and potential solutions, role-playing, narrative construction, and individual and group evaluation of performance. Socialisation sessions were minimally structured, weekly social events in which 10–12 clients, some family members, and 3–4 clinicians participated. In socialisation sessions, clients worked on the same target or goal behaviours that they were working on in individual and group sessions. Baseline recordings were made in all three types of sessions (Figs. 10.2, 10.3, 10.4) and the first treatment-designated situation was the individual therapy session. All of the sessions were video recorded, which readily allowed for calculation of inter-observer reliability for frequency of interruptions. An overall percentage agreement between BR's primary clinician and an observer clinician was used. Over baseline conditions percentage agreement for frequency of interruptions ranged from 79–100% with a mean of 93.8%.

Stage 2: To change a problem behaviour a simple strategy must be used

Stage 2, Step (i)

The treatment phase of CAT is essentially a reinforcement schedule or behaviour modification programme that requires a client to evaluate his/her own behavioural performance. During sessions, the clinician indicated to BR when he had exceeded his agreed goal limit by passing him a token. If he received a token for the session, then he was required to view the video of that session and count the number of interruptions that he observed. This evaluation/counting session took place in the hour session that was set aside for his work on the computer each day. Thus, he lost computer time if he exceeded goal levels and retained it if he did not exceed these levels. It was reasoned that he would learn to recognise his own interruptive behaviour, predict the triggers to this behaviour, and potentially inhibit this behaviour with repeated evaluation of his own performance.

Stage 2, Step (ii)

Figure 10.2 shows the results of CAT in the individual session situation. Baseline recordings were made across 10 individual sessions over a 2-week period and the number of interruptions ranged from 8–14. Treatment (negative consequence) was introduced in session 11. BR was required to view

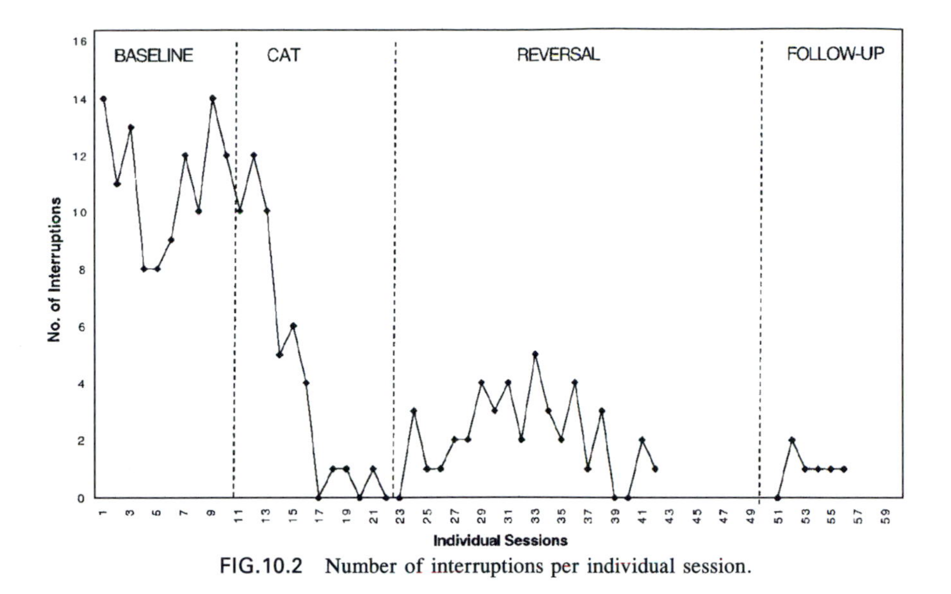

FIG.10.2 Number of interruptions per individual session.

and evaluate the next 6 sessions because he did not reach the agreed goal level of 2 interruptions per session. By session 17 he had reached the goal level and was able to maintain it over the next 4 sessions. The treatment reversal criterion (i.e. return to baseline condition) was set for 5 consecutive sessions in which the behaviour was within the defined goal level of 2 or fewer interruptions. Thus, the reinforcement schedule for individual sessions was discontinued (i.e. baseline conditions were reinstated) in session 22. Overall, performance during the reversal phase remained well below baseline levels with interruptions over the subsequent 21 sessions ranging from 0–5. Performance was within goal levels for 13 of the 21 return-to-baseline sessions and showed relatively good maintenance of reduced interruptive behaviour.

Stage 2, Step (iii)

Baseline recordings in both group and socialisation sessions were continued through the treatment phase for individual sessions. Baseline recordings were made over 14 group sessions (over a 3.5-week period) and 5 socialisation sessions (over a 5-week period). The number of interruptions in the baseline phase for group sessions ranged from 8–19 and for socialisation sessions ranged from 9–25. As expected, reduced structure across the three session types was associated with increased interruptive behaviour. Inspection of the baseline for group sessions shows a possible reduction of interruptive behaviour around sessions 9–14, the time that the treatment phase was conducted in individual sessions. A reduction on baseline recording from week 3 to week 4 in the socialisation sessions is also apparent. These reductions may well represent some carry-over of improved performance (reduced interruptions) to non-treatment situations. However, in neither case does performance approach the designated goal level.

Stage 3: To be successful a treatment response must be stable and generalise to novel situations

Stage 3, Steps (i) and (ii)

Treatment was implemented in group sessions in session 15. The commencement of the treatment phase is marked by an immediate and large decrease in interruptive behaviour (See Fig. 10.3). The designated goal level for groups was reached by the third session following introduction of the negative consequence for interruptive behaviour. Within-goal behaviour was maintained for the subsequent 4 sessions and baseline conditions (reversal) were reinstated in session 22. During the 11 sessions within the reversal phase for group sessions, interruptions remained at a relatively low level (range 0–5). Performance during 7 of these 11 sessions was at or below goal level. At this time the reversal phase for individual sessions was continuing with maintenance of relatively stable performance at a reduced level.

Baseline recordings show that BR's interruptive behaviour was generally high during informal socialisation (range 9–25) (See Fig. 10.4). There is notable variability and a clear downward trend in the number of interrup-

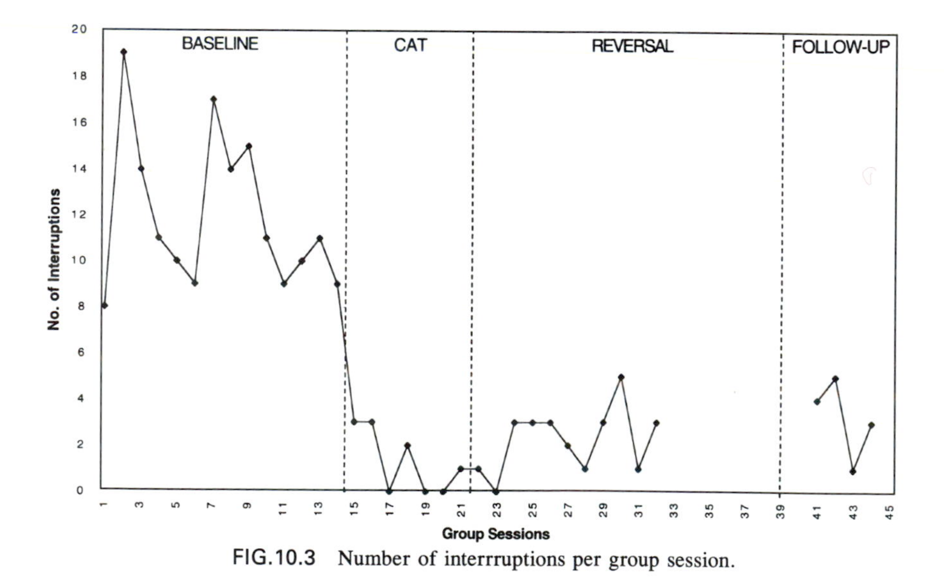

FIG.10.3 Number of interruptions per group session.

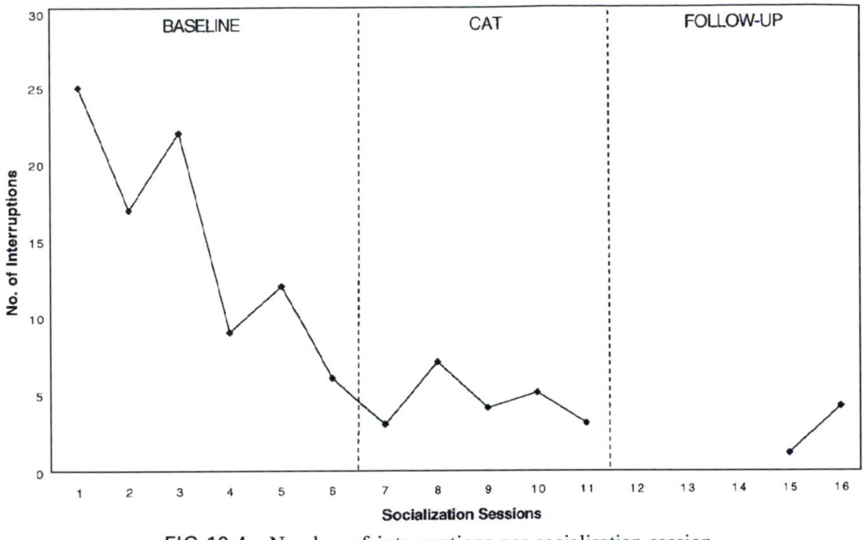

FIG.10.4 Number of interruptions per socialisation session.

tions during baseline recordings in socialisation sessions. Empirically, this trend is problematic with respect to evaluation of the treatment in this setting. BR's interruptions are reducing during the baseline phase and continue to do so during the treatment phase. However, it is worth noting that by session five treatment had already been introduced in individual sessions and group sessions. That is, interruptions had been successfully reduced in two other settings during collection of baseline data in the socialisation sessions. Consequently, the clinicians working with BR considered that the reduction in interruptions during baseline socialisation sessions was likely to reflect a desired carry-over of behaviour change from individual and group settings to the socialisation setting. A treatment carry-over/generalisation interpretation rather than a natural recovery hypothesis was favoured for several reasons. First, BR was more than two years post-injury and consequently less likely to show spontaneous recovery. Second, although his behaviour was characterised by variability there had been no systematic reduction in his interruptive behaviour reported by his family members or previous clinicians prior to commencing CAT. Unfortunately, time and funding constraints did not permit possible clarification of this issue through extension of the baseline recording phase in socialisation sessions and treatment was introduced in socialisation session 6 (week 6). Although there was a significant drop from 12 to 6 interruptions when the treatment phase commenced, BR did not reach goal level in this setting. His performance over the next 4 weeks was 7, 4, 5, and 3 interruptions respectively. These levels reflected much improved performance from his early baseline levels of 25, 17, and 22 interruptions per session. For this particular setting, it could be argued that the goal of two interruptions per session was unrealistic.

Stage 3, Step (iii)

Follow-up recordings were taken one month following termination of the programme (see Figs. 10.2, 10.3, 10.4). Performance was checked in six individual, four group, and two socialisation sessions. BR interrupted on two or fewer occasions in all his individual sessions. Performance was somewhat more variable in group and socialisation sessions ranging from 1–5 interruptions per session. It is interesting to note that he reached goal level for the first time in socialisation sessions during follow-up. Overall, these results were considered extremely promising. BR had shown a relatively stable change in behaviour within treatment situations over a relatively short period of time. This behavioural change meant that BR was much easier to work with and more likely to achieve greater gains in rehabilitation. He was now able to inhibit verbal interruptive responses more effectively.

In order to ascertain the degree to which this behaviour change had carried over to non-treatment situations, BR's mother was asked to rate interruption on the CPS. During the initial interview, she had rated interruption at one (frequent interruptions) on a five-point scale where five represented appropriate interruption and good conversation flow. At follow-up she rated his performance at three indicating that there had been a change in behaviour across non-clinical situations outside of the rehabilitation setting. However, the degree of change was not as strong as that being shown in clinical treatment situations. BR was also asked to rate interruption on the CPS at follow-up. Two important changes had taken place. First, he agreed to rate the behaviour and did not dismiss the request by simply stating he had no problems. Second, he rated the behaviour at four indicating that he did not perceive his current behaviour as entirely appropriate. Somewhere over our period of treatment BR had indeed become more aware of his communication! Finally, it was heartening to note that fellow patients became more willing to communicate with BR. Over the period of treatment he appeared to have become much less of a loner. As therapists, it is appealing to surmise that this increased communication and social integration may at least in part have been due to BR's reduced interruptive and frequently disruptive behaviour during conversation.

Summary

CAT provides an example of a treatment protocol that can be readily applied across communication behaviours and settings with different brain-injured individuals. It provides a framework within which to evaluate therapy by using established single-case methodology practice. It utilises many of the principles and strategies discussed earlier in this chapter, particularly as these pertain to developing awareness as a basis for systematic behavioural change.

CONCLUSIONS

In this chapter we have explored a range of issues relating to the rehabilitation of discourse after severe TBI. Clinicians need to bring to this work a strong background in discourse theory, together with a clear understanding of the neurobehavioural and psychosocial consequences of severe TBI. Every effort needs to be made to employ systematic and flexible assessment procedures incorporating both standardised and ethnographic methodologies. Careful consideration of this assessment data should then form the basis of an individualised management plan for each TBI speaker. The injured person should be an active participant in all stages of discourse therapy, and every effort needs to be made to both maximise the face validity of treatment and maintain motivation over time. It is critical that the efficacy of all intervention is evaluated at the single-case level, so that TBI speakers make real gains towards community re-entry as a consequence of time spent in therapy. This issue is also quite rightly a central concern to funding bodies. Speech-language pathologists need to recognise that their input may not be welcomed by the injured person in the early stages of rehabilitation, when physical recovery is frequently a more pressing (and more tangible) priority. It is crucial, however, that speech-language pathology services be made available in community settings, and over longer time-frames. In this way, input can be provided in the real-life situations in which communicative failure is impacting negatively on the individual in question.

Stumbling along in a clumsy and unsafe manner without the aid of a walking stick is not regarded as optimal physical recovery after severe brain injury. In the same way, it is unacceptable to allow the TBI survivor to re-enter the community with inadequately treated discourse difficulties. Failure to adequately address communication needs carries a high risk of detriment to the individual's ability to resume those life roles that are central to self-esteem and productivity in the real world. The challenges inherent in this therapy are considerable, but the large literature on psychosocial outcome after TBI leaves no doubt about the consequences of neglecting to modify the discourse skills of people who survive this injury.

REFERENCES

Abbott, V., Black, J.B., & Smith, E.E. (1985). The representation of scripts in memory. *Journal of Memory and Language*, *24*, 179–199.

Abrams, D., Barker, L.T., Haffey, W., & Nelson, H. (1993). The economics of return to work for survivors of traumatic brain injury: Vocational services are worth the investment. *Journal of Head Trauma Rehabilitation*, *8(4)*, 59–76.

Allen, C.C., & Ruff, R.M. (1990). Self-rating versus neuropsychological performance of moderate versus severe head injured patients. *Brain Injury*, *4(1)*, 7–17.

Ben-Yishay, Y., Piasetsky, E.B., & Rattok, J. (1987). A systematic method for ameliorating disorders in basic attention. In M. Meier, A. Benton, & L. Diller (Eds.), *Neuropsychological rehabilitation* (pp.165–181). New York: Guilford Press.

Ben-Yishay, Y., & Prigatano, G.P. (1990). Cognitive remediation. In M. Rosenthal, E.R. Griffith, M. Bond, & J.D. Miller (Eds.), *Rehabilitation of the adult and child with traumatic brain injury* (2nd ed.) (pp.393–409). Philadelphia, PA: F.A. Davis Co.

Blair, C.D., & Lanyon, R.I. (1987). Retraining social and adaptive living skills in severely head-injured adults. *Archives of Clinical Neuropsychology*, *2*, 33–47.

Boake, C., & High, W. (1996). Functional outcome from traumatic brain injury. Unidimensional or multidimensional? *American Journal of Physical Medicine and Rehabilitation*, *75(2)*, 1–9.

Body, R., & Campbell, M. (1995) Choosing outcome measures. In M.A. Chamberlain, V. Neumann, & A. Tennant (Eds.), *Traumatic brain injury rehabilitation: Services, treatments, and outcomes* (pp.245–258). London: Chapman & Hall Medical.

Braunling-McMorrow, D., Lloyd, K., & Fralish, K. (1986). Teaching social skills to head-injured adults. *Journal of Rehabilitation*, *Jan/Feb/Mar*, 39–44.

Brooks, D.N., McKinlay, W., Symington, C., Beattie, A., & Campsie, L. (1987). Return to work within the first seven years of severe head injury. *Brain Injury*, *1(1)*, 5–19.

Brotherton, F.A., Thomas, L.L., Wisotzek, I.E., & Milan, M.A. (1988). Social skills training in the rehabilitation of patients with traumatic closed head injury. *Archives of Physical Medicine and Rehabilitation*, *69*, 827–832.

Carpino, L., & Newman, J.F. (1991). Role assessment of the allied health rehabilitation team. *Journal of Rehabilitation Administration*, *August*, 187–190.

Cockburn, J., & Wood, J. (1995). Developing communication skills: A group therapy approach. In M.A. Chamberlain, V. Neumann, & A. Tennant (Eds.), *Traumatic brain injury rehabilitation: Services, treatments, and outcomes* (pp.193–204). London: Chapman & Hall Medical.

Coelho, C.A. (1995). Discourse production deficits following traumatic brain injury: A critical review of the recent literature. *Aphasiology*, *9(5)*, 409–429.

Coelho, C.A., Liles, B.Z., & Duffy, R.J. (1991). Discourse analyses with closed head injured adults: Evidence for differing patterns of deficits. *Archives of Physical Medicine and Rehabilitation*, *72, June*, 465–468.

Coelho, C.A., Liles, B.Z., & Duffy, R.J. (1995). Impairments of discourse abilities and executive functions in traumatically brain-injured adults. *Brain Injury*, *9(5)*, 471–477.

Crisp, R. (1993). Personal responses to traumatic brain injury: A qualitative study. *Disability, Handicap, and Society*, *8(4)*, 393–404.

Crosson, B. (1987). Treatment of interpersonal deficits for head-trauma patients in in-patient rehabilitation settings. *The Clinical Neuropsychologist*, *1(4)*, 335–352.

Damico, J.S. (1985). Clinical discourse analysis: A functional approach to language assessment. In C.S. Simon (Ed.), *Communication skills and classroom success* (pp.165–203). London: Taylor & Francis.

Davis, G.A., O'Neil-Pirozzi, T.M., & Coon, M. (1997). Referential cohesion and logical coherence of narration after right hemisphere stroke. *Brain and Language*, *56,* 183–210.

Deaton, A.V. (1991). Group interventions for cognitive rehabilitation: Increasing the challenges. In J.S. Kreutzer & P.H. Wehman (Eds.), *Cognitive rehabilitation for persons with traumatic brain injury* (pp.191–200). Baltimore, MD: Paul H. Brookes.

DeFilippis, N.A., McCampbell, E., & Rogers, P. (1979). Development of a booklet form of a category test: Normative and validity data. *Journal of Clinical Neuropsychology*, *1*, 339–342.

Douglas, J.M. (1990, March). *Traumatic brain injury: Language and communication deficits*. Paper presented at the New Zealand Speech-Language Therapists Association Biennial Conference, Christchurch, New Zealand.

Douglas, J.M. (1992, February). *Communication awareness training following traumatic brain injury*. Paper presented at the National Australian Association of Speech and Hearing Conference, Melbourne, Australia.

Douglas, J.M., O'Flaherty, C.A., & Snow, P.C. (in press). Measuring perception of communicative ability: The development and evaluation of the La Trobe Communication Questionnaire. *Aphasiology*.

Edwards, J. (1989). *Language and disadvantage* (2nd ed.). London: Cole & Whurr Ltd.

Ehrlich, J., & Sipes, A. (1985). Group treatment of communication skills for head trauma patients. *Cognitive Rehabilitation*, *3*, 32–37.

Elsass, L., & Kinsella, G. (1987). Social interaction after severe closed head injury. *Psychological Medicine*, *17*, 67–78.

Finger, S., & Stein, D.G. (1982). *Brain damage and recovery*. New York: Academic Press.

Flanagan, S., McDonald, S., & Togher, L. (1995). Evaluating social skills following traumatic brain injury: The BRISS as a clinical tool. *Brain Injury*, *9(4)*, 321–338.

Frattali, C.M. (1992). Functional assessment of communication: Merging public policy with clinical views. *Aphasiology*, *6(1)*, 63–83.

Gillis, R.J. (1996). *Traumatic brain injury rehabilitation for speech-language pathologists*. Boston, MA: Butterworth-Heinemann.

Godfrey, H.P.D., Partridge, F.M., Knight, R.G., & Bishara, S. (1993). Course of insight disorder and emotional dysfunction following closed head injury: A controlled cross-sectional follow-up study. *Journal of Clinical and Experimental Psychology*, *15*, 503–515.

Goldstein, G., & McCue, M. (1995). Differences between patient and informant functional outcome ratings in head-injured individuals. *International Journal of Rehabilitation and Health*, *1(1)*, 25–35.

Hannay, H.J., Ezrachi, O., Contant, C.F., & Levin, H.S. (1996). Outcome measures for patients with head injuries: Report of the Outcome Measures Subcommittee. *Journal of Head Trauma Rehabilitation*, *11(6)*, 41–50.

Hartley, L.L. (1995). *Cognitive-communicative abilities following brain injury. A functional approach*. San Diego, CA: Singular Publishing Group.

Hartley, L.L. (1996, November). *A functional approach to the management of cognitive-communicative disorders*. Workshop presented at the Fifth Conference of the International Association for the Study of Traumatic Brain Injury, Melbourne, Australia.

Hartley, L.L., & Griffith, A. (1989). A functional approach to the cognitive-communication deficits of closed head injured clients. *Journal of Speech-Language Pathology and Audiology*, *13(2)*, 51–57.

Hartley, L.L., & Jensen, P.J. (1991). Narrative and procedural discourse after closed head injury. *Brain Injury*, *5(3)*, 267–285.

Heaton, R.K., Chelune, G.J., Talley, J.L., Kay, G.G., & Curtiss, G. (1993). *Wisconsin Card Sorting Test Manual: Revised and expanded*. Odessa, FL: PAR.

Hedberg, N.L., & Stoel-Gammon, C. (1986). Narrative analyses: Clinical procedures. *Topics in Language Disorders*, *7(1)*, 58–69.

High, W.M., Boake, C., & Lehmkuhl, L.D. (1995). Critical analysis of studies measuring the effectiveness of rehabilitation following traumatic brain injury. *Journal of Head Trauma Rehabilitation*, *10(1)*, 14–26.

Hopewell, C.A., Burke, W.H., Weslowski, M., & Zawlocki, R. (1990). Behavioural learning therapies for the traumatically brain-injured patient. In R.L. Wood & I. Fussey (Eds.), *Cognitive rehabilitation in perspective* (pp.229–245). London: Taylor & Francis.

Hudson, R.A. (1980). *Sociolinguistics*. Avon: Cambridge University Press.

Jennett, B. (1972). Some aspects of prognosis after severe head injury. *Scandinavian Journal of Rehabilitation Medicine*, *4*, 16–20.

Jennett, B., & Bond, M. (1975). Assessment of outcome after severe brain damage. *Lancet*, *1*, 480–487.

Johnston, M.V., Hall, K.M., & Banja, J. (1994). Outcomes evaluation in TBI rehabilitation. *Archives of Physical Medicine and Rehabilitation*, *75*, whole supplement.

Johnston, M.V., Hall, K.M., Carnevale, G., & Boake, C. (1996). Functional assessment and outcome evaluation. In L.J. Horne & N.D. Zasler (Eds.), *Medical rehabilitation of TBI* (pp.197–226). Philadelphia, PA: Hanley & Belfus.

Johnston, M.V., & Wilkerson, D.L. (1992). Program evaluation and quality improvement systems in brain injury rehabilitation. *Journal of Head Trauma Rehabilitation*, *7(4)*, 68–82.

Kazdin, A.E. (1982). *Single-case research design*. New York: Oxford University Press.

Kazdin, A.E. (1995). Preparing and evaluating research reports. *Psychological Assessment, 7(3)*, 228–237.

Kearns, K. (1993). Functional outcome: Methodological considerations. In M.L. Lemme (Ed.), *Clinical Aphasiology*, *21* (pp.67–72). Austin, TX: Pro-Ed.

Kossatz, H. (1972). *So ein Dackel! 22 Bildergeschichten für den Sprachunterricht*. Berlin: Tomus-Verlag.

Kraus, J.F., Black, M.A., Hessol, N., Ley, P., Rokaw, W., Sullivan, C., Bowers, S., Knowlton, S., & Marshall, L. (1984). The incidence of acute brain injury and serious impairment in a defined population. *American Journal of Epidemiology*, *119*, 186–201.

Lennox, D.B., & Brune, P. (1993). Incidental teaching for training communication in individuals with traumatic brain injury. *Brain Injury*, *7(5)*, 449–454.

Liles, B.Z. (1993). Narrative discourse in children with language disorders and children with normal language: A critical review of the literature. *Journal of Speech and Hearing Research*, *36*, 868–882.

Liles, B.Z., Coelho, C.A., Duffy, R.J., & Zalagens, M.R. (1989). Effects of elicitation procedures on the narratives of normal and closed head-injured adults. *Journal of Speech and Hearing Disorders*, *54*, 356–366.

Manochiopinig, S., Sheard, C., & Reed, V.A. (1992). Pragmatic assessment in adult aphasia: A clinical review. *Aphasiology*, *6(6)*, 519–533.

McDonald, S. (1993). Pragmatic language skills after closed head injury: Ability to meet the informational needs of the listener. *Brain and Language*, *44*, 28–46.

McDonald, S., & Pearce, S. (1995). The "dice" game: A new test of pragmatic language skills after closed head injury. *Brain Injury*, *9(3)*, 255–271.

McGann, W., & Werven, G. (1995). Social competence and head injury: A new emphasis. *Brain Injury*, *9*, 93–102.

McGrath, J.R., & Davis, A.M. (1992). Rehabilitation: Where are we going and how do we get there? *Clinical Rehabilitation*, *6*, 225–235.

McReynolds, L.V., & Kearns, K.P. (1983). *Single-subject experimental designs in communicative disorders*. Austin, TX: Pro-Ed.

Melvin, J.L. (1989). Status report on inter-disciplinary medical rehabilitation. *Archives of Physical Medicine and Rehabilitation*, *70, April*, 273–276.

Mentis M., & Prutting, C.A. (1987). Cohesion in the discourse of normal and head injured adults. *Journal of Speech and Hearing Research*, *30*, 88–98.

Miller, E. (1984). *Recovery and management of neuropsychological impairments*. Chichester: John Wiley & Sons.

Minichiello, V., Aroni, R., Timewell, E., & Alexander, L. (1995). *In-depth interviewing* (second edition). Melbourne, Australia: Longman.

Naugle, R.I., & Chelune, G.J. (1990). Integrating neuropsychological and "real-life" data: A neuropsychological model for assessing everyday functioning. In D.E. Tupper & K.D. Cicerone (Eds.), *The neuropsychology of everyday life: Assessment and basic competencies* (pp.57–73). Boston, MA: Kluwer Academic Press.

Nelson, K. (1981). Social cognition in a script framework. In J.H. Flavell & L. Ross (Eds.), *Social cognitive development. Frontiers and possible futures* (pp.97–118). New York: Cambridge University Press.

Nofsinger, R.E. (1991). *Everyday conversation*. Newbury Park: Sage Publications.

Pang, D. (1985). Pathophysiologic correlates of neurobehavioural syndromes following closed head injury. In M. Ylvisaker (Ed.), *Head injury rehabilitation: Children and adolescents* (pp.3–70). Boston, MA: College-Hill Press.

Patry, R., & Nespoulous, J.L. (1990). Discourse analysis in linguistics: Historical and theoretical background. In Y. Joanette & H.H. Brownell (Eds.), *Discourse ability and brain damage* (pp.3–27). New York: Springer-Verlag.

Ponsford, J., Sloan, S., & Snow, P. (1995). *Traumatic brain injury: Rehabilitation for everyday adaptive living*. Hove, UK: Lawrence Erlbaum Associates Ltd.

Poole, M.E. (1976). *Social class and language utilization at the tertiary level*. St. Lucia, Queensland: University of Queensland Press.

Prigatano, G.P. (1987). Recovery and cognitive retraining after craniocerebral trauma. *Journal of Learning Disabilities*, *20(10)*, 603–613.

Prigatano, G.P. (1991). Disturbances of self-awareness of deficit after traumatic brain injury. In G. Prigatano & D. Schacter (Eds.), *Awareness of deficit after brain injury* (pp.111–126). New York: Oxford University Press.

Prigatano, G.P., Fordyce, D.J., Zeiner, H.K., Roueche, J.R., Pepping, M., & Wood, B.C. (1984). Neuropsychological rehabilitation after closed head injury in young adults. *Journal of Neurology, Neurosurgery, and Psychiatry*, *47(3)*, 505–513.

Prigatano, G.P., Parsons, O.A., & Bortz, J.J. (1995). Methodological considerations in clinical neuropsychological research 17 years later. *Psychological Assessment*, *7(3)*, 396–403.

Rappaport, M., Hall, K.M., Hopkins, K., Belleza, T., & Cope, D.N. (1982). Disability rating scale for severe head trauma: Coma to community. *Archives of Physical Medicine and Rehabilitation*, *63*, 118–123.

Rees, N.S., & Gerber, S. (1992). Ethnography and communication: Social-role relations. *Topics in Language Disorders*, *12(3)*, 15–27.

Richardson, J.T.E. (1990). *Clinical and neuropsychological aspects of closed head injury*. Hove, UK: Lawrence Erlbaum Associates Ltd.

Robertson, I.H. (1994). Editorial: Methodology in neuropsychological rehabilitation research. *Neuropsychological Rehabilitation*, *4(1)*, 1–6.

Rolan, J., Williams, E., & Crawford, S. (1996). Decision making: A hierarchical program for developing skills in high level problem solving and effective communication. In J. Ponsford, P. Snow, & V. Anderson (Eds.), *International perspectives in traumatic brain injury* (pp.337–341). Proceedings of the 5th International Association for the Study of Traumatic Brain Injury Conference and the 20th Conference of the Australian Association for the Study of Brain Impairment, Melbourne, Australia. Brisbane: Australian Academic Press.

Ross, B.L., & Berg, C.A. (1990). Individual differences in script reports: Implications for language assessment. *Topics in Language Disorders*, *10(3)*, 30–44.

Sbordone, R.J. (1991). Overcoming obstacles in cognitive rehabilitation. In J.S. Kreutzer &

P.H. Wehman (Eds.), *Cognitive rehabilitation for persons with traumatic brain injury: A functional approach* (pp.105–116). Baltimore, MD: Paul H. Brookes.

Schank, R.C., & Abelson, R.P. (1977). *Scripts, plans, goals and understanding*. Hillsdale, NJ: Lawrence Erlbaum Associates Inc.

Schoenfeld, H.A., & Hamilton, L.W. (1977). Secondary brain changes following lesions: A new paradigm for lesion experimentation. *Physiology and Behaviour, 18*, 951–967.

Shadden, B.B., Burnette, R.B., Eikenberry, B.R., & DiBrezzo, R. (1991). All discourse tasks are not created equal. In T.E. Prescott (Ed.), *Clinical aphasiology, 20* (pp.327–341). Austin, TX: Pro-Ed.

Sloan, S., & Ponsford, J. (1995a). Assessment of cognitive difficulties following TBI. In J. Ponsford with S. Sloan & P. Snow. *Traumatic brain injury: Rehabilitation for everyday adaptive living* (pp.65–101). Hove, UK: Lawrence Erlbaum Associates Ltd.

Sloan, S., & Ponsford, J. (1995b). Managing cognitive problems following TBI. In J. Ponsford with S. Sloan & P. Snow. *Traumatic brain injury: Rehabilitation for everyday adaptive living* (pp.103–135). Hove, UK: Lawrence Erlbaum Associates Ltd.

Snow, P. (1995, July). *Cognitive and linguistic factors in discourse assessment following traumatic brain injury*. Australian Society for the Study of Brain Impairment Presidential Address: Second Pacific Rim International Neuropsychological Society Conference, Cairns, Australia.

Snow, P., Douglas, J., & Ponsford, J. (1995). Discourse assessment following traumatic brain injury: A pilot study examining some demographic and methodological issues. *Aphasiology, 9*, 365–380.

Snow, P., Douglas, J., & Ponsford, J. (1997a). Conversational assessment following traumatic brain injury: A comparison across two control groups. *Brain Injury, 11(6)*, 409–429

Snow, P., Douglas, J., & Ponsford, J. (1997b). Procedural discourse following traumatic brain injury. *Aphasiology, 11(10)*, 947–967.

Snow, P.C, Douglas, J.M., & Ponsford, J.L. (in press). Narrative discourse following severe traumatic brain injury: A longitudinal follow-up. *Aphasiology*.

Snow, P., Douglas, J., & Ponsford, J. (1998). Conversational discourse abilities following severe traumatic brain injury: A follow-up study. *Brain Injury, 12*, 911–935.

Snow, P., & Ponsford, J. (1995a). Assessing and managing impairment of consciousness following TBI. In J. Ponsford with S. Sloan & P. Snow. *Traumatic brain injury. Rehabilitation for everyday adaptive living* (pp.33–64). Hove, UK: Lawrence Erlbaum Associates Ltd.

Snow, P., & Ponsford, J. (1995b). Assessing and managing changes in communication and interpersonal skills following TBI. In J. Ponsford with S. Sloan & P. Snow. *Traumatic brain injury: Rehabilitation for everyday adaptive living* (pp.137–164). Hove, UK: Lawrence Erlbaum Associates Ltd.

Sohlberg, M.M., & Mateer, C.A. (1987). Efficacy of an attention process training program. *Journal of Clinical and Experimental Neuropsychology, 9*, 117–130.

Sohlberg, M.M., & Mateer, C.A. (1989). *Introduction to cognitive rehabilitation: Theory and practice*. New York: Guilford Press.

Spencer, J.C. (1993). The usefulness of qualitative methods in rehabilitation: Issues of meaning, of context, and of change. *Archives of Physical Medicine and Rehabilitation, 74*, 119–126.

Stein, N.L., & Glenn, C.G. (1979). An analysis of story comprehension in elementary school children. In R.O. Freedle (Ed.), *New directions in discourse processing* (pp.53–120). New Jersey: Ablex Publishing Corporation.

Stewart-Scott, A., & Douglas, J.M. (1996). Reintegration of post secondary students following traumatic brain injury: A review of the literature. In J. Ponsford, P. Snow, & V. Anderson (Eds.), *International perspectives in traumatic brain injury* (pp.338–392). Proceedings of the

5th International Association for the Study of Traumatic Brain Injury Conference and the 20th Conference of the Australian Association for the Study of Brain Impairment, Melbourne, Australia. Brisbane: Australian Academic Press.

Stewart-Scott, A., & Douglas, J.M. (1998). Educational outcome for secondary and post-secondary students following traumatic brain injury. *Brain Injury*, *12(4)*, 317–331.

Stubbs, M. (1983). *Discourse analysis. The sociolinguistic analysis of natural language*. Oxford: Basil Blackwell.

Togher, L., Hand, L., & Code, C. (1997). Analysing discourse in the traumatic brain injury population: Telephone interactions with different communication partners. *Brain Injury*, *11(3)*, 169–189.

Trenerry, M.R., Crosson, B., DeBoe, J., Leber, W.R. (1989). *Stroop Neuropsychological Screening Test*. Odessa, FL: PAR.

Trudgill, P. (1983). *Sociolinguistics. An introduction to language and society*. London: Penguin Books.

Tupper, D.E., & Cicerone, K.D. (1990). An introduction to the neuropsychology of everyday life. In D.E. Tupper & K.D. Cicerone (Eds.), *The neuropsychology of everyday life: Assessment and basic competencies* (pp.3–18). Boston, MA: Kluwer Academic Publishers.

Ulatowska, H.K., Allard, L., & Chapman, S.B. (1990). Narrative and procedural discourse in aphasia. In Y. Joanette & H.H. Brownell (Eds.), *Discourse ability and brain damage. Theoretical and empirical perspectives* (pp.180–198). New York: Springer-Verlag.

Ulatowska, H.K., Weiss Doyel, A., Freedman Stern, R., & Macaluso Haynes, S. (1983). Production of procedural discourse in aphasia. *Brain and Language*, *18*, 315–341.

Webb, D.M. (1991). Increasing carryover and independent use of compensatory strategies in brain-injured patients. *Cognitive Rehabilitation, May/June*, 28–35.

Wehman, P.H., & Kreutzer, J.S. (1994, September). *Return to work for patients with TBI: Six years of outcome data and program guidelines*. Paper presented at the Fourth Conference of the International Association for the Study of Traumatic Brain Injury, St. Louis, MO.

Wehman, P.H., Kreutzer, J.S., West, M., Sherron, P., Zasler, N., Groah, C., Stonnington, H.H., Burns, C., & Sale, P. (1990). Return to work for persons with traumatic brain injury: A supported employment approach. *Archives of Physical Medicine and Rehabilitation*, *71*, 1047–1052.

Whiteneck, G.G. (1996). *Scoring guidelines for the revised CHART*. Unpublished manuscript: Author.

Whiteneck, G.G., Charliefue, M.A., Gerhart, K.A., Overholser, J.D., & Richardson, G.N. (1992a). Quantifying handicap: A new measure of long-term rehabilitation outcomes. *Archives of Physical Medicine and Rehabilitation*, *73*, *June*, 519–526.

Whiteneck, G.G., Charliefue, M.A., Gerhart, K.A., Overholser, J.D., & Richardson, G.N. (1992b). *Guide for use of the CHART*. Englewood, CO: Craig Hospital.

Whyte, J. (1990). Mechanisms of recovery of function following CNS damage. In M. Rosenthal, E.R. Griffith, M. Bond, & J.D. Miller (Eds.), *Rehabilitation of the adult and child with traumatic brain injury* (2nd ed., pp.79–88). Philadelphia, PA: F.A. Davis Co.

WHO (World Health Organisation) (1980). *International classification of impairments, disabilities and handicaps: A manual of classification relating to the consequences of disease*. Geneva, Switzerland: WHO.

WHO (World Health Organisation) (1997). *ICIDH-2: International classification of impairments, activities and participation*. Geneva, Switzerland: WHO.

Wolf, M.M. (1978). Social validity: The case for subjective measurement or how applied behaviour analysis is finding its heart. *Journal of Applied Behaviour Analysis*, *11*, 203–214.

Wood, R.L. (1984). Behaviour disorders following severe brain injury: Their presentation and psychological management. In N. Brooks (Ed.), *Closed head injury: Psychological, social and family consequences* (pp.195–219). Oxford: Oxford University Press.

Ylvisaker, M.S. & Holland, A.L. (1985). Coaching, self-coaching, and rehabilitation of head injury. In D.F. Johns (Ed.), *Clinical management of neurogenic communicative disorders* (pp.243–257). Boston, MA: Little, Brown & Co.

Ylvisaker, M.S., & Szekeres, S.F. (1994). Communication disorders associated with closed head injury. In R. Chapey (Ed.), *Language intervention strategies in adult aphasia* (3rd ed., pp.546–568). Baltimore, MD: Williams & Wilkins.

Author index

Subject index